THE CYCLIST'S TRAINING BIBLE

4th Edition

JOE FRIEL

BOULDER, COLORADO

1830 55th Street
Boulder, Colorado 80301-2700 USA
303/440-0601 · Fax 303/444-6788 · E-mail velopress@competitorgroup.com

Distributed in the United States and Canada by Publishers Group West

Library of Congress Cataloging-in-Publication Data
The cyclist's training bible / Joe Friel.—4th ed.
p. cm.
Includes index.
ISBN 978-1-934030-20-2 (pbk. : alk. paper)
1. Cycling—Training. I. Title.
GV1048.F75 2009
796.607—dc22

2009000098

For information on purchasing VeloPress books, please call 800/234-8356
or visit www.velopress.com.

Cover design by Erin Johnson
Cover photograph by Don Karle
Interior design by Erin Johnson
Illustrations by Charlie Layton, chapters 12, 13, and 14 and pages 93, 106, and 107
Composition by Eclipse Publishing Services

09 10 11 / 10 9 8 7 6 5 4 3 2 1

To Dirk:

My friend, my training partner, my mentor, my pupil, my son

CONTENTS

FOREWORD

In 1963, while on the faculty of the Romanian Institute of Sport, I was asked to coach one of the country's young and promising javelin throwers. As I looked at the "traditional" training programs at the time, I came to realize that something was missing in the way athletes were trained. Everyone followed the "ancient" program of preparatory, non-specific training during the winter, followed by the competitive phase during the summer and a transition during the fall. Later on, the Russians even called this "periodization." One of the missing links, the change I introduced, refined the sequence and type of strength and endurance training performed for each training period so that athletes ultimately would reach higher levels of strength and endurance. Later, I called this the "periodization of strength" and the "periodization of endurance."

From the 1960s on, Romanian coaches, as well as other Eastern European training specialists, adopted my principles of periodization and dominated world and Olympic competition for many years in many sports. Today, these systems, along with periodization of training for young athletes, are used by most top athletes in Europe and are gaining popularity in the United States as well.

In *The Cyclist's Training Bible,* Joe Friel has carefully provided the competitive road cyclist with all of the tools necessary to design and employ a periodization program following the principles I have laid down. He didn't come to this level of expertise by accident. I have spent time with Joe and know him as a very knowledgeable and masterful coach and teacher who is an authority on periodization. Unlike many other training specialists, Joe has spent many years trying different types of periodization and training schedules to determine what works best for cyclists and other endurance athletes. If he were in Eastern Europe, he would be called a "master coach."

The Cyclist's Training Bible is perhaps the most comprehensive and scientific book ever written on training for road cycling, and yet it is also practical and easy to follow. This book will have you systematically training just as world-class cyclists do. If you scrupulously follow the guidelines presented here, I'm confident your racing performance will dramatically improve.

—Tudor O. Bompa, Ph.D.

Dr. Tudor O. Bompa is considered the "father of periodization." He consults with national Olympic organizations and sports federations throughout the world on the development of training programs for elite athletes.

PROLOGUE TO THE FOURTH EDITION

In 1995 when I started working on the first edition of this book, I viewed it as a personal challenge. It was my first book, and I expected it might sell a few copies. My intent was not to sell a lot of books, but rather to record my training methods and philosophy in an easy-to-use volume for the benefit of the cyclists I worked with as a coach. The book was also for my own satisfaction and growth—having been a teacher, I knew that the best way to ensure that you really understood a subject was to teach it to someone else. That's what *The Cyclist's Training Bible* was all about.

Fourteen years later, the book is still around and going strong. I am contacted daily by curious riders from around the world with challenging questions. Two other books have sprung directly from this one (*The Triathlete's Training Bible* and *The Mountain Biker's Training Bible*), and a Web site (www.TrainingPeaks.com) was launched in 2000 to make the tools and methodology described here accessible to all. I have spoken to thousands of athletes about the concepts described here in clinics around the world. I never cease to be amazed at the book's acceptance in the cycling community and the impact it has had on its readers and their sport.

This is the fourth edition of *The Cyclist's Training Bible* and there have been many revisions and additions. There is not a single chapter that was left unaltered. There have been many advances in sport science over the past few years, and I have incorporated the most up-to-date and reliable information possible in this edition. In general, this includes the research that has provided me with a greater understanding of cycling issues and contributed to my personal growth as a coach. In addition, over the years I have continually tried slight changes in the training of the many athletes I've coached. Some of these produced variations in what I have found to work, and I have revised the book accordingly. Other changes to this edition are in response to the many questions athletes have asked me over the years. Athletes are as eager to understand how best to train for peak performance today as they were when this book first appeared on the scene. They continue to support and question my methods and to offer suggestions. It's been an awe-inspiring journey.

While much has been added to this book for the fourth edition, there is one constant, as described in the original prologue: "I offer this book with the hope that it will make you a better racer and that one day you will return the favor by teaching me something you learned along the course."

—Joe Friel
Scottsdale, Arizona

ACKNOWLEDGMENTS

There are many people who have contributed to this book in some way over the years since I first sat down to write it in 1995. I owe a debt of gratitude not only to those who assisted in various ways during the creation of the first edition, but also to those who came into the process during the second, third, or fourth edition. I would especially like to thank all of my colleagues who helped to produce the concepts included in the version you now hold in your hands: Hunter Allen, Bob Anderson, Dr. Owen Anderson, Gale Bernhardt, Dr. Tudor Bompa, Ross Brownson, Bill Cofer, Dr. Andrew Coggan, Dr. Loren Cordain, Bob Dunihue, Gear Fisher, Donavon Guyot, Greg Haase, Renee Jardine, Nathan Koch, Jennifer Koslo, Dr. Allen Lim, Dr. Jerry Lynch, Chad Matteson, Paraic McGlynn, Gerhard Pawelka, Charles Pelkey, Dr. Andrew Pruitt, Chris Pulleyn, Jill Redding, Mark Saunders, Ulrich and Beate Schoberer, Rob Sleamaker, Amy Sorrells, Oliver Starr, Bill Strickland, Todd Telander, Dave Trendler, Dr. Randy Wilber, Chuck Wurster, and Adam Zucco.

I would also like to thank the many cyclists with whom I have worked during my twenty-some years as a coach. They were often my "lab rats" as new ideas for training came to me, and many of them helped by simply asking the right questions at the right times. Chief among them was my son, Dirk Friel, who throughout a long and successful career as an amateur and pro cyclist continually gave me feedback on what did and didn't work for him.

My wife, Joyce, who provided unconditional support and love as I pursued my dream for more than two decades, contributed immeasurably to making this book a reality.

INTRODUCTION

How should I schedule hard workouts? What is the best way to train during the weeks of my most important races? How many miles do I need before starting speed work? Is it okay to ride the same day I lift? How long should my recovery rides be? What can I do to climb better?

These are a few of the questions I hear from cyclists nearly every day. The athletes who ask these questions are intelligent and curious people—much like you, I'll bet. They have been riding and racing for three or more years, seeing substantial improvements in fitness merely from putting in the miles and competing in races. In the first two years, the competition was fun and they finished well in the races they chose to enter. But now they've moved up in their racing category and things are different. They can no longer expect to improve by just riding a lot and training harder. Usually they find that they have more questions than answers.

The purpose of this book is to provide answers to your training questions in order to help you achieve racing success. The answers aren't always as simple and straightforward as you might like them to be. While the science of training has come a long way over the past thirty years, training is still very much an art.

The answers to the training queries I receive almost always start with "It depends." It depends on what you have been doing prior to this time. It depends on how much time you have to train. It depends on your particular strengths and weaknesses. It depends on when your most important races happen. It depends on your age. It depends on how long you've been seriously training.

I'm not trying to be evasive, but I want to make sure you understand that there usually is more than one way to solve a training problem. If you asked ten coaches to answer the questions that started this introduction, you might get ten different answers. All could be right, as there's "more than one way to skin a cat" or train a cyclist. My aim in this book is to help you answer the questions you have in a way that best suits your own situation. To that end, *The Cyclist's Training Bible* builds on the ideas and concepts presented in each chapter. Following the chapter-by-chapter progression will help you understand the "whys" of my training methods.

In Part I, the self-trained cyclist's need for commitment and a commonsense training philosophy is brought to the fore. Chapter 1 describes what it takes for success in cycling, other than physical talent. Chapter 2 proposes a way of thinking about training that likely runs counter to your tendencies. I hope the Ten Commandments of Training cause you to occasionally stop reading in order to reflect on how to train intelligently.

Part II lays the scientific foundation for the remainder of the book, starting in Chapter 3 with a description of generally accepted concepts that guide the training process. Chapter 4 takes the most critical aspect of training, intensity management, and teaches you how to do it properly. With the ready availability of power meters increasing since the first edition of this book was published, there has been a revolution in how we perceive and monitor the intensity of training. Be prepared to rethink what you know about this important topic.

Part III addresses the idea of training with a purpose and offers a framework for achieving your goals. Chapter 5 shows you how to test your strengths and weaknesses, and Chapter 6 tells you what the results mean in terms of racing.

Part IV is the heart of *The Cyclist's Training Bible.* Here, I take you through the same process I use in designing a yearlong training plan for an athlete. Chapter 7 provides an overview of the planning process. Chapter 8 describes the step-by-step procedures of planning in a workbook format. By the end of this chapter, you will have determined where you're going in the race season and how you will get there. Chapter 9 puts the cap on the process by showing you how to schedule workouts for the season and, more specifically, on a week-to-week and daily basis. It also suggests workouts. If you're doing a stage race during the season, be sure to read Chapter 10 before completing your Annual Training Plan. Chapter 11 offers examples of other cyclists' Annual Training Plans with discussions of the thinking behind their design. You may find these examples to be helpful as you design your own plan.

Part V addresses several other aspects of training that affect the annual plan. In Chapter 12, I explain the importance of strength training for cycling, describe how to incorporate strength training into your periodized plan, and provide illustrations of recommended exercises. Chapter 13 shows how stretching can benefit cycling performance. Training concerns specific to women, masters, juniors, and novices are detailed in Chapter 14. If you are in one of these special groups, it may help you to read this chapter before beginning the planning process laid out in Chapter 8. The importance of keeping a training diary is the topic of Chapter 15. A sample journal is provided that complements the weekly scheduling described in Chapter 9. The discussion of diet in Chapter 16 presents a different way of thinking about eating. Also included is information about supplements and ergogenic aids. Chapter 17 provides guidance for dealing with training problems common to cyclists—overtraining, burnout, illness, and injury. Chapter 18 discusses the most important, but most neglected, aspect of training—recovery.

Before beginning, I want to offer this note of caution: This book is primarily meant for cyclists who have been training and racing for some time. If you are new to the sport or just starting to train, you should first have a medical examination. This is particularly important for those over age 35 who have been inactive. Much of what is suggested here is strenuous and designed for those with highly established levels of fitness and riding experience.

While I believe this book will help most cyclists improve, I do not pretend that it will make everyone a champion. It takes something more than just inspiration and guidance for that. No training program is perfect for everyone. Consider my ways of training critically and take from this book what will benefit you now. I hope you will use it as a training reference for years to come.

As you can see, *The Cyclist's Training Bible* is quite methodical. I hope that you don't feel as some do that analyzing the process of training detracts from the fun of riding and racing. I don't believe it does. Being on a bike is most enjoyable when every starting line is a challenge and every finish line is jubilantly crossed with arms held high. Let's start.

PART I

THE SELF-TRAINED CYCLIST
HISTORICAL PERSPECTIVES

HINTS ON BICYCLE RACING

by Norman Hill

(as it appeared in *Review of Cycling Magazine*, 1943)

In training or conditioning for bike racing, one must remember that for best results it must be considered as a full-time job, and the entire mode of living must be directed toward one objective, namely, the best possible health, which is the basis of all athletic ability.

Another important fact to remember is that adoption of a correct training program will not produce overnight results but must be followed religiously for a period of time. In fact, athletic champions are seldom, if ever, developed with less than several years of constant training and experience.

The correct conditioning program can and will improve anyone's ability but cannot, of course, guarantee that everyone will become a champion, as there are hereditary factors plus an element of luck to be considered. A correct training program can be likened to proper care of a car, the proper care insuring maximum efficiency, performance, and endurance.

1 COMMITMENT

At the base of the climb, which was 12 kilometers long, I started to look around and saw Ullrich, Pantani, Virenque, Riis, Escartin, and Jimenez—all in the top 10 of the general classification—and then me. I was hanging. I was there with these guys for the first time.

—BOBBY JULICH, COMMENTING ON THE MOMENT IN THE 1997 TOUR DE FRANCE WHEN HE REALIZED HE WAS A CONTENDER

TALK IS CHEAP. It's easy to have big dreams and set high goals before the racing starts. But the true test of a commitment to better racing results is not in the talking, but in the doing. It doesn't start with the first race of the season—it's all the things you do today to get stronger, faster, and more enduring. Real commitment means 365 days a year and 24 hours a day.

Talk to the best riders you know. Ask them about commitment. Once you probe past all of the "aw, shucks" stuff, you'll discover how big a role cycling plays in their lives. The better they are, the more you'll hear about life revolving around the sport. The most common remark will be that each day is arranged around training. It's a rare champion who fits in workouts randomly.

Racing to your potential cannot be an on-again, off-again endeavor. It's a full-time commitment—a passion. Excellence requires living, breathing, eating, and sleeping cycling every day. Literally.

The greater the commitment, the more life is centered on the basic three factors of training—eating, sleeping, and working out. Eating fuels the body for training and speeds recovery by replacing depleted energy and nutrient stores. Sleeping and working out have a synergistic effect on fitness: Each can cause the release of growth hormone from the pituitary gland. Growth hormone speeds recovery, rebuilds muscles, and breaks down body fat. By training twice daily and taking a nap, the dedicated rider gets four hits of growth hormone daily, resulting in higher levels of fitness sooner.

In the final analysis, greater fitness is what we're all after. It's the product of three ingredients: stress, rest, and fuel. Table 1.1 illustrates how training, sleeping, and eating can be built into your day.

TABLE 1.1

Suggested Daily Routines

<table>
<tr><th></th><th colspan="2">TWO WORKOUTS DAILY</th><th colspan="2">ONE WORKOUT DAILY</th></tr>
<tr><th></th><th>WORK DAY</th><th>NO-WORK DAY</th><th>WORK DAY</th><th>NO-WORK DAY</th></tr>
<tr><td>6:00 am</td><td>Awake</td><td>Awake</td><td>Awake</td><td>Awake</td></tr>
<tr><td>:30</td><td>Workout 1</td><td>Eat</td><td>Workout</td><td>Eat</td></tr>
<tr><td>7:00</td><td>|</td><td>Stretch</td><td>|</td><td>Stretch</td></tr>
<tr><td>:30</td><td>|</td><td>Personal</td><td>|</td><td>Personal</td></tr>
<tr><td>8:00</td><td>Eat</td><td>|</td><td>Eat</td><td>|</td></tr>
<tr><td>:30</td><td>Shower</td><td>Workout 1</td><td>Shower</td><td>Workout</td></tr>
<tr><td>9:00</td><td>Work</td><td>|</td><td>Work</td><td>|</td></tr>
<tr><td>:30</td><td>|</td><td>|</td><td>|</td><td>|</td></tr>
<tr><td>10:00</td><td>|</td><td>|</td><td>|</td><td>|</td></tr>
<tr><td>:30</td><td>|</td><td>Eat</td><td>|</td><td>|</td></tr>
<tr><td>11:00</td><td>|</td><td>Shower</td><td>|</td><td>|</td></tr>
<tr><td>:30</td><td>Eat</td><td>Nap</td><td>|</td><td>Eat</td></tr>
<tr><td>12:00 pm</td><td>Nap</td><td>Stretch</td><td>Eat</td><td>Shower</td></tr>
<tr><td>:30</td><td>Work</td><td>Personal</td><td>Nap</td><td>Nap</td></tr>
<tr><td>1:00</td><td>|</td><td>Eat</td><td>Work</td><td>Personal</td></tr>
<tr><td>:30</td><td>|</td><td>Personal</td><td>|</td><td>|</td></tr>
<tr><td>2:00</td><td>|</td><td>|</td><td>|</td><td>|</td></tr>
<tr><td>:30</td><td>|</td><td>Workout 2</td><td>|</td><td>|</td></tr>
<tr><td>3:00</td><td>Eat</td><td>|</td><td>|</td><td>|</td></tr>
<tr><td>:30</td><td>Work</td><td>|</td><td>Eat</td><td>Eat</td></tr>
<tr><td>4:00</td><td>|</td><td>|</td><td>Work</td><td>Personal</td></tr>
<tr><td>:30</td><td>|</td><td>Eat</td><td>|</td><td>|</td></tr>
<tr><td>5:00</td><td>End work</td><td>Shower</td><td>End work</td><td>|</td></tr>
<tr><td>:30</td><td>Workout 2</td><td>Nap</td><td>Personal</td><td>|</td></tr>
<tr><td>6:00</td><td>|</td><td>Stretch</td><td>|</td><td>|</td></tr>
<tr><td>:30</td><td>Eat</td><td>Personal</td><td>Eat</td><td>Eat</td></tr>
<tr><td>7:00</td><td>Shower</td><td>|</td><td>Personal</td><td>Personal</td></tr>
<tr><td>:30</td><td>Personal</td><td>Eat</td><td>|</td><td>|</td></tr>
<tr><td>8:00</td><td>|</td><td>Personal</td><td>|</td><td>|</td></tr>
<tr><td>:30</td><td>Eat</td><td>|</td><td>|</td><td>|</td></tr>
<tr><td>9:00</td><td>To bed</td><td>To bed</td><td>To bed</td><td>To bed</td></tr>
</table>

This kind of commitment may not be for you. In fact, there comes a point at which each of us has to check our "want to" against our "have to." Jobs, families, and other responsibilities can't be forsaken for sport. Even the pros must consider other aspects of life. Those elements that contribute to making you a great cyclist may detract from your ability to be a great employee, parent, or spouse. Realistically, there have to be limits to passion; otherwise we'd soon alienate everyone who wasn't equally zealous. A balanced training plan has to take all of these considerations into account.

CHANGE

What can you do to improve your fitness and race performances? The first thing is to make small changes in your life. Balance can be hard to achieve, but remolding daily activities by 10 percent in the direction of better cycling doesn't take much and can bring noticeable improvement. How about committing to hitting the sack thirty minutes earlier each night so that you're more rested? Another small daily change that could bring better results is healthier eating. Could you cut out 10 percent of the junk food every day, replacing it with wholesome foods? What you put in your mouth is the stuff the body uses to completely rebuild and replace each muscle cell every six months. Do you want muscles made from potato chips, Twinkies, and pop or from fruits, vegetables, and lean meat? What can you change?

The Cyclist's Training Bible can help you make some small changes that will bring big results. But what are the most important changes needed for success? What makes a champion a champion?

ATTRIBUTES OF CHAMPIONS

Successful athletes and coaches always ask two questions in their quest for peak athletic performance:

- What does science say?
- How do champions train?

Much of this book is based on answers to the first question, but the second is no less important. Often the top athletes are ahead of science (some, unfortunately, in the abuse of illegal performance enhancements) when it comes to knowing what works and what doesn't. Exercise scientists become interested in certain aspects of training because they seem to work for some athletes. Although we can't pinpoint what percentage of an athlete's success is based on technique, natural ability, or hard work, there are some common traits that the best share—most notably their willingness to work hard at training—not in fits and starts but in a consistent manner over the long haul.

DEDICATION TO IMPROVEMENT

Lance Armstrong, Tiger Woods, and Michael Jordan are often referred to as the greatest athletes of all time in their respective sports. What is it that separates a good athlete from a world-class champion? Is it genetics or opportunity? Nature or nurture? Technique or mental toughness? What we've learned is that it is likely a focus on continual improvement.

Lance Armstrong is a legendary example of constant hard work. He was well-known for keeping up a schedule of daily six-hour rides, repeatedly practicing key routes of the Tour de France, and weighing every bite of food that went into his mouth.

After Tiger Woods won the 1997 Masters Tournament by a record 12 strokes over the second-place finisher, he took time off from the sport in order to improve his swing. After becoming the only man to win the four major tournaments on the PGA Tour in succession, he again went back to work on improving his swing. In doing so, he has single-handedly changed the work ethic among pro golfers.

Being cut from his junior high school basketball team stiffened Michael Jordan's resolve to prove himself. Even after achieving athletic success, however, he was never one to rest on his laurels. He was well-known among basketball fans for staying after practice to work on his "weaknesses."

We know that constant dedication to improvement was critical to the success of each of these athletes. But was it the primary reason they became great? Recent research seems to indicate that it was. This research goes even further, suggesting that it takes ten years of focused work on one's sport to reach the threshold of greatness. That is certainly true for these three athletes. The high level of commitment that they have exhibited provides a model for other athletes hoping to achieve top ranking in their sport.

As a coach for the past three decades, I have found that the research about the length of time required for proficiency applies to cycling. The athlete improves physiologically for about seven years: During this time, athletes learn what it takes, in terms of training, racing, and lifestyle, to succeed in the sport. Then I see continued improvement in performance for at least another three years. This timeline holds true regardless of the age at which the athlete starts training and competing.

Putting aside individual abilities in particular sports, let's look at the common traits that all top athletes share. I find that there are seven such attributes: ability, motivation, opportunity, mission, support system, direction, and mental toughness.

Ability

There's no denying it: Genetics have a lot to do with achievement in sport. There are some obvious examples: tall basketball players, huge sumo wrestlers, small jockeys, and long-armed swimmers are but a few. Such athletes were born with at least one of the physical traits necessary to succeed in their chosen sport.

What are the physical traits common to most of those who are at the pinnacle of cycling? The most obvious are strong, powerful legs and a high aerobic capacity (VO_2max). Other physical traits aren't quite as obvious, such as lung capacity, physical proportions, and muscular power. Lactate threshold (LT) and economy also play a large role in a cyclist's performance. We can't see power, LT, or economy in a rider in the same way we can see body mass or long arms, and they can be improved with proper training. Nevertheless, these factors are somewhat determined by genetics.

So how much natural ability do you have? How close are you to reaching your potential? No one can say for sure. The best indicator may be how you've done in the sport in the past relative to your training. Good results combined with mediocre training may indicate untapped potential. Excellent training with poor results may suggest that potential is lacking—but not necessarily.

If you are new to the sport with less than three years of racing, your results may not tell you much about your ability and potential. In the first three years there are a lot of changes happening at the cellular level—changes that will eventually reveal a rider's ability. This means that even if someone new to the sport is successful, he or she may not continue to dominate. Other beginners may eventually catch up to and surpass the most successful novices. This is often due to the different rates at which the human body responds to training.

Some people are "fast responders" and others are "slow responders." Fast responders gain fitness quickly because, for some unknown reason, their cells are capable of changing rapidly. Others take much longer, perhaps years, to realize the same gains. The problem for slow responders is that they often give up before reaping the benefits of training. Figure 1.1 illustrates the response curve.

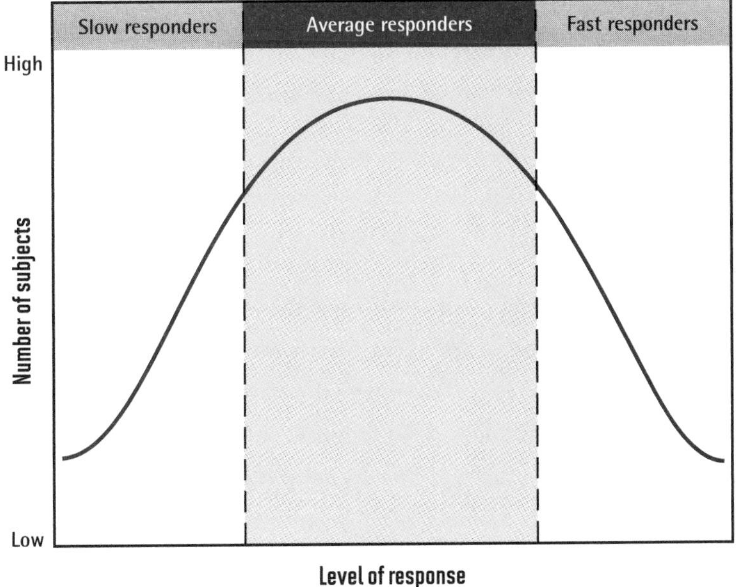

FIGURE 1.1

Response to Training Stimulus

Motivation

The highly motivated cyclist has a passion for the sport. Passion is generally evident in how much time is devoted to riding, caring for the bike, reading books and magazines about cycling, associating with other riders, and simply thinking about the sport.

Those who are passionate about the sport also frequently have a well-developed work ethic. They believe that hard training is what produces good results. Up to a point, that is a valuable trait to have, as success does indeed demand consistency in training. The problem is that the combination of passion for cycling and a strong work ethic sometimes leads to obsessive-compulsive training. These riders just can't stop riding. If they do, their sense of guilt can become overwhelming. For such athletes, training interruptions—such as injuries, business trips, or vacations—are emotionally devastating. This is because although their training pattern may be disrupted, their obsessive motivation is still intact.

This obsessive-compulsive trait is most common in riders who are new to the sport. They may believe that they discovered the sport too late in life and need to catch up with others by training a lot. They may also fear that if they stop training for even a few days, they will revert back to their former, unfit selves. No wonder overtraining is rampant among those in their first three years of racing.

Regardless of when in life you started cycling or how burning your desire is to be good, it's critical that you view excellence in athletics as a journey, not a destination. You will never arrive at the point where you are fully satisfied with your performance—that's the nature of highly motivated people. So achieving some sort of racing nirvana—where you can finally back off—is not going to happen. Obsessive-compulsive training can only be counterproductive. Once you realize this and take a long-term approach to training, your breakdowns from overtraining, burnout, and illness will diminish, allowing you to achieve training with greater consistency and better race performances. You will also experience less mental anguish and frustration when the inevitable setbacks occur.

Cycling is a lifelong sport to be enjoyed for what it brings to your life—superb fitness, excellent health, enjoyable times, and good friends. It is not an opponent to be subdued and conquered.

Opportunity

The chances are great that the best potential athlete in the world is an overweight, sedentary smoker. Right now, sitting in front of a television somewhere, is this person born to be the world champion in cycling and to dominate the sport as no one else ever has. At birth he was blessed with a huge aerobic capacity and all of the other physiological ingredients necessary for success. The problem is that he never had the opportunity to discover his ability, even though the motivation may have been there at one time. Maybe he was born into poverty and forced to work at an early age to help feed the family. Maybe he lives in a war-ravaged corner of the world where staying alive is the number-one priority. Or perhaps cycling just never caught his attention and he instead found success in soccer or playing the piano. We'll never know what he could have been.

The lack of opportunity isn't the only factor that can hold back your growth as a cyclist. If any of the following items are missing, your opportunity to realize your full potential may be compromised:

- A network of roads to ride on
- Terrain variety—flats and hills

- Adequate nutrition
- Good equipment
- Coaching
- Training partners
- Weight-room equipment
- Time to train
- Available races
- A low-stress environment
- Supportive family and friends

This list could go on and on—there are many environmental elements that contribute to your overall opportunity to achieve your potential in cycling. The greater your desire to excel, the more likely you will be to overcome a potential limiting factor. You will work to mold your lifestyle and environment to match your aspirations.

Mission

When you think of champions such as Eddy Merckx, Bernard Hinault, Greg LeMond, and Lance Armstrong, what comes to mind? More likely than not, it is winning the Tour de France. Why do you think of that? Probably because these athletes had a passion for winning the Tour that was, and is, evident for all to see. Their motivation to succeed was exceptional. They were willing to make any sacrifice, ride any number of miles, and do whatever workouts were deemed beneficial to achieving the goal. As they approached the peaks of their careers, riding was the most important thing in their lives. Everything else became just the details of life.

What you can learn from these champions is that motivation and dedication are paramount to achieving your dreams. Your dream may be to win the Tour de France; obviously, the greater the dream, the bigger the mission. But every rider who dreams of improving must bring a certain level of dedication to the job. This sense of being on a mission must come from within. No one else can help you choose your particular dreams or make you become more dedicated to them; even this book cannot do it, ultimately. Only you can do that. But I can tell you that without passion, without a mission, you'll always be just another rider in the peloton.

Support System

The greatest rider with the biggest dreams will never become a champion without a support system—others who also believe in the mission and are committed to it. Surrounding champions are family, friends, teammates, directors, coaches, soigneurs (assistants), and mechanics, all of whom are there to help the champion attain his or her dream. The rider becomes immersed in the we-can-do-it attitude. The mission is no longer singular—it becomes a group effort. Once this is achieved, success is 90 percent assured.

Do you have a support system? Do those around you even know your goals, let alone your dreams? Is there a mentor or close friend with whom you can share your challenges and vision? Again, this book can't develop a support system for you. To start building a support system, offer to help others, perhaps teammates, attain their highest goals. Support is contagious. Give yours to someone else, and the favor will usually be returned.

Direction

Champions don't train aimlessly. Nor do they blindly follow another rider's training plan. They understand that the difference between winning and losing is often as slight as a cat's whisker. They know their training can't be haphazard or left to chance. Merely having a detailed plan provides confidence. It's the final, and smallest, piece in the quest for the dream. Without a plan, the champion never makes it to the victory stand.

Many athletes choose to work with coaches, who can create a personalized plan. Others rely on prestructured plans, adapting them as much as possible to fit their own needs. Obviously, the more personalized the plan, the better, and *The Cyclist's Training Bible* will give you guidelines for creating your own detailed annual plan, one more personalized than a generic workout schedule downloaded from the Internet.

Mental Toughness

Success in cycling requires an enormous amount of hard work physically—but the key to sustaining this level of work over many years is more mental than physical. Being mentally tough is what eventually produces high-level performance in athletes once they have achieved their physiological peak. What does it take to be mentally tough? There are four qualities I look for in athletes who say they want to perform at the highest levels: a desire to succeed, self-discipline, an attitude of believing in themselves, and patience (or perseverance). To evaluate whether you possess these qualities, ask yourself the questions that I ask athletes, which are included below.

Desire to Succeed. Can you train alone, or do you need to be with others to motivate you to complete hard sessions? Do you find a way to work out regardless of environmental conditions such as rain, snow, wind, heat, darkness, or other potential training interruptions?

I find that athletes who regularly train alone tend to have higher levels of mental toughness. Likewise, those who ride in the rain and cold, or who find a way to regularly train despite busy work schedules and family commitments, reach levels of success that elude those who do not take their training that far.

Discipline. Do you shape your training and lifestyle to fit your goals? How important to you are nutrition, sleep, periodization, goal setting, physical skills, attitude, health, and strength? Do your family and friends support you and your goals?

There are athletes who fit training into their lives as much as possible, and those for whom the daily ride is paramount and nearly everything else is secondary. I look for athletes who make workouts, diet, and rest a regular and reliable part of daily life. When those athletes are surrounded by a good support network, they're most likely to stick with a training program.

Belief in Self. Do you go into a race with a success plan? Do you really believe you can succeed even when the conditions are not favorable? When it comes to racing, which do you think more about—the controllable or the uncontrollable variables? Do you accept occasional setbacks as necessary steps on the way to success, or as signs you simply can't do it? Do you believe you can, or question whether you can?

I've seen gifted athletes who didn't believe in their own potential, and I've seen those athletes defeated by physically weaker but mentally tougher competitors. If you don't truly believe that you can improve and win, it will be difficult for a coach to convince you otherwise.

Patience and Perseverance. Are you in this for the long term? Do you need immediate success, or can you postpone it until the time is right, even if that is years in the future? Do you ever skip training for days or even weeks at a time and then try to get into shape quickly?

As discussed earlier, athletes continue to improve physiologically for about ten years, no matter what age they start training. Training to win is a long-term commitment that may have periods of seemingly no progress. Athletes need the patience to work steadily through those periods, knowing that improvement will come later.

My experience has been that if any one of these mental toughness qualities is lacking, the athlete will not achieve his or her lofty career goals. Few athletes have high levels of all these qualities. I've only coached one athlete who I felt had exceptional overall mental toughness. He became a Team USA Olympian.

Mental toughness is perhaps where the nurturing part of the success equation is most evident. Some athletes seem to have internalized these qualities at an early age. Others haven't. What makes the difference? It is probably hundreds of seemingly insignificant interactions that take place on a daily basis from birth through the formative years, experiences that we don't exactly know how to identify or instill.

The best way to improve mental toughness is to work with a sports psychologist in much the same way as you would work with a coach. Sports psychology is a rapidly growing field, and it is becoming increasingly common for athletes at all competitive levels to seek the services of such professionals.

The Cyclist's Training Bible can help athletes who are armed with mental toughness and dedicated to constant improvement. While this book offers individualized, results-oriented, scientific methods, following its program won't guarantee success. But if you already have some ability, if the opportunity has presented itself, if your mission is well defined and your support system is in place, then you're practically there. This just may be the final and decisive element.

2

SMART TRAINING

You can't train luck.

—EDDIE BORYSEWICZ,
RENOWNED POLISH-AMERICAN CYCLING COACH

WHY IS IT that some start their cycling career with little sign of physical talent and years later reach the pinnacle of the sport as elite amateurs or pros? Why do others who excel at an early age end up fizzling and dropping out of the sport before realizing their full potential?

Those who persevere probably had talent all along, but it wasn't immediately evident. More than likely, the young athlete had a parent, coach, or mentor concerned about the long term—someone who wanted to see his or her protégé in full bloom and was wise enough to bring the athlete along slowly and deliberately. The successful athlete's workouts may not have been based on the latest science, but a sensible training philosophy was established early in his or her career.

In contrast, the young cyclist who failed to make it as a senior may have been driven too hard by a parent or coach. The intentions of this adult guide may have been good, but his or her techniques left something to be desired.

When I begin to train an athlete, I start by getting to know him or her fairly well—but it still takes weeks to determine the most effective training methods to employ for that individual. There are many factors to consider in developing an effective training program. A few of them are:

- Years of experience in the sport
- Age and maturity level
- How training has progressed over the long term
- Most recent training program
- Personal strengths and weaknesses

- Local terrain and weather conditions
- Schedule of important races
- Details of the most important races: duration, terrain, competition, previous results
- Recent and current health status
- Lifestyle stress (work and family issues, for example)

The list could go on and on. If you are hoping to find a precise training plan spelled out for you in this book, you must understand that it is not that simple. There are simply too many unknowns for me or anyone else to evaluate you completely without extensive input from you. After all, right now no one knows you as well as you know yourself. Only you can make some of the critical decisions about your training. You do need tools to work with—a set of basic training principles and practices that apply in different ways to different athletes. That's why I've written this book—so that you might understand the basic concepts and do a better job of self-coaching.

SYSTEMATIC TRAINING

This book is about systematic and methodical training. Some riders think that's boring and would rather work out spontaneously. They prefer to train by the seat of their pants—no planning, no forethought, and minimal structure. I won't deny that it is possible to become a good rider without a highly structured system and method. I have known many who have been successful with such an approach. But I've also noticed that when these same athletes decide to compete at the highest levels, they nearly always increase the structure of their training. Structured systems and methods are critical for achieving peak performance. It won't happen haphazardly.

I should also point out that the system and methods described in this book are not the only ones that will produce peak racing performance. There are many systems that work; there are as many as there are coaches and elite athletes. There is no one "right" way—no system that will guarantee success for everyone.

There are also no secrets. You won't find any magic workouts, miracle diet supplements, or all-purpose periodization schemes. Everything in this book is already known and used by at least some cyclists. No coach, athlete, or scientist has a winning secret—at least not one that is legal. Many have developed effective systems, however. Effective training systems are marked by comprehensively integrated components. They are not merely collections of workouts. All of the parts of effective programs fit together neatly, like the pieces of a complex jigsaw puzzle. Furthermore, there is an underlying philosophy that ties the parts together. All aspects of a sound program are based on this philosophy.

THE OVERTRAINING PHENOMENON

Is there a relationship between fatigue and speed? Are there studies showing that if a rider gets really tired in training and does that often enough, he or she will get faster? Does starting workouts with chronically tired legs somehow improve power and other aspects of race fitness?

I pose these questions because so many athletes tell me that there's no improvement unless they feel at least a little sluggish all the time. But when I ask these same athletes why they train, the answer is always, "To get faster for racing." Chronic fatigue is a strange way to get faster.

Recently I did a Web search of the sports science journals to see if any research has found a positive relationship between fatigue and athletic performance. Of the 2,036 studies I came across on this subject, not a single one showed that an athlete performed better if he or she got tired often enough.

All of this leads me to believe that athletes who keep themselves chronically tired and leg weary must be making a mistake. Either that or they have a training secret. But I doubt it. More than likely, the reason for their excessive training is a combination of an overly developed work ethic and obsessive-compulsive behavior.

In fact, there are a few athletes I have been unable to train for this reason. When I allow them to rest in order to go into a hard workout fresh, they interpret the lack of fatigue as a loss of fitness and become paranoid. After a few episodes where they put in "extra" intervals, miles, hours, and workouts, we part company. My purpose in coaching is not to help otherwise well-intentioned athletes keep their addiction going. I'd like to see them race faster, not just be more fatigued and stressed-out than before.

On the other hand, I have trained many athletes in a variety of sports on a program of less training than they were accustomed to. It's amazing to see what they can accomplish once they fully commit to their actual training purpose—to get faster. When riders go into hard workouts feeling fresh and snappy, the speeds and power produced are exceptional. As a result, the muscles, nervous system, cardiovascular system, and energy systems are all optimally stressed. Once they have a few more days of recovery to allow for adaptation, we do it again. And guess what? They are even faster.

PHILOSOPHY

The philosophy of training proposed in *The Cyclist's Training Bible* may seem unusual. I have found, however, that if it is followed, serious athletes improve. Here is my training philosophy: An athlete should do the least amount of properly timed, specific training that brings continual improvement.

The idea of limiting training is a scary thought for some. Many cyclists have become so accustomed to overtraining that it seems a normal state. These racers are no less addicted than drug users. Like a drug addict, the chronically overtrained athlete is continuing a behavior that is destructive to his or her own well-being. That athlete is not getting any better, but still can't convince himself or herself to change.

Read the philosophy statement again. Notice that it doesn't say "train with the least amount of miles." Another way to state it might be "use your training time wisely." For those of us with full-time jobs, spouses, children, a home to maintain, and other responsibilities, using training time wisely is more than a philosophy; it's a necessity.

What this means is that there are times when it's right to do higher-volume training, but not necessarily the highest possible. This is usually in the Base (general preparation) period of training. There are also times when high volume is not wise, but faster, more race-specific training is right. These are the Build and Peak (specific preparation) periods. (Periods are explained in Chapter 7.)

While it seems so simple, there are many who can't seem to get it right. They put in lots of miles when they should be trying to get faster. And when they should be building a base of general fitness, they're going fast—usually in group hammer sessions.

So up to this point in your training and racing experience, how have you been gauging your progress—do you typically go by how tired you are, or by how fast you are? If it's the former, unless you change your attitude you will be doomed to a career of less-than-stellar racing. Once you figure out that fatigue gets in the way of getting faster and you make the necessary changes, you'll be flying.

THE TEN COMMANDMENTS OF TRAINING

To help you better understand this training philosophy I have broken it down into the "Ten Commandments of Training." By incorporating each of these guidelines into your thinking and training, you'll be following this philosophy and getting a better return on your time invested. Your results will also improve regardless of your age or experience.

COMMANDMENT 1: TRAIN MODERATELY

Your body has limits when it comes to endurance, speed, and strength. Don't try too often to find them. Instead, train within those limits most of the time. Finish most workouts feeling like you could have done more. It may mean stopping a session earlier than planned. That's okay. Do not always try to finish exhausted.

Muscles will only contract forcefully a certain number of times before they refuse to pull hard again. When glycogen, the body's storage form of carbohydrate energy, begins to run low, no amount of willpower can fuel the body and slowing down becomes the only option. If such limits are approached frequently and over a long enough period of time, the body's ability to adapt is exceeded, recovery is greatly delayed, and training consistency is interrupted.

The biggest mistake of most athletes is to make the easy days too challenging, so when it comes time for a tough training day, they can't go hard enough. This leads to mediocre training, fitness, and performance. The higher your fitness level, the greater the difference should be between the intensities of hard and easy days.

Many cyclists also think that pushing hard all the time will make them tough. They believe that willpower and strength of character can overcome nature and speed up their body's cellular changes. Don't try it—more tough training is seldom the answer. An organism adapts best when stresses are slightly increased. That's why you've often heard the admonition to increase training volume by no more than 10 percent from week to week. Even this may be high for some.

By progressing carefully, especially with intensity, you'll gradually get stronger and there will be time and energy for other pursuits in life. An athlete who enjoys training will get far more benefits from it than one who is always on the edge of overtraining.

The self-coached cyclist must learn to think objectively and unemotionally. It should be as if you are two people—one is the rider and the other is the coach. The coach must be in charge. When the rider says, "Do more," the coach should question whether that's wise. Doubt is a good enough reason to discontinue the session. When in doubt, leave it out.

Do every workout conservatively, but with a cocky attitude. When the coach stops the hill repeats at just the right time, and the rider says, "I could have done more," stopping is not a loss—it's a victory.

COMMANDMENT 2: TRAIN CONSISTENTLY

The human body thrives on routine. Develop a training pattern that stays mostly the same from week to week—regular activity brings positive change. This does not mean you should do the same workout every day, week after week. Variety also promotes growth. Later in this book you'll see that there are actually slight changes being made throughout the training year. Some of the changes are seemingly minor. You may not even be aware of them, as when an extra hour is added to the training week during the base-building period.

Breaks in consistency usually result from not following the moderation commandment. Overdoing a workout or week of training is likely to cause excessive fatigue, illness, burnout, or injury. Fitness is not stagnant—you're either getting better or getting worse all the time. Frequently missing workouts means a loss of fitness. This doesn't mean, however, that you should work out when ill. There are times when breaks are necessary. For example, what choices do you typically make when you:

- Feel tired, but have a hard workout planned?
- Are afraid of losing fitness while taking time off because you feel wasted?
- Believe your competition is putting in more training time than you are?
- Feel like your training partners are riding too fast?
- Sense there is only one interval left in you?
- Think you could do more, but aren't sure?
- Have a "bad" race?
- Seem to have hit a plateau or even lost fitness?

If your personal philosophy is "more is better," you will answer these questions differently than if it is "do the least amount of properly timed, specific training that brings continual improvement." Do you see the difference?

This is not to say that you shouldn't do hard workouts or that it isn't necessary to push the limits on occasion and experience fatigue as a result. It's obvious that if coming close to your riding potential is your goal, then you must often face and conquer training challenges. The problem arises when you don't know when to back off, when to rest, and when to do less than planned. The inevitable consequences of "more is better" are burnout, overtraining, illness, and injury. Extended or frequent downtime due to such problems inevitably results in a loss of fitness and the need to rebuild by returning to previous, lower levels of training. Riders who experience these problems with some regularity seldom achieve their potential in the sport.

Training consistently, not extremely, is the route to the highest possible fitness and your ultimate racing performances. The key to consistency is moderation and rest. That may not be what you want to hear about in a book on training, but read on to better understand how consistency will make you faster.

COMMANDMENT 3: GET ADEQUATE REST

It's during rest that the body adapts to the stresses of training and grows stronger. Without rest there's no improvement. As the stress of training increases, the need for rest also accumulates. Most cyclists pay lip service to this commandment; they understand it intellectually, but not emotionally. It is the most widely violated guideline. You will not improve without adequate rest.

And to All a Good Night

Quality of sleep may be improved by:

- Going to bed at a regular time every night, including the night before races
- Darkening the room in the last hour before bedtime and narrowing your focus by reading or engaging in light conversation
- Sleeping in a dark, well-ventilated room that is 60 to 64 degrees Fahrenheit (16 to 18 degrees Celsius)
- Taking a warm bath before bed
- Progressively contracting and relaxing muscles to induce total body relaxation
- Avoiding stimulants such as coffee and tea in the last several hours before going to bed
- Restricting alcohol (which interferes with sleep patterns) prior to bedtime

COMMANDMENT 4: TRAIN WITH A PLAN

Planning is at the heart of training, especially when your goals are big ones. You may have heard good athletes say that they don't plan and do quite well anyway. I'd wager they really are following a plan, only it's in their heads and not in writing. Athletes don't become great by training randomly, and you won't either. Fortunately, the heart of this book is all about planning. Chapter 8 provides the details on how I lay out a seasonal plan for an athlete. Chapter 9 covers workout planning, and Chapter 10 discusses stage-race planning.

A strong plan is fundamental to improvement in almost any endeavor of life, yet few self-trained athletes do it. Sometimes I find riders who use a sound plan from a magazine, but as soon as a new issue comes out, they abandon the old plan and take up a new one. Most people will improve if they follow a plan—any plan. It can be of poor design, yet still work. Just don't keep changing it.

This book is all about planning. In Part IV you will learn about annual training plans and weekly scheduling routines. These are the sections you will come back to year after year as you plan for the next season.

Realize that all plans can be tweaked. Although you don't want to start from scratch every month, your plan will not be chiseled into stone. It takes some flexibility to cope with the many factors that will get in your way. These may include a bad cold, overtime at work, unexpected travel, or a visit from Aunt Jeanne. I have yet to coach an athlete who didn't have something interfere with the plan. Expect it, but don't be upset when it happens. Roll with the punches and change the plan to fit the new situation.

I've learned that one of the most critical parts of any plan is the overall goal. Most athletes think they have goals, but few really do. What most call "goals" are actually wishes. They are vague desires for grand achievements that are poorly defined. These often include imprecise words like "faster." When creating a training plan for an athlete, the first question I ask is, "How will you know if this season was successful?" I also have the athlete identify long-term objectives by asking, "What is the greatest accomplishment you'd like to achieve as a cyclist?" These really are dreams, but long-term dreams can eventually become goals. They certainly can help you formulate goals, and in that sense identifying your dreams is a good starting point.

Where do you go from there? To help athletes turn big dreams into specific training goals, I ask questions such as "How much?" "When?" "Where?" "Does this goal make you reach and strive? Is it realistic?" Knowing precisely what you want is critical to success in cycling just as it is in life. Goal setting is discussed in greater detail in Chapter 8.

COMMANDMENT 5: TRAIN WITH GROUPS INFREQUENTLY

There's a real advantage to working out with others—sometimes. Pack riding develops handling skills, provides experience with race dynamics, and makes the time go faster. Riding with friends can also motivate athletes to get on the bike in bad weather or when other commitments threaten to push aside workouts. But all too often, the group will cause you to ride fast at a time when you would be best served by a slow, easy recovery ride. At other times, you will need to go a longer or shorter distance than the group decides to ride. Group workouts too often degenerate into unstructured races at the most inopportune times.

For the winter base-building period, find a group that rides at a comfortable pace. During the spring intensity-building period, ride with a group that will challenge you to ride fast, just as when racing. Smart and structured group rides are hard to find. You may need to create your own. Stay away from big packs that take over the road and are unsafe. You want to get faster, not get killed. Use groups when they can help you. Otherwise, avoid them.

COMMANDMENT 6: PLAN TO PEAK

Your season plan should bring you to your peak for the most important events. I call these "A" races. The "B" races are important, too, but you will not taper and peak for these—just rest for three to four days before them. "C" races are tune-ups to get you ready for the A and B races. A smart rider will use these low-priority races for experience, or to practice pacing, or as a time trial to gauge fitness. If all races are A-level priority, don't expect much for season results.

Peaking also means training for the unique demands of each goal race. The principal factor is race duration. There are many differences in training for a 40 km time trial, a 45-minute criterium, or a 60-mile road race. Beyond this are course profiles such as hilly, rolling, or flat; windy or calm conditions; hot and cold temperatures; courses with lots of or very few turns; off-road and road courses; morning and afternoon start times; and a multitude of other variables. As you work toward peaking, your training should take on more of the coming race's unique characteristics. In Chapter 10 you will learn how to write a race plan that takes into consideration the key variables over which you have control and teaches you how to deal with those you can't control.

This book will show you how to peak for A races two or more times in a season. Each peak may last for up to a couple of weeks. You will still race between peaks, but the emphasis will be on reestablishing endurance, force, and speed skills to prepare for the next peak.

COMMANDMENT 7: IMPROVE WEAKNESSES

What do riders with great endurance, but not much speed, do the most? You guessed it—endurance work. What do good climbers like to do? Not surprisingly, they like to train in the hills. Most cyclists spend too much time working on what they're already good at. What's your weakest area? Ask your training partners if you don't know. I'll bet they do. Then spend more time on that area. *The Cyclist's Training Bible* will help you identify your weaknesses and teach you how to improve them. Understanding your "limiters" is critical to your success in racing. Pay close attention whenever you run across that term in this book.

In endurance sports, with the possible exception of swimming, athletes tend to downplay or even disregard technique. Most athletes, especially those in their first three years in the sport, have lots of room for improvement of their sport-specific skills—

balance, cornering, pedaling, and bike handling. As skills improve, less energy is wasted, which means that you become more "economical" and can go faster using the same effort. Skills and economy for those new to the sport are discussed in Chapter 14.

When identifying your limiters, remember that mental fitness is just as critical as physical fitness. In Chapter 1, I discussed the importance of mental toughness, breaking it down into four elements: having a desire to succeed, mastering self-discipline, believing in yourself, and developing patience. What perhaps ties all these together is having self-confidence. What I look for in an athlete is a quiet, "can-do" attitude, the common denominator for all of the best athletes I have ever known. A great deal of self-doubt is the mark of someone incapable of achieving high goals regardless of physical ability. Working with a sports psychologist can help improve that limiter.

COMMANDMENT 8: TRUST YOUR TRAINING

There's nothing worse than thinking you are making good progress toward achieving your goal and then on race day feeling that you are not physically ready. Few of us trust our training when it comes time to race, but this should be a vague adrenaline-generated fear, not a fact. To ensure that you can feel confident in your training, it's critical to assess it during the year. If you see that you aren't improving as expected in some aspect of fitness, you can correct it and change your training long before race week. There are many ways to assess fitness progress. Chapter 5 addresses some of these.

If you aren't completely confident about your training base, then as the big race approaches, you may worry that you haven't done enough or even train right up to race day. I've seen people the day before an important race go out for a long ride or compete in a hard race because they think it will help. It takes 10 to 21 days of reduced workload for the human body to be fully ready to race, depending on how long and hard the training has been. Cut back before the big races, and you'll do better. Trust me.

COMMANDMENT 9: LISTEN TO YOUR BODY

It is vitally important to do the least amount of training necessary to achieve your goal. When I was a much younger athlete I thought my success depended on doing as much training as possible. What that led to was frequent injury, overtraining, illness, and burnout. It took me many years to listen to my body and figure out what I should be doing—only the training that is necessary to achieve my goals. Once I stopped pushing beyond my body's recovery limits, I improved as an athlete. I've found it works the same way for those I coach.

It's not just my experience. In the early 1990s, after the fall of the Berlin Wall, I attended a talk by the former head of the East German Sports Institute. After conceding that East German athletes had indeed used illegal drugs, which he felt was a minor aspect of their remarkable success, he went on to explain what he saw as the real reason for their great number of Olympic medals. He described how elite athletes lived regulated lives in dormitories. Every morning, each athlete met with a group of experts—an event coach, a physiologist, a doctor or nurse, and a sports psychologist, for example. The group checked the athlete's readiness to train that day and made adjustments as necessary to the schedule. In effect, they were listening to what the athlete's body was saying. The athlete trained only to the level he or she could tolerate that day. Nothing more.

It would be nice if each of us could afford such attention. We can't, so we must learn to listen to our bodies for ourselves. If you listen to what your body is saying, you'll train smarter and get faster. Cyclists who train smart always beat athletes who train hard. *The Cyclist's Training Bible* will teach you how to hear what your body is saying every day—and train smart.

One important note: Even though I coach highly committed athletes, and they work very hard, I have learned the importance of having fun. This may seem obvious, but some athletes are so focused on achieving the right numbers in their logs that they've forgotten why they got involved in the sport in the first place, and it's no longer fun. Many of the pros I talk to are amazed at how much training time the age groupers do on top of working 50 to 60 hours per week, getting the kids to soccer practice, mowing the lawn, doing volunteer work, and attending to myriad other responsibilities. By comparison, the pros have it easy! They just train 30 to 40 hours per week with a few naps sprinkled in. These pros also tell me that if it ever stopped being fun, they would quit racing and get a real job. Fun is the reason each and every one of us participates in cycling. You're probably not earning a living riding a bike—never lose sight of that. You are not defined by your most recent race result. Your kids won't love you any less if you have a "bad" race. The sun will still come up tomorrow. So smile more and frown less; you will enjoy cycling more and do better in the sport because of it.

COMMANDMENT 10: COMMIT TO GOALS

If you want to race farther, faster, and stronger this season than you did last season, you will need to train differently and may even need to make changes in your lifestyle. What could be holding you back? Maybe you need to go to bed earlier. Or perhaps you eat too much junk food. You may benefit from putting in more time at the weight room during the winter to build greater force. Maybe your training partners are holding you back.

After you set your goals in a later chapter, take a look at them and determine how they relate to your lifestyle and training. Determine that if change is needed, you can do it. Only you can control how well you race.

Striving for peak performance is a 24-hour-a-day, 365-day-a-year task. Racing at the highest possible level demands a full-time commitment that is not just training-related. The higher the goals, the more your life must revolve around eating, sleeping, and working out. Eating nutritious food fuels the body for training and helps speed recovery by replenishing depleted energy and nutrient stores while providing the building blocks for a stronger body. Sleeping and working out have a synergistic effect on fitness.

Every day you have lifestyle choices to make about diet, sleep, and other physical and mental activities. The decisions you make, often without even thinking, will impact how well you ride.

A fully committed rider is a student of the sport. Read everything you can get your hands on about cycling, sports nutrition, and the like. Talk with coaches, trainers, athletes, mechanics, race officials, salespeople, and anyone else who may have a unique perspective. Ask questions, but be a bit skeptical. If you're to grow as an athlete, change is necessary. Other knowledgeable people are often the sources for this change.

Training to improve includes keeping a training log. Record workout details, perceptions of effort, stress signals, race results and analyses, signs of increasing or decreasing fitness, equipment changes, and anything else that describes your daily experience. It may all prove helpful down the road. Most athletes also find that keeping a log provides them with a sharper training focus and results in more rapid progress toward their goals.

A word about what I've learned about goal setting: If you set a goal at the start of the season and know you can achieve it even before setting out to train for it, then it wasn't much of a goal, was it? The idea of a goal is to have something to strive for that will cause you to become a better athlete. A good goal will stretch your limits, forcing you to master a new skill, gain strength, or make a lifestyle change. Whatever this "something new" may be, it is critical to your success and requires that you isolate and improve this quality. I call this "fixing the limiters." Chapter 6 offers more on this topic.

Another thing to realize is that the bigger your goals are relative to your abilities, the more things in life must be focused on achieving them. If your goal is to finish with the field in a local, short road race, then you can afford to be a bit sloppy with nutrition, sleep, stress, training partners, friends, stretching, equipment, workout analysis, and strength work—and still do well. But if your goal is to win the race or podium at a national championship, you will need to get everything in your life pointed at cycling success.

Although committing to your goals is critical, bear in mind that each of us has a comfortable level of commitment. For most of us, jobs, families, and other responsibilities cannot be forsaken just to ride a bike. Part of "committing" is finding your own personal balance between training and the rest of life. Chapters 15 through 18 address these issues further.

PART II

FROM LAB TO ROAD
HISTORICAL PERSPECTIVES

TRAINING TIPS AT RANDOM

by Fred Kugler

(as it appeared in *Bicycling Magazine*, April 1946)

A stunt that we have often used in road training is to walk rapidly for about a half a mile but carrying the bicycle with your arm cocked so the bicycle's cross bar is just off your shoulder. This tends to throw your shoulders back and stretches your chest and lungs, developing your grip, wrists, and arms. Change arms in carrying at will, but at no time during your set distance for this exercise let the bike touch the ground or your shoulder. If in a group, it can be made interesting by seeing who can carry their bicycle the farthest, or race to a given point under the above rules. Do this at the beginning or end of a ride, or just before or after a rest stop.

If interest is dull during a training ride, try this. The man in front sticks in ten hard kicks (counting on one foot only), then swings out and drops back to last place, and the next fellow sticks in his ten hard kicks, drops back, etc. You will soon find the going quite tough, that is if each rider really puts in ten good hard kicks.

3 THE SCIENCE OF TRAINING

Having all the sports science knowledge in the world, having all the best coaches, having all the best equipment, will that win a gold medal for you? No. But not having all that can lose it for you.

—CHRIS CARMICHAEL,
LANCE ARMSTRONG'S LONGTIME COACH

IT WAS NOT UNTIL THE 1960s that the study of exercise as a science became widespread, and not until the 1970s that it began to significantly change the way serious cyclists trained. In the 1980s, exercise science made a quantum leap forward. We learned more about the human athlete in those ten years than in the previous eighty.

The earliest scientists learned more from studying the methods of top athletes than they did from independent research in ivory towers. That is still the case today; the people in white lab coats simply seek an explanation for why some athletes succeed and others do not.

Even in the early days of racing, cyclists learned through trial and error that they couldn't develop maximal endurance and maximal power simultaneously. Coaches and athletes found that by first establishing an aerobic endurance base and later adding faster riding, they could come into top form at the right time. This method of training was often imposed on them by the weather. Winter made long, easy rides a necessity, while summer favored faster riding.

Since those leather shoe and wool jersey days, we've learned a lot from the best athletes, coaches, and scientists. It's been a long and winding road. The entire range of training elements, including nutrition, recovery, strength, mental skills, fitness measurement, and workouts, has been explored and greatly refined. Still, many athletes continue to train as if it were 1912. They go out the door day after day with no plan, deciding as the ride develops what they will do. Some are successful despite their backward ways. Could they do better? Probably. Will you improve if you adopt a more scientific way of training as described in this book? I believe you will.

I hope to help you reach toward your potential by taking advantage of the most recent training knowledge available. This knowledge has been gleaned from research studies, from the training methods of top cyclists and coaches, and from athletes and coaches in other sports such as swimming, running, rowing, and triathlon. Some of it is proven beyond doubt, but much is still theory. You need to determine how everything applies to you and your training. Even well-established and proven practices may not be applicable to your unique set of circumstances. Some things may not work for you even though they do for others.

Before getting scientific, I want to explain a few basics about training for cycling. These things may be so elementary that they seem obvious, but I'll describe them just in case.

No one starts out at the top. Many of those who get there make it because they are more patient than others. Training has a cumulative effect from year to year. If it is done correctly, a cyclist should see improvement over time. Don't expect miracles overnight.

Physical and psychological breaks from training are normal and necessary. No one can improve at an uninterrupted pace forever. If you don't build rest and recovery into your training plan, your body will force you to. It doesn't matter how mentally strong you are: You need frequent breaks from training.

If you're new to cycling, the most important thing you can do is ride consistently and steadily for a year. Don't be concerned about all of the details this book will describe until you've put at least one season under your belt. Then you can begin to plug in the finer elements of training.

PHYSIOLOGY AND FITNESS

How can we measure physical fitness? Science has discovered four of its most basic components—aerobic capacity, lactate threshold (LT), aerobic threshold, and economy. The top riders have excellent values for all four of these physiological traits.

AEROBIC CAPACITY

Aerobic capacity is a measure of the amount of oxygen the body can consume during all-out endurance exercise. It is also referred to as VO_2max—the maximal volume of oxygen your body can process to produce movement. VO_2max can be measured in the lab during a "graded" test in which the athlete, wearing a device that measures oxygen uptake, increases the intensity of exercise every few minutes until exhaustion. VO_2max is expressed in terms of milliliters of oxygen used per kilogram of body weight per minute (ml/kg/min). World-class male riders usually produce numbers in the 70 to 80 ml/kg/min range. By comparison, normally active male college students typically test in the range of

40 to 50 ml/kg/min. On average, women's aerobic capacities are about 10 percent lower than men's.

Aerobic capacity is largely determined by genetics and is limited by such physiological factors as heart size, heart rate, heart stroke volume, blood hemoglobin content, aerobic enzyme concentrations, mitochondrial density, and muscle fiber type. It can, however, be improved to a certain extent through training. Typically, in otherwise well-trained athletes, it takes six to eight weeks of high-intensity training to significantly elevate VO_2max peak values.

As we get older, aerobic capacity usually decreases, dropping by as much as 1 percent per year after age 25 in sedentary people. For those who train seriously, especially by regularly including high-intensity workouts, the loss will be far smaller and may not occur until they are well into their thirties or even later.

LACTATE THRESHOLD

Aerobic capacity is not a good predictor of endurance performance. If all of the riders in a race category were tested for aerobic capacity, the race finishing results would not necessarily correlate to their VO_2max test values. The athletes with the highest VO_2max values would not necessarily finish high in the rankings. But the highest value of VO_2max that one can maintain for an extended period of time is a good predictor of racing capacity. This sustainable high value is a reflection of an athlete's LT.

LT, sometimes called "anaerobic threshold," is a critical intensity level for the cyclist, especially one who focuses on short and fast races. The ability to go long and hard near and above LT determines who crosses the line first in hotly contested racing. It measures the level of exercise intensity above which lactate and its associated hydrogen ions begin to rapidly accumulate in the blood. Because LT is marked by the accumulation of acid in the body, it can be readily measured in a lab or clinic.

At the threshold, metabolism rapidly shifts from dependence on the combustion of fat and oxygen in the production of energy to dependence on glycogen—the storage form of carbohydrates. The higher this threshold is as a percentage of VO_2max, the faster the athlete can ride for an extended period of time, as in a race. Once the blood-borne acid reaches a high enough level, there is no option but to slow down in order to clear it from the body.

Sedentary individuals experience LT at 40 to 50 percent of VO_2max. In trained athletes, the LT typically occurs at 80 to 90 percent of VO_2max. So it is obvious that if two riders have the same aerobic capacity, but rider A's LT is 90 percent and B's is 80 percent, then A should be able to maintain a higher average velocity and has quite a physiological advantage in a head-to-head endurance race (unless rider B is smart enough to protect himself from the wind and has a great sprint). Unlike aerobic capacity, LT is highly trainable. Much of the training described in this book is intended to elevate your LT.

AEROBIC THRESHOLD

Aerobic threshold occurs at a much lower intensity than LT but is just as critical to race success. Riding at your aerobic threshold is about the intensity at which the peloton travels. Having excellent aerobic fitness allows you to ride easily in the peloton for hours, if necessary, and still be fresh and ready when race tactics call for a great effort—for a match to be burned, in other words.

The aerobic threshold cannot be pinpointed in a lab, but it is physiologically marked by a slight increase in the depth of breathing accompanied by a sense of moderate-effort intensity. In terms of heart rate, it occurs in zone 2 (heart rate training zones are described in the next chapter; for now, the important thing to note is that zone 2 is quite low). For those in great shape, power output will be quite high at this heart rate. The aerobic threshold will also vary from day to day based on how well rested you are. As with LT, when you are fresh it will be found at a higher power output than when you are fatigued.

Intensity at LT is so great that fatigue may well prevent you from achieving an excessively high heart rate. That is not the case with the much lower-intensity aerobic threshold. Because of high motivation, you may push yourself too hard when fatigued during an aerobic threshold workout. So when it comes to the aerobic threshold, paying close attention to your effort is just as important as watching your heart rate monitor or power meter.

Training in the aerobic threshold zone is perfect for building basic aerobic endurance, which is a primary focus during the Base training period. For this reason, a good portion of each week's training in the Base period should be devoted to training at the aerobic threshold.

ECONOMY

Compared with recreational riders, elite cyclists use less oxygen to hold a given, steady, submaximal velocity. The elite riders are using less energy to produce the same power output. This is similar to automobile fuel-efficiency ratings that tell prospective buyers which cars are gas guzzlers. Using less fuel to produce the same amount of power is an obvious advantage in competition.

Studies reveal that an endurance athlete's economy improves if he or she:

- Has a high percentage of slow-twitch muscle fibers (largely genetic)
- Has a low body mass (weight-to-height relationship)
- Has low psychological stress
- Uses light and aerodynamic equipment that fits properly
- Limits body frontal area exposed to the wind at higher velocities
- Eliminates useless and energy-wasting movements

Fatigue negatively impacts economy as muscles that are not normally called upon are recruited to carry the load. That's just one reason why it's critical to go into important races well rested. Near the end of a race, when economy deteriorates because of fatigue, you may sense that your pedaling and technical handling skills are getting sloppy. The longer the race, the more critical economy becomes in determining the outcome.

Just as with LT, economy is highly trainable. It improves as your overall endurance increases and as your bike skills become refined. This is why I emphasize drill work for pedaling in the winter training months and a commitment to improving skills year-round.

Identifying and defining these four factors in detail probably makes it sound as if fitness can be easily quantified and, perhaps, used to predict or even produce top athletes. Fortunately, that's not the case. The best scientists in the world can take a group of the most fit cyclists into a state-of-the-art lab; test, poke, prod, measure, and analyze them; then predict how they will do in a race—and fail miserably. Labs are not the real world of racing, where many variables beyond the ken of science escape quantification.

TRAINING STRESS

There are five terms used repeatedly in this book that relate to the stresses applied in training: frequency, duration, volume, workload, and intensity. It is important to understand these terms. By carefully changing workout *frequency, duration,* and *intensity* throughout the season, the body's comfortable state is disturbed, forcing it to adapt with the positive changes we call "fitness." This manipulation has to do with *volume* and *workload.* Let's briefly examine each of these terms.

FREQUENCY

Frequency refers to how often training sessions are done. Novice riders may work out three to five times a week and experience a rapid change in fitness, perhaps in the range of a 10 to 20 percent improvement in a short period of time. Experienced cyclists train with greater frequency, often doing two workouts a day at certain times of the year. An Olympic hopeful might work out twelve to fifteen times in a week, but such a high frequency may only produce a 1 percent gain in fitness, since these athletes are already so close to their potential.

Studies have found that training three to five times a week brings the greatest gain for the time invested, and that additional workouts have diminishing returns. If you are trying to realize your racing potential, however, the small gains provided by those additional workouts may be worth it, since the competition will be quite close to you in ability.

Should a novice try to train at the same high level as the more experienced rider, he or she may actually see a decrease in fitness due to overtraining. If the experienced rider trains for a substantial length of time at the novice's low level, there will also be a loss of fitness, but because of undertraining—the stress frequency is too low.

The frequency at which you work out also depends in part on what your body is currently adapted to. For example, even if you're an experienced rider, if you have not trained for several weeks it is best to start with a lower frequency and gradually increase it.

DURATION

Training sessions may vary considerably in length. Those designed to improve aerobic endurance may last several hours. Those allowing for higher-intensity efforts or aiming to promote recovery, in contrast, may be relatively short. Like frequency, workout duration is also partly determined by experience level, with seasoned riders doing the longest sessions. Duration may be measured in time or in distance covered. *The Cyclist's Training Bible* bases training sessions on time.

The appropriate time for long rides is largely determined by the anticipated duration of your races. Typically, the longest workouts are about the same length as the longest race in which you will compete, or even slightly longer. Early in the season, the higher-intensity workouts are done on lower-duration days, but as the racing season approaches, harder workouts incorporate both long duration and high intensity. This prepares the body for the stresses of racing.

VOLUME, WORKLOAD, AND INTENSITY

Frequency and duration are easy to quantify, so athletes often refer to them in describing their training program. They may, for example, say that they rode seven times last week for a total of fourteen hours. This actually only describes a portion of their training—the portion called "volume." Volume is the combination of frequency and duration, and it does, indeed, indicate what an athlete's training is like. But volume is an incomplete description of the stress of training.

A better summary of one's training is "workload," defined as the combination of volume and intensity. By also knowing how hard the rider trained—how much effort or power went into each workout—the stress magnitude is more completely defined. The problem for the average rider is that it's difficult to quantify intensity in the same way that frequency and duration can be quantified. One way to do this is to assign an average exertion level to each training session when it is completed, using a 1 to 10 scale, with 1 being extremely easy and 10 an all-out race effort. By multiplying the number of minutes of the session by the exertion level, the workload is adequately quantified.

Let's say you rode for 60 minutes during a workout that included a warm-up, several high-intensity hill repeats, and a cool-down. Assume that you assigned an average effort level of 7 to this entire session. Your workload might then be expressed as 420 (7 × 60).

To determine weekly workload, which takes into account the frequency of your workouts, add up the daily workload values. By comparing the workloads for a number of weeks, you can see how the stress experienced by the body changes.

Your training is composed of just three basic variables: frequency, duration, and intensity. Volume and workload are derived from these three, and simply help you quantify how these variables change over the course of the season.

Volume Versus Intensity

Which is more important—volume or intensity? Given the finite amounts of physical resources available to the rider, should he or she get in as many miles as possible, or ride fewer miles with higher intensity?

The answers to such questions depend on the rider's level of experience in the sport. Those new to cycling will improve rapidly merely by riding frequently and with relatively high durations. As the rider becomes more experienced—and fit—increases in volume have less and less impact on performance and variations in training intensity become critical.

Training intensity is the stressor that athletes most often get wrong. They ride a little too intensely when they should be taking it easy and, as a consequence, are slightly tired when a high-intensity workout is needed. All training therefore shifts toward mediocrity as the easy rides become too hard and the hard rides too easy. For most cyclists, getting the intensity right is the key to moving up to the next level of performance. Chapter 4 offers greater detail on this complex issue.

FATIGUE

Were it not for fatigue we would all be champions. How quickly and to what extent we experience fatigue is a great determinant of our fitness level—and increasing stamina to counteract it is a primary reason for training. The fittest athletes are those who can best resist its slowing effects.

Fatigue has several causes, but the ones the cyclist is most concerned with are:

- Lactate accumulation
- Glycogen depletion
- Muscle failure

A sound training program improves fitness by stressing the systems of the body associated with these causes of fatigue. Let's briefly examine each.

LACTATE ACCUMULATION

Energy for pedaling the bike comes largely from two sources—fat and carbohydrates. The body's storage form of carbohydrates is called "glycogen." As glycogen is broken down to produce energy, lactic acid appears in the working muscle cells. The lactic acid gradually seeps out of the cells and into the surrounding body fluids, where it is picked up in the bloodstream. As it leaves the cells, hydrogen ions are released, and the resulting salt is called "lactate." If the concentration of lactate becomes great enough, its acidic nature reduces the ability of the muscle cells to contract, causing the rider to slow down.

Lactate is always present in the blood, as the body uses carbohydrates along with fat for fuel at all levels of exertion—including the exertion involved in reading this page. But during exercise, as the use of glycogen increases, there is a concurrent rise in blood lactate levels. At low levels, the body has no trouble removing and buffering the acid. But as the intensity of exercise shifts from aerobic (light breathing) to anaerobic (labored breathing), the lactate eventually reaches so great a level that the body is no longer able to remove it at the same rate it is produced. The resulting lactate accumulation causes short-term fatigue. The only way the rider can deal with it now is to slow down so that lactate production is decreased and the body can catch up.

This type of fatigue occurs during brief but extremely high-intensity efforts such as long sprints, bridging to a break, or climbing a hill. Thus, the way to improve your body's ability to clear and buffer lactate is by doing short-duration interval workouts that replicate these race conditions.

GLYCOGEN DEPLETION

Fat is the primary source of fuel for every ride you do, but as the intensity of the ride varies, the contribution of carbohydrates to the energy demand rises and falls considerably. Figure 3.1 illustrates this shift.

Carbohydrates are stored in the muscles and liver as glycogen and in the blood as glucose. A well-nourished athlete has about 1,500 to 2,000 kilocalories of glycogen and glucose packed away, depending on body size and fitness level. That's not much energy. Most of this, about 75 percent, is in the muscles.

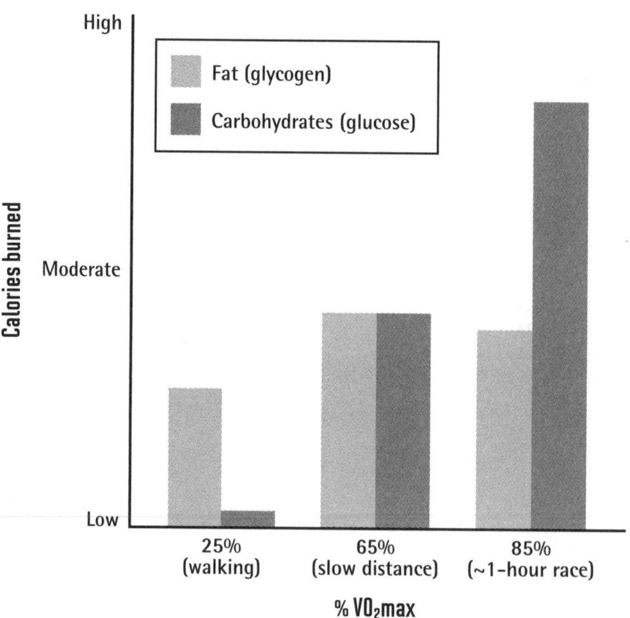

Adapted from Romijn et al. 1993.

FIGURE 3.1

Fuel Demand at Varying Levels of Aerobic Capacity

The problem is that when glycogen and glucose stores run low, exercise slows considerably, since the body must now rely primarily on fat for fuel, as shown in Figure 3.1. In cycling, this is called "bonking" or "hitting the wall." It means you're out of gas.

A 2.5-hour race may have an energy cost of 3,000 kilocalories, with perhaps half of that coming from carbohydrate sources. If the rider starts with a low level of glycogen on board and these carbohydrate calories are not replaced during the race, he or she may be forced to abandon the race. The same sorry results may also occur if the rider pedals the bike uneconomically or if his or her general aerobic fitness is poor.

Research reveals that a well-trained athlete is capable of storing greater amounts of carbohydrates while using them more sparingly than an untrained person. The diet you habitually eat also determines how much fuel is socked away and how rapidly it is used up. This is discussed in greater detail in Chapter 16.

MUSCLE FAILURE

Exactly what causes the cyclist's working muscles to fail to contract forcefully near the end of a long and grueling race is unknown. It is probably related to chemical failure at the point of connection between the nerve and the muscle, or caused by a protective mechanism in the central nervous system intended to prevent muscle damage.

High-intensity training may help to fortify the body against muscle failure by training the nervous system to recruit more muscles for endurance activity. Working out at high intensity, as when doing intervals, involves more fast-twitch muscles than riding long and slow, which favors slow-twitch muscles. Fast-twitch muscles are not called upon until the effort becomes so great that the slow-twitch muscles can no longer handle the effort. As fast twitchers are recruited to support the slow twitchers during what is basically an endurance activity, such as intervals, they begin to take on some of the slow-twitch characteristics. This is of great benefit to the endurance athlete.

PRINCIPLES OF TRAINING

The principles upon which periodization training is based are individualization, progression, overload, and specificity. Bear with me here, as these terms may sound somewhat scientific and theoretical. However, understanding the principles will make you a better cyclist—one capable of smart self-coaching.

INDIVIDUALIZATION

The capacity of an athlete to handle a given workload is unique. Each athlete is like an ecosystem in that various factors work together in a particular balance to form an integrated whole. An ecosystem has to do with environmental factors, but the factors influencing the athlete are threefold: sociocultural, biological, and psychological. Each of these categories has the potential to impede or promote improvement.

Sociocultural factors, such as lagging career progression, economic pressure, or poor interpersonal relationships, often undercut how much time and energy, both mental and physical, are available for training. Examples of biological factors are allergies, use of drugs, and inadequate nutrition. These factors may restrict the individual's physical ability to train successfully. Psychological factors are perhaps the most overlooked, yet they are the most likely to compromise the benefits of training. Some examples are fear of failure, low self-esteem, and the unreasonable expectations of others.

In addition, some athletes are "fast responders" while others are "slow responders." This means that if you and a teammate do exactly the same training in precisely the same way, you probably won't find that you reach a common level of fitness by a given race. Being a slow or a fast responder is probably mainly genetic—you may have inherited a body that changes at a given rate. Generally, four to eight weeks of a given type of training are necessary to show significant results. Although you can't change how quickly your body responds, you can learn to design your training program around your unique characteristics.

The bottom line is that you cannot simply do what others are doing and expect to get the same benefits—or any benefits at all. What is an easy day for one rider may be a race effort for another. Chapters 5 and 6 will address the issue of individualizing training to fit your unique set of abilities.

PROGRESSION

Have you ever done a workout so hard that you were sore for days afterward and did not have the energy to even ride easily? We've all done that. Such a workout violated the progression principle. The body didn't get stronger; it lost fitness. The workout caused you to waste two very precious resources: time and energy.

The workload must be gradually increased, with intermittent periods of rest and recovery, as the athlete focuses fitness for the most important races of the season. The stresses must be greater than the body is accustomed to handling. The workloads, especially the intensity component, must be increased in small increments, usually of 5 to 15 percent. Increasing the workload in this way allows the cyclist to avoid overtraining and injury, yet provides enough stress to allow adaptation to occur. Workload increases are largely individual matters, especially with regard to intensity. Chapters 5 and 6 will guide you through the maze of building race fitness progressively.

OVERLOAD

The object of training is to cause the body to positively change in order to better manage the physiological stresses of racing. In order to stress the body, it must be presented with a load that challenges its state of fitness. Such a load will cause fatigue, followed by recovery and eventually a greater level of fitness known as "overcompensation" (see Figure 3.2).

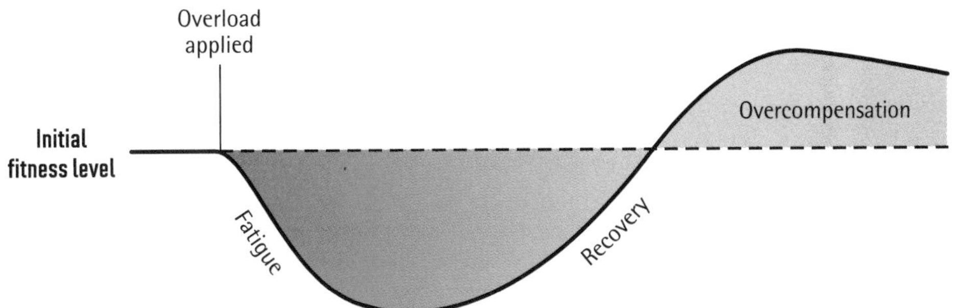

FIGURE 3.2
Effect of Training Overload

Top-level performance is the result of years of well-planned overload resulting in adaptation. This optimum training repeatedly places measured stresses on the athlete. If the workloads are of the right magnitude—slightly more than the body can handle—adaptation occurs and fitness steadily improves.

It's important to note that overload happens during workouts, but adaptation occurs during rest. It is as if the potential for fitness is produced by training, but the realization of fitness occurs during subsequent rest. If you repeatedly shortchange your rest, you will not improve, but will actually lose fitness. This is called "overtraining." The biggest mistake I see self-coached athletes make is disregarding their need for rest. Smart athletes know when to abandon a workout early. They know when to do less instead of more. In short, they understand and listen to their bodies, and you must learn to do the same. In Chapter 15, I'll teach you some techniques to help you refine this skill.

If the load of training is decreased for extended periods, the body adapts to lower levels of fitness. We call this being out of shape. But once a rider has reached optimal fitness, it can be maintained with infrequent but regular and judiciously spaced stress, allowing for increased recovery between hard workouts.

SPECIFICITY

The principle of specificity states that the stresses applied in training must be similar to the stresses expected in racing. Sometimes the workload must include long, steady distances. At other times, brief bouts of high intensity are required to bring the needed changes. Riding slow and easy all the time is just as wrong as always going hard. In Chapter 6, I'll explain how to isolate the various stresses required in road races and show you how to blend them into a comprehensive program.

4

INTENSITY

Every time I suffer I'm a better man because of it.

—LANCE ARMSTRONG

RECREATIONAL CYCLISTS generally believe that the more miles they ride, the better they will race, regardless of what they do with those miles. To some extent they are right, as there does seem to be a minimum of miles or hours that a given athlete must ride in order to boost fitness to a sufficient level to race well. Above that threshold, however, adding more miles has less benefit than increasing the intensity. It's not how many miles you ride but what you do with the miles that counts most.

Of the three basic elements of training—frequency, duration, and intensity—the most important element to get right is intensity. Oddly enough, this is the part cyclists all too often get wrong. Most train too intensely when they should be going easy. Then when it's time to go fast, they are a little too tired to push their limits. As a result, all of their training becomes moderate. They race the same way: Stay with the pack until it's time to put the hammer down. Then they're off the back wondering how they got there.

In the context of this chapter, intensity refers to the effort or power output that closely simulates that of the A-priority events for which you are training. For a road race or criterium this may mean a wide variety of intensities, including steady efforts near LT while in a fast-traveling group, aerobic-capacity intensities for several minutes while chasing down a break, or an all-out intensity for sprinting. For a time trial, century ride, or ultra-marathon, the intensity will be much more narrowly defined. The intensity necessary to produce peak fitness must be well defined in order to create a sound training program.

Developing peak fitness is like building a house. The most important part of the house is its foundation. Without a solid foundation, the house will settle, its walls will crack, and it will have little value. If the foundation is constructed well, the house will be solid and last a long time. The same can be said of training to race. A solid foundation built on a base of easy miles is necessary before the finish work—intervals, hill repeats, and fast group rides—is added. Once the foundation is well established, workouts that mimic the intensities expected in the race pay dividends. Do these same intense workouts too soon, and your house will shift and crack.

Another explanation that has stood the test of time likens a good training program to a pyramid. The broader the base of the pyramid (easy aerobic training), the higher the peak will be (fast racing speed).

The bottom line is that high-intensity training needs to be undertaken with thought and planning in order to peak at the right times of the year. Too much, too soon, and you won't be able to maintain the fitness. Too little, too late, and you're off the back. Learn to apply the intensity concepts in this chapter and you'll avoid overtraining and undertraining; your racing fitness will be high when the time is right.

MEASURING INTENSITY

What's going on inside a cyclist's body during a race or workout? How does a rider know whether to go faster or back off during a time trial? Is a workout too hard or too easy? How is it possible to finish with enough left for a sprint?

The answers to these and other questions come down to keeping close tabs on your use of energy. By measuring intensity and comparing the information with what you have learned about your body in training and racing, you can make decisions as new situations such as breakaways, headwinds, and hills occur. Today's technology allows an athlete to measure intensity quickly and accurately.

The oldest, and still one of the best, gross indicators of intensity is perceived effort. An experienced cyclist is able to judge his or her intensity quite accurately by taking a subjective survey of the entire body at work. This is a skill honed by years of riding, making mistakes, and relearning as fitness changes.

Perceived exertion is quantifiable using the Borg Rating of Perceived Exertion (RPE) Scale (see Table 4.1) and is frequently used by scientists to determine an athlete's workout level.

TABLE 4.1

Borg Rating of Perceived Exertion Scale

TRAINING PURPOSE	RATING	EXERTION
Recovery	6	
	7	Very, very light
	8	
	9	Very light
Aerobic development	10	
	11	Fairly light
	12	
Tempo development	13	Somewhat hard
	14	
Subthreshold development	15	Hard
	16	
Superthreshold development	17	Very hard
Aerobic capacity development	18	
	19	Very, very hard
	20	

Some athletes are so good at using an RPE scale that in a laboratory graduated-effort test they can pinpoint their LT precisely just from feel.

There are two other ways of measuring intensity that are related more or less to specific systems of the body. The first is to monitor heart rate, which provides an indication of how hard the entire cardiovascular system is working. The other is to monitor power output—that is, the ability of the muscular system to drive the pedals. Let's see how these and other methods can be utilized in measuring training and racing intensity.

The body is made up of several interconnected and mutually beneficial systems, such as the energy production, cardiovascular, and nervous systems. Regardless of what method of intensity measurement you use, when you monitor some aspect of your physiological response to training you are taking a peek into your body through only a small window. Since the systems are linked, however, you can draw conclusions about the entire body—once you have the experience and knowledge to do so with some degree of accuracy. I'll help you with the knowledge part in this chapter; you'll need to acquire the experience by using what you learn here.

ENERGY PRODUCTION SYSTEM: LACTATE

The metabolic system provides fuel to muscles in the form of carbohydrates, fat, and protein. Within the muscle, these fuels are converted to a usable energy form called adenosine triphosphate (ATP). This process happens either aerobically or anaerobically.

As we saw in Chapter 3, aerobic energy production occurs while you are riding easily. It relies primarily on fat and to a lesser extent on carbohydrates for fuel and uses oxygen in the process of converting fuel to ATP. The slower you go, the greater the reliance on fat and the more carbohydrates are spared. As the pace of your ride increases, there is a gradual shifting away from fat and toward carbohydrates as the fuel of choice. At high efforts, around 15 to 17 RPE, oxygen delivery no longer keeps up with the demand, and you begin producing ATP anaerobically, meaning "without oxygen."

Anaerobic exercise relies heavily on carbohydrates for fuel. As carbohydrates are converted to ATP, a by-product called lactic acid is released into the muscle. This causes the familiar burning and heavy-legged sensations you've experienced while riding hard. As lactic acid seeps through the muscle-cell walls into the bloodstream, it gives off a hydrogen molecule and becomes lactate. Lactate accumulates in the blood and can be measured by taking a sample from the finger or earlobe. The unit of measurement used in labs is millimoles per liter (expressed as mmol/L). Since carbohydrates are in use during both of these types of energy production, to a lesser extent in aerobic exercise and more so anaerobically, lactic acid is always being produced. Even while you are reading this book, your muscles are producing measurable amounts of lactic acid.

By measuring lactate, an athlete, or likely his or her coach, can determine—with some degree of accuracy depending on skill level and equipment used—several key aspects of fitness, such as:

- *Lactate threshold.* As previously described, this is the level of exertion at which metabolism shifts from aerobic to anaerobic, marked by lactate being produced so rapidly that the body can't keep up with its removal. Lactate thus accumulates in the blood. I often explain LT using an analogy. If I slowly pour water into a paper cup that has a hole in the bottom, the water will run out as fast as I pour it in. This is what happens to lactate in the blood at low levels of exertion. If I pour faster, there comes a point when the water begins to accumulate despite the fact that some is still leaking out through the hole. This is similar to the LT point that is achieved at higher levels of exertion. LT is an important concept that will be used throughout this book.

TABLE 4.2

Lactate Levels and Training

TRAINING PURPOSE	RPE	LACTATE (mmol/l)
Recovery	<10	<2
Aerobic	10–12	2–3
Threshold	13–17	3–5
Aerobic capacity	18–19	5–12
Anaerobic capacity	20	12–20

- *Training zones.* Training and racing intensities may be determined based on lactate levels (see Table 4.2).
- *Physiological improvement.* The faster you can ride or the more power that you can generate without accumulating high levels of lactate, the better your racing fitness.
- *Economy of pedaling.* Smoother pedaling means less effort to attain a given speed or distance and therefore less lactate accumulation in your muscles.
- *Equipment selection.* Optimal crankarm length, saddle height, and handlebar adjustment create a greater pedaling economy, which then produces lower levels of lactate in your muscles.
- *Recovery interval.* Reduced levels of lactate indicate that you are ready for the next work interval in a workout.

The key piece in achieving all of these benefits is the ability to accurately measure lactate in a "field" setting (using an indoor trainer or track) rather than in a lab—in other words, inexpensively. Until recently, the only way to measure lactate was in a lab using an analyzer such as the YSI 2300, the accepted standard in the United States. Its size, expense, and electricity requirements, however, made it impractical for field use.

In the past few years, less expensive portable lactate analyzers have been introduced to the U.S. fitness market, but these are not for the average rider's use, either. Using such a device effectively requires extensive skill that comes only with the experience of sampling hundreds of athletes. Instead, as a cyclist you need to learn, here and in the chapters that follow, how to roughly estimate your LT in the field by being aware of your level of exertion and that "burning" feeling you get in your legs. Once you learn how to do make this assessment, you can combine your perceived level with the more accurate information gathered by a coach or a lab technician for a reasonably precise gauge of your lactate level.

MUSCULAR SYSTEM: POWER

Power is a measure of work compared with time. It is expressed in watts, named for James Watt, the inventor of the steam engine. In physics, power is described in a formula as

$$\text{Power} = \text{work} \div \text{time}$$

At the risk of oversimplification, we can say that in cycling "work" is essentially gear size and "time" is cadence. So if gear size is increased and cadence kept steady, power rises. Or, if cadence is increased (time per revolution of the crank is decreased) while using the same gear size, power also rises.

Several scientific studies have found that power is closely related to performance. If the average power output increases, race velocity also increases. The same cannot always be said for heart rate, as explained above; that is why power monitoring is such an excellent tool for bicycle training. It is the most effective way for the serious rider to gauge intensity.

The downside of power monitoring, as compared with heart rate, is equipment cost. While the price of power meters has come down since their introduction in the late 1980s, they are still more expensive than heart rate monitors. However, power meters are becoming more affordable each year, and you can expect the cost of the equipment to continue to fall in the coming years.

Power-based training begins with determining one's "critical power profile." This is a visual representation of the ability to produce power at various durations. Finding and graphing average power output for the critical power (CP) durations of 12 seconds and 1, 6, 12, 30, 60, 90, and 180 minutes produces a curve, or profile (Figure 4.1).

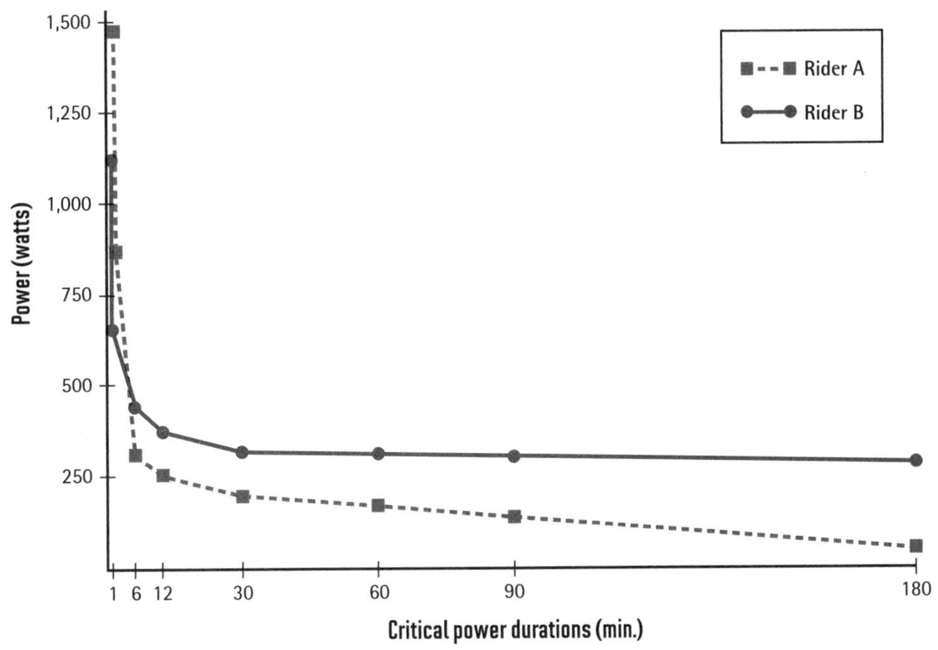

FIGURE 4.1

Critical Profiles of Two Riders

Note that the profiles in Figure 4.1 are considerably different for the two riders. Rider A is capable of producing far greater power than rider B for short durations. Although rider B lacks short-duration power, the generally shallower slope indicates much greater endurance capability. In an all-out sprint near the finish line, rider A has an advantage, but rider B has the upper hand as the duration increases.

Once you've established your critical power for a duration of 60 minutes (CP60), you and your coach will be able to set up your power training zones. Table 4.3 shows you how to do this using the system created by Hunter Allen and Andy Coggan and described in their book *Training and Racing with a Power Meter.*

TABLE 4.3

Power Zones Based on CP60

ZONE 1	ZONE 2	ZONE 3	ZONE 4	ZONE 5	ZONE 6	ZONE 7
Recovery	Aerobic	Tempo	Threshold	Aerobic capacity	Anaerobic capacity	Power
<56%	56–75%	76–90%	91–105%	106–120%	121–150%	>150%

CARDIOVASCULAR SYSTEM: HEART RATE

The introduction of the portable heart rate monitor in the early 1980s brought about a profound change in how athletes approached training. It is now a commonly used training device, second only to the handlebar computer in popularity.

From the time heart rate monitors first hit the market until about 1990, they were "gee whiz" toys—they were fun to play with, but the numbers didn't mean much. Now that nearly everyone has one, athletes are becoming more astute in their use. At criteriums, road races, and time trials around the country you can find most cyclists wearing them to regulate or monitor exertion.

A heart rate monitor is much like the tachometer in an automobile. Neither one tells how fast you're going, but rather how hard the engine is working. Just as a car can rev up the engine without moving and redline the tachometer, heart rate can zoom while you are running in place.

SIDEBAR 4.1

Don't Be a Slave to Your Heart Rate Monitor

Ten years ago hardly anyone had a heart rate monitor. Now almost everyone has one. Generally, I'm glad to see that trend, but there's a downside: It seems that we're becoming overly concerned with heart rate. Let me explain.

Before heart rate monitors, when an athlete started a hard workout such as intervals, he or she continually gauged how the session was going and might decide to cut the session short or extend it based on the resulting observations. The usual basis for this pre–heart rate monitor decision was rate of perceived exertion (RPE). RPE is based on a subjective reaction to breathing, lactate accumulation, fatigue, and other less well-defined sensations occurring during exercise. From these somewhat vague data the athlete would make decisions. What was good about this system was that it forced athletes to stay in tune with what their bodies were feeling. The downside was that it took experience to develop the skills to know what the sensations meant.

But now, with heart rate monitors, many athletes largely ignore their RPE and focus solely on what their heart rates are. Although it can be useful to know your heart rate when training, heart rate is not the only metric that should be monitored. In fact, doing so can actually cause problems. Why? For one thing, heart rate monitors do not give you a complete picture of the body's workload. Nor do they necessarily even give you an accurate picture, as many factors besides the workout itself—such as heat, diet, and stress, to name just a few—may affect heart rate.

Heart rate by itself does not tell you how well you're performing in a workout or a race, and yet many athletes try to draw conclusions from one number. For example, something I hear all the time is, "I couldn't get my heart rate up so I stopped the workout." Is a low heart rate bad? It could be, but then again, it might be good. One of the physiological side effects of improving aerobic fitness is an increased heart-stroke volume—more blood is pumped per beat. That means a reduced heart rate for any submaximal level of exertion. So a low heart rate in a workout or race may be telling you that your fitness is high and that you are doing well; if that is the case, you should by all means keep going, not stop.

The other erroneous conclusion that athletes often draw is that a high heart rate is good. I sometimes hear the boast, "It was easy to get my heart rate up today," as if that statement translated into "I'm in good shape." Again, that's not necessarily true. We could take a sedentary person off the street, put him on a bike, and force him to ride fast. Guess what? His heart rate would rise very easily. We might even be able to achieve a maximal pulse with very little power output. If his heart rate achieved the same max as that of a fit rider, it would really tell us nothing about either one of them. You see, there is no difference between the maximal heart rate of a very fit athlete and that of an obese couch potato. The less fit you are, the easier it is to get your heart rate up to max.

When testing athletes I have found that when they are in very good race shape, their maximal heart rates appear to drop. I don't know exactly why that is. It may have something to do with their aerobic system adapting so well to endurance training that the muscular system is incapable of driving it any higher.

Another misuse of the heart rate monitor number is drawing conclusions about one's state of well-being. "My resting heart rate is high (or low) so I must be overtrained," a cyclist

Continued >

< Sidebar 4.1 continued

might say. It is not possible, however, to look at resting or exercising heart rates and draw such a conclusion. If it was, sports scientists would have stopped looking long ago for a way to gauge overtraining—something they have not been able to find.

Heart rate by itself tells you nothing about performance or well-being. It must be compared with something else to have meaning. For example, when it comes to cycling performance, comparing heart rate with power (for example, on a CompuTrainer or with a Power-Tap or SRM) is an excellent way to determine gains in fitness. If heart rate is low and power is normal to high when compared with previous performances, then fitness is high. If heart rate is high and power is high, then the athlete is probably still building fitness. This is a good way to gauge when the Base period should come to an end.

If heart rate is low and power is also low, then the athlete may be experiencing fatigue, lifestyle stress, or even overtraining. There are other possibilities in this combination, so all we know is that something is not right; we cannot pinpoint the exact problem without further information.

Metrics other than power could also be used in conjunction with heart rate to help draw conclusions about the athlete's status. For example, what would low heart rate and high RPE be telling you? This is saying that fitness and well-being are probably good. What would you say about high heart rate and low RPE? Common sense would suggest that something isn't right. Think your way through the various possibilities.

The main point here is that heart rate alone tells you only one thing—you are still alive. Drawing conclusions only from what your monitor says on a given day is folly. Use the information that this miraculous training tool gives you, but don't rely on it alone.

Knowing how hard the heart is working is important information that allows you to make decisions as a workout progresses. Sometimes motivation, or lack of it, gets in the way of rating your perceived exertion during high-quality training sessions.

Be aware that a low heart rate is not always a bad sign. In fact, a low workout heart rate relative to what experience has shown to be more common for you can be a good sign. As your aerobic fitness improves, typically your heart rate will decline because your heart is becoming stronger and more efficient. By the same principle, a high heart rate is not always a good sign.

For a cyclist, knowing lactate threshold heart rate (LTHR) is as important as knowing a bicycle's frame size. But forget about trying to find maximum heart rate. Not only does this require great motivation—as in a gun to the head—but it's not as good an indicator as LT.

Heart rate training zones are best based on LTHR, since the percentage of maximum at which one becomes anaerobic (lactate accumulates) is highly variable. For example, one cyclist may have an LTHR that is 85 percent of his maximum heart rate, while another goes anaerobic at 90 percent of max. If both riders train at 90 percent of max, one is deeply anaerobic and the other is at threshold. They are not experiencing the same workout or getting the same benefits. If, however, both train at 100 percent of LT, or any other percentage of LT, they are experiencing the same exertion level and reaping the same benefits.

Finding LT requires scientific precision, but don't let that scare you away. It's actually a simple procedure. I'll describe how to do it in the next chapter. I prefer to first determine LTHR and then establish heart rate training zones on either side of it.

One "easy" way to estimate your LTHR is to time trial while wearing a monitor (the method is easy, not the time trial). The distance of the individual time trial could be 5 kilometers, 10 kilometers, 8 miles, 10 miles, or 40 kilometers. The test can be done as an established race or as a workout you do alone. The average heart rate from this test will serve as a predictor of your LT. Since you will undoubtedly have higher motivation in a race than when doing this test alone, the results should be interpreted differently. Table 4.4 provides a basic formula for determining LTHR from an individual time trial.

TABLE 4.4

LT Heart Rates Based on Individual Time Trial

DISTANCE	AS RACE	AS WORKOUT
5 km	110% of LT	104% of LT
10 km	107% of LT	102% of LT
8–10 miles	105% of LT	101% of LT
40 km	100% of LT	97% of LT

Example: A 10-mile individual time trial is done as a race when the athlete is rested and highly motivated. The athlete's average heart rate is 176, and we will assume the rider is working at 105 percent of LT (see the second column of Table 4.4). Since 176 divided by 1.05 is 167, this rider's LTHR is 167. (See bold number 167 and read to left and right in Table 4.6 for heart rate training zones.) Table 4.4 may also be used to determine the heart rate to be used in an individual time trial. For example, a 40 km individual time trial should be ridden at 100 percent of LT.

Another simple test that can be done alone and has proven to provide a fairly accurate estimate of LTHR is to ride a 30-minute time trial alone. Ten minutes into the time trial, click the lap button on your heart rate monitor. The average heart rate for the last 20 minutes of your time trial is a reasonable estimate of LTHR. As with all of these tests, the more frequently you repeat the test, the more accurately you can estimate LTHR.

You may even be able to use your workouts to help confirm what was previously found in tests to be LTHR. Simply pay attention to your heart rate whenever you feel yourself initially becoming anaerobic. This level of intensity will be marked by burning sensations in your legs and the onset of heavy breathing.

Once you've found your LTHR, you can determine your heart rate training zones by using Tables 4.5 and 4.6.

Since we'll be referring to them frequently, I've numbered each heart rate zone. Zones 1 through 4 are aerobic zones, and zones 5a, 5b, and 5c are anaerobic.

TABLE 4.5 Heart Rate Training Zones Based on LTHR

ZONE	RPE	PURPOSE	% OF LTHR
1	<10	Recovery	65–81
2	10–12	Aerobic	82–88
3	13–14	Tempo	89–93
4	15–16	Subthreshold	94–100
5a	17	Superthreshold	101–102
5b	18–19	Aerobic capacity	103–105
5c	20+	Anaerobic capacity	106+

Heart rate varies with the individual sport. If you're crosstraining in the winter by running, your LTHR for running will be different from your LTHR for cycling, and your training zones will differ accordingly. You should therefore determine your heart rate zones for each sport you train in, or else use the LTHR measure only for cycling and go only by RPE for other sports.

RACE-FIT SYSTEMS

Getting into top racing form means optimizing the performance of each of the three race-fit systems. A cyclist with a great muscular system but poor energy and cardiovascular systems won't last long on the roads. It takes all three systems working together. These systems must go through many changes during the training year for you to race effectively and attain your goals. Following is a partial list of changes that occur as a result of training.

Energy Production System

- Greater utilization of fat and sparing of glycogen
- Enhanced conversion of lactate to fuel
- Increased stores of glycogen and creatine phosphate
- Improved ability to extract oxygen from blood

Muscular System

- Increased force generation within a muscle fiber
- Enhanced recruitment of muscle fibers
- More economical movement patterns
- Enhanced endurance qualities

Cardiovascular System

- More blood pumped per heartbeat
- Greater capillarization of muscle fibers
- Increased blood volume
- Enhanced oxygen transportation to the muscles

MULTISYSTEM TRAINING

RPE, heart rate, and power each offer unique benefits for the serious cyclist when it comes to monitoring the intensity of a workout or race. RPE provides a subjective yet comprehensive view of what you are encountering when on the bike. Heart rate offers a

TABLE 4.6

LTHR and Heart Rate Training Zones

Find your LTHR in the "Zone 5a" column (bold number). Read across to left and right for training zones.

ZONE 1	ZONE 2	ZONE 3	ZONE 4	ZONE 5A	ZONE 5B	ZONE 5C
Recovery	Aerobic	Tempo	Subthreshold	Super-threshold	Aerobic Capacity	Anaerobic Capacity
90–108	109–122	123–128	129–136	**137**–140	141–145	146–150
91–109	110–123	124–129	130–137	**138**–141	142–146	147–151
91–109	110–124	125–130	131–138	**139**–142	143–147	148–152
92–110	111–125	126–130	131–139	**140**–143	144–147	148–153
92–111	112–125	126–131	132–140	**141**–144	145–148	149–154
93–112	113–126	127–132	133–141	**142**–145	146–149	150–155
94–112	113–127	128–133	134–142	**143**–145	146–150	151–156
94–113	114–128	129–134	135–143	**144**–147	148–151	152–157
95–114	115–129	130–135	136–144	**145**–148	149–152	153–158
95–115	116–130	131–136	137–145	**146**–149	150–154	155–159
97–116	117–131	132–137	138–146	**147**–150	151–155	156–161
97–117	118–132	133–138	139–147	**148**–151	152–156	157–162
98–118	119–133	134–139	140–148	**149**–152	153–157	158–163
98–119	120–134	135–140	141–149	**150**–153	154–158	159–164
99–120	121–134	135–141	142–150	**151**–154	155–159	160–165
100–121	122–135	136–142	143–151	**152**–155	156–160	161–166
100–122	123–136	137–142	143–152	**153**–156	157–161	162–167
101–123	124–137	138–143	144–153	**154**–157	158–162	163–168
101–124	125–138	139–144	145–154	**155**–158	159–163	164–169
102–125	126–138	139–145	146–155	**156**–159	160–164	165–170
103–126	127–140	141–146	147–156	**157**–160	161–165	166–171
104–127	128–141	142–147	148–157	**158**–161	162–167	168–173
104–128	129–142	143–148	149–158	**159**–162	163–168	169–174
105–129	130–143	144–148	149–159	**160**–163	164–169	170–175
106–129	130–143	144–150	151–160	**161**–164	165–170	171–176
106–130	131–144	145–151	152–161	**162**–165	166–171	172–177
107–131	132–145	146–152	153–162	**163**–166	167–172	173–178
107–132	133–146	147–153	154–163	**164**–167	168–173	174–179
108–133	134–147	148–154	155–164	**165**–168	169–174	175–180
109–134	135–148	149–154	155–165	**166**–169	170–175	176–181
109–135	136–149	150–155	156–166	**167**–170	171–176	177–182
110–136	137–150	151–156	157–167	**168**–171	172–177	178–183
111–137	138–151	152–157	158–168	**169**–172	173–178	179–185
112–138	139–151	152–158	159–169	**170**–173	174–179	180–186
112–139	140–152	153–160	161–170	**171**–174	175–180	181–187
113–140	141–153	154–160	161–171	**172**–175	176–181	182–188
113–141	142–154	155–161	162–172	**173**–176	177–182	183–189
114–142	143–155	156–162	163–173	**174**–177	178–183	184–190
115–143	144–156	157–163	164–174	**175**–178	179–184	185–191
115–144	145–157	158–164	165–175	**176**–179	180–185	186–192
116–145	146–158	159–165	166–176	**177**–180	181–186	187–193
116–146	147–159	160–166	167–177	**178**–181	182–187	188–194
117–147	148–160	161–166	167–178	**179**–182	183–188	189–195
118–148	149–160	161–167	168–179	**180**–183	184–190	191–197
119–149	150–161	162–168	169–180	**181**–184	185–191	192–198
119–150	151–162	163–170	171–181	**182**–185	186–192	193–199
120–151	152–163	164–171	172–182	**183**–186	187–193	194–200
121–152	153–164	165–172	173–183	**184**–187	188–194	195–201
121–153	154–165	166–172	173–184	**185**–188	191–195	196–202
122–154	155–166	167–173	174–185	**186**–189	190–196	197–203
122–155	156–167	168–174	175–186	**187**–190	191–197	198–204
123–156	157–168	169–175	176–187	**188**–191	192–198	199–205
124–157	158–169	170–176	177–188	**189**–192	193–199	200–206
124–158	159–170	171–177	178–189	**190**–193	194–200	201–207
125–159	160–170	171–178	179–190	**191**–194	195–201	202–208
125–160	161–171	172–178	179–191	**192**–195	196–202	203–209
126–161	162–172	173–179	180–192	**193**–196	197–203	204–210
127–162	163–173	174–180	181–193	**194**–197	198–204	205–211
127–163	164–174	175–181	182–194	**195**–198	199–205	206–212

window into the cardiovascular system and thus a glimpse of the workload the body is experiencing. A power meter reports what the body is accomplishing. Power is a measure of performance rather than an indicator of the physiological stress experienced. Each can be valuable in the training process when the interpretation of the data is correct.

Using all three of these measures is like seeing a picture in three dimensions instead of only one or two—training makes more sense. Whether or not a number is assigned, RPE should be an integral method of monitoring intensity in all workouts. This will pay dividends in races where closely observing heart rate and power is not possible. RPE is the "stake in the ground"—the supreme reference for all intensity monitoring. You must become good at using it. Heart rate is best used for steady-state training, particularly when conducted below LT. It is especially effective during long, aerobic rides and for recovery workouts. Focus on power for intervals, hill training, sprint-power training, and all anaerobic workouts. I've seen significant improvement in race performance when riders have begun training with power meters. This is unquestionably the future of bicycle training. Mastering and appropriately applying each of these intensity monitoring systems has the potential to dramatically improve your training and, therefore, your racing.

MEASURING WORKLOAD

Now that you have three systems for monitoring intensity, it's possible to quantify workload. Recall from the previous chapter that workload is the combination of frequency, duration, and intensity of training. Knowing your workload allows you to keep track of the weekly training stress loads you are placing on your body and enables you to compare those loads from week to week. Such information is valuable for avoiding overtraining. When you know how much stress training is likely to produce, you can plan your daily workouts accordingly and schedule adequate recovery periods. Quantifying your workload can also ensure more effective periodization of your training (see Chapter 7 for details on periodization). What follows are descriptions of three methods of measuring workload.

Rate of Perceived Exertion

At the end of a training session, assign an average workout RPE using a scale of 6 to 20 (as defined in Table 4.1). Then multiply this RPE value by the number of minutes in the session. For example, if a 60-minute session including intervals had an average RPE of 14, the workload for this day would be 840 ($60 \times 14 = 840$).

Heart Rate

Using a heart rate monitor with a time-by-zone function, it's possible to know how many minutes were spent in at least three zones (with a three-zone monitor, all five zones may be observed by switching zones during the ride). By multiplying each of the zone's numeric identifiers (zone 3, for example) by the number of minutes spent in each zone and then adding them up, workload for a week or any other period of time may be determined.

For example, if you completed a 60-minute ride that included 20 minutes in zone 1, 25 minutes in zone 2, and 15 minutes in zone 3, the cumulative workload would be 115. Here's how that number was derived:

Time in Zone 1	20 x 1 = 20
Time in Zone 2	25 x 2 = 50
Time in Zone 3	15 x 3 = 45
Total	115

Power

Power meters offer a quick way of monitoring workload—session kilojoules (kJ), often referred to as "E" (for energy), are displayed on the power meter. This is a measure of energy expended. One kilocalorie (kcal or calorie) is equal to 4.184 kJ. Energy used in training is a nearly perfect way of expressing workload.

If you use WKO+™ training analysis software (more about that later), workload is expressed as a "Training Stress Score." This is a way of comparing your power for the workout with the intensity of the ride as a factor of your CP60 combined with the workout duration. CP60 is the highest average power you can maintain during an all-out 60-minute effort.

SIDEBAR 4.2

Should You Buy a Power Meter?

Should you buy a power meter? If I was your coach you'd have to. I require every cyclist I work with to use one. Why do I do that? Because I know athletes are more likely to achieve their race goals by training—and racing—with power than without. I've seen it happen with every athlete I've coached since power meters hit the market a few years ago.

Don't get me wrong, heart rate monitors are great training devices, too. They are another requirement of mine. But heart rate monitors are even more beneficial than they were before, now that there are power meters. Now there is something to compare heart rate with besides how you feel, which makes the information much more valuable.

But let's get back to why you should use a power meter.

They are more valuable to the serious rider than a lighter frame or faster wheels. Given the choice, I'd recommend a power meter every time. Why? Let's start with a basic reason—getting the intensity right for workouts.

Power meters remove most of the guesswork that goes into training and racing. For example, I've known athletes who, when doing intervals with heart rate monitors, don't call the work interval "started" until their heart rates reach the targeted level. With a power meter you soon learn that the interval starts as soon as the power hits the

Continued >

< Sidebar 4.2 continued

targeted zone—which means right away. Training the heart is not the main objective of doing intervals—or any workout, for that matter. For most workouts, what happens in the muscles is really the key to your fitness and racing ability. Heart rate monitors, though quite valuable to training, have many believing that training is just about the heart. It isn't.

Also, with only a heart rate monitor, how do you get the intensity right in the first minute or so of the first few intervals in a workout? Heart rate certainly can't be relied on then, as it is low at that point and still rising for the first couple of minutes. Are you going too hard or too easy? How do you know? A power meter tells you precisely, and right away.

Using a power meter in a time trial is almost like cheating. When everyone else is fighting the wind, or flying downwind, or guessing how hard to go when climbing, the rider with a power meter is just rolling along at the prescribed power. He or she will produce the fastest possible time given the conditions so long as the optimal target power has been determined through training and observed closely during the race. Although something similar can be done with heart rate, there are some confounding factors, such as cardiac drift, the acute effect of diet, and the slow response on hills, that make heart rate monitors less than optimal as training tools.

Power meters also provide highly accurate details about how your fitness is changing throughout the season. I test the athletes I coach regularly using a combination of heart rate and power. This testing procedure is described later in this chapter. Without this information I really wouldn't know for sure whether they were making progress. I might think they were, based on other observations, but I'd just be guessing. With a power meter I know exactly how much progress each athlete has made.

There are many benefits of training with power. Perhaps the best indicator of their value for performance is the elite athletes who use them. Power meters are common with professional road cyclists—and for an obvious reason: They have mortgages to pay, and a power meter will help them do that.

TRAINING TIME BY INTENSITY ZONE

How much time should you spend in each heart rate zone over the course of a season? This is a question often asked by cyclists, and with good reason. The answer would tell you exactly what you needed to know to design a program of purposeful and effective training. Unfortunately, it's not an easy question to answer.

Training intensity is determined by many variables, the most important being the event for which you are training. There are significant differences between preparing for a 40 km time trial and a criterium. Preparing for a 40 km time trial requires a lot of steady training just below and at LT, but for a short criterium a great deal of interval work is done above LT. Obviously one cannot train in the same heart rate zones for both events.

It's not really possible to say how much time most athletes should spend in each zone over the course of the season because every athlete is different. There is no generic "cyclist" and no perfect one-size-fits-all training plan. There are differences in the types of races each athlete does, differences in their limiters, and differences in their race priorities. But let's take a stab at mapping out a very general estimate.

Figures 4.2 through 4.4 suggest what training time by heart rate zone for an entire season might look like, assuming that a given type of race is always an A-priority. The purpose of these figures is not to give you specific numbers or volumes to shoot for, but rather to suggest how training intensity might generally be distributed. The examples might serve as a rough guide for you as you make decisions about how many low-intensity and high-intensity workouts to schedule in your training.

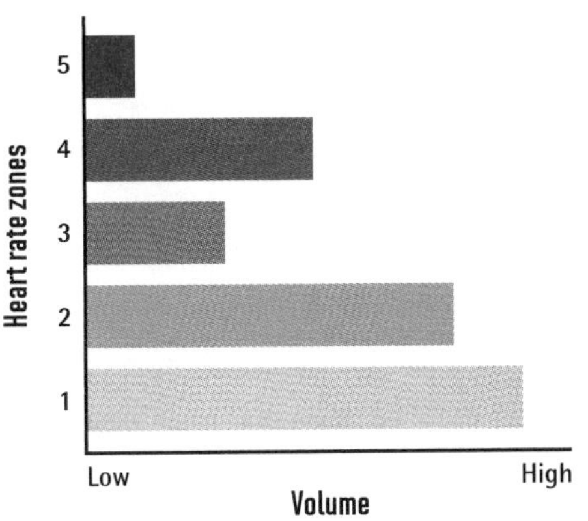

FIGURE 4.2

Time Trial Periodization

Relative distribution of intensity over the course of a season when training for 30- to 90-minute bicycle time trials.

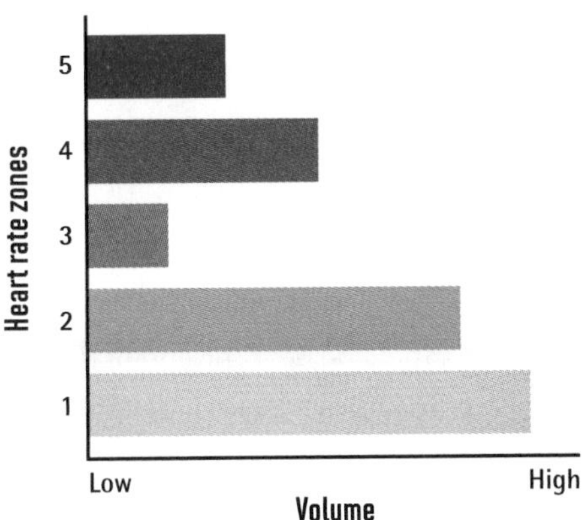

FIGURE 4.3

Criterium Periodization

Relative distribution of intensity over the course of a season when training for bicycle criterium-type races lasting 30–90 minutes.

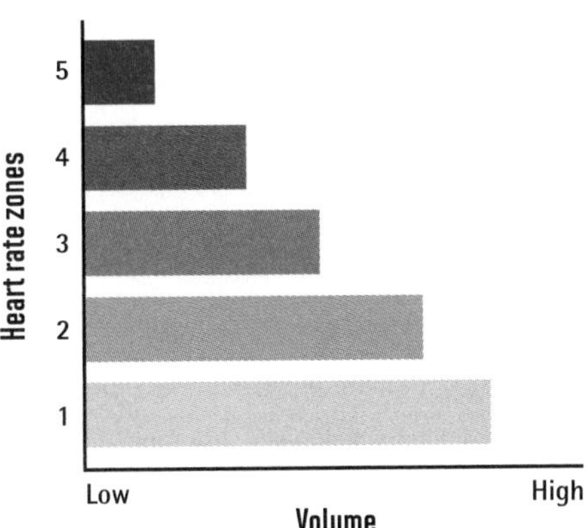

FIGURE 4.4

Road Race Periodization

Relative distribution of intensity over the course of a season when training for bicycle road races lasting 90 minutes to 6 hours.

MEASURING FITNESS

It is impossible to map out a useful training plan for an athlete without knowing about his or her fitness. This is why any good coach will make it a priority to evaluate an athlete's baseline fitness level before designing a program. You will also want to be able to accurately measure how your fitness is progressing during the training period. But what should these baseline and ongoing evaluations measure? Here are some techniques for evaluating overall fitness at any point in time during training.

COMPARING HEART RATE WITH POWER

Let's begin by pulling together some of the intensity concepts I've already introduced—aerobic threshold, heart rate, and power.

For the serious rider, it is important to know when enough aerobic threshold training has been done to establish a good base for the bottom of the fitness pyramid. To figure this out, look at heart rate and power to see if the two are staying closely linked, with little or no cardiac drift. Cardiac drift is the tendency of the heart rate to rise even though power remains steady, and in an aerobically fit athlete it is minimal. The following explains an advanced method that you may use to determine whether aerobic fitness is as good as it should be near the end of the Base period. This is a number-crunching exercise that requires a power meter and WKO+ software.

On a bike with a power meter, complete an aerobic threshold ride. Then upload the power meter's heart rate and power data to the WKO+ analysis software. The software will separate the aerobic threshold portion of the ride into two halves. For each half, the average power is divided by the average heart rate to establish a ratio. The results are then compared by subtracting the first half ratio from the second half ratio and dividing the remainder by the first half ratio. This produces a power-to-heart-rate ratio percentage of change from the first half to the second half of the aerobic threshold ride. Don't worry, the software will do all of this calculating for you. But just so you understand the concept, here is an example of how power–to–heart rate ratio percentage of change is calculated:

First half of aerobic threshold portion of ride:
Power average: 180 watts
Heart rate average: 135 bpm
First half power-to-heart rate ratio (180 ÷ 135): 1.33

Second half of aerobic threshold portion of ride:
Power average: 178 watts
Heart rate average: 139 bpm
Second half power-to-heart-rate ratio (178 ÷ 139): 1.28
Second half ratio minus first half ratio (1.33 – 1.28): 0.05

Remainder divided by the first half ratio (0.05 ÷ 1.33): 0.038

Power-to-heart rate shift: 3.8 percent

If your power-to-heart rate shift is less than 5 percent, as in the above example, the workout is said to be "coupled," meaning the power and heart rate graph lines stay close to parallel, as shown in Figure 4.5. That's good: It means that you have a low level of cardiac drift. But if the power-to-heart rate ratio shift is greater than 5 percent, the workout is "decoupled," as shown in Figure 4.6. Note that the two lines on this graph do not remain parallel for the entire aerobic threshold portion of the workout. That level of cardiac drift indicates that you have a low level of Base period fitness.

Note how heart rate remains parallel with power for only part of the aerobic portion of the workout shown in Figure 4.6. The decline in power indicates a lack of aerobic fitness for long durations.

There are two ways to do an aerobic threshold coupling workout. You can ride while keeping heart rate steady to see what happens to power. Or you can maintain a steady power output and see what heart rate does. In the Base period, it's generally better to maintain a steady heart rate, while for the Build period you should keep power steady.

In the early Base period, you should start these aerobic threshold rides at 20 to 30 minutes and then increase them weekly. Do two of these each week during Base. When you can do an aerobic threshold ride for two hours while your heart rate and power remain coupled, you can consider your aerobic threshold fitness fully developed. Congratulations! Your primary goal of the Base period has been accomplished. Assuming your force and speed skills are also well advanced, you are now ready to move on to more advanced goals such as building muscular endurance, anaerobic endurance, and power.

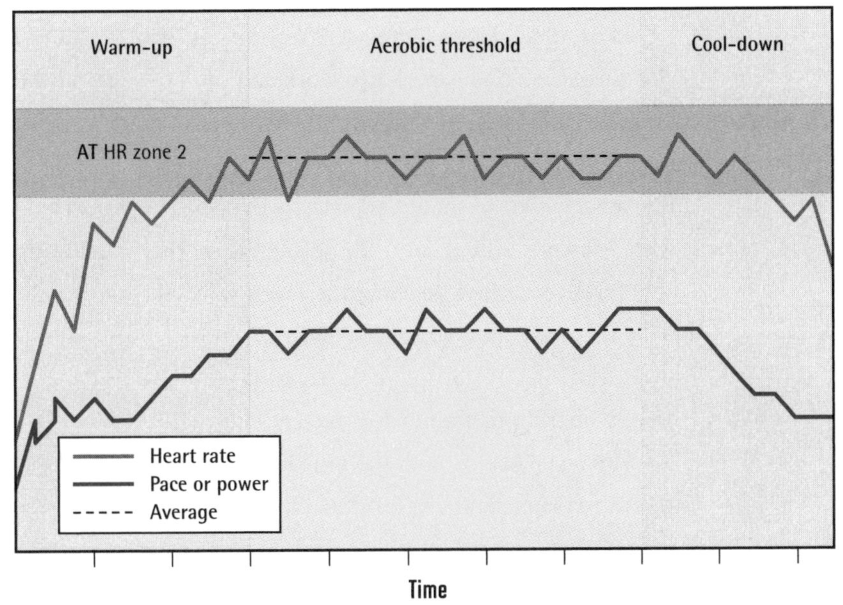

FIGURE 4.5

Coupled Aerobic Threshold Workout

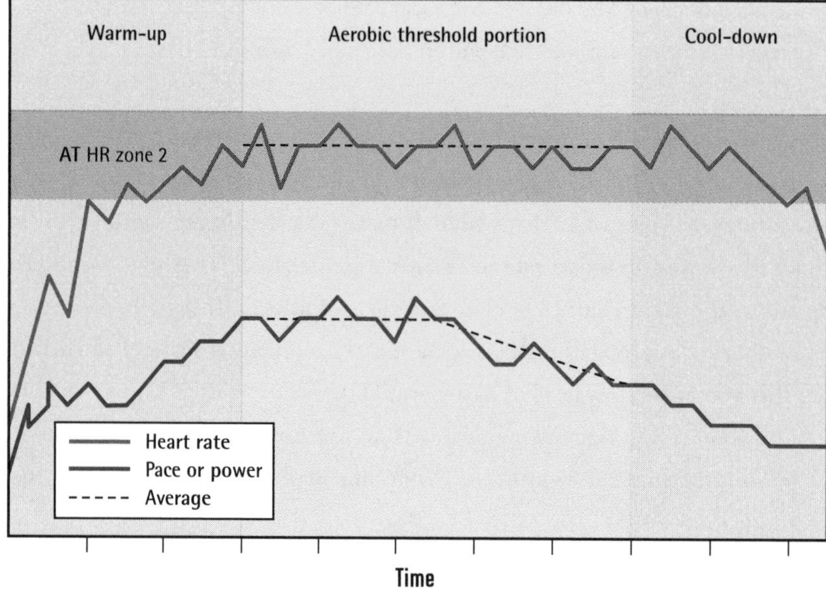

FIGURE 4.6

Decoupled Aerobic Threshold Workout

In the Build period, you will need to maintain your endurance by doing an aerobic threshold ride about every two weeks.

If you don't have a power meter, you can still do aerobic threshold workouts using your trusty heart rate monitor. You will have to make decisions about your aerobic endurance fitness based strictly on perceived exertion. Over time, the effort at aerobic-threshold heart rate will seem to be getting easier, and you should find yourself riding faster over the same course at the same heart rate.

CUMULATIVE WORKLOAD

Whichever method you use, record your daily workload in a training log. By totaling the daily workloads, expressed as kilojoules or Training Stress Scores, you can calculate a cumulative workload for the week. This cumulative workload serves as an indicator of how difficult the week was. By comparing it with past weeks, you can quickly see what is happening to the training stress load.

In general, the cumulative workload should increase as the year progresses from the start of the training season in early winter until the spring races. This should not be a straight-line progression, however. It instead should follow a wave-like pattern that allows the body to gradually adapt and grow stronger. Figure 4.7 shows how the cumulative weekly workload advances through one portion of the training year.

Unfortunately, there is no rule of thumb for determining what a given athlete's workload should be. It varies considerably with the individual, so experience is the best teacher. By comparing your weekly cumulative workloads with your training and racing performances, it's possible to plan optimal training patterns while avoiding overtraining. But always bear in mind that optimal workload is a moving target that is dependent on

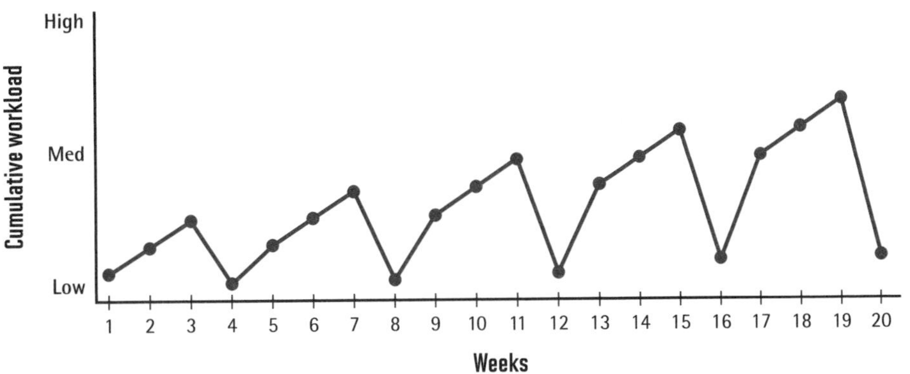

FIGURE 4.7

Cumulative Progression of Workload

accumulated fitness, time of the training year, health, psychological stress, and other variables. Cumulative workload history provides a better starting point than merely guessing how you should train today and in the future.

FATIGUE, FITNESS, AND FORM

Although all of the discussion on the topic of periodization in this book sounds very scientific, measuring its results has largely been a leap of faith. Coaches and athletes have simply trusted that organizing workouts in a certain way produces peak readiness on race day. During training it has always been possible to take "snapshots" of your fitness every four weeks or so by doing aerobic or LT tests. But since the physiological changes are generally quite small—on the order of 1 percent—variables such as weather, the warm-up, and even a few cups of coffee can easily make it appear that there was either great progress or none over the previous few weeks. So you are back to trusting your instincts about whether you are becoming fitter.

Now all of that is changing. With power meters and new software designed by Hunter Allen and Andrew Coggan, it is possible to graph and manage the daily changes in your race preparation. The software is called WKO+ (available through http://TrainingPeaks.com) and is compatible with all power meters on the market as of 2008.

One of the most powerful features of WKO+ is its performance management chart, which allows you to track periodization and progress toward your race goals. Figure 4.8 is based on this chart for the early season for one of the athletes I coach. This is a good example of the future of training technology. If you are serious about your race performance, such software will allow you to keep a close eye on your progress and respond quickly when small periodization changes are necessary to stay on track toward your goals.

There are three aspects of training represented by the lines on Figure 4.8. All are derived from formulas determined by certain power-based variables—normalized power, intensity factor, and Training Stress Score. These reflect the intensity, duration, and frequency of your bike workouts. To learn more about these details, see Allen and Coggan's book, *Training and Racing with a Power Meter*.

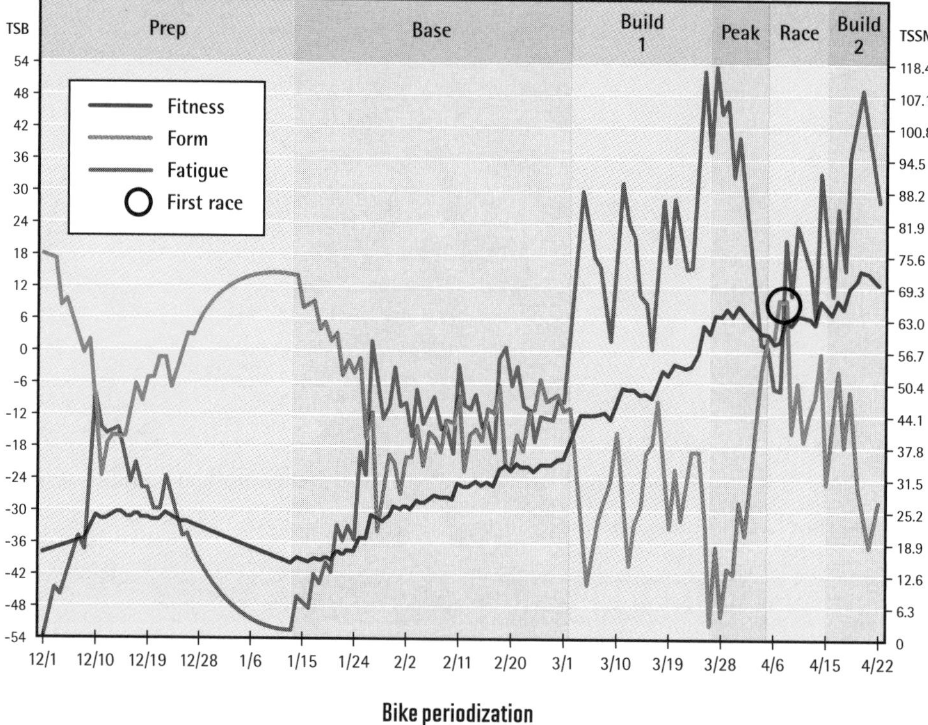

FIGURE 4.8

Performance Chart for Sample Athlete

The gray line on Figure 4.8 represents *fatigue.* It closely approximates what you would subjectively describe after a few days of hard training, and it responds very quickly to high and low levels of training stress. Notice the spikes and valleys. These indicate alternating hard and easy workout days. The spikes show increased training stress from long duration or high intensity as well as the frequency of such workouts. The valleys represent short, easy rides or days off the bike.

The dark red line is for *fitness.* When this line rises, fitness is improving. Relative to fatigue, fitness responds slowly to training stress. Notice that it isn't a straight line. Fitness is never static; it is always changing, either positively or negatively. Also, fitness only increases after an earlier increase in fatigue. Fitness and fatigue go hand in hand. This makes sense, as being fatigued means you trained hard, and hard training produces greater fitness. Although a few days of extended rest are necessary every three or four weeks to prevent overtraining and burnout, you must be careful not to make the break too long, or too much fitness will be lost. The software allows you to monitor these changes. Effectively balancing rest and stress is tricky when it comes to fitness.

The light red line on Figure 4.8 represents *form,* which may also be described as race "restedness." This use of the word "form" comes from late-nineteenth-century British horse racing when bettors would review a page of previous race results for the horses in that day's race—a form. A horse was said to be "on form" when racing well. Cycling adopted the term.

Form rises when you back off from hard training to rest more. It falls when you train frequently with high intensity or long workouts. On the left side of the graph, you see a 0 (zero) in the center of the scale. When the lighter red line is above this point, the athlete is "on form."

So now let's take a look at my athlete's early-season periodization and see how it worked out. Along the fitness curve, I've indicated his early-season periods: Prep, Base, Build, Peak, and Race (circle). The second Build period following the Race period is the start of his return to hard training in preparation for the next A-priority race on his schedule.

As described earlier, the Prep period is a time when the athlete is just getting back into training following a break at the end of the previous season. In this case, it was December through early January. He had a family vacation planned for the last three weeks of this period and did not have a bike available. Here, since he wasn't riding, you can see the steady drop in both fatigue and fitness. Accompanying that drop is a rise in form. He was really rested but, of course, his bike fitness was becoming increasingly poor.

In the Base period he returned to steady and consistent training. He spent time on the indoor trainer working on aerobic endurance, muscular force, and pedaling speed skills. The steady rise in fatigue and fitness with a drop in form all indicate that training was going as expected.

During the first Build period, I began to increase the intensity of his training by including muscular endurance and anaerobic endurance rides. These consisted primarily of intervals and tempo rides while maintaining the three basic abilities he established during the Base period—endurance, force, and speed skills. Both fatigue and fitness rose at a greater rate, and form dropped to his lowest point of the early season because of this increase in the training load. I made slight adjustments to stress and rest along the way because the chart revealed how he was responding to training.

In the short Peak period, he did only a few hard workouts with lots of rest between them. Notice how fatigue dropped dramatically while fitness decreased only slightly. The most important change here is the rapid rise in form, which increased above the zero line mentioned above. At his first race he was not only at a high level of fitness, he was also well rested. This was confirmed by his perception of feeling ready on race day as well as by his exceptional race performance. He was *on form*.

Following this first race of the season, he went on a mountain-biking vacation for a few days and resumed hard training on his return. As you can see by where the graph ends, he was well on his way to the second peak of the season, which produced even better results.

PART III

TRAINING WITH A PURPOSE
HISTORICAL PERSPECTIVES

THE RACING CYCLE

by Willie Honeman

(as it appeared in *Bicycling Magazine*, October 1946)

The Novice, with rare exceptions, will find himself lacking in one or more of the following: (1) ABILITY TO REPEAT, in other words ride five or six times at one race meeting, (2) ABILITY TO CARRY A SPRINT, (3) ABILITY TO RIDE AROUND THE MAN IN FRONT, (4) NO ENDURANCE, (5) CONCERN ABOUT NERVOUSNESS, (6) DISCOURAGED UPON FAILURE TO PLACE.

An important point to keep in mind is that nothing can be accomplished by a rider in Racing if he does not try to improve on his Weak Points in Training. To ride around the Track or Road accepting pace (known as sitting in) at a slow speed and with no purpose will accomplish nothing toward the rider's preparation for a coming event.

5 TESTING

Motivation can't take you very far if you don't have the legs.

—LANCE ARMSTRONG

WHAT ARE MY STRENGTHS as a cyclist? What aspects of performance should I focus on in training? Am I making progress toward my long-term goals? How can I improve my race results?

These are questions the serious bicycle racer must ask several times every year. For the novice cyclist, they can be difficult to answer, because there is so much self-discovery to come. Even an experienced rider may find it hard to answer them. The problem is that athletes often "can't see the forest for the trees." It is always difficult to evaluate yourself objectively. Most people need someone else's studied opinion—often a coach's or a concerned teammate's—to get the answers to such questions. Because the purpose of this book is to help you become your own coach, I'm going to encourage you to take an honest look at yourself. When you learn to do this, you will be on your way to emphasizing the right things in training and race preparation.

You may not like what you discover about yourself. Several years ago, a master rider asked me to coach him. He described how, when it came to climbs, he had been unable to hang on with the peloton in the previous season, and was off the back early in most races. Although unhappy with the situation, he wasn't completely dejected. He had given it a lot of thought and decided that the problem was a lack of power. So over the course of the winter he had taken a plyometrics class with a trainer who worked with professional power athletes such as football players.

My new charge had attended workouts four times a week that winter and had been so committed to improving that he had ended up with stress fractures in both feet. What he wanted to know was how I could help him improve his power.

The first thing I did was to test his power on his CompuTrainer. We discovered that he had tremendous power, despite inactivity for several weeks due to the stress fractures. He easily ranked in the top 5 percent for maximum power generation of all the masters I had ever coached. We also found, however, that he couldn't sustain the power output for even a few seconds and that his anaerobic endurance was poor. Once he crossed the red line and became anaerobic on a short climb or a long, intense effort, he quickly fatigued. Maximum power generation wasn't holding him back at all. I subsequently set up a program for him that would improve his anaerobic endurance and lactate tolerance. He went on to have a much-improved race season.

You also may have reached a conclusion about your strengths and weaknesses that is not true. By pursuing the wrong course of training, you're expending both time and energy and may still end up with very little to show for your trouble. It is not unusual at all for riders to concentrate on the wrong abilities in training. What is most common among cyclists is to focus primarily on strengths. Good climbers, for example, prefer to spend their training time climbing rather than working on time trialing, even though it is the lack of time trialing skills that is the cause of their lackluster results in A-priority stage races.

I call these race-specific weaknesses "limiters." Knowing what limits your race performance is like finding the weak link in a chain. Once you strengthen this link, your results immediately improve. But if you only work on your strengths and the weak link remains weak, your race performance will stay much the same from year to year.

Of course, your limiters may never become strengths, but you must always be trying. The trick is to improve the limiters without letting the strengths deteriorate. That's what I want to teach you to do in the planning chapters of this book. For now, let's discover what your strengths and limiters are.

There are two general categories of assessment that should be done each year to see where to focus your training during the Base and Build periods. Performance assessment is done on the bike, and self-assessment is done with paper and pencil. There are three times during the season when it is beneficial to conduct an assessment:

- Near the end of the last Race period of the season, complete a performance assessment to establish a high-fitness baseline.
- At the start of the Base period, do both performance and self-assessment to determine what is needed for training in the coming months.
- At the end of the Base period, repeat the performance assessment to measure progress before starting the Build period.

I cover these training periods in detail in Chapter 7.

By the end of this chapter, you'll be able to score yourself in several performance-related areas. Using the resulting data, you will then compare your capabilities with the specific demands of cycling and develop a customized training program specific to your needs.

Some athletes are not keen on testing and prefer to make decisions intuitively based on what they have discovered in races. That may work for some, but for most it results in little more than guesswork. Jumping to inaccurate conclusions based more on emotion than on fact is rarely helpful or productive. By completing all of the assessments included here, you'll be on the road to training more effectively than you've ever done before. Imagine what that could mean for your next race season.

PHYSICAL ASSESSMENT

Before you start back into training for a new season, it's a good idea to have your doctor give you a complete physical exam. The older you become, the more important this is. It's most likely that nothing unusual will be found. Then again, your doctor may discover something important, such as skin cancer, high blood pressure, high cholesterol, or prostate or breast cancer. Conditions such as these are much easier to treat in their early stages than they are later on. Getting an annual physical exam is just a good preventive practice regardless of how active you are, but it is even more important for you as an athlete because you will be putting more stress on your body than the average person. Of course, your doctor will probably give you a clean bill of health. Then you are ready to take the next step.

I also advise every athlete to make a preseason appointment with a physical therapist. Look for one who has experience working with endurance athletes. Some insurance plans allow you to go directly to a physical therapist without a doctor's prescription. If your health insurance does not cover such a visit to a physical therapy center, be prepared to pay for a costly one-hour screening (at least \$100–\$200). What you will learn is well worth the cost.

The physical therapist will do a head-to-toe exam looking for potential injury sites due to lack of strength, limited flexibility, or physical imbalances. He or she can tell you how to modify your training to improve the condition or how to adjust equipment to allow for your unique weaknesses.

We all have physical imperfections. You may discover that you have leg-length discrepancies, both functional and physical; weak core muscles that allow your body to be moved from side to side and rotated when it should be still; tight muscles and tendons; muscle imbalances; limited range of motion in your joints; poor posture; or scoliosis. These may be hereditary, caused by long-ago injury, or simply the result of the repetitive motions of riding a bike for many years. The physical therapist can suggest strengthening or stretching exercises to correct these imperfections.

The physical therapist may also wish to refer you to a bike-fit specialist. Although your bike shop may have measured you for a custom bike, a fit specialist will take that process several steps further by assessing your working position on the bike in some detail. This usually involves taking several laser measurements as you ride on a trainer. The specialist may recommend cleat spacers, shoe orthotics, slight changes in the bike's stem or crank length, or a special type of saddle.

At least once each year, generally in the early Base period, I send my athletes to the lab for metabolic testing, sometimes called gas analysis. Athletes usually refer to this as a "VO_2max test," but it goes well beyond discovering your VO_2max. Most think this test reveals their potential for high-level performance. It does not tell you this any more than competing in a race shows your potential for future races. But this test does quantify your current level of fitness from many different angles.

Metabolic testing assesses your current fitness level and can also provide useful information about heart rate zones, bike power zones, how much fat and carbohydrates you use at various intensities, and how efficient you are when pedaling a bike. Lab testing also helps to establish your personal rate of perceived exertion on a given scale (for example, a scale of 1 to 10, where 1 is easy and 10 is hard) so that you can think about effort more precisely in the future. All of this will help fine-tune your training plan.

That's a lot to be gained from one test session that takes only about an hour to complete. If you are self-coached, the technician can help you make sense of the test results and may even offer suggestions on how to use the information to train more effectively.

This can also be an investment of at least $100 to $200. Look for a facility that specializes in athlete testing, not one that caters to those at risk for heart disease or aging populations. Athlete testing centers are becoming increasingly available in bike shops, health clubs, and physical therapy centers. Some coaches even provide this service.

By repeating the test at the start of each major period of the season, especially the Base 1, Build 1, and Peak periods, you can closely monitor your training progress. These tests also serve as great motivators when you don't have a race scheduled for some time.

Once you have completed a physical assessment, you're ready to determine your current fitness level with a lengthy performance assessment.

PERFORMANCE ASSESSMENT

There are several tests that can gauge your physiological status. It is best to use them comparatively. Establish a baseline in each of the tests that you choose, and then retest yourself at intervals throughout the year to see how your physical ability is changing. It is not necessary to repeat all of the tests throughout the season. Focus on the ones that seem to best reflect your limiters. This may come down to one test of all of those described here. By regularly gauging your progress with it, you can ensure that the training program is on track—or that it isn't.

When retesting, it is important that you eliminate as many variables as possible from one test to the next. For example, the warm-up procedure needs to be the same. Some other elements that should remain stable from test to test are diet, hydration, level of fatigue, equipment, bike setup, tire pressure, and time of day.

If at any time during a test you feel light-headed or nauseated, stop immediately. You are not attempting to achieve a maximum heart rate on any of the tests described here, but it is necessary to attain a very high level of exertion.

Here are the tests broken down by category.

SPRINT POWER TEST

Tests done on the bike are usually the best indicators of racing performance. With a power meter, a CompuTrainer, or in a laboratory, measure your maximum power and average sustained power. The following CompuTrainer sprint power test describes how this is done with a CompuTrainer. With a power meter, perform the test on the road in the same way. The course should be about 0.2 mile (352 yards, or 322 meters) and either flat or slightly uphill. Mark the start and finish points so you can find them in the future for retests.

SPRINT POWER TEST ON COMPUTRAINER

TEST

CompuTrainer Setup

You will need one or two assistants to record information and possibly to spot for safety (there is a risk of the bike tipping over with a maximal effort). Set up and calibrate the equipment as described in the user's manual. Warm up for about 10 minutes and calibrate the equipment. Select a course that is 0.2 mile long.

Test

1. Following your warm-up, take two or three increasingly powerful practice starts of 8–12 seconds each to determine the best gear to start the test. The start is with the rear wheel stopped. If the rear wheel slips, tighten and recalibrate it.
2. During the test you may stand or sit and shift gears at any time. If you are a large or powerful rider, you'll want a spotter on either side of the bike to prevent tipping. You may also bolt the CompuTrainer to a sheet of plywood to prevent tipping.
3. When ready to begin the test, stop your rear wheel and have an assistant press the start button on the handlebar control unit.
4. Sprint the 0.2-mile course as fast as you can. It will probably take 25–40 seconds.
5. At the completion of the test, record maximum watts and average watts.
6. Recover by spinning in a light gear with minimal resistance for several minutes.

If you can conduct the test in a lab, the applicable protocol will probably be something called a "Wingate Power Test." The technician should be able to explain what the results mean. He or she will probably not be able to tell you how your performance compares that of other cyclists, however. Once you've completed the power test, use Table 5.1 to help you further interpret the results.

TABLE 5.1

Power Ranges of Cyclists

RANKING	SCORE	MEN MAX (watts)	MEN AVG (watts)	WOMEN MAX (watts)	WOMEN AVG (watts)
Excellent	5	1,100+	750+	1,000+	675+
Good	4	950–1,099	665–749	850–999	600–674
Average	3	800–949	560–664	720–849	500–599
Fair	2	650–799	455–559	585–719	410–499
Poor	1	<650	<455	<585	<410

Don't be disheartened if your maximum is lower than expected. Identifying your weakness, especially if it is also a limiter (it prevents you from attaining better results in A-priority races), means that you know what to start improving. For a power weakness, you must work on your ability to quickly generate force against the pedals if you're going to improve. A low average power is a warning to improve lactate tolerance, as we saw in the case of the masters athlete mentioned previously. I will discuss how to improve both force and lactate tolerance in later chapters. If you score 4 or 5 for both, the quick application of force and lactate tolerance are among your strength areas. You're probably a very good sprinter in this case, and we'll need to keep looking for your weakness.

Average power output will vary more throughout the year than maximum power will. While testing in the winter, you may find average power lower than in the summer months when race fitness is high. That's because you quickly lose the ability to tolerate lactate after racing season is over and your body no longer experiences it on a routine basis.

GRADED EXERCISE TEST

The graded exercise test can be done with a CompuTrainer or power meter. Most laboratory testing facilities at hospitals, clinics, and universities also conduct a very sophisticated ergometer stress test that measures aerobic capacity and also determines lactate threshold (LT). Some may even sample blood to determine lactate profiles, as described in Chapter 4. Expect to pay dearly for a lab test.

One of the measures to be gleaned from the graded exercise test is your lactate threshold heart rate (LTHR) and power. In the scientific world, there are different definitions for the point at which LT is reached. I've found that labs frequently use the more conservative of these definitions. That approach yields a low threshold heart rate and power level for a racer. If you're a master, the lab technicians may also be reluctant to allow you to continue the test until fatigue sets in, choosing instead to stop the test prematurely. They don't want you to die in their labs. Again, it is helpful to find a reputable lab and work out these issues before scheduling your testing. It goes without saying that being honest about your limits is of the utmost importance.

If you're new to racing or have coronary risk factors such as a history of heart disease in your family, high cholesterol, high blood pressure, a heart murmur, or dizziness after exercise, then you should only conduct this test in a laboratory under the close supervision of a physician, preferably one who is familiar with your personal health history.

It is also possible to conduct the graded exercise test using an indoor trainer or stationary bike. To use a trainer, you will need a handlebar computer sensor for the rear wheel. Power outputs will not be known, but you can measure speed instead. Accurate and reliable stationary bikes are hard to find for such precise measurement. Look for one that digitally displays power or speed. Do not use a health club bike that shows speed or power with a needle or sliding gauge. These are far too inaccurate.

If using a power meter, use an indoor trainer of any type and follow the CompuTrainer protocol.

GRADED EXERCISE TEST ON COMPUTRAINER

CompuTrainer Setup

You will need an assistant to record information. Set up and calibrate the equipment as described in the user's manual. Warm up for about 10 minutes and calibrate the equipment. Select a flat course that is 8–10 miles (12–16 km) long. You won't use all of it.

Test

1. Throughout the test, you will hold a predetermined power level (plus or minus 10 watts). Start at 100 watts and increase by 20 watts every minute until you can no longer continue. Stay seated throughout the test. Shift gears at any time.
2. At the end of each minute, tell your assistant your exertion level using the RPE guide (place this where you can see it during the test).
3. Your assistant will record your exertion rating and your heart rate at the end of the minute and instruct you to increase power to the next level.
4. The assistant will also listen closely to your breathing to detect when it becomes noticeably labored for the first time in the test. This point is defined as the VT, or ventilatory threshold.

RPE SCALE	
6	
7	Very, very light
8	
9	Very light
10	
11	Fairly light
12	
13	Somewhat hard
14	
15	Hard
16	
17	Very hard
18	
19	Very, very hard
20	

5. Continue until you can no longer hold the power level for at least 15 seconds.
6. The data collected should look something like this:

Power (watts)	Heart Rate (bpm)	RPE
100	110	9
120	118	11
140	125	12
160	135	13
180	142	14
200	147	15
220	153	17 (VT)
240	156	19
260	159	20

Now let's determine your LT. It may be estimated from the test data by observing four indicators: RPE, VT, time above LT, and power percentage. For the experienced rider, LT typically occurs when RPE is in the range of 15 to 17. A rough estimation of LT may be made by noting the heart rates that fall into this RPE range. If you are new to cycling, you may be unsure about rating your RPE. However, the more experience you gain on the bike at various intensities, the easier this task will become.

LT may also be estimated by your assistant's estimation of VT, when your breathing becomes labored. If this falls in the range of RPE 15 to 17, it narrows the possibilities even more. Realize, however, that it can be quite difficult for someone who has never determined VT before to do it accurately. Another general rule to go by when attempting to determine LT is that a rider will typically not be able to continue for more than five minutes on this type of test once LT has been reached. So your LT is likely within the last five datapoints collected.

Power output may also be used to estimate LT for the experienced rider, as it generally is found at about 85 percent of the maximum power achieved on the test. From these four indicators you should be able to closely estimate LTHR. The more times you complete the test, the more refined the estimate of LT becomes.

TEST

GRADED EXERCISE TEST ON INDOOR TRAINER

Indoor Trainer Setup

- Test must be done with a bike that accurately displays speed (or watts).
- Select "manual" mode.
- You will need an assistant to record information.
- Warm up on equipment for 5 to 10 minutes.

Test

1. Throughout the test, you will hold a predetermined speed or power level. Start at 15 miles per hour (or 100 watts) and increase by 1 mile an hour (or 20 watts) every minute until you can no longer continue. Stay seated throughout the test. Shift gears at any time.
2. At the end of each minute, tell your assistant how great your exertion is using this guide (place this where it can be seen).
3. Your assistant will record your exertion rating and your heart rate at the end of the minute and instruct you to increase speed (watts) to the next level.
4. The assistant will also listen closely to your breathing to detect when it becomes labored. This is the ventilatory threshold (VT).
5. Continue until you can no longer hold the speed (watts) for at least 15 seconds.
6. The data collected should look something like this:

RPE SCALE

6	
7	Very, very light
8	
9	Very light
10	
11	Fairly light
12	
13	Somewhat hard
14	
15	Hard
16	
17	Very hard
18	
19	Very, very hard
20	

Speed (mph)	Power (watts)	Heart Rate (bpm)	RPE
15	100	110	9
16	120	118	11
17	140	125	12
18	160	135	13
19	180	142	14
20	200	147	15
21	220	153	17 (VT)
22	240	156	19
23	260	159	20

LACTATE THRESHOLD TEST ON ROAD

If you will be training with either a heart rate monitor or a power meter, this test will give you a good indication of your LT relative to your heart rate and power. Most riders find this road test to be far easier to conduct than either of the aforementioned LT tests.

TEST

LACTATE THRESHOLD TEST ON ROAD

1. Complete a 30-minute time trial on a flat to slightly uphill road course. (This may also be done on an indoor trainer, although most riders find it harder to perform on a trainer than on the road.)
2. To determine or confirm your LTHR, click the lap button on your heart rate monitor 10 minutes into the time trial. Your average heart rate for the last 20 minutes is a good estimation of LTHR.
3. If you are training with a power meter, your average power output for this test also functions as an approximation of LT power. It will establish your CP30 (as described in Chapter 4) as well.

The more times you do this or any of these tests during the year, the more reliable your training zones will be.

Testing for LT reveals two elements of your race fitness: power at LT and anaerobic endurance. It also locates your LTHR—a key element of your training when using a heart rate monitor. In order to derive the full benefit of a workout, you should regulate the intensity of that workout using LTHR as a guide to set zones, as listed in Table 4.6.

Power at LT is a good indicator of performance and will allow you to train the muscular system with a power meter or CompuTrainer. Anaerobic endurance is important in criteriums and during the sustained, high-intensity efforts of road races. Most race-fit athletes can last four or more minutes beyond their LT on the indoor trainer LT test. If you are unable to achieve that, then anaerobic endurance is one of your weaknesses. Many athletes find this to be the case at the start of the winter Base period, so don't be concerned if it is early in the season and you are unable to last long on the test. Table 5.2 shows how to rank your efforts in this test.

TABLE 5.2

Anaerobic Endurance Time from LT to End of Test

RANKING	SCORE	TIME (min.)
Excellent	5	>5:00
Good	4	4:00–4:59
Average	3	3:00–3:59
Fair	2	2:00–2:59
Poor	1	<2:00

The LT test also serves as an excellent baseline of your fitness. By graphing the results from two or more successive tests, you can see the changes in your fitness throughout the year. Construct a graph by plotting heart rate on the vertical axis and power on the horizontal axis. The Conconi Test, developed by Italian physiologist Francesco Conconi in the early 1980s, applied the method to Francesco Moser's training program in preparation for his attempt on the world hour record. The test relies on the establishment of the LTHR as the point at which the line on such a graph deflects or bends downward. I've found very few athletes who have an obvious deflection in their graph, so don't be concerned with looking for this in your test results.

Figure 5.1 illustrates the tracings of a LT test performed on two separate occasions. The first was conducted at the start of the Base period and the second following 12 weeks of Base training. Notice that the tracing for Test 1 has shifted to the right and slightly down. This shows that the athlete has a lower heart rate than before at any given power level. That illustrates one effective way of measuring progress. Another way of looking at it is that power has increased for every given heart rate. While the LTHR (indicated as LT) has not changed in 12 weeks, power has.

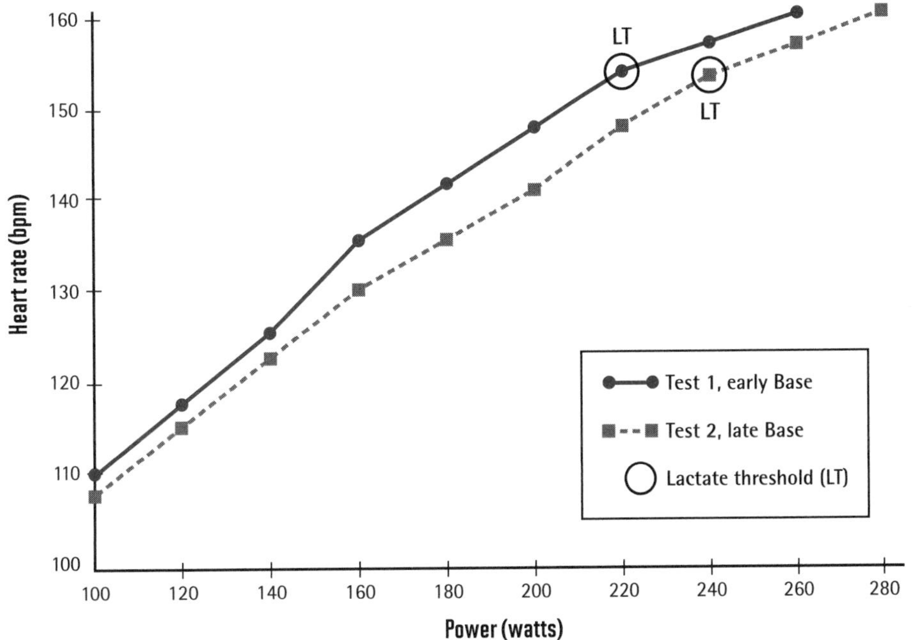

FIGURE 5.1

Comparison of Lactate Threshold Tests

CRITICAL POWER TESTS

If you have a power meter, establishing power-based training zones will allow you to make better use of the unit in training while also providing you with valuable comparison points for fitness throughout the season. If you also establish and periodically update a personal critical power profile, as shown in Figure 4.1, you will have a visual representation of how your performance is changing over time.

TEST

TEST FOR ESTABLISHING CRITICAL POWER PROFILE

Complete five time trials, preferably over the course of several days.

12 seconds
1 minute
6 minutes
12 minutes
30 minutes

Each test is a maximum effort for the entire duration. Once your profile is established, you may want to update only certain critical power points along the curve in subsequent tests without completing the entire battery.

There is a learning curve associated with testing your critical power profile. It's common to start out too fast on each time trial and then fade near the end. It may take two or three attempts over a few days or even a few weeks to get the pacing right. To reduce the need for such continued testing, it's best to start each time trial test at a lower power output than you think is appropriate. This will pay off with fewer test failures. Begin this testing in the early Base period, add at least one other battery of follow-up tests, and complete all before beginning the Build period. (These periods are explained in Chapter 7.)

The longer durations of 60, 90, and 180 minutes may be estimated from the profile graph by extending the slope of the CP12 to CP30 line in Figure 5.1. You may also get an estimation of the values for these extended datapoints with the use of a little math. To estimate 60-minute power, subtract 5 percent from your 30-minute average power result. For an approximation of 90-minute power, subtract 2.5 percent from the 60-minute power. Subtracting 5 percent from the 90-minute power figure estimates 180-minute power.

Keep in mind that power points beyond 30 minutes are estimates only and may well be inaccurate. That's acceptable, because training with a power meter as a guide is normally only recommended for shorter durations, as when doing intervals, hill repeats, sprints, or tempo efforts. Long, steady rides are best done using heart rate or perceived exertion to regulate intensity.

Once all of these power datapoints are established, you are ready to determine your critical power training zones as shown in Table 4.3.

APPLYING TEST RESULTS

Establishing a profile and completing selected tests is not enough—you must now determine what all of these data mean for your training. Again, keep in mind that the results of these tests are only as good as the effort put into controlling the many variables discussed earlier. Sloppy testing provides no basis for measuring fitness. Also remember that there are variables not completely under your control, such as weather. In addition, the changes in fitness can be so slight—2 percent or less—that field testing may not be sophisticated enough to detect them. Because of these confounding factors, it might appear in subsequent tests that fitness is slipping even though you sense an improvement. Your feelings and indications of fitness from workouts are valid—don't completely disregard them in an attempt to train "scientifically."

SPRINT POWER TEST

The purpose of this test is to determine whether sprinting is a weakness or a strength for you. Table 5.1 will help you determine that. Bear in mind that even if it is a weakness, it is not necessarily a limiter. If your race goals do not include events that often come down to a sprint for the line, then it is merely a weakness but not a limiter.

While it seems that good sprinters are born that way, this does not mean that your sprinting cannot improve. Good sprinters have several things in common. The first is that they have a tremendous ability to instantaneously recruit a large number of muscle fibers to initiate and finish the sprint. They also can generate tremendous force on the pedals owing to a high level of total body strength. And they can turn the pedals at a very high cadence. These are all characteristics that can be trained. Some will find such training produces quick and easy results, while others who do not have the sprinter body type will not realize as much gain.

GRADED EXERCISE TEST

As mentioned earlier, this test provides a snapshot of your aerobic fitness and helps to establish an LTHR. Both are applicable only to you. Comparing the heart rate data of this test with another rider's will be of little or no value. Comparing your present results with those of future tests is quite revealing, however. Figure 5.1 is a graph of an initial test (Test 1) and a follow-up test done several weeks later (Test 2).

In subsequent tests, an improvement in aerobic fitness is evident if the slope of the line moves to the right and down. This indicates, as mentioned earlier, that for any given power level, heart rate has dropped. Or, to look at it another way, for any given heart rate, power is greater.

Notice in Figure 5.1 that the LTHR has not changed from Test 1 to Test 2, although LT power has increased. This is typical of the results seen in experienced and generally well-conditioned riders during their Base period. A novice, or someone who has had a long break from training, in contrast, may expect to see the LTHR rise slightly in subsequent tests.

LACTATE THRESHOLD TEST ON ROAD

The analysis for this test is very straightforward. Your heart rate average for the last 20 minutes of the 30-minute, all-out time trial done on the road as a workout is a close approximation of LTHR. If you compete in a time trial as a race, take 5 percent of your average heart rate and add it to the average to estimate LT.

If you do only this test or the graded test, it's a good idea to continue evaluating your LTHR on future training rides. When riding steadily at this heart rate, you should be aware of labored breathing and a feeling of burning tightness in the legs, and your RPE should be about 15 to 17. As with all testing, the more often you perform the LT road test, the better you will become at both conducting the test and evaluating the results.

CRITICAL POWER TESTS

The data gathered for the critical power tests should be graphed to produce a Power Profile as shown in Figure 5.2. The longer critical power durations may be estimated by extending the slope of the line for CP12 to CP30. This method provides rough estimations that may be a bit low or high, depending on your aerobic-anaerobic fitness balance. For example, in the early winter months, your aerobic fitness is probably better than your anaerobic fitness. As a result, your CP12 may be lower than what would be found in the summer months, thus causing the extended slope of the line to be high on the right end. Follow-up tests done over the ensuing winter and spring months will help to correct this overestimation.

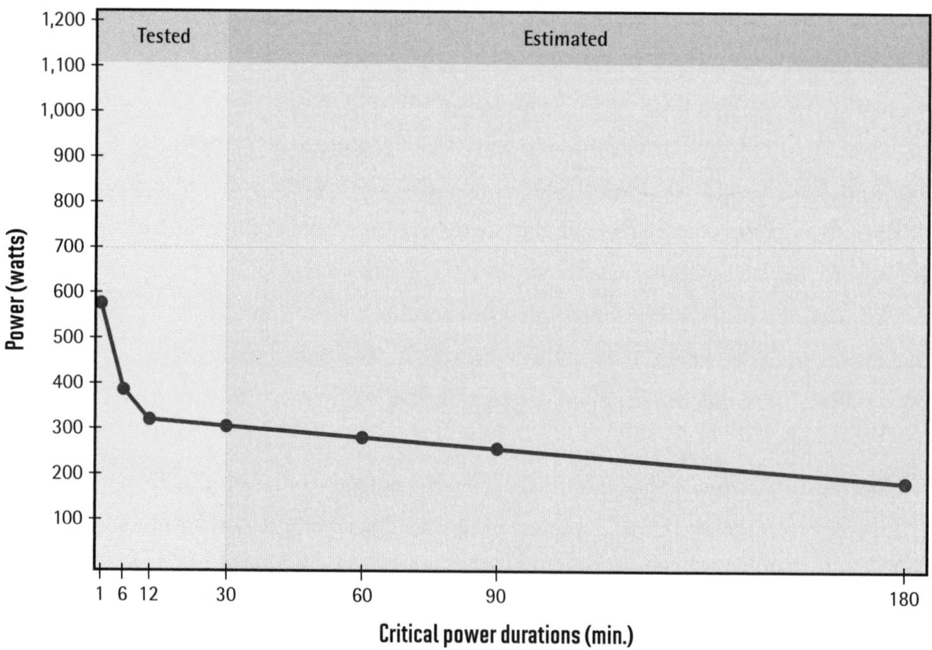

FIGURE 5.2

Sample Power Profile

What should your Power Profile look like? That depends somewhat on the courses you race on. A short-duration race contested on a course with short, steep hills favors a rider with high CP1 and CP6 power, whereas a longer race with rolling hills and long, steady climbs favors those with high CP12 and CP30 power. In theory, those power zones that are trained in most frequently will improve the most. So comparing your Power Profile with the course and race requirements of your most important races of the season can provide you with guidance for determining exactly how to train. Chapter 6 provides greater detail on this issue.

SELF-ASSESSMENT

By now you've collected a lot of data on yourself—but none of it is of any value unless you use it to improve your training and racing. Completing the three profiles in Sidebars 5.1–5.3—to determine your proficiencies, mental skills, and natural abilities—will take you a step closer to applying this new knowledge. Chapter 6 takes you even further by providing a system for improvement in weak areas.

If you have the equipment to conduct the performance assessment tests, you now have a good idea of some of your areas of strength and weakness. Chances are, however, that you don't have access to sophisticated equipment. You can still get a pretty good understanding of your capabilities by asking yourself the right questions and, of course, answering them honestly. Even if you were able to do the performance testing, you should evaluate your proficiencies, mental skills, and natural abilities at the start of every training year. Before reading any further, complete the three profiles that follow. Then I will explain your scores.

SIDEBAR 5.1

Proficiencies Profile

Read each statement below and decide if you agree or disagree with it as it applies to you. Check the appropriate answer. If unsure, go with your initial feeling.

A = Agree D = Disagree

A D

___ ___ 1. I'm quite lean compared with others in my category.

___ ___ 2. I'm more muscular and have greater total body strength than most others in my category.

___ ___ 3. I'm usually capable of single-handedly bridging big gaps that take several minutes.

___ ___ 4. I'm capable of enduring relentless suffering for long periods of time, perhaps as long as an hour.

___ ___ 5. I can climb long hills out of the saddle with most others in my category.

___ ___ 6. I can do wheelies and hop and jump my bike better than most.

___ ___ 7. I can spin at cadences in excess of 140 rpm with no difficulty.

___ ___ 8. I look forward to the climbs in races and hard group workouts.

___ ___ 9. I'm comfortable in an aerodynamic position: aero bars, elbows close, back flat.

Continued >

< Sidebar 5.1 continued

_____10. I have a lot of fast-twitch muscle based on my instantaneous sprint speed, vertical jump, or other indicator.

_____11. While I suffer, I seldom "blow up" on climbs even when the tempo increases.

_____12. In a race, I can ride near my LT (heavy breathing) for long periods of time.

_____13. In a long individual time trial, with the exception of turnarounds and hills, I can stay seated the entire race.

_____14. In a pack sprint, I feel aggressive and physically capable of winning.

_____15. When standing on a climb, I feel light and nimble on the pedals.

Scoring: For each of the following sets of questions count the number of "agree" answers you checked.

Question numbers		Score
1, 5, 8, 11, 15	Number of "agrees" _____	Climbing _____
2, 6, 7, 10, 14	Number of "agrees" _____	Sprinting _____
3, 4, 9, 12, 13	Number of "agrees" _____	Time trial _____

SIDEBAR 5.2

Mental Skills Profile

Read each statement below and choose an appropriate answer from these possibilities:

1 = Never	2 = Rarely	3 = Sometimes
4 = Frequently	5 = Usually	6 = Always

___1. I believe my potential as an athlete is excellent.

___2. I train consistently and eagerly.

___3. When things don't go well in a race, I remain positive.

___4. In hard races, I can imagine myself doing well.

___5. Before races, I remain positive and upbeat.

___6. I think of myself more as a success than as a failure.

___7. Before races, I am able to erase self-doubt.

___8. The morning of a race, I awake feeling enthusiastic.

___9. I learn something from races when I don't do well.

___10. I can see myself handling tough race situations.

___11. I'm able to race close to my ability level.

___12. I can easily picture myself training and racing.

___13. Staying focused during long races is easy for me.

___14. I stay in tune with my exertion levels in races.

___15. I mentally rehearse skills and tactics before races.

___16. I'm good at concentrating as a race progresses.

___17. I make sacrifices to attain my goals.

___18. Before an important race, I can visualize doing well.

___19. I look forward to workouts.

___20. When I visualize myself racing, it almost feels real.

___21. I think of myself as a tough competitor.

___22. In races, I tune out distractions.

___23. I set high goals for myself.

___24. I like the challenge of a hard race.

___25. When the race gets hard, my concentration improves.

___26. In races, I am mentally tough.

___27. I can relax my muscles before races.

___28. I stay positive despite late starts or bad weather.

___29. My confidence stays high the week after a bad race.

___30. I strive to be the best athlete I can be.

Scoring: Add up the numerical answers you gave for each of the following sets of questions and rate the associated categories according to the scoring chart below.

Question numbers		**Score**
2, 8, 17, 19, 23, 30	Total _____	Motivation _____
1, 6, 11, 21, 26, 29	Total _____	Confidence _____
3, 5, 9, 24, 27, 28	Total _____	Thought habits _____
7, 13, 14, 16, 22, 25	Total _____	Focus _____
4, 10, 12, 15, 18, 20	Total _____	Visualization _____

Total	**Ranking**	**Score**
32–36	Excellent	5
27–31	Good	4
21–26	Average	3
16–20	Fair	2
6–15	Poor	1

SIDEBAR 5.3

Natural Abilities Profile

Read each statement below and decide if you agree or disagree with it as it applies to you. Check the appropriate answer. If unsure, go with your initial feeling.

A = Agree D = Disagree

A	D		
___	___	1.	I prefer to ride in a bigger gear with a lower cadence than most of my training partners.
___	___	2.	I race best in criteriums and short road races.
___	___	3.	I'm good at sprints.
___	___	4.	I'm stronger at the end of long workouts than my training partners.
___	___	5.	I can squat and/or leg press more weight than most in my category.
___	___	6.	I prefer long races.
___	___	7.	I use longer crankarms than most others my height.
___	___	8.	I get stronger as a stage race or high-volume training week progresses.
___	___	9.	I comfortably use smaller gears with higher cadence than most others I train with.
___	___	10.	I have always been physically quicker than most other people for any sport I've participated in.
___	___	11.	In most sports, I've been able to finish stronger than most others.
___	___	12.	I've always had more muscular strength than most others I've played sports with.
___	___	13.	I climb best when seated.
___	___	14.	I prefer workouts that are short but fast.
___	___	15.	I'm confident of my endurance at the start of long races.

Scoring: For each of the following sets of questions, count the number of "agree" answers you checked and rate the categories accordingly.

Question numbers		Score
1, 5, 7, 12, 13	Number of "agrees" _____	Strength _____
2, 3, 9, 10, 14	Number of "agrees" _____	Skill _____
4, 6, 8, 11, 15	Number of "agrees" _____	Endurance _____

There are three proficiencies that determine success in cycling:

- Climbing
- Sprinting
- Time trialing

It's an unusual cyclist who scores a 4 or 5 on each of these. Body size and shape, aerobic capacity potential, and muscle type often determine which of these is your strength. Just because you are a good sprinter, however, doesn't mean that you should neglect climbing. What value is it to have a tremendous sprint but be unable to climb, and so arrive at the finish long after the winners? You must work to improve your limiters. Any proficiency in which you scored a 3 or lower needs work if it is a race-specific weakness—a limiter. Just how much work you need depends on the types of races you plan to be doing. We'll explore that issue in the next chapter.

MENTAL SKILLS

Mental skills are the most neglected aspect of racing for serious cyclists at all levels. I've known talented riders who, except for their lack of confidence, were capable of winning or always placing well, but were seldom contenders. Their heads were holding them back.

More than likely, you scored a 4 or 5 in the area of motivation. I always see this in the athletes I coach. If you didn't, then it may be time to take a long look at why you train and race bicycles.

A highly motivated and physically talented rider who is confident, has positive thought habits, can stay focused during a race, and has the ability to visualize success is practically unbeatable. A physically talented athlete without these mental qualities hopes to finish with the peloton. If you are weak in this area, and you can work closely with a good sports psychologist, by all means do so. The next best thing would be to read a book by one of the top sports psychologists in the field. In the Bibliography I've included some books that I have found to be helpful in improving mental skills. Some may be difficult to find, as they are out of print; try looking for them on Web sites that carry hard-to-find books, such as alibris.com.

NATURAL ABILITIES

Some people were born to be cyclists. Their parents blessed them with the physiology necessary to excel on two wheels. Others were born to be soccer players or pianists. Many of us who are cyclists have chosen to race a bike regardless of our genetic luck. Passion for the sport means a lot and can help overcome many physiological shortcomings.

The right mix of three basic abilities determines success in any sport:

- *Endurance:* The ability to continue for a long time.
- *Strength:* The ability to generate force against a resistance.
- *Speed skills:* The ability to make the movements of the sport at a required speed.

For example, an Olympic weight lifter must generate a tremendous amount of force and needs a fair amount of skill, but requires very little endurance. A pole vaulter needs tremendous skill, a moderate amount of strength, and little endurance. A marathon runner doesn't need much strength, only a little skill, but great endurance. Every sport is unique in terms of the mix of these three elements and therefore requires unique methods of training.

Road cycling puts a premium on endurance, but strength for climbing hills and skill for sprinting and pedaling correctly are also important elements of the formula. This unique combination of abilities is one of the reasons that cycling is such a difficult sport for which to train. A cyclist can't just put in a lot of miles to develop huge endurance and disregard strength and skill. It takes a mix of all three to excel.

The Natural Abilities Profile you completed provides a snapshot of your individual capabilities for the three elements of fitness for cycling. A score of 4 or 5 for one of the abilities indicates a strength area. If all of your scores are 4 or 5, you undoubtedly have been a good athlete in many sports. A score of 3 or lower indicates a weakness, one that may partly be due to heredity and partly to lack of training. You can't change your genes, but you can change your body, to some extent, and your training. That's what you'll find out how to accomplish in the next chapter.

MISCELLANEOUS FACTORS

There is a fourth category for self-assessment included in the Cyclist Assessment at the end of this chapter—miscellaneous factors. Most of these are quite subjective, but try to rate them using the same 1–5 scale used in the other profiles. The following brief comments may help you to do this.

- *Nutrition.* Could your nutrition improve? Do you eat a lot of junk food? On a scale of 1 to 5, how strict is your diet? If it is very strict, with no junk food, circle 5. If nearly all you eat is junk food, circle 1.
- *Technical equipment knowledge.* How well do you know your bike's inner workings? Could you repair or replace anything that may need it? If you're a certified mechanic, circle 5. If you're unable to repair even a flat tire, circle 1.
- *Race strategy.* Before starting every race, do you have a master plan of what you will do under various circumstances? If so, mark 5. If you never give race strategy any thought and just react to what happens, circle 1.
- *Body composition.* Power-to-weight ratio is extremely important in cycling. Evaluate your weight side of the ratio. Are you carrying excess flab that, if removed, would make you a better climber? Use the following scale:

Excess weight	10 or more pounds	7–9 pounds	4–6 pounds	1–3 pounds	No excess weight
Rating	1	2	3	4	5

- *Support of family and friends.* For those who are not fans of the sport, cyclists may seem somewhat strange. Those we are closest to have a tremendous effect on our psychological stress. How supportive are your family and friends of the time you spend training and racing? If they are 100 percent supportive, circle 5. If you have no support and are ridiculed by those who are close to you, or if they try to convince you not to devote so much time to riding, circle 1.
- *Years of racing experience.* How many years have you been training and racing? Circle that number. If more than five years, still circle 5. Experience plays a significant role in high-level training and racing.
- *Tendency to overtrain.* Do you come on strong about December, and are you ready to quit by June every year? If so, you're prone to overtraining—circle 1. Or do you frequently take rest breaks throughout the year and stay enthusiastic for training and racing right up until the last race on the calendar? If you're one of the few racers with such wisdom and patience, circle 5.

You've now evaluated yourself in several key areas. To compile the results, mark your score for each on the Cyclist Assessment form (Sidebar 5.4). All of those with a score of 4 or 5 are strength areas. Scoring a 3 or lower indicates a weakness. For each item, briefly comment on what you learned about yourself. Later on we'll come back to this form and use it to help design your training plan for the year.

At the top and bottom of the Cyclist Assessment form, there are spaces for you to write in your goals for the season and your training objectives. Don't do anything with these sections yet. The next chapter takes a closer look at how to go about correcting some of the weaknesses that may be holding you back from better racing. In Chapter 7, the assessment will come together as you complete the last sections at the bottom of the form and begin the process of designing an annual training plan for better racing results.

SIDEBAR 5.4

Cyclist Assessment

SEASON GOALS

1.

2.

3.

SPRINT POWER TEST	**Score** (5 = Best, ? = Unsure)	**Comments**
Maximum power	? 1 2 3 4 5	____________
Average power	? 1 2 3 4 5	____________

Continued >

< Sidebar 5.4 continued

GRADED EXERCISE TEST

Lactate threshold power ? 1 2 3 4 5 ____________________

Anaerobic endurance ? 1 2 3 4 5 ____________________

PROFICIENCIES PROFILE

Climbing ? 1 2 3 4 5 ____________________

Sprinting ? 1 2 3 4 5 ____________________

Time trialing ? 1 2 3 4 5 ____________________

To improve weaknesses:

MENTAL SKILLS PROFILE

Motivation ? 1 2 3 4 5 ____________________

Confidence ? 1 2 3 4 5 ____________________

Thought habits ? 1 2 3 4 5 ____________________

Focus ? 1 2 3 4 5 ____________________

Visualization ? 1 2 3 4 5 ____________________

To improve weaknesses:

NATURAL ABILITIES PROFILE

Endurance ? 1 2 3 4 5 ____________________

Strength ? 1 2 3 4 5 ____________________

Skill ? 1 2 3 4 5 ____________________

To improve weaknesses:

MISCELLANEOUS FACTORS

Nutrition ? 1 2 3 4 5 ____________________

Technical equipment knowledge ? 1 2 3 4 5 ____________________

Race strategy ? 1 2 3 4 5 ____________________

Body composition ? 1 2 3 4 5 ____________________

Support of family and friends ? 1 2 3 4 5 ____________________

Years of racing experience ? 1 2 3 4 5 ____________________

Tendency to overtrain ? 1 2 3 4 5 ____________________

TRAINING OBJECTIVES TO ACHIEVE GOALS

1.

2.

3.

4.

5.

6

RACING ABILITIES

Things worth having are not easy to obtain. Once obtained, those items must be treated with care and respect or they slip away.
—GALE BERNHARDT, ELITE COACH

YOU HAVE IDENTIFIED your strengths and weaknesses as a cyclist. Based on your results from the tests in Chapter 5 and your previous race experience, you should have a good idea what makes you the rider you are. You now know that many factors play a role in your performance: physical, mental, nutritional, technical, strategic, and more. In this chapter, as with most in this book, we will focus on the physical aspects of training.

Back in the 1970s when I began to study training seriously from a scientific perspective, I was convinced that if I could find a diagram that illustrated what training was all about, I'd have a better grasp of the subject. For years I played around with various drawings, always trying to find the one that made it clear. Could training be a straight-line continuum? Might a circle best explain what happens in training for competition? Or maybe a three-dimensional spiral best shows what training is all about. Nothing seemed to work.

Then I discovered the writings of Dr. Tudor Bompa, a Romanian scientist and coach who has written extensively about periodization. In his work he uses a simple diagram to describe training. This was it! Once I got a handle on the components of his diagram, training became simple. His figure not only helped me to simplify the elements of training, it also provided a third dimension: time.

In this chapter I'll introduce you to the Bompa diagram, which now serves as the basis for all I do when training athletes. While it appears to be very simple, there are many subtle nuances that require some consideration. But once you have grasped the concepts, the process of training—and the answers to many of the questions you have about how to train—will become evident.

First, I would like to further explore the concept of "limiters" that was touched upon in Chapter 5 so you can better relate the Bompa diagram to your own strengths and weaknesses and accurately apply the model to your training.

LIMITERS

There are aspects of your physical fitness that hold you back when it comes to race performance. You discovered some of these weaknesses in Chapter 5. Although it would be nice if you could eliminate all of your weaknesses and have only strengths, it is neither realistic nor all that necessary for you to aim that high. More than likely, only one or two of these shortcomings stand between you and better race results. These key weaknesses are your "limiters."

Performance in a race depends on how well your individual strengths match the requirements of the event. If it is a good match, your peak performance is just what it takes to race at the front. But this is rare. Usually, racing is more like a lottery: You compare your ticket to the winning numbers and find out that you had five of the six numbers right—close, but no million-dollar prize. Having two of the three qualities necessary to race well isn't good enough. The one you're missing is the limiter. By correcting it, regardless of your other weaknesses, you're a contender. So it's really not weaknesses that should concern you, it's limiters.

A limiter is a race-specific weakness. For example, let's say you are training for a hilly, A-priority road race that is always won or lost on the last climb, and one of your weaknesses is climbing. This weakness is obviously a limiter—it prevents you from performing at the level required for success in that race. You may have another weakness, such as sprinting, but this would not be a limiter for this race. So while you have two weaknesses—climbing and sprinting—only one is limiting your performance in this important event.

In this chapter you will learn what is necessary to race well in the types of races you do, and which of those requirements you are missing. Later, I'll show you how to strengthen your limiters.

BASIC RACING ABILITIES

In Chapter 5, I mentioned the three basic abilities required in all sports: endurance, force, and speed skills. Different types of races, from hilly or flat to long or short, require different mixes of these abilities. Athletes should start their training year with a focus on these three basics. The basics should also form the foundation of the novice cyclist's development in the sport for the first year or two.

Think of the basic racing abilities as the corners of a triangle (see Figure 6.1). We will build on this image as we go into further detail in this chapter. Therefore, although endurance, force, and speed skills sound simple enough, it may be helpful to explain how those terms are used here.

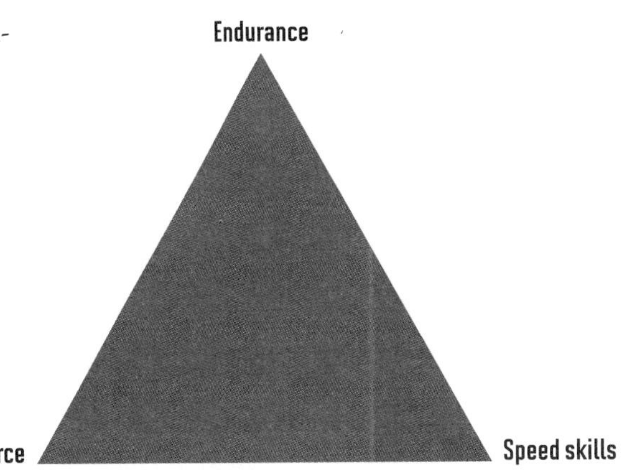

FIGURE 6.1

Basic Abilities Triangle

ENDURANCE

Endurance is the ability to continue working by delaying the onset of fatigue. Within the context of this book, it implies an aerobic level of exertion. Endurance is specific to the event. For example, a one-hour race does not require the endurance to ride for five hours.

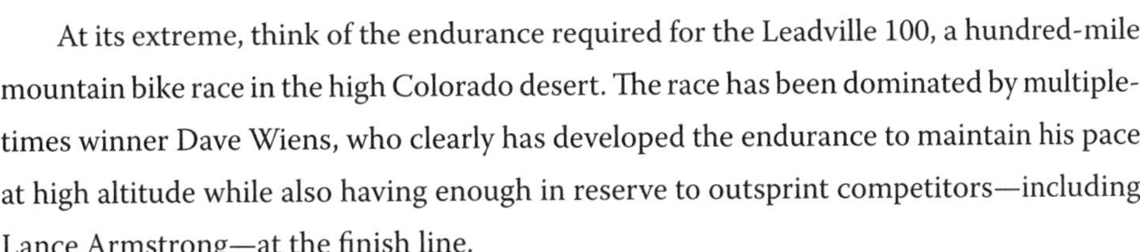

At its extreme, think of the endurance required for the Leadville 100, a hundred-mile mountain bike race in the high Colorado desert. The race has been dominated by multiple-times winner Dave Wiens, who clearly has developed the endurance to maintain his pace at high altitude while also having enough in reserve to outsprint competitors—including Lance Armstrong—at the finish line.

As with other aspects of fitness, you build endurance by starting with general endurance training and then progressing to more specific training. This means building a foundation of aerobic endurance by developing the capabilities of the cardiorespiratory system (heart, lungs, blood, blood vessels). Early in the season and especially in cold climates, cyclists achieve this by pursuing crosstraining activities such as skiing or running. If you are strongly committed to riding your bike year-round, consider cyclocross training in the winter, since it combines running with cycling and lets you hone your handling skills. As the season progresses, your training will become more specific as you extend the length of your longest training rides. Toward the end of your first Base period (typically 8 to 12 weeks in its entirety), you would steadily increase the duration of these rides to a minimum of two hours or to the length of the longest race you are entering, whichever is longer.

There is a wealth of scientific research showing that endurance training improves aerobic capacity (VO_2max), increases the number of capillaries supplying blood to the working muscles, increases the density of mitochondria (the cells where energy is created from fat in the muscle), raises blood volume, and decreases heart rate during exercise at a given intensity. Endurance is the base upon which road racing is built, but experienced cyclists often take it for granted and fail to fully develop their abilities in this area. I have found that most riders improve their performances if they concentrate on endurance for several weeks, riding long at a moderate effort, before beginning to do fast group rides and interval workouts. It takes a great deal of patience to become aerobically fit.

For the novice cyclist, endurance is the key to progress. After all, the sport of road racing is primarily an endurance sport. If you don't have the endurance to finish the race, it doesn't matter how well developed any of your other abilities may be. This ability has to be nurtured before others are emphasized.

FORCE

Force, or strength, is the ability to overcome resistance. In cycling, force comes into play on hills and when riding into the wind. It also has a lot to do with how big a gear you can turn anytime you want to go fast. You probably already know some "force" riders on your own team or in your riding group. They're the ones who like to mash a big gear at a slow cadence. Think Ivan Basso and Jan Ullrich pounding up the Alps in the Tour de France.

You develop muscular force by progressing from general to specific training during the year. This starts with weight lifting early in the season and eventually becomes big-gear repeats and then hill work. This progression, by the way, is typical of the general to specific preparation so common in proper training. When lifting weights, you are engaged in general training, as no bike is involved, but when you're suffering through big-gear hill repeats your training is specific to the demands of the sport. I mention this now because it will be an important theme in the development of all the race abilities described here.

Improving force isn't just about being able to hammer a big gear. A review of the scientific literature reveals a number of studies suggesting that athletes who increase their muscular force improve their performance in all cycling efforts, from well above the LT down to the aerobic threshold. This is probably because such training has two effects: It causes certain fast-twitch muscle fibers to take on the characteristics of slow-twitch muscle fibers, and it increases the size and ability of the slow-twitch muscles to overcome resistance. What this means is that, over time, all the muscle fibers learn to work together to generate more power for the same effort. No matter what the course looks like, you'll be able to ride it in a bigger gear and a faster speed.

SPEED SKILLS

Speed skills are the ability to move quickly and efficiently. Racers with strong speed skills can pedal smoothly at a high cadence and negotiate turns quickly without wasted movement. "Speed skills" is not used here as a synonym for velocity, although this is a related issue. As speed skills improve, so do race times and performances. Some aspects of this ability, such as pedaling at 200 rpm, are typically genetic. Athletes with world-class power have been found to have a high percentage of fast-twitch muscles that are capable of rapid contraction, but they tend to fatigue quickly.

Cycling speed is affected by both cadence and gear size, as illustrated by the following formula:

Bike speed = stroke rate x gear size

To ride a bike fast, you can either turn the pedals around at a high rate, use a high gear, or do a little of both. That's all there is to it.

Of course, in the real world of bike racing there's more to it than just that. We need to factor in aerobic capacity (VO_2max), LT, and economy. These make it possible to maintain a high cadence and big gear over time. The most highly trainable of these factors for the fit athlete is economy.

Economy is defined as how much effort you use when pedaling at a given power output. The goal is to make quick movements with little wasted energy. By improving your economy you can go faster using the same effort. This is the ability I call "speed skills"—one of the critical corners of the training triad.

As with force, speed-skills training progresses from the general to the specific. The goal for this ability is to pedal comfortably (in other words, with a lower energy expenditure) at a higher cadence than you are now capable of doing. Several scientific studies have demonstrated that leg turnover is trainable, given the right types of workouts and consistency of purpose. Such training starts with drills (general) and slowly moves toward riding with a higher cadence than you currently employ (specific).

An easy way to determine how economically you pedal is to simply see what the highest cadence is that you can maintain for several minutes in a low gear. Lance Armstrong proved to be a master at this during his Tour de France victory years, when he raced time trials at a remarkably high 110 to 120 rpm. When he first came onto the world cycling stage in the early 1990s, he was a "masher," turning the cranks at 80 to 90 rpm. By the late 1990s he had completely overhauled his pedaling mechanics to be much more economical—and more competitive as a result.

Economy can be improved if you work at it. This will result in faster race times and better results, but it will take time to accomplish. One study using Swedish runners found that economy continued to improve 22 months after VO_2max had plateaued. It takes a long-term dedication, not just a brief experiment of only a few workouts.

Are you already so economical that further work is unnecessary? That's unlikely. In the early 1980s, American running legend Steve Scott improved his economy by a whopping 6 percent just before setting a world record for the mile. If an elite runner who already had excellent economy could improve by so much, what can the rest of us do? A 1 percent enhancement in pedaling economy could shave 30 to 40 seconds off your 40 km time trial. What would a 6 or even a 10 percent improvement mean for your performance?

ADVANCED RACING ABILITIES

The triangle diagrammed in Figure 6.1 may now be further defined. The basics of endurance, force, and speed skills make up the corners, but each of the sides of the triangle represents a more advanced ability. These are the abilities the experienced athlete will emphasize in the later periods of training, once the basic abilities have been more fully developed.

MUSCULAR ENDURANCE

Muscular endurance is the ability of muscles to sustain a high load for a prolonged time. It is the combination of the basic force and endurance abilities. In the world of cycling, muscular endurance is the ability to repeatedly turn a relatively high gear for a relatively long period of time. For the road cyclist, this is a critical ability. Muscular endurance is what allows you to ride in a fast-moving group without suffering, to be fast in time trials, and to hang with the leaders on a very long, steady grade.

Excellent muscular endurance is evidenced by a high level of fatigue resistance when turning a big gear. It is so critical to performance in road cycling that we will work on it almost as much as the more basic ability of pure endurance.

The "general" aspect of muscular endurance training is the development of the accompanying corners—endurance and force. Once these abilities are deep-rooted, muscular endurance training begins, starting with long repeats (endurance) in a higher-than-normal gear (force). The intensity is not high at first, being well below the LT, but eventually such training approaches and often surpasses threshold effort. As the early-season training progresses, the work intervals gradually get longer, but the recovery intervals remain quite short—about one-fourth of the work interval duration.

FIGURE 6.2 Higher Abilities Triangle

ANAEROBIC ENDURANCE

Anaerobic endurance is the ability to resist fatigue at high cadence while turning a big gear. In advanced athletes, it is the blending of speed skills and endurance. Anaerobic endurance is fundamental to races in which long sprints determine success. A rider with the ability to maintain sprint speed for several hundred meters can often dictate the outcome of a race, either as a strong lead-out or as a solo effort. Aerobic endurance is also present in the rider who is capable of single-handedly bridging a gap. Another time when this ability is needed is when climbing steep hills that take only a couple of minutes to ascend. In short, fast events such as criteriums, anaerobic endurance is challenged by the many surges that take place. Such rapid changes of effort cause the creation of high levels of lactic acid. Without well-developed anaerobic endurance, a rider would quickly fatigue as lactate accumulates.

Clearly, any rider who wants to compete at the highest levels must fully hone his or her anaerobic endurance. But for the novice, anaerobic endurance training is to be avoided for at least the first year. The training is very stressful and can lead to injury, overtraining, and burnout. The recovery requirements for this type of training are also the highest of all.

POWER

Power is the ability to apply maximum force in the shortest time possible. It results from having high levels of the basic abilities of force and speed skills. Well-developed power, or the lack of it, is obvious on short hills, in sprints, and in sudden pace changes.

Since it is based on the speed skills and force components of the triangle, power depends on the nervous system and the muscles and how they interact. The nervous system must send signals to the proper muscles, initiating their contraction at just the right times. The muscles then must produce a large contraction force.

Training for greater power involves short, all-out efforts in the power CP0.2 zone (12 seconds) or at RPE 20, followed by long rests to allow the nervous system and muscles to fully recover. Inadequate recovery will diminish the value of this workout. The repetitions are quite short—in the neighborhood of 8 to 12 seconds or less. Heart rate monitors are of no use in power training.

Attempting to improve power while fatigued is counterproductive. Such training is best done early in a training session when you are rested and the nervous system and muscles are most responsive. This is not to say that you should never work on sprinting late in a workout. You should at some time in the season prepare to sprint when tired, as that is what usually happens in a race. But when trying to improve power earlier in the season, be sure you are well recovered.

MEETING THE DEMANDS OF RACING

Let's return to the discussion of limiters, which were previously defined as race-specific weaknesses. By now you should have a good idea of what your physical-ability limiters are. The basic abilities of endurance, force, and speed skills are easily identified. The advanced abilities are somewhat more difficult to recognize. But since the higher abilities are based on the combination of the basic abilities, a weakness in basic abilities produces a weakness in the higher abilities. For example, if your endurance is weak, it will limit both muscular endurance and anaerobic endurance. If endurance is good but force is lacking, muscular endurance and power are negatively affected. Poor speed skills mean low power and inferior anaerobic endurance.

As mentioned, the types of races you do determine what strengths are needed and how your weaknesses limit you. Matching your abilities to the demands of the event is critical for success. Let's examine how that works.

There are several variables that define the demands of a road race. For example, races vary in course length and in terrain characteristics (whether they have hills, corners, and so on). Other variables include wind, temperature, and humidity. Perhaps the most significant variable in road racing is the competition. Matching your physical fitness to the demands of the most important events you are entering produces the best results.

The longer the race is, the more it favors the basic abilities. Conversely, the shorter the race, the more important the higher abilities become. In preparing for a longer race, endurance is paramount, but force is also necessary to deal with hills, and good fuel economy resulting from good speed skills conserves energy. Muscular endurance plays an important role, but training for anaerobic endurance and power is of lower value.

In the same way, a short race such as a criterium favors the higher abilities, especially anaerobic endurance and power. That doesn't mean that endurance and force aren't needed—it just means they're not needed to the same extent as they are for the endurance events. Speed-skills training is critical for short races, and muscular endurance also plays a role.

Training for an important event means first deciding what is important for success and then improving your limiters while maintaining strengths that already fit its demands.

Besides the event-specific ability limiters discussed here, there are other factors that may also hold you back from achieving race goals. One of the most critical is a lack of time to train. This is perhaps the most common limiter. If this is a limiter for you, then refer back to the specificity of training, discussed in Chapter 3. Essentially, when time becomes scarce, your training must increasingly simulate racing. As training volume declines, workout intensity specific to the event increases. The next chapter helps you decide how many weekly training hours are reasonable and necessary.

TRAINING OF ABILITIES

As you can see from the brief discussion of abilities, there are training patterns that progress from the general to the very specific. Figure 6.3 illustrates this concept. At the start of the training year, much of the work is general in nature, meaning that it may not include a bicycle or may involve riding in an unusual fashion, as when doing drills. Force (strength) training serves as a good example of the progression from general to specific. Early in the training year, weight workouts take up a large portion of training time. Later in the winter, weight-room training is cut back as the number of hilly rides increases—especially in a high gear with low cadence. Eventually, the athlete may progress to hill repeats or hill intervals and, finally, to racing on hilly courses—the most specific of force-related work.

Each ability has a unique method of training associated with it throughout the season. What follows is a brief and simplified summary of how to train abilities from the start of the season through the end. In Chapter 8, I provide details of how to blend all of the abilities, and in Chapter 9, I furnish workout menus and the criteria for selecting workouts for each of these abilities. In the meantime, you can refer to Table 6.1 for some tangible ideas on how to train your basic and specific racing abilities.

ENDURANCE

Endurance training starts in early winter with aerobic crosstraining activities such as Nordic skiing or in-line skating. These modes of training will provide enough stress to the heart, lungs, blood, and blood vessels to improve their endurance qualities. By midwinter, the program calls for a gradual phasing-in of on-bike training and the gradual elimination of crosstraining. Late-winter or early-spring rides should increase until they are at least as long as the longest race of the upcoming season. By this point, you have already established a good level of stamina and have begun to favor high-intensity workouts over endurance training. During the Transition period from the end of the race season to the beginning of the Base period, you can maintain a minimum level of endurance with crosstraining.

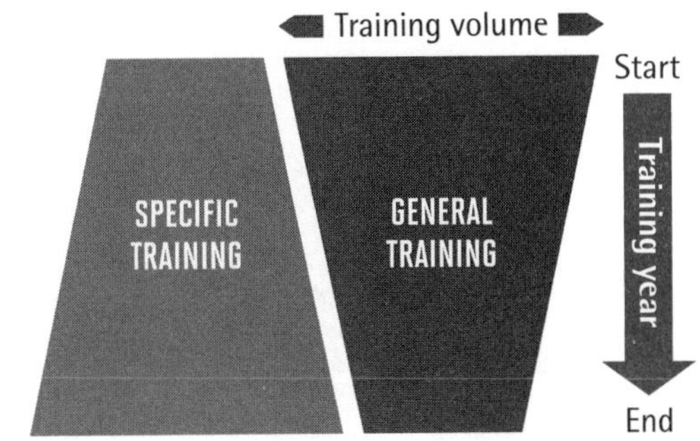

FIGURE 6.3 Training Progression

During the Build period, the emphasis on endurance lessens slightly as intensity increases. Once the season begins, an athlete's endurance level has largely been set; it is then typically maintained with long rides, but these are less frequent now than in the Base period. The focus at that point switches more to the advanced abilities of muscular endurance, anaerobic endurance, and power.

FORCE

Force development begins in early winter with training in the weight room. If you have followed the schedule, you should attain the maximum strength necessary by the end of Base 1 near midwinter. You should then shift your emphasis toward improving your force when on the bike. Depending on the weather, late winter is the best time to begin riding in the hills. Later, hill work may evolve into hill intervals and repeats, depending on your weaknesses. A rider can work to maintain strength throughout the season with weight-room training and hill work. This approach is especially helpful for women and masters, who sometimes have trouble building and maintaining muscle mass.

SPEED SKILLS

Like force development, speed-skills development improves pedaling economy, much like force. Frequent drill work, especially in the winter months, teaches big and small muscles exactly when to contract and when to relax. As the muscles involved in pedaling are activated with precise harmony, precious fuel is conserved. Just as with endurance and force, speed-skills training begins in the late fall or early winter, depending on the race schedule, and continues at a maintenance level throughout the rest of the season.

TABLE 6.1 Training Racing Abilities

ABILITY	WORKOUT FREQUENCY*	INTERVALS DURATION**	ZONES WORK	RECOVERY***	RPE	HEART RATE	POWER	BENEFIT	EXAMPLE
Endurance	1–4/week Continuous	20 min.–6 hrs.	N/A	N/A	2–6	1–3	CP180	Delay fatigue Build slow twitch Economy	3 hrs. on flat course
Force	1–2/week Intervals	20–90 min.	30 sec.–2 min.	1:2	7–9	4–5b	CP12–60	Muscular strength Economy	Seated hill repeats
Speed skills	1–4/week	20–90 min.	10–30 sec.	1:2–5	9–10	N/A	CP1	High cadence Economy	30-sec. spin-ups
Muscular endurance	1–2/week	30 min.–2 hrs. Intervals/ continuous	6–20 min.	3–4:1	7–8	4–5a	CP30–90	Strength endurance Race-pace comfort Boost LT velocity	4 x 6 min. (2 min. RI)
Anaerobic endurance	1–2/week	30–90 min.	3–6 min. 30–40 sec.	2:1–2 2–3:1	9	5b	CP6	Raise VO_2max VO_2max velocity Lactate clearance Lactate tolerance	5 x 5 min. (5 min. RI) 4 x 40 sec. (20 sec. RI) 5 sec. RI between sets
Power	1–3/week	20–90 min.	8–12 sec.	1:10	10	N/A	CP0.2	Muscular power Fast starts Short hills Sprints	10 x 8 sec. (80 sec. RI)

* Varies with individual, time of season, and time available to train.
** Total workout time including the portion of workout that develops the ability.
*** Work interval-to-recovery interval ratio. Example, 3:1 means rest ("off") 1 minute for every 3 minutes of work ("on") time.
Note: min. = minutes, sec. = seconds, hrs. = hours, RI = recovery ("off") interval

Economy is largely determined by biomechanics—how efficiently you move your legs while pedaling. This is a nervous-system function and as such requires focusing on technique rather than fitness. For example, good pedaling skills are based on a slight amount of "ankling" (Figure 6.4). This means using your ankle like a movable hinge instead of a rigid crowbar. On flat terrain, the ankle slowly opens during the upstroke, allowing the heel to rise slightly above the toes by the 12 o'clock position. On the downstroke the ankle closes a bit, so that the heel is even with or slightly below the toes by the 3 o'clock position. On a climb, ankling may be a bit more pronounced.

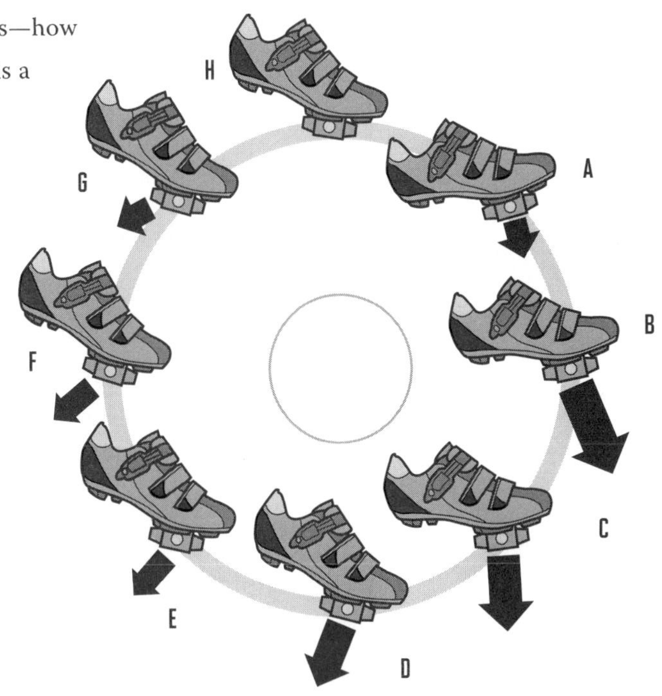

Adapted with permission from Cavanagh and Sanderson 1986.

FIGURE 6.4 Pedaling Biomechanics: Foot Position and Resultant Force

Focusing your technique to improve speed skills involves concentrating on making adjustments in a few precise movement patterns and then taking a relatively long break before trying it again. It's best to call it a day before fatigue sets in and you get sloppy. Once technique begins to break down, you are no longer refining the skill—you're simply allowing bad habits to become ingrained.

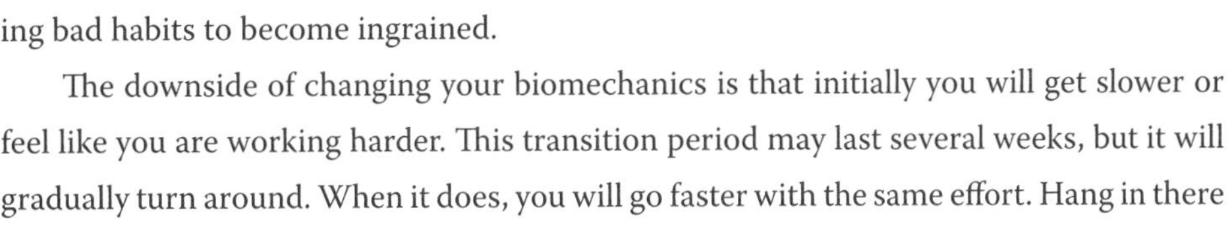

The downside of changing your biomechanics is that initially you will get slower or feel like you are working harder. This transition period may last several weeks, but it will gradually turn around. When it does, you will go faster with the same effort. Hang in there until then.

MUSCULAR ENDURANCE

Muscular endurance work begins in midwinter with sustained efforts of several minutes in heart rate zone 3 or power zone CP90. By late winter, it gradually progresses to interval training in heart rate zones 4 and 5a or power zones CP30 to CP60. The work intervals gradually get longer as the recovery intervals shorten. By spring, the athlete is riding for up to an hour in these zones. The effort is much like "controlled" time trialing and tremendously effective in boosting both aerobic and anaerobic fitness with little risk of overtraining. Throughout the Race period, muscular endurance is maintained.

POWER

Power may be the most misunderstood aspect of training in cycling. Most athletes do sprints with brief recovery periods to try to improve their power. They are really working on anaerobic endurance. You can improve power with brief sprints at near-maximum exertion followed by long recovery intervals. Natural sprinters love these workouts. Those with little power—riders possessing great endurance and little speed skills or force—find them painful and dread them. For these cyclists, the blending of speed-skill and force training into power development will lead to an effective jump at the start of sprints.

ANAEROBIC ENDURANCE

Anaerobic endurance training includes lactate tolerance repetitions and intervals to develop aerobic capacity. At the start of the Build period of training, the experienced athlete should phase into interval training to bring his or her aerobic capacity to a peak. During the last weeks of the Build period, lactate-tolerance work trains the body to dissipate lactate from the blood and to buffer its usual effects.

There are two types of anaerobic endurance workouts, and both are interval based. One is done at a power output roughly equivalent to what you would experience at the highest levels of your aerobic capacity (VO_2max). If you have a power meter, this is your CP6 zone. If you train only with a heart rate monitor or rate of perceived exertion, the heart rate zone is 5b and the RPE is 18 to 19 on the 6–20 scale. The work intervals are about three minutes long with equal recovery intervals. As the season progresses and fitness improves, the work intervals are shortened.

The second type of anaerobic endurance interval workout prepares you for the stresses that are common when repeated surges occur. Short repetitions (less than a minute long) at very high power outputs are completed with only short recoveries between them. This is exactly what you experience in a criterium.

The idea of these workouts is to challenge the body's lactate-clearance and buffering systems so that eventually you will be able to remove and cope with so much lactate so quickly that staying with such a demanding event becomes considerably easier—but never easy. This is not the sort of training you want to do frequently or for many weeks. This is the most demanding of all workouts.

Anaerobic endurance training is quite stressful and should not be a part of the novice cyclist's regimen. Both speed skills and endurance should be well established, with at least two years of training, before these workouts are attempted on a regular basis. The likely results of too much anaerobic endurance work too soon are burnout and overtraining.

ABILITY REGIONS

In this section, it may sound as if I'm encouraging you to specialize in a particular category of races. I'm not. My purpose here is to show you how to blend the six abilities previously discussed to produce optimal performance for specific types of races. Your strengths will favor success in some of these, but it is likely that you will still need to improve limiters for complete mastery. This section will also help you see how strengths and limiters can be blended into a comprehensive training program.

To understand the requirements of various types of races, Figure 6.5a is another look at the triangle depicted in Figure 6.2, with further refinements.

Note that the triangle is divided into six regions, each representing a specific set of ability requirements. By now, you should be able to position yourself within one of the regions based on your known strengths. For example, if endurance is your number-one ability and force is second, then you are a Region I cyclist—high in muscular endurance with a tendency toward endurance. If two or all three of the natural abilities are equal for you, then your proficiencies may help define your region. Sprinters usually fit into the speed-skills regions (IV, V), climbers into the force regions (II, III), and time trialists into the endurance regions (I, VI).

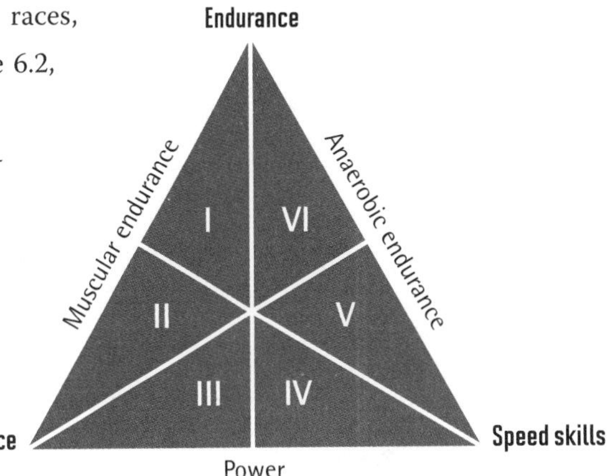

FIGURE 6.5a

Racing Abilities: Overview of Regions

Races may also be divided into these same six regions based on their type, distance, and terrain. If you are a Region I cyclist, then you will do best in Region I races. The triangle can also help you decide what to work on in order to perform better in a particular region.

Following are race descriptions by ability regions, including a prioritizing of the needed abilities for each race type. Obviously, your strengths will require less training time than your limiters. Chapter 8 teaches you how to blend the training of the various abilities, and Chapter 9 provides detailed workouts to support each of these ability requirements.

In each region you can see the highest priorities for your training highlighted in the corresponding diagram. There is not an implied order of training, but rather an emphasis on training for optimal performance in that region. Given that you have time and energy constraints on your training (due to career, family, home maintenance, and so on), you must decide what is most important and focus on that. If any of the three critical abilities in a given list is your personal weakness and they are needed for an A-priority race, then you must give that limiter top priority when it comes to training. The remaining three abilities in each list have limited value for the corresponding races and should be given lower priority in training. Do not avoid these areas, but assign them less training time and energy. If one of your strengths falls into one of the last three abilities, you need to place only minor emphasis on it.

REGION I: LONG, FLAT TO ROLLING RACES

Region I includes the long, flat to rolling races that are so common in the northwestern European countries, the Netherlands and Belgium. In the United States, races of more than 100 miles like these are becoming harder to find. Wind direction, team tactics, and mental tenacity go a long way toward determining the outcome of these races. Riders with excellent endurance and time trialing proficiency are likely to emerge victorious. These races are also likely to come down to a pack sprint.

Also included in this region are time trials that are 30 kilometers or longer. Indeed, time trialing proficiency is critical to performance in Region I races. If your weakness is time trialing, you need to put a great deal of emphasis on muscular endurance training in order to race well. Good time trialists have exceptional LT relative to their aerobic capacities and maximum power outputs. They develop the ability to ride comfortably in an aerodynamic position and minimize wasted energy in pedaling. They also have a superior ability to concentrate despite great suffering. Figure 6.5b shows Region I priorities.

FIGURE 6.5b

Racing Abilities, Region I

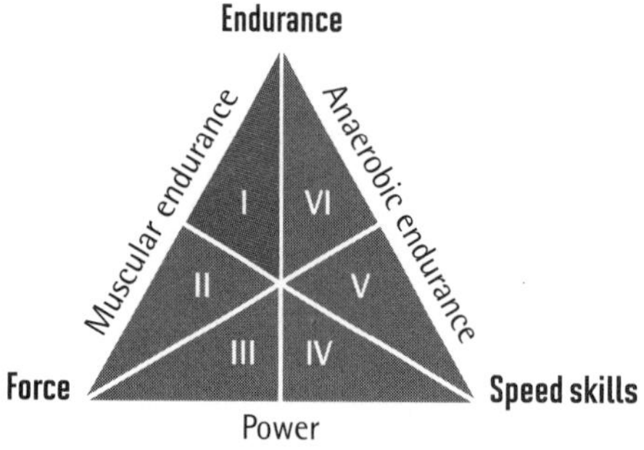

Region I Priorities	
Primary	1. Endurance
	2. Muscular endurance
	3. Force
Secondary	4. Anaerobic endurance
	5. Speed skills
	6. Power

REGION II: TIME TRIALS AND SHORTER ROAD RACES

Region II races include time trials of about 15 to 30 kilometers and road races of less than three hours. Hills are usually the element that determines outcomes. These are common road races in U.S. cycling.

Climbing is a central proficiency skill for Region II. What makes for champion climbers? Typically, they have less than two pounds of body weight for every inch of height. They are capable of generating high wattage per pound of body weight in sustained efforts. This requires a high LT-power output and a large aerobic capacity. Natural climbers have an economical climbing style and are especially nimble on the pedals when out of the saddle on a climb. Figure 6.5c shows Region II priorities.

FIGURE 6.5c

Racing Abilities, Region II

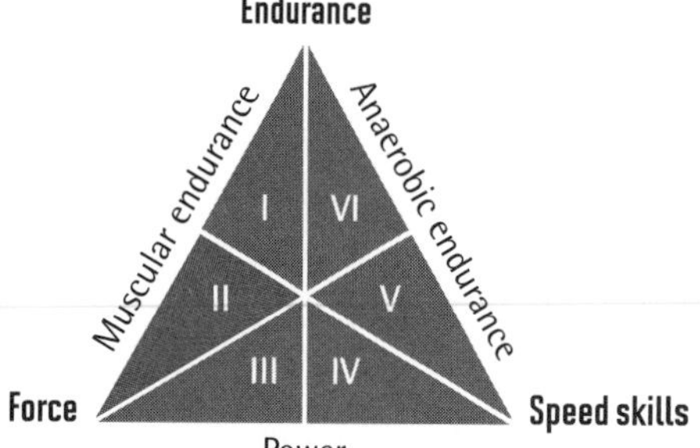

Region II Priorities	
Primary	1. Force
	2. Muscular endurance
	3. Endurance
Secondary	4. Power
	5. Speed skills
	6. Anaerobic endurance

REGION III: SHORT TIME TRIALS

Region III in road racing is found only in short prologues of stage races. These are generally individual time trials on hilly courses taking only a few minutes to complete. As such, there is no need for the road racer to train for these events. The stage racer must simply grin and bear the agony. Figure 6.5d shows Region III priorities.

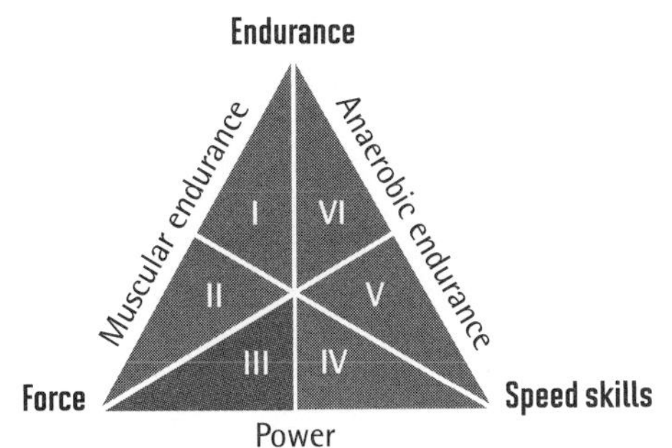

Region III Priorities	
Primary	1. Force
	2. Speed skills
	3. Power

FIGURE 6.5d

Racing Abilities, Region III

REGION IV: TRACK RACING AND SPRINTING

Region IV is in the domain of the track racer, especially the match sprinter. Training for this region is not within the scope of this book, but Figure 6.5e shows Region IV priorities.

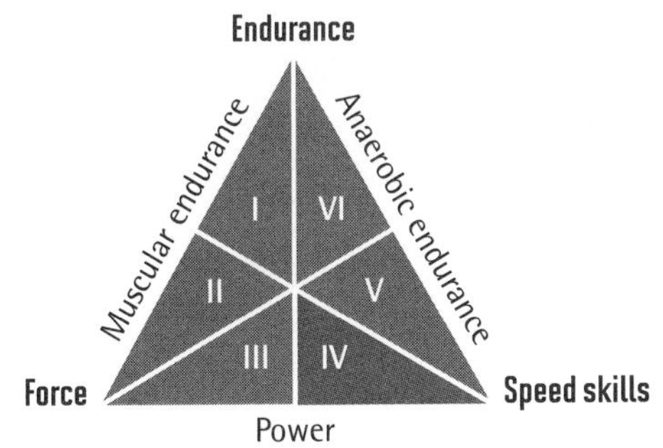

Region IV Priorities	
Primary	1. Power
	2. Speed skills
	3. Anaerobic endurance

FIGURE 6.5e

Racing Abilities, Region IV

REGION V: SHORT CRITS

Region V includes short criteriums that are typical of many masters, women's, and juniors races. These are 45 minutes or less and have a high requirement for speed skills and anaerobic endurance. You must also realize that while this is a short event with much sprinting, it is still an endurance race. Don't disregard the development of this primary ability.

Short criteriums attract riders who are good sprinters. They usually have great total body strength and a capacity to produce extremely high power outputs instantaneously. This power is often marked by the ability to produce vertical jumps in excess of 22 inches. Champion sprinters have the dynamic balance of a gymnast and can turn the cranks at extremely high cadences. In close-quarters sprints, they race aggressively with no thought given to "what would happen if . . ."—they are confident in their ability to win the close one. Figure 6.5f shows Region V priorities.

FIGURE 6.5f

Racing Abilities, Region V

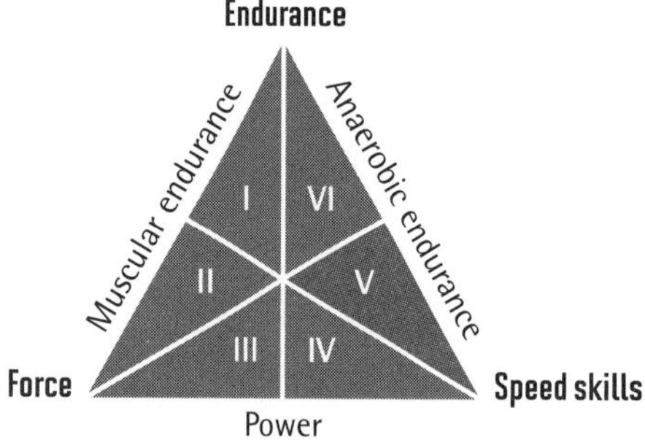

Region V Priorities	
Primary	1. Speed skills
	2. Anaerobic endurance
	3. Endurance
Secondary	4. Power
	5. Force
	6. Muscular endurance

REGION VI: LONG CRITS AND CIRCUIT RACES

Region VI races are long criteriums and circuit races. This is the most common type of race in the United States. Notice that the primary quality of criterium racing is still endurance. Criteriums, however, require less endurance ability than longer road races do. The ability to maintain speed and repeatedly sprint out of corners is necessary for success, as are superb bike-handling skills when cornering, bumping, and balancing.

If, in a particular race, a hill or hills are the deciding factor, then force may replace speed skills as a success characteristic. Figure 6.5g shows Region VI priorities.

FIGURE 6.5g

Racing Abilities, Region VI

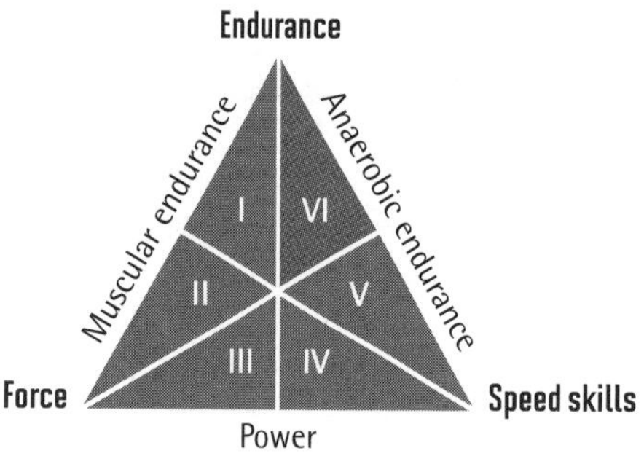

Region VI Priorities	
Primary	1. Endurance
	2. Anaerobic endurance
	3. Speed skills
Secondary	4. Muscular endurance
	5. Force
	6. Power

If you want to be a better cyclist, your limited training time will force you first to identify any personal limiters that exist in the prioritized abilities for each region and dedicate yourself to the drills and repetition that will bring improvement. It is good to realize even the most dedicated cyclist can't be good at everything. Be deliberate with your training, but don't forget the value of cultivating your pure enjoyment of cycling.

PART IV

PLANNING
HISTORICAL PERSPECTIVES

MODERN EUROPEAN TRAINING METHODS

by Jack Heid

(as it appeared in *Cycling Almanac*, 1951)

No one can tell you exactly how to train. It is something you have to work out according to the time at your disposal and the roads and companionship available. However, there are some basic things that you can make your training plans around, which you can copy from my present training methods that I assure you I copied from the European "masters" who have taught me to the point that I feel I have the ability to stay with many of them.

No matter how much training you do on the road with 70 gear or lower, you cannot go stale. You must get in the hours and the mileage. There is no substitute for it. Great riders like Harris and Coppi, who have entirely different actual racing styles, attest to this. Road riders here sit on their bikes all day and do 150 miles one day and the other they rest in the woods doing calisthenics and much deep breathing.

For my track training, I first get on the track and ride around slowly for 5 minutes to warm up. Then we get into a group and for about one-half hour change off pace every 500 yards (about one lap of the track) traveling at 20 mph. Then we all take a 15-minute rest and then go out taking turns leading out for sprints of 250 yards. We have three or four of these 15-minute turns, always resting off the track between. The same can be done on a piece of road measured off for 250 yards.

Developing a jump can be practiced afterwards by coming to an almost dead stop and jumping hard to get up top speed, then rolling slowly to a stop and duplicating this procedure. Don't do too much in one day if you don't feel like it—don't ever force yourself in training.

7

PLANNING TO RACE

The method is the same for you as it is for the pros. What is different is the workload.

—MICHELE FERRARI, ITALIAN CYCLING COACH

WHY DO YOU TRAIN? Is it to enjoy fresh air, the companionship of friends, travel to exotic places, and the feeling of fitness? Or is it to prepare for the peak experience of racing near your limits?

Certainly all of these play a part in getting you out the door and onto a saddle, but since you're reading this book, I suspect the latter choice is correct. All of us want to see how well we can perform, to get new glimpses of our potential, to push the limits of fitness, and to bask in the glow of success.

This chapter lays the groundwork for Chapters 8 and 9, in which you will develop your own personalized training plan.

TRAINING SYSTEMS

Cyclists typically gravitate to one of three training systems in order to prepare for racing. Each has produced champions. Most athletes don't consciously select a system—it just happens. They roll out of the driveway every day and then do what they feel like once on the road, or they meet with a group and let the top riders determine the day's workout. This is not the way to achieve your true potential as a bicycle racer. The road to racing success begins with understanding where you are headed and how you will get there. The starting point is a decision to train purposefully. Until you replace haphazard workouts with systematic training, approaching your potential is highly unlikely.

Selecting a training system has a lot to do with this decision. Let's examine the three training systems most commonly used by cyclists: race into shape, always fit, and periodization.

RACE INTO SHAPE

The most common training system used by cyclists is racing into shape. It traces its roots back to the days of wool jerseys and nail-on cleats. Even in the age of power meters, fingertip shifters, and titanium components, racing into shape is still the system used by most cyclists. It's easy to do—there are only two steps.

Step 1 involves building a large aerobic base by pedaling 1,000 miles easily. Nearly every rider I talk with knows this number and speaks of it with quiet reverence. Interestingly, the 1,000-mile goal does work well for some athletes. But it doesn't work for everyone. For some it is way too much, and for others it is not nearly enough.

Once you have established aerobic endurance, step 2 commences, and it involves just one thing: racing. The idea is that by going to a race every weekend and club races at midweek, a high level of fitness will result.

There are some good reasons to train this way, the most important being that the fitness developed is specific to the demands of racing. What could be more similar to racing than racing? There are, however, some problems. Training this way is very unpredictable. It's just as likely that great fitness will occur at the wrong time as at the right time relative to the most important races of the season. Another problem is that there is no planned rest. Racing into shape frequently leads to overtraining. It is also likely to lead to premature burnout. Every time you put your wheel on a starting line, there is an emotional investment. After some number of these in a short period of time, the rider loses enthusiasm. It's as if you have only so many matches to burn, and once they are all used up, the body and mind are unwilling to continue.

ALWAYS FIT

In warmer climates such as Florida, southern California, and Arizona, cyclists often try to stay in racing shape year-round. The cooler weather and availability of training races throughout the winter entice them to keep a constant level of fitness by doing the same training rides every week. Due to weather constraints, athletes in other parts of the country never even consider this system. That's a good reason why sloppy weather and frigid temperatures are probably an advantage for training.

The greatest issues facing the always-fit trainer are boredom and burnout. After 220 to 250 days of high-level training, an athlete becomes toast. Burnout is not a pretty sight. All interest in training, racing, and life in general vanishes. It sometimes takes months to regain enthusiasm for riding, if it's regained at all. (Chapter 17 discusses burnout in detail.)

Another problem has to do with physiology. After about twelve weeks of training in the same way, improvement seems to plateau. And since fitness is never stagnant, if it's not improving, it must be getting worse. Trying to maintain fitness at a high level all the time really means trying to minimize losses. It just doesn't work.

PERIODIZATION

Periodization is the system used by most successful athletes today, and the one I propose you use. The rest of Part IV describes how to incorporate it into your training.

In Chapter 6, I mentioned periodization in relation to the works of Romanian scientist Dr. Tudor Bompa, who contributed the Foreword to this book. In the late 1940s, Soviet sports scientists discovered that they could improve athletic performance in their athletes by varying the training stress throughout the year rather than maintaining a constant training focus. This finding led to the development of annual training plans that varied the stress of training over periods of time in various ways. The East Germans and Romanians further developed this concept by establishing goals for the different periods, and the system of periodization was born. Bompa so refined the concept that he is known as the "father of periodization." His seminal work, *Theory and Methodology of Training,* introduced Western athletes to this training system. The most recent edition of this work is called *Periodization: Theory and Methodology of Training.* While athletes and coaches have "Westernized" periodization, they have done so largely without the help of science. Scientific literature offers little in the way of direction as to a long-term training approach for endurance athletes.

The basic premise of all periodization programs is that training should progress from the general to the specific. For example, early in the season, the serious cyclist uses much of the available training time to develop general strength with weights, while also cross-training and doing some riding. Later in the season, more time is spent on the bike in conditions that simulate bicycle racing. Although there is no scientific evidence to support such a pattern of training, logic seems to support it. In fact, most of the world's top athletes adhere to this principle.

Of course, periodization means more than simply training more specifically. It also involves arranging the workouts in such a way that the elements of fitness achieved in an earlier phase of training are maintained while new ones are addressed and improved. This modular method of training means making small changes in workouts during four- to eight-week periods. The body will gradually become more fit with such a pattern of change.

Flexibility of training, or lack of it, may be the biggest obstacle facing a cyclist using periodization. Once a rider has outlined a plan, there is often a reluctance to vary from it. Successful periodization requires flexibility. I've never coached an athlete who got through an entire season without a cold, work responsibilities, or a visit from Aunt Bessie getting in the way of the plan. That's just the way life is. An annual training plan should never be viewed as "final." You must assume from the outset that there will be changes due to unforeseen and unavoidable complications. Remember this in the next chapter when you sit down to write your training plan.

Another problem with periodization is all the scientific mumbo jumbo that goes along with it. The language of periodization seems to confuse many, including coaches. Figure 7.1 illustrates the terms that are used for blocks of time in periodization. For the purposes of this book, when referring to specific mesocycle periods, the terms in Figure 7.1 are used: Preparation, Base, Build, Peak, Race, and Transition.

FIGURE 7.1

The Training Year

Macrocycle	TRAINING YEAR							
Mesocycle	Preparation					Competition		Transition
	General preparation			Specific preparation		Pre-comp	Competition	Transition
	Prep	Base 1	Base 2	Build 1	Build 2	Peak	Race	Transition
Microcycle	1 2	3 4 5	6 7 8	Weeks 9–42			43 44 45 46	47 48 49 50 51 52

TRAINING PERIODS

The reason for dividing the season into specific periods in a periodization plan is that this division allows for emphasis on specific aspects of fitness, while maintaining others developed in earlier periods. Trying to improve all aspects of training at the same time is impossible. No athlete is capable of handling that much simultaneous stress. Periodization also allows for two of the training principles discussed in Chapter 3—progressive overload and adaptation.

Figure 7.2 diagrams the process of periodization, describes the focus of each mesocycle period, and suggests a time frame for each period.

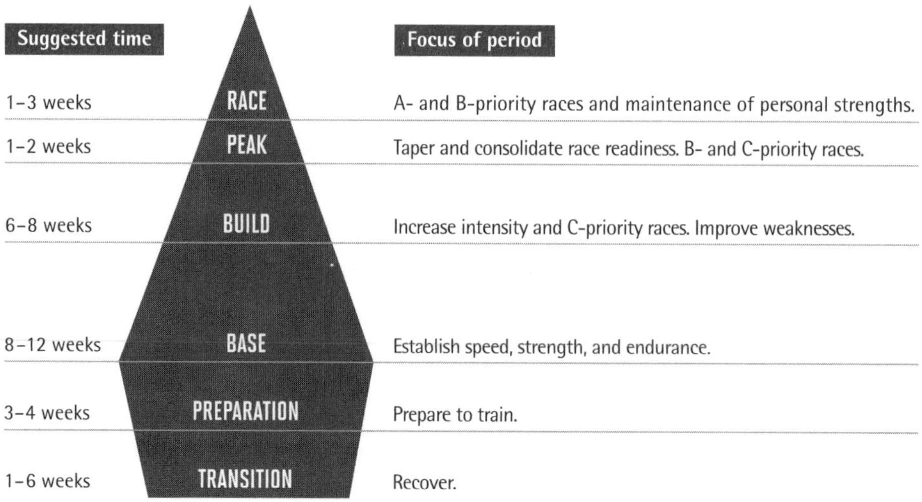

FIGURE 7.2

Using Training Periods to Peak at Selected Times

If you add up the suggested times for each period, you'll find a range of 21 to 38 weeks—well short of a year. The reason for this periodization scheme is that cyclists seem to perform best when they peak two or three times a year. Multipeak seasons allow for adequate rest and recovery, are less likely to cause burnout or overtraining, and are more likely to keep training and racing fun. If you do things right—instead of losing fitness as a long race season progresses—each subsequent peak is higher than the previous one. In Chapter 8, I'll explain how to design such a multipeak season.

In the remainder of this chapter, I'll introduce you to each period in detail. I'll describe every aspect of periodization and provide suggestions for how to train the racing abilities discussed in Chapters 5 and 6. As you read about each period, use Figure 7.3 to see how volume and intensity blend in a hypothetical racing season. Although your own blend will not look exactly like Figure 7.3, it will probably come close. The elements common to most periodization plans are increased volume at the start of the training year and increased intensity as volume declines later on. Notice that there are reduced-volume recovery weeks scheduled periodically throughout the Base and Build periods. These are important—don't pass them up.

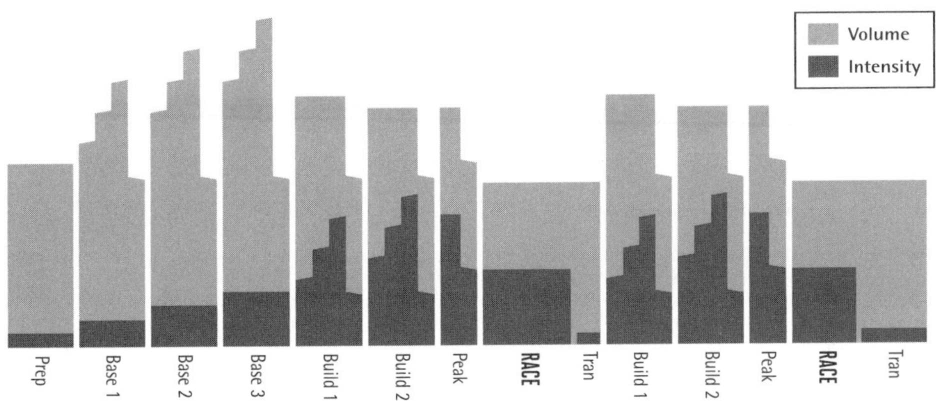

FIGURE 7.3 Volume and Intensity Throughout Training Periods

Accompanying each period description in the following section is a diagram that illustrates the mix of racing abilities for that period. It is especially important to note that the portion devoted to each ability is not exact. The amount of time spent working on each fitness ability will vary with the individual's strengths and limiters. Use the chart only as a rough guide for how to use your training time.

PREPARATION PERIOD

The Preparation period generally marks the start of the training year and is included only if there has been a long transition following the end of the racing season. It is usually scheduled for the late fall or early winter, depending on when the last race was held and the length of the transition.

The purpose of this period is to prepare the athlete's body for the periods to follow. It's a time of training to train (Figure 7.4a). Workouts are low intensity with an emphasis on aerobic endurance, especially in the form of crosstraining. Activities such as running, vigorous hiking, cross-country skiing, snowshoeing, swimming, and in-line skating will maintain or improve cardiorespiratory fitness (heart, blood, blood vessels, and lungs). The total volume of training is low when compared with most other periods.

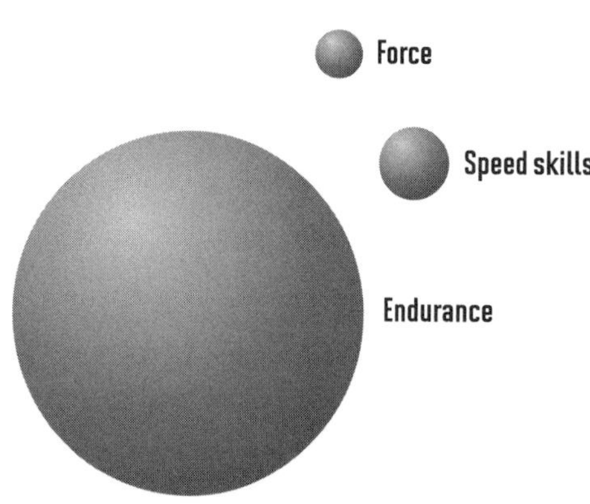

FIGURE 7.4a
Preparation

Strength training begins with the Anatomical Adaptation (AA) phase, which prepares the muscles and tendons for the heavier stresses to follow later. (Strength training is discussed in detail in Chapter 12.)

Speed skills can be developed through drills, usually done on an indoor trainer or rollers. This will reawaken the legs to spinning fluidly in smooth circles.

BASE PERIOD

The Base period is the time to fully establish the basic fitness abilities of endurance, force, and speed skills. Base is generally the longest period of the season, lasting eight to twelve weeks. Some athletes are careless with Base training, ending it too soon. It is essential that the basic abilities have a strong foothold before you launch into high-intensity training.

In warm-winter areas, there may be races available during this period, but I usually advise my athletes to avoid these. They are often demoralizing to athletes who are following a periodization plan because some of the other riders (the always-fit ones) will be in better shape at this point in the game. If you must do one of these races, treat it as a workout and do not take the results seriously. Remember that it is okay to abandon the race. These races are of no consequence for the season ahead.

Since this is such a long period and there will be many changes taking place in your fitness throughout, the Base period is divided into three segments: Base 1, Base 2, and Base 3. The volume of training grows in each segment as crosstraining phases into on-bike training. Intensity also rises slightly as the Base period progresses (refer back to Figure 7.3).

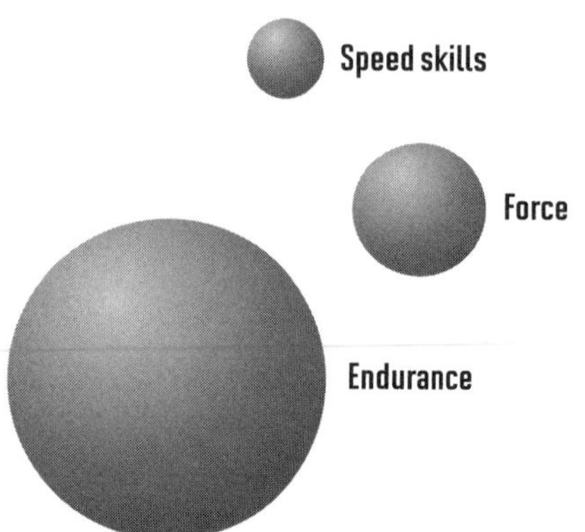

FIGURE 7.4b
Base 1

Base 1 marks the start of steady increases in volume to boost aerobic endurance and increase the body's resilience to large workloads (Figure 7.4b). In the more northern latitudes, you accomplish most of this through crosstraining. Cyclists in warm-winter states should still consider crosstraining instead of spending all of their time on a bike. It's a long season, and many of the elements of fitness developed now can be accomplished off the bike.

Strength training in Base 1 places an emphasis on establishing Maximum Strength (MS) with the use of high-resistance loads and low repetitions. The shift to these greater loads should be gradual so as not to cause injury.

Speed-skills work continues just as in the Preparation period with drills that emphasize high cadence and smooth technique on a trainer or rollers.

In Base 2, on-bike endurance work begins to replace crosstraining as the volume rises (Figure 7.4c). As the road rides become longer, the companionship of a group helps the time to pass faster. Be careful, however, not to ride with groups that turn these endurance rides into races. This time of year you will find many "Christmas stars"—riders who are in great race shape in the winter, but aren't around when the serious racing starts in the summer.

You should plan to do the majority of your road workouts each week on continuously rolling to hilly courses that place controlled stress on the muscular system. The best courses at this time of the season keep effort below the LT and allow cadences of 80 rpm and higher while seated as you climb hills. Staying in the saddle is important for these workouts so that you can develop greater hip extension strength for the next period.

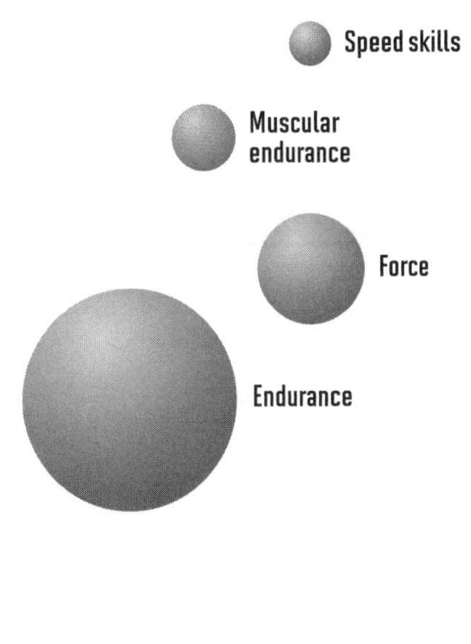

FIGURE 7.4c
Base 2

Weight-room training shifts toward maintenance of strength gains made in the previous period. Also, speed-skills work moves outside, weather permitting. Otherwise, indoor workouts continue. Whenever possible, use the road to refine your sprinting form.

Muscular endurance training is also introduced in Base 2, with tempo workouts based on heart rate or power output (see Chapter 4 for details).

Base 3 marks a phasing-in of higher-intensity training with the introduction of hill work done at or slightly above LT (Figure 7.4d). In Base 2, somewhat hilly

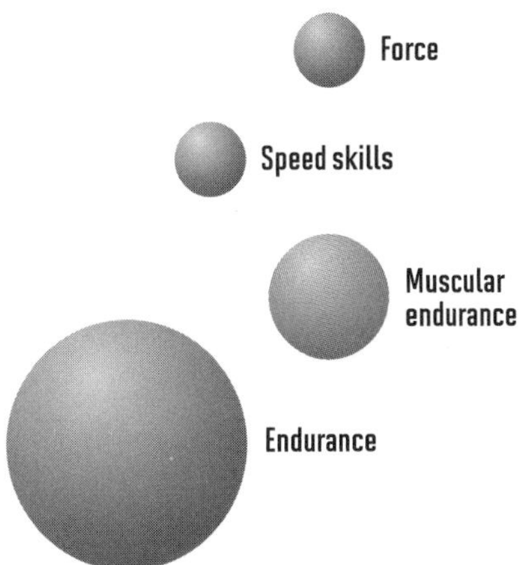

FIGURE 7.4d
Base 3

courses ridden in the saddle complemented the weight-room workouts by creating greater hip extension force. Now you should seek out serious hills with long climbs, still riding them mostly in the saddle.

The total weekly volume of training progresses to the highest point of the season in Base 3, with aerobic endurance rides on the road accounting for about half of all training time. The longest workouts now should be at least as long as your longest race of the season or two hours, whichever is longer. Group rides are still the best way to get in these long efforts. Some in the group may be ready for higher-intensity training, so these rides will typically become faster. It's okay to occasionally put the hammer down in a sprint for the city limits sign, but don't turn these rides into races. This is not easy to do, as the pressure to "race" will be high. Be patient and sit in. Your objective is to get as fast as you can with low-effort rides before turning up the heat in the next period. Later in the season, you'll be glad you held back.

Muscular endurance training is increased, and weight workouts continue as maintenance. Several weekly workouts should now take you to the LT intensity training zones.

Speed-skills work, done mostly as form sprints, must now be on the road.

BUILD PERIOD

A multi-peak season includes two or more full Build periods. These periods are shown in Figure 7.3. As you can see, Build 1 maintains the volume of training at a relatively high level, although less than what was achieved in three of the previous eight weeks. That means that when it is time to return to Build 1 after the first Race period, you may need to reestablish endurance, force, and speed skills.

The Build period is marked by the introduction of anaerobic endurance training. Just as with force, hill work, and muscular endurance training, this should be done cautiously to avoid injury.

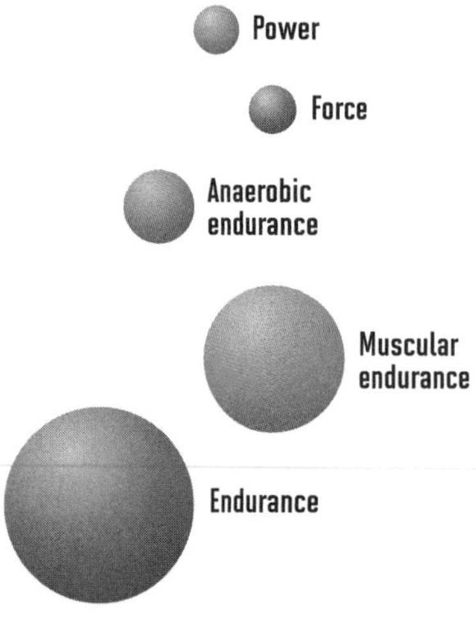

There will probably be criteriums and road races throughout this period. These should mostly be low priority, and you can regard them as a substitute for anaerobic endurance training. Anaerobic endurance workouts may also include intervals and fast group rides.

During Build 1, endurance work is reduced, but it is still a prominent focus of training (Figure 7.4e). At this time in the season such rides may occur less frequently than in the Base period. You will be much better served by doing your long, easy endurance

Power
Force
Anaerobic endurance
Muscular endurance
Endurance

FIGURE 7.4e
Build 1

rides during this period with one or two teammates rather than with a large group. Use the group rides for the development of muscular endurance and anaerobic endurance. Overtraining can easily occur during this phase of training, so pay close attention to your fatigue level. If you feel dead in the saddle during a group ride, for example, don't work hard with the group. Either sit in, getting as much of a free ride as you can, or turn off and ride alone. Be smart. You're not doing this to impress your friends. Save that for the races.

Force training in the weight room is either eliminated or cut back to one day a week now as the duration of such sessions gets shorter. Try to maintain your strength in the weight room, but don't try to achieve new goals. For the athlete limited by force, hill work continues to be a primary focus. This may be in the form of muscular endurance or anaerobic endurance intervals done on a hill. Appendix C offers a workout menu with further suggestions.

Anaerobic endurance workouts can be done with one or two other riders close to your ability. Muscular endurance training is best done alone to prepare you for the focus you will need in time trialing and to keep you in the narrow threshold training zones.

Power may now replace speed-skills work, and power training can be combined with other workouts, such as anaerobic endurance sessions. If you choose to do this, initially incorporate the power-training portion of your routine early in the workout when your legs are still fresh. In Build 1, don't make the common mistake of doing power training at the end of workouts. Reserve that portion of the session for anaerobic endurance and muscular endurance work. In Build 2, power may be shifted to the end of workouts to simulate the demands of sprinting late in a race (Figure 7.4f).

Build 2 slightly decreases the volume of training while increasing the intensity. Notice in Figure 7.3 that intensity increases during each of the three weeks, just as volume increased in the Base period. By now you should be experiencing greater levels of fatigue, and you will need to continue being cautious with anaerobic intensity. If you are unsure whether you should do a certain workout, be wise and either leave it out or shorten it. The mere fact that you're questioning it is enough reason to back off. When in doubt, leave it out.

Training in Build 2 emphasizes intensity to a greater extent than previous weeks did. Anaerobic endurance and muscular endurance sessions become longer, while recovery intervals decrease. At this point, muscular endurance should involve long, continuous exertions, just as in time trialing.

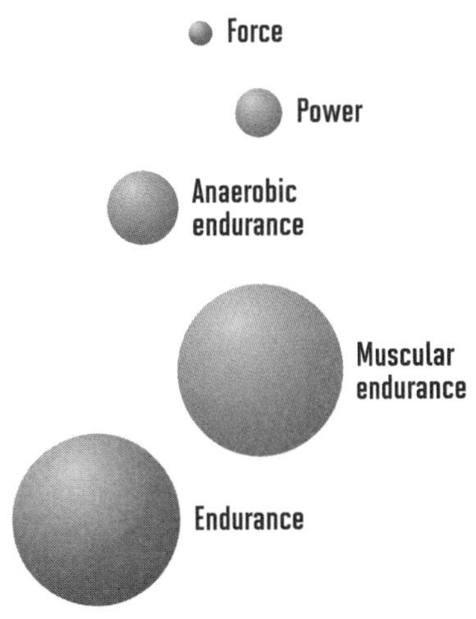

FIGURE 7.4f
Build 2

Weight-room training remains at once a week, if at all, and follows a strength maintenance plan. Riders for whom force is not a limiter may stop weight training in this period. I recommend, however, that masters and women continue, but the choice is up to you. Power training may continue, as in Build 1.

SIDEBAR 7.1

Balancing Fitness, Fatigue, and Form

There are three elements of physical preparation to balance over the course of your training—fatigue, fitness, and form. Fatigue is a measure of how great your workload has been over the past few days. High-intensity and long-duration workouts produce fatigue and fitness simultaneously—hard training makes you tired and also makes you more fit. But fitness increases much more slowly than fatigue. Three hard workouts in three days will produce a lot of fatigue, but only a tiny increase in fitness. So fitness is best measured in weeks, whereas fatigue is measured in days.

Form has to do with how well rested you are. You can have high form (if you are well rested and have a low level of fatigue), but low fitness (if you have allowed yourself too much rest). The trick to preparing for a race is to reduce fatigue, maintain fitness or allow only a slight decrease, and increase form. So how do you achieve that ideal?

You can see how fitness, fatigue, and form fluctuate in the athlete's performance chart shown below. It's easy to see the demands placed on the athlete within each period

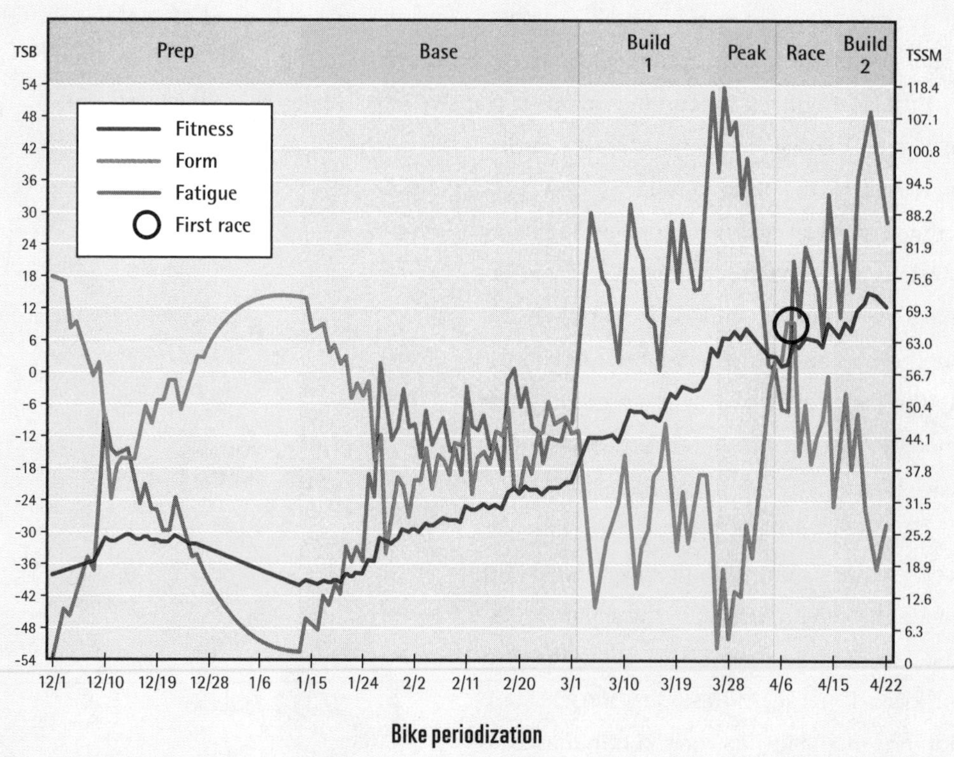

Bike periodization

of training by following the athlete's fatigue. As intensity increases with an increased focus on muscular endurance and anaerobic endurance in the Build period, fatigue builds, culminating in the race-intensity workouts of the Peak period. Consequently, form suffers with the increased fatigue, but in both the recovery weeks and the taper prior to the athlete's first race, form is buoyed by the reduction in fatigue.

The athlete's overall fitness is steadily increasing over the course of the five months shown in the chart, proving that the athlete's training is in fact paying off.

PEAK PERIOD

The Peak period is when you consolidate racing fitness, but it's an easy place to make mistakes when self-training. Athletes often don't understand that it is a time to reduce volume and keep intensity levels high. Recovery between workouts is critical. The idea is to be rested and ready to push the limits of the fitness envelope when it's time for a quality workout. These workouts may also be B- or C-priority races that serve as tune-ups for the A-priority races to follow.

Peaking consists of two to three weeks of short, race-intensity workouts that simulate the conditions of the race every 72 to 96 hours. If you don't have nearby races to substitute for these workouts, see the "Race-Intensity Workouts" section of Appendix C for guidelines on how to structure these workouts.

The Peak period should be longer if you are training for a longer race, if you have a particularly high fitness level, if you are injury prone, or if you are an older athlete. Each Peak workout will gradually get shorter as you progress through the Peak period. Total weekly volume also drops rapidly in order to incorporate more rest. The workout intensity is key to maintaining fitness and should be at maximum race level, *at least* power zone 3 or moderately hard.

The two or three days of easy workouts between race simulations are designed to erase fatigue and elevate form. Each of these workouts should also get shorter as peaking progresses. A good Peak period balances intensity and rest so that you come into race readiness at the right time (Figure 7.4g). In the "Balancing Fitness, Fatigue, and Form" sidebar you can refer to the athlete's

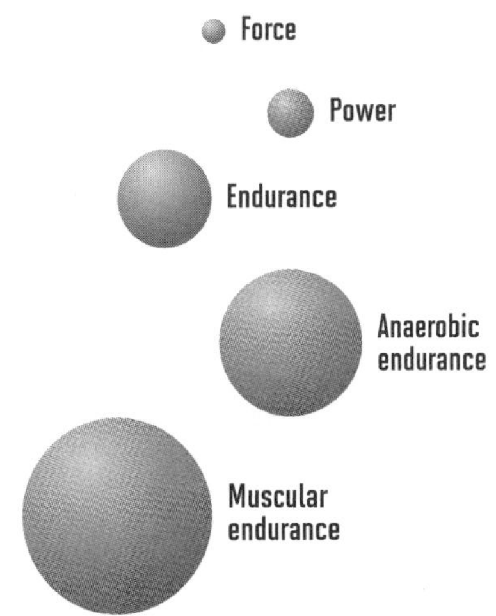

FIGURE 7.4g

Peak

performance chart for an example of how this happens in the real world. To tap your greatest potential on race day you'll want to see a dramatic decrease in fatigue in the days leading up to the race, while form rises steadily and fitness drops only slightly.

Tapering during the Peak period sometimes causes athletes to question whether they are doing enough work. If you've designed your season correctly and followed the plan, you will be ready. And even if you aren't ready, there's nothing you can do about it now.

The purpose of periodization is to reach peak form just as the most important races occur. Since these races are seldom on back-to-back weekends and may be separated by several weeks, it's usually necessary to peak more than once. I've found that the athletes I train race best when they peak two times each season. I believe you'll find that this works for you as well. Chapter 8 will help you design a twin-peaks season using the same procedure I use when training riders.

RACE PERIOD

This is what you've been waiting for. The fun time of the year is starting. Now all that's needed is to race, work on strength areas, and recover. The races will provide adequate stress to keep your systems working at an optimal level. Your anaerobic fitness should stay high. In weeks when there are no races, a race-effort group ride is the best option.

During the Race period, you really want to emphasize rest but still need to do just a bit of intensity to maintain fitness (Figure 7.4h). Now is not the time for long-duration workouts. Instead, do three or four workouts this week in which you complete several 90-second intervals at expected race intensity or at least in power zone 3, as described above, with 3-minute recoveries. Five days before the race, do five of these 90-second efforts. Four days beforehand, do four times 90 seconds. Continue this pattern throughout the week.

The easiest day of race week should be two days before the race. This is usually best as a day off, but for the high-volume athlete it could be a short and easy ride. The day before should also include some race-like intensity within a very brief session: for example, a 30- to 60-minute bike ride including a few short efforts at race intensity or higher.

Until this point, you've been working on your limiters. Now is the time to emphasize your strength areas and take them to a new level. If muscular endurance is one of your strengths, time trial at midweek. If you're a strong sprinter, work on that. If climbing is your forte, then climb. Make your strength as strong as possible.

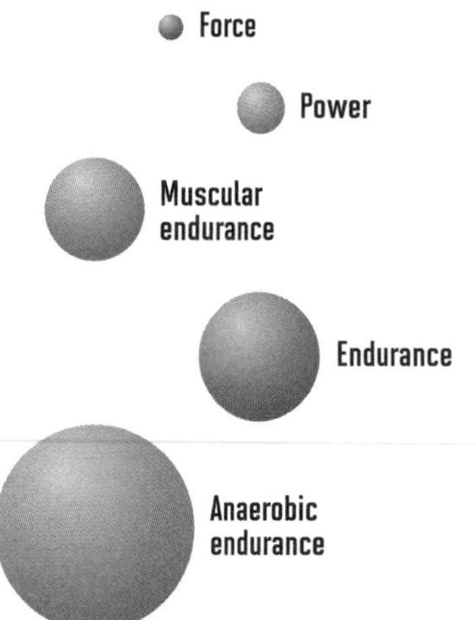

FIGURE 7.4h
Race

TRANSITION PERIOD

The Transition period is a time of rest and recovery following a Race period. A transitional rest should always be included after the last race of the year, but one may also be inserted early in the season following the first Peak period to prevent burnout later in the year. Early-season Transition periods may be brief, perhaps only five to seven days, whereas at the end of the season such a break may be four weeks or so.

The Transition period should have little regimentation (Figure 7.4i). My only admonition is to do what you feel like doing during this period, as long as it is low intensity and low volume. Crosstraining is a good idea. Use this time to recharge your batteries. The time away from your bike will pay off with higher motivation for training and racing later on. This rest period also allows healing of minor muscle damage to occur and reduces psychological stress.

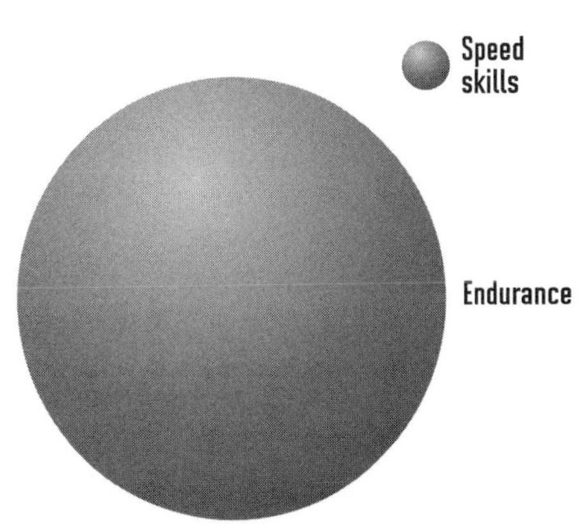

FIGURE 7.4i
Transition

PERIODIZATION ALTERNATIVES

All of the training suggestions in this book are based on the linear periodization model illustrated in Figure 7.3. Although it is the one that is easiest to understand and has become the most common way of organizing the training season for endurance athletes, it is not the only periodization model. There are several models that are common in endurance sports.

LINEAR PERIODIZATION

The linear periodization model, otherwise known as "classic" periodization, is the one I use. The season begins with a focus on training volume as you do long and frequent workouts at low intensity. This way of starting off the season creates a high level of aerobic endurance fitness while building injury resistance through low-intensity stress. Then, in the Build period, you decrease volume by doing less frequent long sessions while increasing the intensity of your training. This improves the advanced abilities of muscular endurance, anaerobic endurance, and power, as described in Chapter 6, as you get closer to the target race.

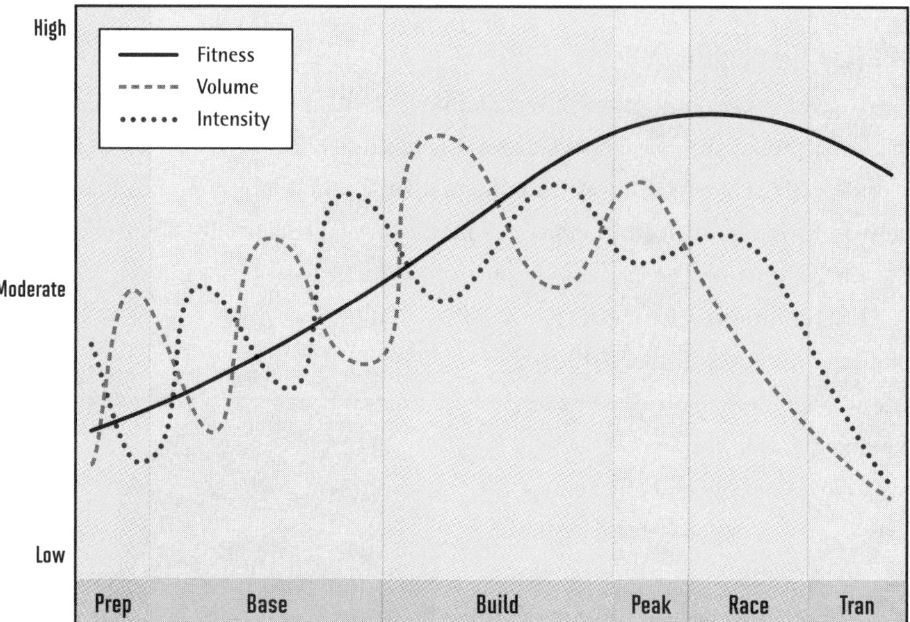

FIGURE 7.5

Undulating Periodization

UNDULATING PERIODIZATION

Figure 7.5 shows one way the "undulating periodization model" may be employed. Essentially, volume and intensity are rising and falling alternately as the season progresses. In this way, undulating periodization changes the short-term focus to include more variety. A variation of this method involves rotating several of the abilities weekly. For example, you might work on endurance one day, anaerobic endurance a couple of days later, and force a couple of days after that, with recovery days in between. The next week may alternate muscular endurance, speed skills, and power.

Because the variety built into this model maintains motivation, I sometimes use it late in the season after general fitness is well established. It also works well with strength training in the early Base period by alternating the Anatomical Adaptation, Max Transition, and Max Strength phases, either within a week or within a single session of training.

Whether this method works as a yearlong training model for endurance athletes is still unclear, and for that reason I would not recommend it for road cyclists. Weight lifters using this model have shown greater improvements in strength performance than weight lifters following the linear model, but researchers do not yet know what is going on at the cellular level and cannot yet pinpoint the physiological reason for the advantage.

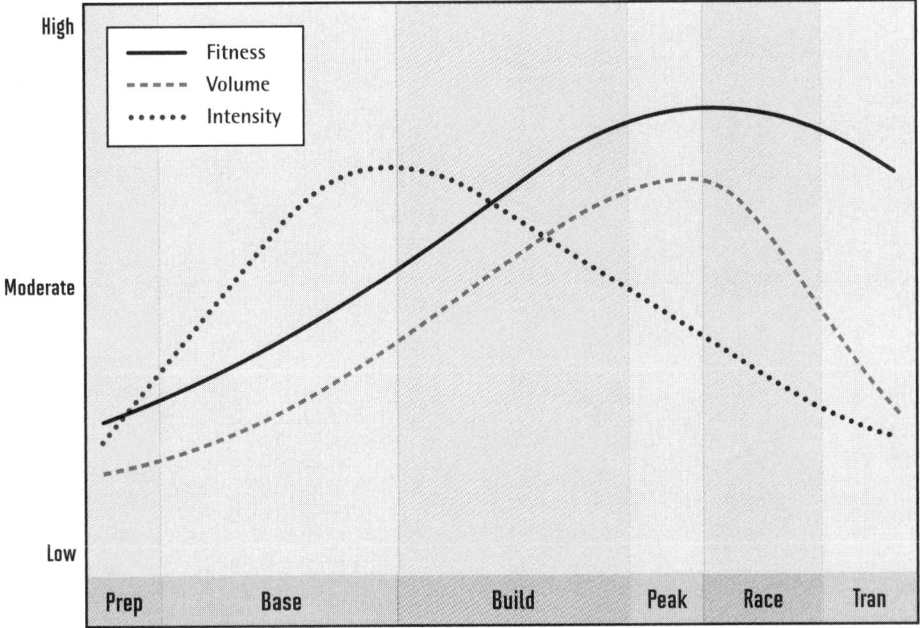

FIGURE 7.6
Reverse Linear Periodization

REVERSE LINEAR PERIODIZATION

Figure 7.6 shows the reverse of the classic periodization model shown in Figure 7.3. In reverse linear periodization training, intensity is high in the Base period, whereas volume increases most significantly in the Build period. This model works best for athletes training for long, steady events such as century or even double-century rides. Combining high intensity with low volume early in the season boosts aerobic capacity (VO_2max). Lower-intensity, longer workouts later in the season develop aerobic endurance. This method can therefore bring you into excellent fitness for particularly long events but is not as effective for shorter races.

The periodization platform you choose should be one that you understand and are committed to. Linear periodization is generally the easiest model to understand and put into place, and it is still the model used by most athletes around the world, regardless of their levels of performance. The other models have very little established research behind them, and training guidelines are therefore lacking. Trying to create and follow such a plan would involve a lot of trial and error and would likely result in uneven performances. With linear periodization, you will know you are following a well-researched, proven plan for success.

8

THE TRAINING YEAR

I used to train too much, too many hours. In my first year as a pro I trained thirty-five hours a week, which is too hard.

—TONY ROMINGER

NOW IT'S TIME to begin designing an annual training plan. The best time of year to do this is shortly after the end of your last Race period, when you're ready to start the Preparation period. If you've purchased this book after your season has already begun, it's still a good idea to plan the rest of your year. Better late than never.

I'm about to take you through a simple six-step process of annual planning that will have you on the way to a better season before you even turn a crank. This will require some writing; use a pencil as you'll need to make changes later. The Annual Training Plan worksheet is in Appendix B. You should make a copy before starting to work. If you prefer to work on a computer, you will find an electronic version of the Annual Training Plan along with other tools for self-coaching at www.TrainingBible.com.

The danger of following a methodical process to arrive at a training plan is that you'll be so engrossed in procedures and numbers that you might forget to think in a realistic way. The purpose is not simply to write a plan, but to race better than ever before. At the end of a successful season, you'll realize how important it was to have a written plan.

Writing and following an annual training plan are somewhat like climbing a mountain. Before you take the first step, it's a good idea to know where the peak of the mountain is and how you plan to get there. It also helps if you know what problems you're likely to encounter along the route so you can be prepared to deal with them. While ascending the mountain, you'll stop occasionally to look at the peak and check your progress. You may decide to change the route based on new conditions, such as bad weather or unexpected obstacles. Arriving at the peak, you'll be elated, but looking back down you will remember all of the challenges you overcame along the way and how the plan gave you direction.

Remind yourself throughout this chapter that you're not writing an annual plan to impress anyone or simply to feel organized. The purpose is to create a useful and dynamic guide for your training. You will refer to the plan regularly to make decisions as your training progresses. The plan will help you to keep an eye on the goal and not get lost in "just going to races." A training plan is dynamic in that you will frequently modify it as new circumstances arise.

THE ANNUAL TRAINING PLAN

It's time to get started planning. As you complete the six steps presented in this chapter, you will:

1. Define your goals for the upcoming season.
2. Establish training objectives that will support your goals.
3. Establish your annual training hours.
4. Prioritize your planned races.
5. Divide your season into training periods.
6. Assign hours to each week of training.

In Chapter 9, you will complete the annual plan by assigning weekly workouts based on abilities. This probably sounds like a lot to accomplish. It is, but the system I've set out here will make it easy to do.

You'll find a working version of the Annual Training Plan in Appendix B. Notice that there are several parts to the plan. At the top left of the page are spaces for annual hours, season goals, and training objectives. The column on the left assigns a number to each week of the year. You should write in the date of the Monday of each week of the season. For example, if your first week of training at the start of the next season will be the week of November 3–9, write "Nov. 3" in week 1, then fill in the dates in the same way for the remaining weeks of the coming season. There is a column to list the races, their priorities (Pri), the period, and weekly hours for each week. The small boxes down the right-hand side will be used to indicate categories of workouts by abilities as listed at the top of the page. Chapter 9 will explain this last part.

STEP 1: DETERMINE SEASON GOALS

Start with the destination: What racing goals do you want to accomplish this season? It could be to upgrade to a higher racing category, to place in the top five at the district road race, or to finish a stage race. Studies have shown that clearly defined goals improve one's ability to achieve them. A successful mountain climber always has the next peak in the back of his or her mind. If you don't know where you want to go, you will find at the end of the season that you have gone nowhere.

Don't get goals confused with wishes and dreams. The athletes I train sometimes dream about what they wish to accomplish, and I encourage them to do so. Dreaming is healthy. Without dreams there is no vision for the future, no incentive. Dreams can become realities. But wishes and dreams take longer than one season to accomplish. If you can achieve it this season, no matter how big it is, it's no longer a dream—it's a goal. Also, dreams become goals when there is a plan for accomplishing them. So we are dealing strictly with goals for the purpose of planning a season.

Let's be realistically optimistic. If you had trouble finishing club rides in the past season, winning a stage race this season is a wish, not a goal. "But," you say, "if I don't set high goals, I'll never achieve anything." That's true, but the problem with wishes is that you know deep down that you really aren't capable of achieving them this season, so there's no commitment to the training required. A challenging goal will stretch you to the limits, and may require you to take some risks, but you can imagine yourself accomplishing it in the next few months. Ask yourself: "If I do everything right, can I imagine success with this goal?" If you can, it's a good goal. But if you can't even conceive of achieving it now, you're wasting your time. It's just another dream.

There are four principles your goals must adhere to:

1. *Your goal must be measurable.* How will you know if you're getting closer to it? Businesspeople know if they're achieving their financial goals because they have a measurable way to gauge how close they are getting: They simply count their money. You also need to have measurable ways to gauge your progress. Rather than saying "get better" in your goal statement, you might say, "I will complete a 40 km time trial in less than 58 minutes."
2. *Your goal must be under your control.* A successful person does not set goals based on what other people might do. "If Jones misses the break, win XYZ race" is not a goal that demands your commitment. "Make the winning break at the Boulder Road Race," however, gets your juices flowing.
3. *Your goal must stretch you.* A goal that is too easy or too hard to achieve is the same as having no goal. For a Category III racer, winning the National Pro Championship this year is more than a stretch, even though it's a great dream. But "Finish the club's 8-mile time trial" isn't much of a challenge. Upgrading to Category II would perhaps be an excellent stretch, however, and could be a realistic goal.
4. *Whatever your goals, state them in the positive.* Whatever you do while reading this paragraph, don't think about pink elephants. See what I mean? Your goal must keep you focused on what you want to happen, not what you want to avoid. Guess what happens to people who set a goal such as "Don't lose the Podunkville Criterium." You got it: They lose—because they didn't know what they were supposed to do. Knowing what not to do is of little benefit.

The goal should also be racing-outcome oriented. For example, don't set a goal of climbing better. That's an objective, as we'll see shortly. Instead, commit to a faster time for the Mount Evans Road Race, for example. Here are some other examples of racing-oriented goals to help you formulate your own:

Finish in top 10 in district Category III road race.
Break 1 hour in 40 km time trial in August.
Finish in top 5 in two out of three A-priority criteriums.
Upgrade to Category II.
Rank in top five in district Category III B.A.R.
Finish in top 3 in masters nationals road race.
Place in top 25 Category III G.C. at Mike Nields Stage Race.

After establishing a racing-oriented goal, you may have one or two others that are important to you. Give them the same consideration you did the first goal. Stop at three goals so things don't get too complicated in the coming months. All of your goals should be listed at the top of the Annual Training Plan.

STEP 2: ESTABLISH TRAINING OBJECTIVES

In Chapter 5, you determined your strengths and weaknesses. Then you completed the Cyclist Assessment form (Sidebar 5.4). Look back at that form now to refresh your memory: What are your strengths and weaknesses? Which of your weaknesses is a limiter?

I described the concept of limiters in Chapter 6. These are key race-specific weaknesses that hold you back from being successful in certain races. In that chapter I also explained abilities required for different types of races. If you compared your weaknesses with the requirements for the type of race that interests you, you should know your limiters. For example, a hilly race requires good force and climbing proficiency. A weakness in either of these areas means you have a limiter for A-priority, hilly races. You must improve in that area if you're to be successful in hilly races.

Read your first season goal. Do any of your weaknesses (indicated by a score of 3 or lower on the Cyclist Assessment) present a limiter for this goal? If so, you'll need to train to improve that specific weakness. List the limiter under "training objectives." In the coming weeks of the Annual Training Plan, you'll work on improving this race-specific weakness. Chapter 9 will show you how to do that. For now, the challenge is to know when you have improved a limiter—in other words, being able to measure progress.

There are several ways to measure how far you have come toward meeting specific types of goals. Tests specific to your goals and objectives (see Chapter 5) can be repeated periodically throughout the season. Races and workouts also serve as good progress indicators. Table 8.1 provides examples of training objectives for hypothetical limiters associated with specific goals. You should write your training objectives for each goal in a similar manner so that you know how to determine when you have made progress. Notice that time limits are set for each objective. To accomplish the goal, you must meet the training objective by a certain time of the season. Too late is as good as never.

TABLE 8.1

Defining Training Objectives

GOAL	TRAINING OBJECTIVE TO ADDRESS LIMITERS
Top 10 finish in district Category III road race	1. **Improve muscular endurance:** Complete a sub-57-minute 40 km TT in June. 2. **Improve climbing:** Squat 320 pounds by end of Base 1.
Break one hour in 40 km time trial in August	1. **Improve focus:** Feel more focused in tempo workouts and races by July 31 (subjective measurement). 2. **Improve muscular endurance:** Increase LT power to 330 watts by end of Base 3.
Finish in top five in two out of three A-priority criteriums	1. **Improve speed endurance:** Increase speed score on Natural Abilities Profile by end of Base 3. 2. **Improve sprinting:** Increase average watts to 700 on power test by end of Base 3.
Upgrade to Category II	1. **Improve climbing:** Increase power-to-weight index by 10% by end of Base 3. 2. **Improve training consistency:** Complete all BT workouts in Build period.
Rank in top five in district in Category III B.A.R.	1. **Improve speed:** Spin at 140 rpm and remain in contact with the saddle (no bouncing) by February 12. 2. **Improve speed endurance:** Continue for four minutes beyond 165 heart rate on LT test by end of first Build 2 period.
Finish in top three in masters nationals road race	1. **Improve sprint:** Produce 950 watts on max power test by end of Base 3. 2. **Improve climbing:** Climb Rist Canyon in 28 minutes by May 31.
Place in top 25 in Category III G.C. at Mike Nields Stage Race	1. **Improve muscular endurance:** Climb Poudre Canyon six times in 10 weeks prior to race. 2. **Improve time trialing:** Lower 8-mile TT self-test to 19:12 by April 15.

By the time you are done with this part of the Annual Training Plan, you will probably have three to five training objectives listed. These are short-term standards against which you will measure progress.

STEP 3: SET ANNUAL TRAINING HOURS

The number of hours you train in the coming season—including on the bike, in the weight room, and crosstraining—partly determines the stress load you carry. It is a balancing act: An annual volume that is too high will probably result in overtraining; if it's too low, you begin to lose endurance. Setting annual training hours is one of the most critical decisions you will make about training. If you make an error here, make it on the side of too few hours.

Before discussing how to arrive at this number, I'd like to make a case for training based on time rather than on distance. Training by miles encourages you to repeat the same courses week after week. It also causes you to compare your time on a given course today with what it was last week. Such thinking is counterproductive. Using time as a basis for training volume allows you to go wherever you want, so long as you finish within a given time. Your rides are more enjoyable because there is more variety and less concern for today's average speed.

How do you determine annual hours if you haven't kept track of time in the past? Most cyclists keep a record of the miles they've ridden. If you have such a record, divide the total by what you guess the average speed to have been—18 miles per hour would be a reasonable guess. If you've also crosstrained and lifted weights, estimate how many hours you have put into those activities in the past year. By adding all of the estimates together, you have a ballpark figure for your annual training hours.

Looking back over the past three years, you can easily see trends in training volume. If so, did you race better in the high-volume years, or worse? There were undoubtedly other factors in your performance at those times, but this kind of analysis may help you to decide what your training volume should be for the coming season.

Even without records of annual miles or hours trained, you may be able to produce an estimate. That will give you a starting point. To do this, jot down on a piece of paper what a typical training week looks like for you—neither your highest nor your lowest volume. Add these daily times and multiply by 50 for a very rough gauge of how many hours you train annually.

Table 8.2 offers a rough guideline of the annual hours typical of cyclists by racer category. This should not be considered a "required" volume. I know of many riders with ten or more years of racing who put in fewer hours than those suggested here for their category and yet race quite well. The volume of training has a lot to do with developing endurance. With endurance already established by years of riding, you can shift your emphasis toward intensity.

TABLE 8.2

Suggested Annual Training Hours

CATEGORY	HOURS/YEAR
Pro	800–1,200
I–II	700–1,000
III	500–700
IV	350–500
V	200–350

Note: Juniors typically fall into Category V.

Limiting the number of hours you spend on the bike produces better results than struggling through an overly ambitious volume. If you have a job, a family, a home to maintain, and other responsibilities, be realistic—don't expect to train with the same volume as the pros. Training is their job.

If, however, you have not been competitive in the past, and fall well below the suggested annual hours for your category, it may be wise to consider increasing your volume to the lower figure in your category range so long as this is not more than a 15 percent increase. Otherwise, increases in your annual hours from year to year should be in the range of 5 to 10 percent.

If something limits your training time and can't be flexed, be honest about it, or you'll just set yourself up for frustration. Determining annual hours in this case is based strictly on what is available. Write your annual training hours at the top of the Annual Training Plan. Later you'll use that figure to assign weekly training hours.

STEP 4: PRIORITIZE RACES

For this step you need a list of the races you will be doing. If the race schedule has not been published yet, go back to last year's race calendar and guess which days they'll be held on. Races nearly always stay on the same weekends from year to year.

On the Annual Training Plan, list all of the races you intend to do by writing them into the "Race" column in the appropriate row by date. Remember that the date indicated is the Monday of that week. This should be an inclusive list of tentative races. You may decide later not to do some of these races, but for now you should assume you'll do all of them.

The next step is to prioritize the races into three categories—A, B, and C—using the criteria that follow. If your team is well organized, the team manager may have some input on the priorities of the season, so check with him or her before going further.

A Races

Pick out the three or four races—no more than this—that are most important to you this year. A stage race counts as one race, and two A-priority races on the same weekend count as one race. An A-priority race isn't necessarily the one that gets the most press or has the biggest prize purse. It could be the Nowhereville Road Race, but if you live in Nowhereville, that could be the big race of the year for you.

The A-priority races are the most important on the schedule and all of your training will be designed around them. The purpose of training is to build and peak for these A races.

It's best that these races either be clumped together within two or three weeks or widely separated by eight or more weeks. For example, two of the races may fall into a three-week period in May, and the other two could be close together in August. Then again, two may occur in May, one in July, and the other in September. The idea is that in order to come to a peak for each of these most important races, you will need a Preparation period of several weeks. During this time between A races, you can still race, but you won't be in top form. Realize that every time you go through the tapering and peaking process you lose some base fitness. So if your A-priority races occur frequently with little time to reestablish the most basic abilities of fitness between them, your performance will suffer. This is why you should limit the number of A races you enter to three or four and keep them widely separated on the calendar. It's generally best for the single most important race of the year to come near the end of the season when your fitness is likely to be at the highest level possible.

If your A races aren't neatly spaced or grouped as I've described here, don't worry. Season priorities are not determined by the calendar, but rather by your goals. A schedule that doesn't conveniently space or group the races makes planning and coming to a peak much more difficult, as you will see, than one that follows this principle. But it is not impossible to work with this kind of race season if it can't be helped. In the "Pri" column, write in "A" for all of your A-priority races. Again, there should be no more than three or four of these.

B Races

These are important races and you will still want to perform well, but they are not as critical as the A races. You'll rest for a few days prior in preparation, but you will not build to a peak for each race. There may be as many as twelve B-priority races. As with the A-priority events, stage races count as one, as do two B races on the same weekend. In the "Pri" column, write in "B" for all of these races.

C Races

You now have up to sixteen weeks dedicated to either A or B races. That's most of the racing season. All the other races on the list are C-priority. C races are done for experience, as hard workouts, as tests of progress, for fun, or as tune-ups for A races. You will "train through" these races with no peaking and with minimal rest before each one. It's not unusual to decide at the last moment not to do one of these low-priority events. If your heart isn't in it, you'd be better off training that day—or resting.

Be careful with C races. They are the ones in which you are most likely to crash or go over the edge into a state of overtraining, since you may be tired or lack the motivation to perform well. They are also often done haphazardly or with confused objectives. There should be a reason for every race in your schedule, so decide before a C race what you want to get out of it. The more experienced you are as a racer, the fewer C races you should do. Conversely, juniors and Category IV and V riders should do several to gain experience.

Just because you classified a race as a C-priority doesn't mean that you won't give it your best shot. It only means that this is a workout and you're probably coming into it carrying a bit of fatigue. You may still give it everything you've got, if that fits with your purpose for doing a given race. If you do not finish at the front, however, don't let it demoralize you; you were not at your peak because you planned it that way—it was just a C race in your schedule. You are saving your peak performance for your A races.

STEP 5: DIVIDE YEAR INTO PERIODS

Now that you know the times in the year when you want to be in top form (where the A-priority races are listed), you can assign periods. Chapter 7 described the six training periods of the year. To refresh your memory, Table 8.3 summarizes each.

Find the week of your first A race on the schedule, and in the "Period" column, write in "Race." This first Race period extends throughout your clumping of A races and could be as long as three weeks. Count (up the page) two weeks from "Race" and write in "Peak." Now work backward three (for those over 40 years of age or so) or four weeks from Peak and write "Build 2." Using duration as indicated in Table 8.4, do the same for Build 1 (3–4 weeks), Base 3 (3–4 weeks), Base 2 (3–4 weeks), Base 1 (3–4 weeks), and Prep (3–4 weeks). The first part of the year is now scheduled.

Go to your second A race and write in "Race" as you did above. Count backward two weeks and write in "Peak" again. Then count back three or four weeks for Build 2 and another three or four for Build 1. It's not necessary to repeat the Base period unless: (1) your first peak has a two- or three-week Race period; (2) you feel that your base abilities, especially endurance and force, are lacking; or (3) you included a Transition period following your first Race period of the season (which, by the way, is a very good idea).

TABLE 8.3

Periodization Summary

PERIOD	DURATION	TRAINING FOCUS
Preparation	3–4 weeks	General adaptation with weights, crosstraining, and on-bike drills.
Base	8–12 weeks	Establish strength, speed, and endurance. Introduce muscular endurance and hill work.
Build	6–10 weeks	Develop muscular endurance, speed endurance, and power.
Peak	1–2 weeks	Consolidate race readiness with reduced volume and race tune-ups.
Race	1–3 weeks	Race, refine strengths, and recover.
Transition	1–6 weeks	Rest and recover.

It's unlikely that the Build-Peak period between your two Race periods will work out exactly with this number of weeks assigned to each period. Once you have the second Race period scheduled, it may be necessary to change the lengths of the various periods so that you can both improve your fitness and allow for scheduled rest weeks. Remember that the purpose of assigning periods at this point is to make sure you are ready for the A-priority races. Only you can determine what this means in terms of training, since you are the only one who knows what your fitness is like at a given point in the season. It may well be necessary to change your plan for the second peak of the season once you reach that point. Again, when you first develop the Annual Training Plan early in the year it is merely a guide to get you started. Be prepared to change it as you progress through the various stages.

It's a good idea to schedule a five- to seven-day Transition after your first Race period to allow for recovery and to prevent burnout later in the season. A Transition period at this time always pays off with higher enthusiasm for training and greater fitness for late-season races. Following the last Race period of the season, schedule a longer Transition period.

If this step in the planning process seems confusing, you may want to look ahead to Chapter 11, where you can see how the annual plan takes shape in several different case studies.

STEP 6: ASSIGN WEEKLY HOURS

Throughout the season there is a wave-like pattern of increasing and decreasing volume. Figure 7.3 illustrates this. The purpose of this pattern is to ensure that endurance is main-

TABLE 8.4 Weekly Training Hours

		ANNUAL TRAINING HOURS								
PERIOD	WEEK	200	250	300	350	400	450	500	550	600
Prep	All	3.5	4.0	5.0	6.0	7.0	7.5	8.5	9.0	10.0
Base 1	1	4.0	5.0	6.0	7.0	8.0	9.0	10.0	11.0	12.0
	2	5.0	6.0	7.0	8.5	9.5	10.5	12.0	13.0	14.5
	3	5.5	6.5	8.0	9.5	10.5	12.0	13.5	14.5	16.0
	4	3.0	3.5	4.0	5.0	5.5	6.5	7.0	8.0	8.5
Base 2	1	4.0	5.5	6.5	7.5	8.5	9.5	10.5	12.5	12.5
	2	5.0	6.5	7.5	9.0	10.0	11.5	12.5	14.0	15.0
	3	5.5	7.0	8.5	10.0	11.0	12.5	14.0	15.5	17.0
	4	3.0	3.5	4.5	5.0	5.5	6.5	7.0	8.0	8.5
Base 3	1	4.5	5.5	7.0	8.0	9.0	10.0	11.0	12.5	13.5
	2	5.0	6.5	8.0	9.5	10.5	12.0	13.5	14.5	16.0
	3	6.0	7.5	9.0	10.5	11.5	13.0	15.0	16.5	18.0
	4	3.0	3.5	4.5	5.0	5.5	6.5	7.0	8.0	8.5
Build 1	1	5.0	6.5	8.0	9.0	10.0	11.5	12.5	14.0	15.5
	2	5.0	6.5	8.0	9.0	10.0	11.5	12.5	14.0	15.5
	3	5.0	6.5	8.0	9.0	10.0	11.5	12.5	14.0	15.5
	4	3.0	3.5	4.5	5.0	5.5	6.5	7.0	8.0	8.5
Build 2	1	5.0	6.0	7.0	8.5	9.5	10.5	12.0	13.0	14.5
	2	5.0	6.0	7.0	8.5	9.5	10.5	12.0	13.0	14.5
	3	5.0	6.0	7.0	8.5	9.5	10.5	12.0	13.0	14.5
	4	3.0	3.5	4.5	5.0	5.5	6.5	7.0	8.0	8.5
Peak	1	4.0	5.5	6.5	7.5	8.5	9.5	10.5	11.5	13.0
	2	3.5	4.0	5.0	6.0	6.5	7.5	8.5	9.5	10.0
Race	All	3.0	3.5	4.5	5.0	5.5	6.5	7.0	8.0	8.5
Trans.	All	3.0	3.5	4.5	5.0	5.5	6.5	7.0	8.0	8.5

tained and to permit increases in intensity without overly stressing the body's systems. In this step, you'll write in the weekly training hours using Table 8.4 as a guide.

Now that you have an estimate of annual hours and have divided the year into periods, you're ready to assign weekly training hours. Find the annual training hours in Table 8.4. In the columns beneath the annual hours, weekly hours are in half-hour increments. On the left-hand side of the table are all of the periods and weeks. By reading across and down, determine the number of hours for each week and write those in under "Hours" on the Annual Training Plan. If you are over 40 years of age or have scheduled some three-week periods during the season, leave out week 3 for each of these periods. There is a more complete discussion of training for older riders in Chapter 14.

You have now completed the Annual Training Plan, with the exception of the workouts portion, which we will tackle in the next chapter.

ANNUAL TRAINING HOURS											
650	700	750	800	850	900	950	1,000	1,050	1,100	1,150	1,200
11.0	12.0	12.5	13.5	14.5	15.0	16.0	17.0	17.5	18.5	19.5	20.0
12.5	14.0	14.5	15.5	16.5	17.5	18.5	19.5	20.5	21.5	22.5	23.5
15.5	16.5	18.0	19.0	20.0	21.5	22.5	24.0	25.0	26.0	27.5	28.5
17.5	18.5	20.0	21.5	22.5	24.0	25.5	26.5	28.0	29.5	30.5	32.0
9.0	10.0	10.5	11.5	12.0	12.5	13.5	14.0	14.5	15.5	16.0	17.0
13.0	14.5	16.0	17.0	18.0	19.0	20.0	21.0	22.0	23.0	24.0	25.0
16.5	17.5	19.0	20.0	21.5	22.5	24.0	25.0	26.6	27.5	29.0	30.0
18.0	19.5	21.0	22.5	24.0	25.0	26.5	28.0	29.5	31.0	32.0	33.5
9.0	10.0	10.5	11.5	12.0	12.5	13.5	14.0	15.0	15.5	16.0	17.0
14.5	15.5	17.0	18.0	19.0	20.0	21.0	22.5	23.5	25.0	25.5	27.0
17.0	18.5	20.0	21.5	23.0	24.0	25.0	26.5	28.0	29.5	30.5	32.0
19.0	20.5	22.0	23.5	25.0	26.5	28.0	29.5	31.0	32.5	33.5	35.0
9.0	10.0	10.5	11.5	12.0	12.5	13.5	14.0	15.0	15.5	16.0	17.0
16.0	17.5	19.0	20.5	21.5	22.5	24.0	25.0	26.5	28.0	29.0	30.0
16.0	17.5	19.0	20.5	21.5	22.5	24.0	25.0	26.5	28.0	29.0	30.0
16.0	17.5	19.0	20.5	21.5	22.5	24.0	25.0	26.5	28.0	29.0	30.0
9.0	10.0	10.5	11.5	12.0	12.5	13.5	14.0	15.0	15.5	16.0	17.0
15.5	16.5	18.0	19.0	20.5	21.5	22.5	24.0	25.0	26.5	27.0	28.5
15.5	16.5	18.0	19.0	20.5	21.5	22.5	24.0	25.0	26.5	27.0	28.5
15.5	16.5	18.0	19.0	20.5	21.5	22.5	24.0	25.0	26.5	27.0	28.5
9.0	10.0	10.5	11.5	12.0	12.5	13.5	14.0	15.0	15.5	16.0	17.0
13.5	14.5	16.0	17.0	18.0	19.0	20.0	21.0	22.0	23.5	24.0	25.0
11.0	11.5	12.5	13.5	14.5	15.0	16.0	17.0	17.5	18.5	19.0	20.0
9.0	10.0	10.5	11.5	12.0	12.5	13.5	14.0	15.0	15.5	16.0	17.0
9.0	10.0	10.5	11.5	12.0	12.5	13.5	14.0	15.0	15.5	16.0	17.0

CHANGING THE ANNUAL TRAINING PLAN

Once you have created an Annual Training Plan, there are two blunders you must avoid. The first is the more common—ignoring the plan and simply training as you always have. I hope that once you've put in the time to create a solid plan, one that will help produce your best race results ever, you won't disregard it. That would be a considerable waste of both your planning time and your training time. The second mistake is the opposite—to pay *too much* attention to the plan and not make changes when dictated by new circumstances. I'm not talking about circumstances like wanting to go on the group ride on a scheduled rest day. I mean those times when you realize that you are making inadequate progress, or you begin missing workouts because something unexpected has happened. Be realistic in these situations and adapt the plan as needed.

INADEQUATE PROGRESS

When you're not making the progress you had expected, you must make strategic changes in your plan. You'll know whether you're making progress because you will perform a test and compare the results with your training objectives as described in Step 2 above. The test could be a field test, a test done in a clinic, or a C-priority race. Figure 8.1 shows how to handle the results. Basically, you will compare them with your planned objectives and see if you are on track or not quite up to par. If your progress is good, you will continue following the plan. If you're not happy with your progress, you must reevaluate the plan and decide what must change.

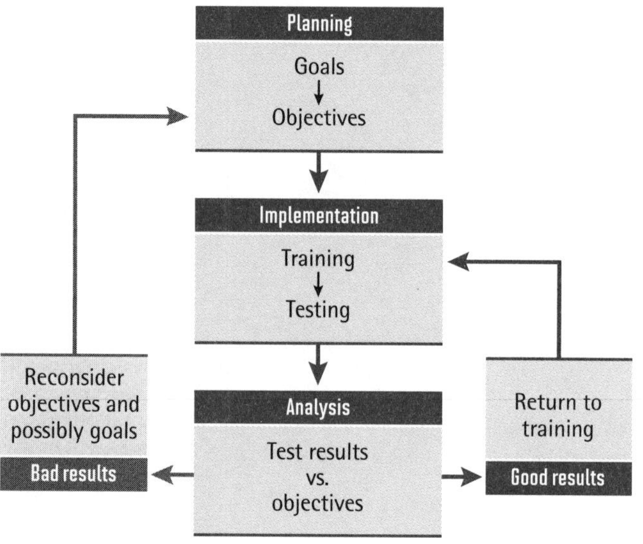

FIGURE 8.1

Planning, Implementation, and Analysis Model

What could need changing? It could be that you didn't spend enough time in the Base period and some of your basic abilities are lacking. This is the most common mistake athletes make—they can't wait to get to the hard training of the Build period, so they cut the Base period short. The solution is simply to go back to Base 3 for a few weeks to strengthen endurance, force, and speed skills. Of these, if you have made the Base period shorter than it should have been, poor endurance is the most likely problem.

Or it may be that your objectives, and perhaps even your goals, were set unrealistically high. This mistake is especially common in athletes in the first couple of years of bike racing. After you've had a chance to implement the plan and test your progress, it may become clear that you expected too much. Give some thought to revising your goals and objectives at this point.

Another common cause of poor progress is simply doing the wrong sort of training. The problem may be that you are spending too much time training your strengths while giving your limiters only lip service. As explained in Chapter 6, the focus of most of your training must be on those race-specific weaknesses—limiters—that are holding you back. The tendency among self-coached athletes is to spend more training time on what they are already good at than on their weaknesses. Realize that it is only by training your limiters that you will obtain better results.

Doing too many group workouts can be a problem. If you are going along with the group, you may not be focusing on what you really need to focus on for that workout session. There are times when having training partners can be very beneficial, but group workouts are often detrimental, especially in the Base period. You may be working either too hard or too easy, depending on the skills and experience of your riding partners. Look for partners who are of similar ability, and decide on a workout before starting. Unstructured group workouts tend to become "races." In the Build period this may be beneficial, but only if done in moderation. If your objectives for the ride are compatible with those of the group, then go ahead and take advantage of the camaraderie.

MISSING WORKOUTS—OR MORE

It happens to everyone. Your training is going well, you've been consistent, and you can tell that your fitness is progressing. Then your job throws you a curve ball and you have to miss a day or more of training. Or you catch a winter virus and don't train for four days while your body is fighting it off. Maybe your knee becomes inflamed and the doctor says no riding for two weeks, or you decide you're too tired to train and need an extra day off. What should you do? Should you try to fit in the missed workouts at a later time by wedging them in between the others? Or do you just continue on as if nothing happened? How will this affect your race preparation? Here is how to handle such dilemmas.

Missing Three or Fewer Days

For a downtime of just a few days, continue training with no adjustments. The worst thing you can do is try to fit in the lost workouts. That will not only set you up for poor training quality due to accumulated fatigue but also increase the potential for a breakdown, such as an overuse injury, an illness, or the early stages of overtraining.

Missing Four to Seven Days

If you've missed more than a few days, some rearranging is required. You'll need to readjust your workouts for up to two weeks, but you won't be able to do all of the missed workouts plus those originally planned over that time period. You'll need to be selective. The most important workouts to retain are the ones related to your limiters. Reorganize your schedule so that you can do most of those, although that may mean skipping some of the workouts that maintain your strengths. Be sure to include easy days just as you would normally do in training. Don't try to cram more hard training into fewer days.

Missing One to Two Weeks

If you miss one or two weeks of training, step back one mesocycle and omit an entire chunk of the training you had planned to do in the future, rather than trying to merge the lost workouts into your existing plan. For example, say you missed two weeks of training in Build 2. When ready to train normally again, go back to Build 1 for two weeks and do the appropriate workouts. Adjust your plan by cutting out two weeks of training that were scheduled to take place later in the season. One way to do this is to make Build 2 three weeks long instead of four and omit Peak 1.

Missing More Than Two Weeks

Missing a significant block of time, such as two weeks or more, requires a return to the Base period, as one or more of the basic abilities—endurance, force, or speed skills—has probably been compromised. If you were already in the Base period when the training time was lost, step back one mesocycle. Let's say you were in Base 3 and had to miss three weeks of training for some reason. Return to Base 2. If you were in Build 2 when it happened, go back to Base 3 and then continue on from this new starting point. You will need to make major revisions to your Annual Training Plan to accommodate this change by omitting some portion of Build 2 and by possibly shortening the Peak period from two weeks to one.

No matter which of these unfortunate situations occurs, you will have less fitness on race day than you had originally hoped. You can't force in the extra workouts, because there is a limit to how much stress your body can handle. You can't force it to become just as fit on less training. This is why it is so important to avoid taking high risks in training; if you become injured, you could miss critical training hours while forced to take time off to recuperate. In any case, remember that missing some training isn't a disaster, it's simply a situation that you need to manage. Adjust your plan and move on.

NEVER COMPROMISE RECOVERY

Consistency is the key to success in athletic training. If you train inconsistently as a result of frequent physical breakdowns or mental burnout, you will never achieve a high level of race readiness. To maintain consistent training, you must provide adequate recovery days every week. One of those days should be very light. For an athlete who trains fewer than 10 hours each week, this could mean a day off; for someone who does 15 hours a week, it could mean doing an hour of weight lifting instead of riding; and for a 20-hour-per-week athlete, it could mean a two-hour, easy ride on the light day. The other weekly recovery workouts should be done at a low intensity—in heart rate zone 1 or 2.

There are two common ways to blend recovery days and high-stress training days within a training week. For the rider who is fairly new to the sport or who recovers slowly, alternating hard and easy days generally works best, as in the following example:

Monday	Day off
Tuesday	Long or intense ride
Wednesday	Short, very low-intensity ride
Thursday	Long or intense ride
Friday	Short, very low-intensity ride
Saturday	Long, high-intensity ride
Sunday	Long, low-intensity ride

An experienced rider, or one who recovers very quickly, might see better results from grouping high-stress workouts on back-to-back days and having an easy day for recovery:

Monday	Day off or light training
Tuesday	Long or intense ride
Wednesday	Long or intense ride
Thursday	Long or intense ride
Friday	Short, very low-intensity ride
Saturday	Long, high-intensity ride
Sunday	Long, low-intensity ride

Not everyone respects recovery days. I often see self-coached athletes miss workouts or become frustrated with their progress, then overcompensate by making their recovery days harder. That's exactly the wrong thing to do. You will only create more fatigue and lower your workout quality on the harder days. The solution in this case is to make the hard training days harder and the easy days easier. Making workouts harder means either making them longer, doing them at a higher intensity, or doing more high-intensity volume, such as more intervals. Whatever your approach, never compromise recovery to gain fitness. It doesn't work.

9

PLANNING WORKOUTS

The novelty of riding thirty-hour weeks wore off a long time ago.

— STEVE LARSEN

IF THERE'S ONE THING you're getting out of this book so far, I hope it's that training should be purposeful and precise to meet your unique needs. Training haphazardly brings results initially, but to reach the highest level of racing fitness, carefully planned workouts are necessary. Before starting any training session, from the easiest to the hardest, you must be able to answer one simple question: What is the purpose of this workout?

When training for high performance, each workout should have one of three purposes: improvement of ability, maintenance of ability, or active recovery. How these three are mixed into every week of training ultimately determines how well you race. The previous chapter explained how to map out your Annual Training Plan. This chapter focuses on the individual weeks.

ANNUAL PLAN WORKOUT CATEGORIES

By now you should be familiar with my system of planning based on strengths and limiters. Your daily workouts will be determined by those limiters, so if you haven't already identified them, please refer back to Chapters 5 and 6. Knowing what you need to work on will make your plan purposeful and precise.

You are not going to schedule every workout for all fifty-two weeks of your Annual Training Plan now. With the exception of endurance maintenance workouts, you will only be determining the "breakthrough" (BT) workouts. These are the ones that provide the stress to start the adaptive process described earlier. Active recovery workouts, the ones you do between the BTs, will not be scheduled now, but they will quickly become a part of your weekly plan, as you will soon see.

You should base these workouts on the abilities listed at the top of the Annual Training Plan (see Appendix B). Notice that there are two categories of workouts added to the abilities we've discussed before: "Strength Phase" and "Testing." It may be helpful before you start this planning step to review all of the workout columns listed.

STRENGTH

In this column you will schedule weight-room workouts. This is an aspect of cycling training that is often neglected, especially by riders whose limiter is force. It has been my experience that measurable results on the bike are more evident from this type of training than any other in athletes who lack the ability to apply force to the pedals. They are always amazed at how strong they feel riding in the spring after a winter of weight training.

The details of the strength phases listed below are discussed in Chapter 12, but with a little information you can complete the "Strength" column now by penciling in the abbreviations for the various phases. Here's how to determine the duration of each weight-room phase. You can flip ahead to Chapter 11 for examples of completed Annual Training Plans.

Preparation Period: Anatomical Adaptation (AA) and Maximum Transition (MT)

On your Annual Training Plan, for the first two or three weeks of the Preparation period, write in "AA" under the "Strength" column. This weight-room phase prepares the body for the stresses that are to follow. It's a period of high repetitions and low weight loads. For the last week of the Preparation period, include one or two weeks of MT (Maximum Transition). As the name implies, MT is a transitional phase that prepares you for the heavier lifting of the next phase.

Base 1 Period: Maximum Strength (MS)

Write in "MS" for each week of Base 1. In this period you will be lifting heavy loads but with only a few reps. If you are a masters athlete who is training in three-week periods, extend MS by one week into the Base 2 period in order to schedule four total MS weeks.

All Other Periods: Strength Maintenance (SM)

For the remainder of the season, basic strength is maintained with brief workouts and heavy loads. Riders in their twenties with good force may omit weight-room strength training from their schedules starting with Build 1. All women and men over about forty years of age are advised to continue the SM phase of weights throughout the season. Do not schedule any weight training during the week of an A-priority race.

ENDURANCE

Racing on the roads is primarily an endurance sport. The ability to delay the onset of fatigue during long rides is what sets road racers apart from track racers. For this reason, the "Endurance" column will be frequently selected on the Annual Training Plan form. You will work on endurance in some form nearly every week of the year, for once you have lost endurance, the time required to fully restore it is exorbitant. That's not to say that there won't be fluctuations in your endurance throughout the season. Following an extended Race period, your endurance is likely to wane, and you must work to rebuild it by returning to the Base period before you are able to attain another high peak.

FORCE

The "Force" column refers to on-bike workouts intended to improve muscle dynamics, while the "Strength" column consists of off-bike workouts usually done in the weight room. If you don't live in a vertically challenged region, use hills for on-bike force training. Later on, in Appendix C, I refer to hills by percentage grades. Here's a guide to help you select the proper types of hills for specific workouts.

- *2–4 percent grade:* Slight hill. In a car on a 2 percent grade, you may not even know there is a grade. You could easily ride these hills in the big chainring. These are often described as "gently rolling hills."
- *4–6 percent grade:* Moderate hill. These hills get your attention in races, but are seldom determining factors. You could ride them in the big chainring, but may drop down to the small chainring.
- *6–8 percent grade:* Steep hill. These are the steepest hills you generally find on state and federal highways. Such hills, especially if they're long, often determine the winning move. These are usually climbed in the small chainring.
- *8–10 percent grade:* Very steep hill. These hills are always a determiner in a race. They are climbed only in the small chainring. A workout on such a hill is challenging for riders of all abilities.
- *10+ percent grade:* Extremely steep hill. These hills are most often found in remote areas or in the mountains. In more populated areas, they are usually quite short. Everyone climbs them in the small chainring. Some riders have difficulty just getting over them. They make you cry for your mother.

If you live on the plains of Kansas or in Florida's flat coastal terrain, don't despair. The real benefit of hills is that they offer greater resistance. You can achieve a similar result with big gears and headwinds while sitting up, or on a good indoor trainer. Highway overpasses offer short hills with about a 4 percent grade. Multilevel parking garages are great for simulating mountain climbs—just remember to ask the attendant's permission first and time your visit for off-peak hours.

SPEED SKILLS

Do not get speed skills confused with anaerobic endurance. While working on speed skills you are not doing intervals or hammering on group rides. The purpose of workouts in this column is always to improve mobility—the ability to handle the bike efficiently and effectively while turning the cranks quickly and smoothly. In the Base period, many of these workouts will be drills on a trainer or rollers that exaggerate the mechanics of pedaling—typically in a low gear at a high cadence—in order to become more fluid and supple. On the road, speed-skills training involves form sprints, high-cadence pedaling, and the handling skills necessary for sprinting.

MUSCULAR ENDURANCE

Muscular endurance is the ability to turn a relatively high gear for a long time, as in time trialing. In many ways, this ability is at the heart of road racing. As it is one of the primary ingredients of road-racing fitness, you need to emphasize it throughout the training year regardless of your limiters. All of the legendary champion road cyclists—Eddy Merckx, Bernard Hinault, Greg LeMond, Connie Carpenter, Miguel Induráin, and Jeannie Longo—had great muscular endurance. You will be developing this ability starting in the first Base period and will continue to do so in various forms right through the Race period.

ANAEROBIC ENDURANCE

Anaerobic endurance involves continuing to work hard even though the body is crying out for relief. It is necessary during long sprints and short climbs. If this skill is a limiter for you (as it is for nearly every other athlete), schedule anaerobic endurance workouts at the start of the first Build period. Anaerobic endurance training is excellent for improving aerobic capacity (VO_2max).

POWER

For the rider whose ability limiter is power, these workouts mean the difference between success and failure in criteriums that require racers to accelerate quickly out of corners and contest field sprints. Workouts for power depend on speed and force, so these more basic abilities must be improved first. Power training may be included primarily in the Build and Peak periods.

TESTING

Throughout the Base and Build periods, make progress checks about every four to six weeks. It's important for you to know how your abilities are developing in order to make adjustments to your training.

WEEKLY TRAINING BY PERIOD

The following sections will help you complete the weekly workouts portion of the Annual Training Plan. As the rest and recovery weeks are usually neglected, but are in some ways the most important parts of the entire plan, I will start with them.

If you are at all confused about how to fill in your Annual Training Plan, see the examples provided in Chapter 11.

RECOVERY WEEKS

In your annual plan, you've already reserved every fourth week (every third week for over-forty riders) during the Base and Build periods for recovery and rest from accumulated fatigue. Without such regular unloading of fatigue, fitness won't progress for long. Your plan already assigns reduced weekly hours during these weeks; now we'll assign the specific workouts. (For more detail on recovery weeks, see Chapter 18.)

For each of the R&R weeks, place an "X" in the "Endurance," "Speed Skills," and "Testing" columns. Other than one weight-room session, that's all for those weeks. The idea is to recover from the collected stress; feel rested by week's end; maintain endurance (with a late-week long ride), speed skills, and force; and test your progress, once you are rested. It may take you only three to five days to feel fully recovered, so that's when the testing should be done. In the Build period, there may be a B or C race at week's end in place of a test.

In the workout menu in Appendix C (under "Testing"), I'll describe the tests you will do during recovery weeks.

Now you're ready to complete workouts for the other weeks of the year. You'll refer to the "Workout Menu" in Appendix C later to fill in the details of what you schedule here.

PREPARATION PERIOD

Place an "X" in the "Endurance" and "Speed Skills" columns for each week of the Preparation period. Endurance training during this period concentrates on improving the endurance characteristics of the heart, blood, and lungs. Crosstraining by running, swimming, hiking, or cross-country skiing accomplishes the desired results while limiting the number of times each week that you're on an indoor trainer in the early winter months. Be cautious with your volume of indoor riding as it can be mentally and emotionally draining.

BASE 1

Again, mark the "Endurance" and "Speed Skills" columns for each week of the Base 1 period. During this period, endurance training shifts slightly toward more time on the bike and less in crosstraining modes. Weather, however, is often the determining factor for the type of endurance training done now. A mountain bike is an excellent alternative during this period when the roads and weather don't cooperate. A good indoor trainer, especially a CompuTrainer, also provides an excellent way to train throughout the Base period when you can't get on the roads.

BASE 2

Place an "X" in the "Endurance," "Force," "Speed Skills," and "Muscular Endurance" columns for each week of the Base 2 period. As you will see in the "Workout Menu" (Appendix C), you should conduct force and muscular endurance workouts at moderate heart rates and power outputs during this period. Endurance training should be mostly on the road by now with very little crosstraining. You will be doing some force work in the form of endurance rides on rolling courses, staying in the saddle on the uphill portions. This can be an integral part of endurance training.

BASE 3

Mark the "Endurance," "Force," "Speed Skills," and "Muscular Endurance" columns for each week of the Base 3 period. Training volume tops out during this period. Intensity also rises slightly with the addition of more hill work and higher-effort muscular endurance work.

BUILD 1

Schedule workouts for endurance and muscular endurance for each week of the Build 1 period. Also select your greatest limiter and mark that column. If you are not sure which limiter to schedule, choose the "Force" column. If you don't select power or anaerobic endurance, also mark the "Speed Skills" column. A criterium may take the place of an anaerobic-endurance or power workout, and road races and time trials may be substituted for force and muscular endurance sessions. Early-season races in this period are best as C-priority. Schedule each Build 1 period on your Annual Training Plan in this same way.

BUILD 2

Check off the "Endurance" and "Muscular Endurance" columns for each week of the Build 2 period. Then mark two of your limiters. If you are not sure which limiters to work on, or if you have only one limiter, mark the "Force" and "Anaerobic Endurance" columns. Speed skills will be maintained with either anaerobic endurance or power training. If there are B or C races scheduled during this period, substitute them for workouts. A criterium takes the place of either a power or an anaerobic endurance workout. Depending on the terrain, you may substitute a road race or a time trial for a force or muscular endurance workout. The week of B-priority races, schedule only one limiter. Remember that you're training through C-priority races. Mark all Build 2 periods on your plan in the same manner.

PEAK

Place an "X" in the "Muscular Endurance" column and also choose your next greatest limiter for each week of the Peak period. If you are unsure of your next limiter, select anaerobic endurance. You may substitute races for workouts using the same criteria as in the Build periods. C races in the Peak period are excellent tune-ups for the approaching A-priority races, as they get you back into a racing mode again. If there are no races but you have a hard club ride available, that may be one of your anaerobic endurance sessions. There should be a race-specific intensity workout every 72 to 96 hours in a Peak week. Refer to Appendix C for race-specific intensity workouts. If you have more than one Peak period scheduled for the year, mark all in this same way.

RACE

During each week of this period, you should either race or complete a race-effort group ride. If there is no group ride or race available, substitute an anaerobic endurance workout. Also mark "Speed Skills" and your strongest ability other than endurance. If you are not sure about your strength, mark the "Muscular Endurance" column. All Race periods should be marked just as the first one was.

TRANSITION

Mark the "Endurance" column, but keep in mind that this is a mostly unstructured period. By "mostly," I mean that your only purpose is to stay active, especially in sports that you enjoy other than cycling. These can even be team games, such as soccer, basketball, volleyball, or hockey. Such sports require some endurance and also encourage quick movement. Don't become a couch potato, but don't train seriously, either.

WEEKLY ROUTINES

Now that your Annual Training Plan is complete, with each week sorted into periods, the only issue left to decide is the weekly routine—on which day to do which workout and for how long. That's no small task. You could have the best possible plan, but if you do not blend workouts in such a way as to allow for recovery and adaptation, then it's all for nothing. The problem is that you must blend both long- and short-duration workouts with workouts that are of high and low intensity.

Chapter 15 provides you with a weekly training journal in which to record each day's scheduled workouts and results. For now, let's consider ways to determine each day's routine.

Keep in mind that the workout options listed in Figure 9.1 (pages 144–145) are just that—options. These are not intended to be the only ways to organize a week. There are many possibilities. When it comes to selecting a workout for a given day, choose one option—do not do all of the options. Your selections should address your limiters, as discussed in Chapter 6.

PATTERNS

Figure 9.1 illustrates a suggested pattern for blending duration (or volume) and intensity for each week of the training periods plus the recovery and race weeks. Duration and intensity are indicated as high, medium, and low or recovery. Obviously, what is high for one cyclist may be low for another, so these levels are meaningful only to you. Also, what constitutes high duration or high intensity in the Base 1 period may be moderate by Build 1 as your fitness improves. Recovery days may be active recovery (on the bike) or passive (complete rest), depending on your experience level.

Notice in the Base period that duration is high or medium, four times each week, while intensity is either medium or low, except in Base 3, when one high-intensity day is included. Also note in the Build period that intensity increases and duration decreases. In Build 2, there are no moderate workouts—everything is either high or low. This is to allow for adequate recovery, since there is so much high-intensity work during this period. In Build 2, both high duration and high intensity are combined once each week for the first time. Training in this period takes on many of the characteristics of racing. Note that "high duration" and "high intensity" are relative to the A-priority event you are training for. The average intensity of a criterium is typically higher than that of a road race, whereas the duration of road races is generally higher than that of criteriums. The minimum high-duration workout is two hours.

The last two "Race" sections of Figure 9.1 also suggest a blending of duration and intensity for A- and B-race weeks. Of course, A-race weeks immediately follow a Peak period or a previous Race period week, so rest would already be built into your schedule. B-race weeks would not necessarily have that advantage.

The workout codes suggested for each day are the alphanumeric codes used in the "Workout Menu" in Appendix C. Weight-room training has not been included in the suggested weekly patterns, since some cyclists lift three times per week and others only once or twice. Also, some riders, such as masters, may lift year-round, while others prefer to stop once racing begins. It is best to substitute a weight-room workout for "E" category workouts. Weight training is best done the day after a long or "breakthrough" (BT) workout. A BT session is stressful and challenging so you should try to avoid doing weights the day before a BT. If weight training must be done the same day as a BT workout, lift after riding.

DAILY HOURS

In the "Hours" column of your Annual Training Plan, you have already indicated the volume for each week of the season. All that remains is to decide how those hours should be allocated during the week. Table 9.1 (pages 146–147) offers a suggested breakdown.

In the left-hand column, find the hours you scheduled for the first week of the season. By reading across to the right, you'll find the weekly hours broken down into daily amounts. For example, find 12:00 in the "Weekly Hours" column. To the right are seven daily hours—one for each day of the week: in this case, 3:00, 2:30, 2:00, 2:00, 1:30, 1:00, and Off. This means the long workout that week will be three hours. The other daily hours may be divided between two workouts in the same day, especially in the Base period when volume is high. In fact, there are some advantages to working out two times a day, such as an increase in quality for each workout (see next section, "One Workout or Two?").

When it comes time to schedule hours for a given week, use Table 9.1 along with Figure 9.1 to assign high, medium, and low durations for each day of the week.

ONE WORKOUT OR TWO?

Instead of doing a single three-hour ride, is it just as good to do two 90-minute rides on the same day? The answer depends on the purpose of the workout. If your purpose is to improve speed skills, force, muscular endurance, power, or anaerobic endurance, the answer is yes. In fact, in all of these cases, two rides on the same day are far preferable to a single long ride because of the built-in recovery period between rides.

If your purpose is to improve endurance for long events, however, two workouts on the same day are seldom beneficial. One long workout is better than two shorter ones in this case. Here's why. The physiological benefits of endurance workouts require that you stress not only the many parts of the aerobic system—primarily the heart, lungs, and blood—but also the muscular and nervous systems. In addition, energy-, hormone-, and enzyme-production improvements are necessary for aerobic fitness to increase.

For example, look at how the body produces energy from fat and carbohydrates during moderate-intensity exercise. As you start a workout, the body relies heavily on carbohydrate stores to provide energy. But as the duration of the workout increases, there is a steady shift from carbohydrate burning to fat burning. Shifting into this fat-burning condition as soon as possible is one of the benefits of aerobic exercise that improves endurance. Riding twice for 90 minutes rather than taking one three-hour ride means you will spend less time that day using fat for fuel and therefore produce a smaller benefit for the energy-production system.

One longer workout is better for stimulating this and all of the previously listed endurance functions. There is also a psychological benefit that comes from completing long workouts.

TIMING OF WORKOUTS

Figure 9.1 suggests days on which to do different types of workouts, but this pattern may not work for your particular lifestyle, job, facility availability, and training group. How, then, do you schedule your training sessions? By taking all of the above factors into account and designing your own customized training week, one that you can repeat week

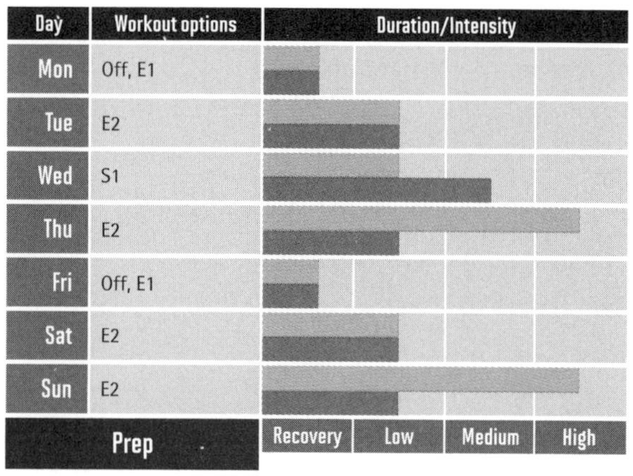

Day	Workout options
Mon	Off, E1
Tue	E2
Wed	E2
Thu	E2
Fri	S1, S2
Sat	E2
Sun	E2

Duration/Intensity: Recovery | Low | Medium | High

Base 1

Day	Workout options
Mon	Off, E1, S4
Tue	E2
Wed	E2
Thu	S1, S2, S3, S5
Fri	E1
Sat	T1
Sun	E2

Duration/Intensity: Recovery | Low | Medium | High

Base Recovery

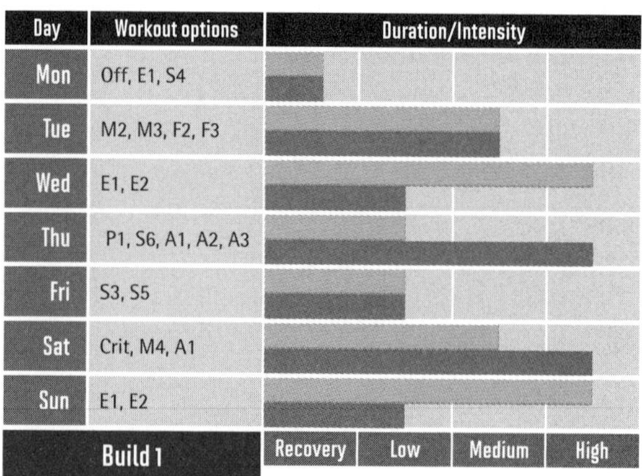

Day	Workout options
Mon	Off, E1
Tue	E2
Wed	F3, A2, P1, M2, A3, P2, M3, A4, P3, M5, A5, S6, M6, A6
Thu	E1, E2
Fri	E2, S5
Sat	E2
Sun	Crit, M4, M7, A1, A2

Duration/Intensity: Recovery | Low | Medium | High

Peak

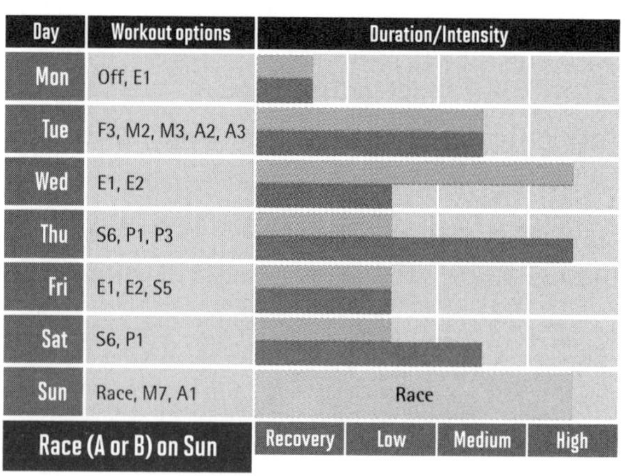

FIGURE 9.1

Weekly Training Patterns

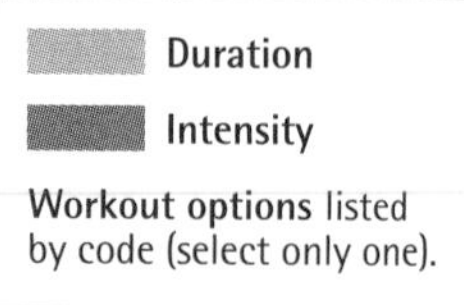

Base 2

Day	Workout options	Duration/Intensity
Mon	Off, E1	
Tue	E3, M1	
Wed	E2	
Thu	S1, S2	
Fri	F1	
Sat	E2	
Sun	E2	
		Recovery / Low / Medium / High

Base 3

Day	Workout options	Duration/Intensity
Mon	Off, E1, S4	
Tue	M1, M2	
Wed	E2	
Thu	E3, S1, S3, S5	
Fri	E2	
Sat	F1, F2	
Sun	E2	
		Recovery / Low / Medium / High

Build 2

Day	Workout options	Duration/Intensity
Mon	Off, E1, S4	
Tue	M2, M3, M4, M5, M6, F3	
Wed	E1, E2	
Thu	S6, A5, A1, A6, A2, P1, A3, P2, A4, P3	
Fri	S3, S5	
Sat	RR, M7, A1	
Sun	E1, E2	
		Recovery / Low / Medium / High

Build Recovery

Day	Workout options	Duration/Intensity
Mon	Off, E1, S4	
Tue	E2	
Wed	E2	
Thu	S1, S2, S3, S5	
Fri	E1	
Sat	T2	
Sun	E2	
		Recovery / Low / Medium / High

Race (A or B) on Sat

Day	Workout options	Duration/Intensity
Mon	Off, E1	
Tue	E2	
Wed	S1, P1, P3	
Thu	E1, E2, S5	
Fri	S6, P1	
Sat	Race, M7, A1	Race
Sun	E1, E2	
		Recovery / Low / Medium / High

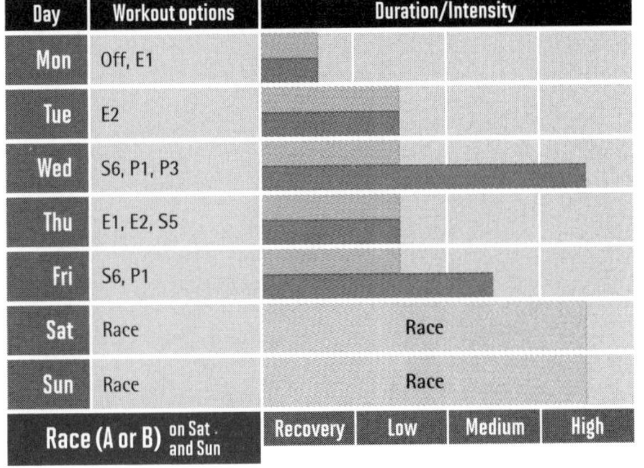

Race (A or B) on Sat and Sun

Day	Workout options	Duration/Intensity
Mon	Off, E1	
Tue	E2	
Wed	S6, P1, P3	
Thu	E1, E2, S5	
Fri	S6, P1	
Sat	Race	Race
Sun	Race	Race
		Recovery / Low / Medium / High

TABLE 9.1
Daily Training Hours

WEEKLY HOURS	LONG RIDE	DAILY RIDES (may be two-a-day workouts)					
3:00	1:30	0:45	0:45	Off	Off	Off	Off
3:30	1:30	1:00	1:00	Off	Off	Off	Off
4:00	1:30	1:00	1:00	0:30	Off	Off	Off
4:30	1:45	1:00	1:00	0:45	Off	Off	Off
5:00	2:00	1:00	1:00	1:00	Off	Off	Off
5:30	2:00	1:30	1:00	1:00	Off	Off	Off
6:00	2:00	1:30	1:00	1:00	1:00	Off	Off
6:30	2:00	1:30	1:00	1:00	1:00	Off	Off
7:00	2:00	1:30	1:30	1:00	1:00	Off	Off
7:30	2:30	1:30	1:30	1:00	1:00	Off	Off
8:00	2:30	1:30	1:30	1:30	1:00	Off	Off
8:30	2:30	2:00	1:30	1:30	1:00	Off	Off
9:00	3:00	2:00	1:30	1:30	1:00	Off	Off
9:30	3:00	2:00	1:30	1:30	1:00	0:30	Off
10:00	3:00	2:00	1:30	1:30	1:00	1:00	Off
10:30	3:00	2:00	2:00	1:30	1:00	1:00	Off
11:00	3:00	2:00	2:00	1:30	1:30	1:00	Off
11:30	3:00	2:30	2:00	1:30	1:30	1:00	Off
12:00	3:00	2:30	2:00	2:00	1:30	1:00	Off
12:30	3:30	2:30	2:00	2:00	1:30	1:00	Off
13:00	3:30	3:00	2:00	2:00	1:30	1:00	Off
13:30	3:30	3:00	2:30	2:00	1:30	1:00	Off
14:00	4:00	3:00	2:30	2:00	1:30	1:00	Off
14:30	4:00	3:00	2:30	2:30	1:30	1:00	Off
15:00	4:00	3:00	3:00	2:30	1:30	1:00	Off
15:30	4:00	3:00	3:00	2:30	2:00	1:00	Off
16:00	4:00	3:30	3:00	2:30	2:00	1:00	Off
16:30	4:00	3:30	3:00	3:00	2:00	1:00	Off
17:00	4:00	3:30	3:00	3:00	2:00	1:30	Off
17:30	4:00	4:00	3:00	3:00	2:00	1:30	Off
18:00	4:00	4:00	3:00	3:00	2:30	1:30	Off
18:30	4:30	4:00	3:00	3:00	2:30	1:30	Off
19:00	4:30	4:30	3:00	3:00	2:30	1:30	Off

after week for the entire season with only minor changes as new circumstances arise. Here's how to do that.

Anchor Workouts

These are workouts that must occur on given days each week and over which you have little or no control. For example, if your team or club rides on Wednesdays and Saturdays, that's when you must plug these sessions into your weekly plan. If you lift weights and the

WEEKLY HOURS	LONG RIDE	DAILY RIDES (may be two-a-day workouts)					
19:30	4:30	4:30	3:30	3:00	2:30	1:30	Off
20:00	4:30	4:30	3:30	3:00	2:30	2:00	Off
20:30	4:30	4:30	3:30	3:30	2:30	2:00	Off
21:00	5:00	4:30	3:30	3:30	2:30	2:00	Off
21:30	5:00	4:30	4:00	3:30	2:30	2:00	Off
22:00	5:00	4:30	4:00	3:30	3:00	2:00	Off
22:30	5:00	4:30	4:00	3:30	3:00	2:30	Off
23:00	5:00	5:00	4:00	3:30	3:00	2:30	Off
23:30	5:30	5:00	4:00	3:30	3:00	2:30	Off
24:00	5:30	5:00	4:30	3:30	3:00	2:30	Off
24:30	5:30	5:00	4:30	4:00	3:00	2:30	Off
25:00	5:30	5:00	4:30	4:00	3:00	3:00	Off
25:30	5:30	5:30	4:30	4:00	3:00	3:00	Off
26:00	6:00	5:30	4:30	4:00	3:00	3:00	Off
26:30	6:00	5:30	5:00	4:00	3:00	3:00	Off
27:00	6:00	6:00	5:00	4:00	3:00	3:00	Off
27:30	6:00	6:00	5:00	4:00	3:30	3:00	Off
28:00	6:00	6:00	5:00	4:00	3:30	3:30	Off
28:30	6:00	6:00	5:00	4:30	3:30	3:30	Off
29:00	6:00	6:00	5:30	4:30	3:30	3:30	Off
29:30	6:00	6:00	6:00	4:30	3:30	3:30	Off
30:00	6:00	6:00	6:00	4:30	4:00	3:30	Off
30:30	6:00	6:00	6:00	5:00	4:00	3:30	Off
31:00	6:00	6:00	6:00	5:00	4:00	4:00	Off
31:30	6:00	6:00	6:00	5:00	4:30	4:00	Off
32:00	6:00	6:00	6:00	5:30	4:30	4:00	Off
32:30	6:00	6:00	6:00	5:30	4:30	4:30	Off
33:00	6:00	6:00	6:00	5:30	5:00	4:30	Off
33:30	6:00	6:00	6:00	6:00	5:00	4:30	Off
34:00	6:00	6:00	6:00	6:00	5:30	4:30	Off
34:30	6:00	6:00	6:00	6:00	5:30	5:00	Off
35:00	6:00	6:00	6:00	6:00	6:00	5:00	Off

club availability or your work schedule only allows this to occur on Mondays and Fridays, that is when these anchor workouts must be placed in your weekly plan. Your longest bike ride may also be an anchor workout, since most working people and students must do these on the weekend.

The first step in designing your customized training week is to create a sample seven-day schedule and write in your anchor workouts on the appropriate days. Use a pencil, as you may still have a little juggling to do.

Time-Flexible Workouts

The remaining workouts may be done on other days of the week of your choice. If you are a high-training-volume athlete and do six or more workouts each week, then scheduling one of those each day will be fairly straightforward. But if you do only three or four weekly rides, spacing them becomes very important.

For example, if you ride three times each week, you would not want those rides to be on Saturday, Sunday, and Monday with no riding for the next four days. With that many days off the bike, you would lose any physical gains you made every week. Instead, separate the rides by two or three rest days. For example, perhaps you could ride on Sundays, Tuesdays, and Fridays. Once you've determined the best days for these time-flexible workouts, add them to your sample weekly schedule.

Daily Order of Workouts

You probably have little or no control over the time of day for your anchor workouts. But with the flexible workouts, you must schedule the time to address one important concern: You must allow for recovery so that the hard workouts are just that—hard. In designing your optimal week, arrange the high-intensity sessions, such as intervals, fast group rides, and hill work, so that you go into them with legs that are fresh and not cooked from the workout the day before.

For example, in the Base 1 period, strength training is a high priority. Those workouts should be arranged so that you are fresh for them, which means riding easily the day before a weight session. But in all the following periods, on-bike training trumps weight training. Adjust the workout days accordingly on your sample weekly schedule.

Time Between Workouts

If you are doing two or more workouts on the same day, it is generally best to provide for some rest and rejuvenation between them. You will reap greater benefits from your training if you are at least partially recovered from the day's first session before starting the next. The time between workouts should include refueling and is best spent sitting down whenever possible.

It may take a few tries, but once you've accounted for all of these factors you will have your own customized weekly plan. This plan will optimize your available time and produce the greatest race readiness possible given your lifestyle.

STAGE RACE TRAINING

10

There are a lot of feelings about racing you can never communicate. They're your own, and only you can identify with them.

—ALEXI GREWAL, 1984 OLYMPIC GOLD MEDALIST, ROAD CYCLING

FOR THE SERIOUS CYCLIST, a stage race is often the most important event of the year. With a season made up mostly of 1-hour criteriums and 60-or-so-mile circuit races, few riders are ready to take on five or more days of back-to-back races including time trials, 90-minute crits, 75-mile circuits, and 100-mile road races in the mountains. Throw in the toughest competitors in the region, prize money, and crowds, and it's easy to see why stage races are often the high point of the season and the ultimate measure of a road racer.

For training purposes we will separate stage races into two broad categories—short events with four or fewer stages, and long events with five or more stages. Short stage races require no specific preparation for the cyclist who frequently competes in two races on the same weekend. Long stage races, however, are a whole different game demanding exceptional raw endurance, muscular endurance, and usually force for climbing. Combine that with the need to recover quickly in order to be ready for the next stage, and it's apparent why long stage races have such a high attrition rate. It's survival of the fittest.

Training to race well in a long stage race requires a focused six- to eight-week training program to prepare for the unique stresses. Stage races require peak fitness and well-thought-out recovery methods. And you must achieve all this, of course, within the context of an ongoing weekly race schedule.

It is important not to take stage race preparation lightly. The stress resulting from high-volume training, high intensity, and short recovery times can threaten an athlete's health, fitness, work performance, and family relations. Overtraining is a definite possibility. Approach this training with great caution.

CRASH CYCLES

Training for a long stage race is much like doing several short stage races in the weeks building up to the event. High-quality workouts are gradually brought closer together with the purpose of overloading the body's systems. Success in that endeavor results in a delay in recovery, further increasing the stress load. This process is sometimes called "crashing"—a descriptive if somewhat ominous-sounding term for what occurs as your body adapts to this type of training load.

With the inclusion of a recovery period following the crash, there is a greater-than-normal training adaptation known as "supercompensation."

Two important studies have looked at supercompensation resulting from crash cycles. In 1992, a group of seven Dutch cyclists crashed for two weeks by increasing their training volume from a normal 12.5 hours per week to 17.5 hours. At the same time, their high-intensity training went from 24 to 63 percent of their total training time. The immediate effect was a drop in all measurable aspects of their fitness. But after two weeks of recovering with light training, they realized a 6 percent improvement in power. Their time trial improved by an average of 4 percent, and they had less blood lactate at top speed compared with pre-crash levels. Not bad for two weeks of hard training.

A similar study in Dallas put runners through a two-week crash cycle with positive results similar to the Dutch study. The second study also found an increase in the aerobic capacities of the runners. Again, it took two weeks following the crash cycle to realize the gains. Other studies suggest that a high-stress crash and recovery cycle and the subsequent supercompensation can result in an increase in blood volume, greater levels of hormones that cause muscle growth, and an improved ability to metabolize fat.

Be careful with crashing. The risk of overtraining rises dramatically during such a buildup. If the typical signs of overtraining appear, such as a greatly changed resting heart rate or feelings of depression, cut back on the intensity of training immediately. High-intensity training is more likely than low-intensity work to magnify or cause overtraining.

THE TRAINING PLAN

Designing a stage race training plan is a complex task—almost as complex as designing an entire season. The key is to decide, just as you did when putting together your Annual Training Plan, what it takes to achieve your goals in the targeted stage race and how those demands match your own strengths and limiters. The key limiters for long stage races typically are endurance, muscular endurance, and force for climbing. Speed skills, power, and anaerobic endurance play a lesser part, depending on the number and relative importance of criteriums, which seldom play a significant role in the outcome of the general classification. The objective of winning a criterium stage, however, would increase the importance of anaerobic endurance in stage race planning and preparation. Otherwise, the amount of endurance, muscular endurance, and force training you do will primarily determine your success.

For an A-priority stage race, start by finding out exactly what the stages will be, their order, how much time separates them, the terrain, and what the weather is expected to be—especially heat, humidity, and wind. Then try to simulate these conditions as closely as possible during the buildup weeks.

Let's take a look at how the eight weeks of training leading up to a stage race would look if we were to emphasize the above limiters. This suggested plan assumes that base fitness is well established. That means you have been putting in adequate miles, hills, pedaling drills, and weight-room training, if appropriate, for at least six weeks before starting.

Weeks 1–2	Build 1
Week 3	Recovery
Weeks 4–5	Build 2
Week 6	Recovery
Week 7	Peak
Week 8	Race

Notice that quality workouts are clumped together in two Build weeks of high volume and intensity, with each followed by a week of recovery. The workload (combined volume and intensity) is not as great in the Build 1 period as in the Build 2 period, so the first Recovery period is only one week. A Recovery week and a reduced-volume Peak week follow Build 2, allowing fitness to soar.

Three-week cycles are used instead of the more typical four-week cycles to help your system deal with the greater accumulated stress and more frequent need for recovery with this type of training plan. If there's any question about your readiness for a breakthrough workout, don't do it. It's better to be mentally and physically sharp, but somewhat undertrained, than the opposite. As always, when in doubt, do less intensity.

Also, note in Figure 10.1 that the most intense workouts are clumped closer together in Build 2 than in Build 1. This is the basis of crash training—providing increasing dosages of high intensity within short spans of time and then allowing for complete recovery.

During the Build weeks, be sure to practice recovery techniques following each of the intense workouts. These techniques include massage, stretching, fuel replacement, high fluid intake, and extra rest. For a cyclist, recovery also entails an effort to spend less time on your feet and elevate your legs when possible. (See Chapter 18 for a complete discussion of recovery methods.) Find out what works best for you, and be ready to use the best options between stages when it comes time to race. Once you have built your fitness, quick recovery is the key to stage racing success.

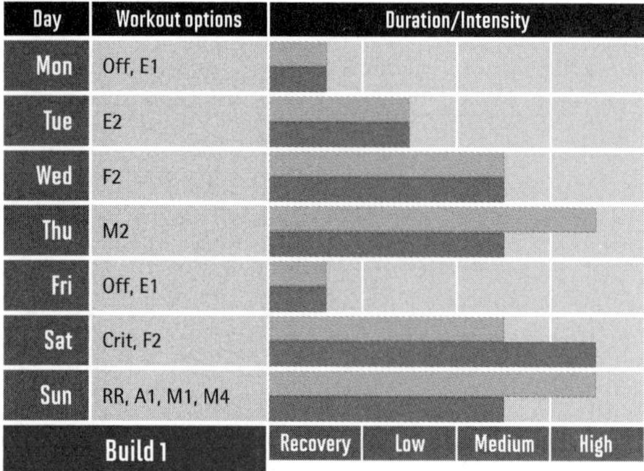

Day	Workout options
Mon	Off, E1
Tue	E1
Wed	E2
Thu	F2
Fri	M5, M6
Sat	Crit, F3
Sun	RR, A1, M6, M7
Build 2	

Day	Workout options
Mon	Off, E1
Tue	E1
Wed	E2
Thu	S5, S6
Fri	Off, E1
Sat	Crit, TT
Sun	E2
Build Recovery	

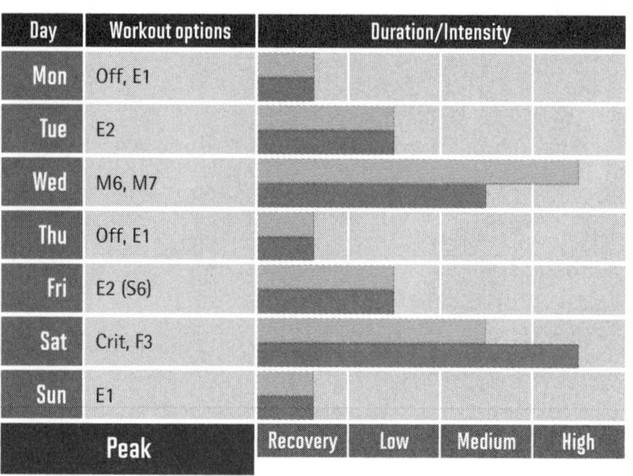

FIGURE 10.1

Weekly Training Patterns for Stage Races

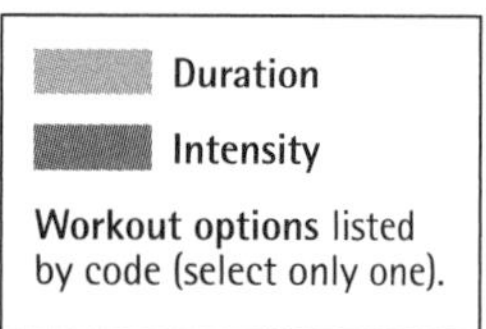

Following the stage race, while the glow of the accomplishment is still fresh, take one or two weeks to transition back to normal training. You've just had a major physiological crash, and your body needs to recover from it fully. As always, be sure to allow yourself a Transition period—a break from structured training that allows the mind and body to recover, rest, and feel refreshed.

If you don't reduce your training to allow your body to catch up with all of the stress it has experienced, you are likely to wind up overtrained or burned-out. Stage races must be treated with respect.

If your endurance was good going into the stage race, you may find, once you return to training, that your fitness is greater than it was before. That's the supercompensation kicking in again. If you finished all the stages despite questionable endurance, full recovery is likely to take longer than two weeks, and you may feel as if you lost fitness. That's called overtraining. The danger of overtraining is a good reason not to attempt a stage race until you know you're ready.

THE RACE PLAN

As with any race, attaining the performance and results you want in a stage race largely depends on having an effective strategy. A race strategy is nothing more than a plan for each stage that covers the variables over which you have control. You don't, for example, have control over the weather or over the fitness level of your competition. You can, however, plan for how to respond to various weather conditions, or how to position yourself relative to other riders. If you ride for a well-managed team, your role in each stage will be well defined. Unfortunately, many teams are not so well organized.

Any plan, even a sketchy one, is better than none at all. Typically, the longer the stage, the more complex the plan. The plan for a short criterium or time trial will include only a few items, whereas a plan for a long road race will include many possible tactics to achieve team or individual goals.

The plan is most effective when written down, and I like to have athletes do this about a week before the race. If you have a coach, share your plan with him or her. If not, discuss it with another teammate to make sure it is reasonable and that you haven't overlooked something important. See Sidebar 10.1, "Sample Race Plan."

The race plan takes shape during the previous twelve weeks as you're preparing for the stage race. One week before the race, you should have a pretty good idea of what you are capable of doing in the various stages. Start with your season's goal for this A-priority event. Does it still seem reasonable? Has your training gone as expected? If so, it should be easy to prepare the plan. If not, consider what you are capable of doing—either at a higher or lower level than originally thought—and create a plan that addresses the revised goal.

Of course, there could be more than one race goal, with some goals more important than others. There is no limit on secondary goals. For example, you might have a secondary goal of helping a teammate win a stage, of completing a time trial in a given time, or of simply building a higher level of fitness to boost your race performances in the following weeks.

Consider yourself a student of bike racing. When you attend races as a spectator or watch them on television, pay close attention to what is happening. Notice how the various teams' tactics play out. Bike racing is like playing chess on wheels. Understanding what your opponent is trying to accomplish will improve your defense while allowing you opportunities to have a better offense. A good resource for helping you grow as a tactical rider is Thomas Prehn's book *Racing Tactics for Cyclists* (VeloPress 2003).

Tactics are important because the outcomes of road races are usually determined by 2- to 4-minute episodes that create a separation of riders. The most common of these

SIDEBAR 10.1

Sample Race Plan

ATHLETE: John H.

RACE: Hoosierville Stage 2 Road Race.

RACE DATE: July 18.

START TIME: 10 a.m.

RACE CATEGORY: 35+.

COURSE: Five laps on an 8-mile circuit with one 0.5-mile climb of about 6–8 percent grade, then a winding descent. The climb is about 1.5 miles from the finish. Overall, a rolling course with four corners and not many windbreaks. The course favors my strengths.

EXPECTED WEATHER: Hot with temps in high 80s at start time. No rain expected. Has been windy in past.

PRE-RACE MEAL: My usual, which works well for me.

RACE NUTRITION: Sports drink only.

WARM-UP: The race should start fast, so I will make sure I'm ready. Warm-up will include 20 minutes on the turbo trainer, steadily lifting my power and heart rate, followed by 3–5 jumps on a short hill near the start.

START POSITION: The road is narrow at the start, so I want to be in the first or second row. There will probably be about 50 riders total.

RACE GOAL: Primary: win the stage. Secondary: top 3.

LAST YEAR'S RESULTS: 5th.

HOW THE RACE PLAYED OUT LAST YEAR: There were several attempts to establish breaks early on, but none of them worked until Tom R. got away with Ralph H. on the climb with a little over a lap to go. They worked well together. Before we organized a chase, Bill P. took off alone. We closed the gap and almost caught Bill at the line. I was second in the sprint to Ron R.

EXPECTED COMPETITION: Three of the top four from last year. Tom R., who won last time, has a team that isn't as strong this year. I expect him to make a move to get away early, probably on the climb. Bill P., the National TT Champ, usually tries to solo late in the race. He has no team to support him. Ralph H. will sit in all day hoping for a sprint. He will use his team to pull back breaks and set him up for the finish. No one else is really a strong contender, and I don't expect the other teams to be active either.

STRATEGY: Roger, Jim, and I will stay near the front of the peloton. We will watch for moves from Tom, Bill, and Ralph. Roger and Jim will help other teams chase down any breaks early on. I will go with any moves made by Tom, Bill, or Ralph and try to minimize how much work I do, saving something for the finishing sprint. I expect these moves to come on the 4th or 5th lap on the hill or after the second corner, when we are likely to hit a guttering crosswind. I'll be near the front and on the left side of the group as we approach each of these points.

occur on hills, in crosswinds, and in the lead-out to the finish line for a sprint. If you improve your anaerobic endurance, you'll be physically ready for these critical moments. Having the tactical savvy to position yourself correctly is an altogether different matter, however. Physical fitness can easily be established by training alone, following the guidelines in Chapter 6 and the sample workouts in Appendix C. But to become adept at proper positioning for hills, wind, and sprints, you need to ride with a group. This is the primary reason to train with others.

Most riders who engage in group training do so without any purpose other than to "get in a hard workout." Group rides become more useful, however, if you take time to consider the types of tactical situations you need to master in order to improve your race performance. There are several common positioning mistakes that riders make: becoming boxed in on the right-hand side of the road when approaching a hill, ending up too far back in the peloton when coming into a crosswind section, and being on the front on an approach to a sprint finish, for example. Group rides are excellent opportunities to improve your tactical skills in such situations.

Of course, stage races are not just made up of road races, although they play a big role in the General Classification. Criteriums seldom have much impact on the GC. Finishing the race with the main field will generally maintain a GC contender's ranking. Time trials, however, are another story. In many stage races, especially those with flat road race courses, the time trial is the chief determiner of the final GC. Getting on your time trial bike once a week for the last eight weeks leading up to the race and doing a muscular endurance workout (see Appendix C for examples) will do wonders for your stage race preparation and final ranking.

11

CASE STUDIES

If I trained the same way two years running, the results weren't ever the same. Something always changes.

—MIGUEL INDURÁIN

BY NOW IT SHOULD BE CLEAR that there is no single training plan for all athletes. Not only do individual abilities and limiters vary, but so do goals, available time, race schedules, experience, and so on. When you put all of these variables into the mix for a particular athlete in a given year, the resulting schedule is unique. It cannot readily be used by another rider because training must match the individual's needs. The Annual Training Plan you've been developing is for you and you alone.

Although it may have seemed easy to design a schedule, there is more to it than at first appears. As I said earlier, training is as much an art as a science. What I've described so far is the science. The schedule you've written is largely based on scientific principles, and it will undoubtedly serve you well. As you become more experienced at writing your own schedules, however, it will become apparent that bending or even breaking the rules can sometimes help you devise a plan that is better suited to your needs. This chapter provides a few examples of that. The following plans were developed for four very different cyclists, using the same steps outlined in the earlier chapters. But each athlete had a unique set of circumstances that required bending the rules in some way.

CASE STUDY 1: SINGLE-PEAK SEASON

PROFILE

Tom Brown, 39, is a sales manager for an electronics retail store. He works six days weekly, averaging over 50 hours a week. Married with two daughters, ages 8 and 10, Tom is in his third year of racing. He races with masters, mostly in road races, as he is uncomfortable with the high-speed cornering of criteriums. In his first two years, he was satisfied with simply finishing road races, but at the end of last season he began to see improvement, probably due to increased endurance.

Tom's greatest limiter for cycling is endurance, primarily because of too many missed workouts in the past two years. His job promises to place fewer demands on his time this season, and he has a greater commitment to riding consistently now. With regular training, his endurance will undoubtedly improve.

The Mental Skills Profile pointed to a lack of confidence as another serious limiter for Tom. Even though he set goals around three of the biggest races he could participate in, he lacks confidence when talking about them. Physiological testing revealed that he has the ability to achieve the goals, which seemed to bolster his self-esteem. He has been asked to read books on mental skills training for athletes and apply the techniques. In August, he will repeat the Mental Skills Profile.

His maximum power tested high, but his power at lactate threshold was relatively low. He is limited by low muscular endurance, a major weakness when it comes to road racing.

PLAN

Due to the weather in Regina, Saskatchewan, where Tom lives, training in the winter is difficult at best. He prefers to cross-country ski from October through February rather than ride an indoor trainer. He participates in a few ski races, mostly in the late winter, which in Regina extends into March. Winter is also the busiest time of year for his business, so he has less time to train then. His Annual Training Plan projects a longer-than-normal Preparation period for these reasons.

I encouraged Tom to train more than the 6-hour weeks scheduled through the winter Preparation period whenever he could. As this will be mostly on skis, I suggested he get on the trainer once or twice each week to do speed-skills drills.

Since the road-racing season is so short in Regina, and all of Tom's A-priority races are clumped near the end of the season, there is only one Peak period. Notice that in weeks 33 and 35, his hours are increased and endurance workouts are added. This change to the usual Race period layout is to help Tom maintain his endurance, which could easily erode with all of the races. This will better prepare him for a century in week 36. By that time his anaerobic endurance will be better suited for 50-mile road races than for 100-mile efforts, so the century will be done at a conservative speed.

SAMPLE WEEKS

In the Base period, Tom's training emphasizes aerobic endurance with a gradual increase in muscular endurance work. He also needs to work on cornering, so his training throughout the Base period includes many skill-development sessions. Table 11.1 shows

Sample Annual Training Plan (Single-Peak Season)

Athlete: *Tom Brown* Annual hours: *350*

Seasonal goals:

1. *Top 50 finish in Masters Nationals Road Race.*
2. *Top 25 at Provincial Masters Road Race.*
3. *Top 15 G.C. for masters at Tumbler's Classic Stage Race.*

Training objectives:

1. *Improve endurance: Start 90% of all workouts scheduled for season.*
2. *Improve confidence: Finish all races by August 4.*
3. *Read Mental Toughness by March 3 and use skills.*
4. *Improve confidence: Higher score on Mental Skills Profile by August 4.*
5. *Improve muscular endurance: Increase power on LT test by May 25.*

Wk#	Mon	Race	Pri	Period	Hours	Details	Weights	Endurance	Force	Speed Skills	Muscular Endur.	Anaerobic Endur.	Power	Testing
01	1/6			Prep	6:00	XC Ski	AA	X		X				
02	1/13							X		X				
03	1/20							X		X				
04	1/27							X		X				
05	2/3							X		X				
06	2/10						↓	X		X				
07	2/17						MS	X		X				
08	2/24			↓	↓	↓		X		X				
09	3/3			Base 1	7:00			X		X				
10	3/10				8:30			X		X				
11	3/17				9:30			X		X				
12	3/24			↓	5:00	*AT Test	↓	X		X				*
13	3/31			Base 2	7:30		SM	X	X	X	X			
14	4/7				9:00			X	X	X	X			
15	4/14				10:00			X	X	X	X			
16	4/21	Regina RR	C	↓	5:00	*Race **AT Test		X		X	*			**
17	4/28			Base 3	8:00			X	X	X	X			
18	5/5				9:30			X	X	X	X			
19	5/12				10:30			X	X	X	X			
20	5/19	Saskatoon RR	C	↓	5:00	*Race **LT Test		X		X	X	*		**
21	5/26			Build 1	9:00			X	X	X	X			
22	6/2							X	X	X	X			
23	6/9	Regina RR	C		↓	*Race		X	X	X	*			
24	6/16			↓	5:00	*TT Test		X		X				*
25	6/23	Race Across Saskatoon	B	Build 2	8:30	*Race		X	X		*	X		
26	6/30	Prince Albert SR	B			*Race		X			*	*		
27	7/7				↓			X	X		X	X		
28	7/14			↓	5:00	*TT Test		X		X				*
29	7/21	Canada Cup RR	C	Peak	7:30	*Race					*	X		
30	7/28			↓	6:00		↓				X	X		
31	8/4	Tumbler's Classic SR	A	Race	5:00	*Race					*	*		
32	8/11	Provincial RR	A		↓	*Race					*	X		
33	8/18				7:00		SM	X	X			X		
34	8/25	Nationals RR	A		5:00	*Race			X			*		
35	9/1				6:00		SM	X	X			X		
36	9/8	Harvest Century	B	↓	↓	*Race	↓		X		*			
37	9/15			Tran										
38	9/22													
39	9/29													
40	10/6			↓										
41	10/13			Prep	6:00	XC Ski		X		X				
42	10/20							X		X				
43	10/27							X		X				
44	11/3							X		X				
45	11/10							X		X				
46	11/17							X		X				
47	11/24							X		X				
48	12/1							X		X				
49	12/8							X		X				
50	12/15							X		X				
51	12/22							X		X				
52	12/29			↓	↓	↓		X		X				

his daily training schedule for weeks 19 and 22 of his Annual Training Plan. I've selected these two weeks because they provide a good example of how training can change from Base 3 to Build 1. Note the increase in the intensity of his workouts from Base 3 (upper table) to Build 1 (lower table). I also chose these two weeks because they represent some of Tom's highest-volume training, since they come shortly before his early-season races and important fitness tests.

TABLE 11.1

Tom Brown, Weeks 19 and 22

	DAY	TRAINING SESSION (see Appendix C for details)	DURATION (hrs:min)
Week 19 (Base 3)	Mon.	Weights: Strength Maintenance (SM)	1:00
	Tue.	Muscular Endurance: Tempo (M1)	1:30
	Wed.	Speed Skills: Cornering (S3)	1:00
	Thur.	Endurance/Force/Speed Skills: Fixed Gear (E3)	1:30
	Fri.	Endurance: Recovery (E1) or day off	1:00
	Sat.	Endurance: Aerobic (E2)	2:30
	Sun.	Endurance: Recovery (E1)	2:00
Week 22 (Build 1)	Mon.	Weights: Strength Maintenance (SM)	1:00
	Tue.	Muscular Endurance: Hill Cruise Intervals (M3)	1:00
	Wed.	Speed Skills: Cornering (S3)	1:00
	Thur.	Force: Long Hills (F2)	1:30
	Fri.	Day off	0:00
	Sat.	Muscular Endurance: Hill Cruise Intervals (M3)	2:00
	Sun.	Endurance: Aerobic (E2)	2:30

CASE STUDY 2: LOTS OF TIME AND LIMITERS

PROFILE

Lisa Harvey is a 27-year-old Category II cyclist who has been racing for four years. She works full-time as an engineer with an aeronautics company in the Phoenix, Arizona, area. She usually puts in 45 hours per week on the job and has weekends off. She lives with a roommate, has few family or community-related commitments, and is able to ride with only minimal restrictions on her time. Her training in the past was free-form—she did what she wanted, when she wanted, *if* she wanted. As a result, many of her basic abilities are weak.

Lisa has good power, owing primarily to her ability to turn the cranks at high cadence. She has always been a good sprinter. Her limiters are force, climbing, and muscular endurance. Her endurance is not as bad as the other limiters but nevertheless needs to be improved.

PLAN

Someone Lisa's age without major demands on her time should be able to train 500 hours annually; however, Lisa has broken down frequently over the past two years with a cold and sore throat. These illnesses may be due to her habit of piling on too many hard workouts without adequate rest, so we will make sure her recovery practices are adequate. We will also examine her diet to see if it is a factor. Recurring illness can be related to getting too little in the way of micronutrients (substances such as vitamins and minerals that your body needs to function properly). Athletes are prone to illness when they eat too many starchy foods and too few nutrient-dense foods, especially vegetables.

Lisa trained about 400 hours last year, based on her records, so she will start at the same level. Her ability to cope with a structured training regimen that includes frequent rest and recovery should allow her to avoid such problems. At the end of Base 2, we will evaluate her capacity for handling the workload to that point and increase the volume if it seems manageable.

Lisa has two Race periods planned, the first in June, with two A-priority races in five weeks, and the second in September, with back-to-back A races (see her Annual Training Plan, page 162). A short Transition period follows the first Race period to allow her to recover so that she can reach a higher peak later on. It's possible that this Transition period will be only five days off the bike, as that should be adequate for someone her age. Because there are only seven weeks from the end of the Transition to the start of the second Peak period, we will shorten Build 2 by one week. We will not, of course, remove the recovery week. Build 1 will be left intact, as her basic abilities need more time to develop. We may even decide to go back to Base 3 at this point if testing reveals that her endurance and force are not responding to training to the extent that we would like them to.

In this seven-week Build period, there will undoubtedly be other races that she wasn't aware of when she drafted the plan. She can substitute these races for workouts. If a B race falls in a non-R&R week, the volume will be reduced by about 20 percent so that she can go into these races fairly well recovered.

The last Race period is five weeks, finishing with a C race—the last race of the season—which is in week 40. There's no reason to try to build a higher level of fitness following week 37, with only three weeks remaining in the race season. Therefore, Lisa's C race in week 40 is being treated like an A race, except that we will add more endurance work in the preceding two weeks.

SAMPLE WEEKS

Table 11.2 shows Lisa's training for weeks 32 and 33 when she has races scheduled. The C-priority criterium race in week 32 is short, 45 minutes, but with warm-up and cool-down she will ride about 90 minutes that day. Nothing is changed about her normal Build 2

Sample Annual Training Plan (Lots of Time and Limiters)

Athlete: *Lisa Harvey* Annual hours: *400*

Seasonal goals:

1. *Break 1:04 at State Time Trial.*
2. *Finish in top 20 at La Vuelta Stage Race.*
3. *Finish in top 15 at State Road Race.*

Training objectives:

1. *Improve climbing: Climb S. Mountain in less than 32 minutes by May 25.*
2. *Improve muscular endurance: Complete 40-min. threshold workout by May 11.*
3. *Improve endurance: Complete at least five 10+ hour training weeks by Mar. 16.*
4. *Improve strength: Increase all max lifts by at least 15% by Feb 16.*

Wk#	Mon	Race	Pri	Period	Hours	Details	Weights	Endurance	Force	Speed Skills	Muscular Endur.	Anaerobic Endur.	Power	Testing
01	1/6			Base 1	10:30		MS	X		X				
02	1/13			↓	5:30	*AT Test	↓	X		X				*
03	1/20			Base 2	8:30		SM	X	X	X	X			
04	1/27				10:00			X	X	X	X			
05	2/3				11:00			X	X	X	X			
06	2/10			↓	5:30	*Test Max		X		X				*
07	2/17			Base 3	9:00			X	X	X	X			
08	2/24				10:30			X	X	X	X			
09	3/3				11:30			X	X	X	X			
10	3/10			↓	5:30	*AT Test		X		X				*
11	3/17			Build 1	10:00			X	X	X	X			
12	3/24	Arrowhead RR	C			*Race		X	X	X	*			
13	3/31				↓			X	X	X	X			
14	4/7			↓	5:30	*TT Test		X		X				*
15	4/14	Congress-Yarnell RR	C	Build 2	9:30	*Race		X	X		*	X		
16	4/21							X	X		X	X		
17	4/28	Fountain Hills RR	C		↓			X	X		*	X		
18	5/5	Festival RR	C	↓	5:30			X		X	*			
19	5/12			Peak	7:30				X	X	X	X		
20	5/19			↓	6:00		↓		X	X	X	X		
21	5/26	La Vuelta SR	A	Race	5:30	*Race				X	*	*		
22	6/2	Thunder Road TT	B	Build 2	9:30	*Race	SM	X	X		*	X		
23	6/9	Climb to the Stars TT	B	↓	↓	*Race		X	X		*	X		
24	6/16	Grand Canyon State RR	B	Peak	6:00	*Race	↓		X	X	*	X		
25	6/23	Wupatki	A	Race	5:30	*Race				X	*	X		
26	6/30			Tran										
27	7/7	High Country RR	C	Build 1	10:00	*Race	SM	X	X	X	*			
28	7/14							X	X	X	X			
29	7/21				↓			X	X	X	X			
30	7/28			↓	5:30	*TT Test		X		X				*
31	8/4			Build 2	9:30			X	X		X	X		
32	8/11	Falcon Field Crit.	C		↓	*Race		X	X		X	*		
33	8/18	Road to Nowhere TT	B	↓	5:30	*Race		X		X	*			
34	8/25			Peak	7:30			X	X		X			
35	9/1			↓	6:00		↓		X		X			
36	9/8	State TT	A	Race	5:30	*Race				X	*	X		
37	9/15	State RR	A		↓	*Race				X	*	X		
38	9/22				7:30		SM	X		X	X	X		
39	9/29				6:00			X		X	X	X		
40	10/6	Mt. Graham RR	C	↓	5:30	*Race	↓			X	*	X		
41	10/13			Tran										
42	10/20						SM							
43	10/27													
44	11/3													
45	11/10													
46	11/17			↓			↓							
47	11/24			Prep	7:00		AA	X		X				
48	12/1							X		X				
49	12/8							X		X				
50	12/15			↓	↓	*AT Test	↓	X		X				
51	12/22			Base 1	8:00		MS	X		X				
52	12/29			↓	9:30		↓	X		X				

TABLE 11.2

Lisa Harvey, Weeks 32 and 33

	DAY	TRAINING SESSION (see Appendix C for details)	DURATION (hrs:min)
Week 32 (Build 2)	Mon.	Weights: Strength Maintenance (SM)	1:00
	Tue.	Muscular Endurance Force: Hill Cruise Intervals (M3)	1:30
	Wed.	Endurance: Aerobic (E2) on TT bike	1:00
	Thur.	Force: Moderate Hills (F1)	1:00
	Fri.	Endurance: Recovery (E1) or day off	1:00
	Sat.	Race: Falcon Field Crit (C priority)	1:30
	Sun.	Endurance: Recovery (E1)	2:30
Week 33 (Build 2)	Mon.	Weights: Strength Maintenance (SM), easy on legs	1:00
	Tue.	Speed Skills: Sprints (S6)	1:00
	Wed.	Endurance: Aerobic (E2) on TT bike	1:00
	Thur.	Speed Skills: Form Sprints (S5)	1:00
	Fri.	Day off	0:00
	Sat.	Endurance: Aerobic (E2) on TT bike. Include a few race efforts of 90 sec.	1:00
	Sun.	Race: Road to Nowhere TT (B priority)	1:30

training routine for this week, since the race is a low priority and being treated as a hard workout. Note that this does not mean she won't give it her best effort. It would be a mistake to go into any race with the idea of holding back. Lisa realizes, however, that since she hasn't rested before this race, her results are likely to be subpar.

The following weekend she will have a B-priority, 30 km time trial on Sunday. As it comes at the end of a recovery week, Lisa should feel rested and ready for a hard effort and might expect good results, even though the time trial is not her specialty. Notice that while Lisa's Annual Training Plan called for 5 hours and 30 minutes (5:30) of total training time this week, she has scheduled 6:30 instead. You must not be a slave to the volume numbers in your Annual Training Plan. They are there as general guidelines only. To train only 5:30 in week 33 would have required her to take another day off, with a resulting drop in fitness. Given the lower-than-normal intensity of the early part of this week and the already shortened training hours, she should recover nicely and be ready to race well on the weekend.

CASE STUDY 3: THREE RACE PEAKS

PROFILE

Sam Crooks, 37, is a dentist in Johnson City, Tennessee. He is married and has two children by a former marriage, who sometimes spend the weekend with him and his wife. When the kids are visiting, Sam reduces his training and racing schedule in order to spend more time with them.

Sam is a Category III cyclist and has been racing for four years in both Category III and masters races. He competes mostly in criteriums. He is dedicated to racing and training and fits in workouts whenever he can around his busy schedule. This means training on his lunch hour and before and after work. He rarely misses a workout.

Maximum power and speed skills are Sam's strong points, making him an excellent criterium racer, but his marginal endurance, climbing, and muscular endurance limit his performance when it comes to road races and time trials. He has what it takes to win the district masters criterium, but he'll be taken to his limits with his goals: a top-five finish in the Johnson City Stage Race and a top-twenty at the Greenville Road Race.

PLAN

Sam has a long season ahead of him, with races starting in early March and extending into mid-October. His A-priority races are widely separated, with one in late May, a pair in July, and the last in October. Because of this spread, I scheduled Sam for three Race periods (including a period with two A-priority races in July). His first race peak is in late May, and I decided to maintain his peak for the district time trial in week 21, since he needs to concentrate more on muscular endurance training. A bit more focus on time trial training will help him accomplish that. Sam's Annual Training Plan is shown on page 165.

The second Race period is followed by a one-week Transition, which comes fairly late in the season. This Transition period may be extended by another three to five days if Sam loses enthusiasm after completing the Greenville Road Race. With a break in the racing and ten weeks until the next A race, that shouldn't present a problem.

In the second Race period, endurance workouts have been added to weeks 27 and 28, since he will be coming into two road races in weeks 29 and 30—one is an A race, and endurance is one of his limiters. If the week 27 and 28 criteriums are on Saturdays, he will ride long on the two Sundays. If they're Sunday races, he'll do endurance rides following the races. He has increased his hours for these two weeks to allow for the longer rides.

The last Peak period of the season (early October) will be preceded by a four-week Build 2 period, because the last race is a group of criteriums and he will want to emphasize anaerobic endurance coming into them. By that point, Sam will have solidly established endurance and muscular endurance.

After such a long season, Sam may be in need of a longer Transition period starting in October, so it has been extended to six weeks.

SAMPLE WEEKS

Here is a great example of how to schedule two race weeks. The upper portion of Table 11.3 includes Sam's first race of the season, which appears on the schedule during his highest-volume week of the year—Base 3, week 8. Getting in about 15 hours this week will be a challenge for Sam, given his work schedule. There are two rides scheduled for Wednesday that week. The first will likely be done indoors on a trainer before work,

Athlete: *Sam Crooks* Annual hours: *500*

Sample Annual Training Plan (Three Race Peaks)

Seasonal goals:
1. *Win District Masters Criterium.*
2. *Top 5 at Johnson County Stage Race.*
3. *Top 20 at Greenville Road Race.*

Training objectives:
1. *Improve climbing strength: Increase squat by 20% by Jan. 12.*
2. *Improve muscular endurance: Sub-57-min. 40 km at District Time Trial.*
3. *Improve endurance: Train on a 500-annual-hr. schedule.*

Wk#	Mon	Race	Pri	Period	Hours	Details	Weights	Endurance	Force	Speed Skills	Muscular Endur.	Anaerobic Endur.	Power	Testing
01	1/6			Base 1	7:00	*AT Test, Test squat	MS	X		X				*
02	1/13			Base 2	10:30		SM	X	X	X	X			
03	1/20				12:30			X	X	X	X			
04	1/27				14:00			X	X	X	X			
05	2/3			↓	7:00	*AT Test		X		X				*
06	2/10			Base 3	11:00			X	X	X	X			
07	2/17				13:30			X	X	X	X			
08	2/24	Crossville RR	C		15:00	*Race		X	X	X	*			
09	3/3			↓	7:00	*TT		X		X				*
10	3/10			Build 1	12:30	1 Strength/wk		X	X		X	X	X	
11	3/17	Anderson Crit.	C			*Race		X	X			*	X	
12	3/24				↓			X	X		X	X	X	
13	3/31	Korbel Crit.	B	↓	7:00	*Race		X		X		*		
14	4/7			Build 2	12:00			X	X		X	X	X	
15	4/14	Raccoon Mtn RR	C			*Race		X	*		*	X	X	
16	4/21	Athens Crit.	C		↓	*Race		X	X		X	*	X	
17	4/28			↓	7:00	*TT		X		X				*
18	5/5	McMinnville Crit.	B	Peak	10:30	*Race		X			X	*	X	
19	5/12	Drummond Crit.	C	↓	8:30	*Race					X	*	X	
20	5/19	Johnson Cty SR	A	Race	7:00	*Race	↓			X	*	*		
21	5/26	District TT	B	↓	7:00	*Race	SM			X	*	X		
22	6/2	Roann RR	C	Build 1	12:30	*Race		X	X		*		X	
23	6/9	Crossville Crit.	B		10:00	*Race		X	X		X	*	X	
24	6/16			↓	7:00	*TT		X		X			X	*
25	6/23	Charleston Crit.	C	Peak	10:30	*Race		X		X	X	*	X	
26	6/30	Murfreesboro Crit.	B	↓	8:30	*Race				X	X	*	X	
27	7/7	District Crit.	A	Race	8:00	*Race		X		X	X	*		
28	7/14	Gaffney Crit.	B	Peak	10:30	*Race		X		X	X	*	X	
29	7/21	Asheville RR	B	↓	8:30	*Race	↓			X	X	*	X	
30	7/28	Greenville RR	A	Race	8:00	*Race				X	*	X		
31	8/4			Tran										
32	8/11			Base 3	11:00		SM	X	X	X	X			
33	8/18				13:30			X	X	X	X			
34	8/25			↓	7:00	*TT		X		X				*
35	9/1			Build 2	12:30			X	X		X	X	X	
36	9/8	Carolina Cup	B		10:00	*Race		X	X		X	X	X	
37	9/15				↓			X	X		X	X	X	
38	9/22	A to Z RR	B	↓	7:00	*Race		X		X	*			
39	9/29	Apple Dash	C	Peak	10:30	*Race		X			*	X	X	
40	10/6			↓	8:30		↓				X	X	X	
41	10/13	Michelin Classic Crit.	A	Race	7:00	*Race				X	X	*		
42	10/20			Tran										
43	10/27				7:00									
44	11/3													
45	11/10													
46	11/17													
47	11/24			↓	↓									
48	12/1			Prep	8:30		AA	X		X				
49	12/8							X		X				
50	12/15							X		X				
51	12/22			↓	↓		↓	X		X				
52	12/29			Base 1	10:00		MS	X		X				

since in February it will be dark in the morning. The second Wednesday ride will be immediately after work, and since the sun goes down early he may need to start this ride from his office to get it in before dark. After Saturday's C-priority race, Sam will ride for an hour to cool down. And with a long ride on Sunday, Sam will be able to complete his biggest week in years. As he will have built up to this high-volume week over a period of several months, his endurance should be at an all-time high by week's end. Following a recovery week, he should be ready to start into the Build period with much lower volume but more intensity.

Of course, all of his plans for a high-volume week could be for naught should this wind up being a week that his children are visiting. As with most riders, there are many complications in trying to create the perfect training plan, and you must be willing to be flexible.

The lower portion of Table 11.3 shows one of Sam's lowest-volume weeks of the season, a week that ends with an A-priority race on Sunday. The emphasis this week will be on maintaining anaerobic endurance by doing intervals at his aerobic-capacity power (CP6). Notice that the number of intervals decreases during the week, and that there are relatively long recoveries after each interval to prevent excessive fatigue. The day off on Friday will help ensure that he is rested going into the weekend. It is better to take the day off, or do a very easy ride, two days before the race rather than the day before. After a day of complete rest the day before a race, riders often complain of being "flat" on race day. Some high-intensity training on Saturday should prevent this.

TABLE 11.3

Sam Crooks, Weeks 8 and 30

	DAY	TRAINING SESSION (see Appendix C for details)	DURATION (hrs:min)
Week 8 (Base 3)	Mon.	Weights: Strength Maintenance (SM)	1:00
	Tue.	Endurance: Aerobic (E2)	1:30
	Wed.	A.M.—Endurance: Aerobic (E2) P.M.—Force: Long Hills (F2)	1:00 1:30
	Thur.	Endurance: Recovery (E1)	1:30
	Fri.	Speed Skills: Form Sprints (S5)	1:30
	Sat.	Race: Crossville RR (C priority). Ride for 1 hr. after race (E1).	3:30
	Sun.	Endurance: Aerobic (E2)	3:30
Week 30 (Race)	Mon.	Day off	0:00
	Tue.	Anaerobic Endurance: 5 x 90 sec. @ CP6 (3 min. recoveries). Otherwise ride aerobic (E2).	2:00
	Wed.	Anaerobic Endurance: 4 x 90 sec. @ CP6 (3 min. recoveries). Otherwise ride aerobic (E2).	1:30
	Thur.	Anaerobic Endurance: 3 x 90 sec. @ CP6 (3 min. recoveries). Otherwise ride recovery (E1).	1:00
	Fri.	Day off	0:00
	Sat.	Power: 1 set of 5 Jumps (P1)	1:00
	Sun.	Race: Greenville RR (A priority)	2:30

CASE STUDY 4: SUMMER BASE TRAINING

PROFILE

Randy Stickler, 25, is a college student living in Fort Collins, Colorado. He has been racing since age 14 and has been on the national team participating as a Category I cyclist in several high-profile races in the United States and in international competition. He carries a full load at Colorado State University, majoring in watershed management. Classes and studying limit his available riding time during the week, but on the weekends he has plenty of time to train. In the summer, he will be doing an internship that will keep his riding time somewhat restricted on weekdays.

Randy's greatest abilities are endurance, force, muscular endurance, power, and climbing. With so much on his side, it's no wonder that he is a force to be reckoned with in every race he enters. He believes his limiter is anaerobic endurance, but since he determined this from early-winter testing, his concern is somewhat suspect. Nearly everyone has poor anaerobic endurance in the winter months. Randy's short sprint is excellent, but his longer sprints fade in races.

PLAN

Randy is capable of training about 1,000 hours a year. However, with the restrictions on his time due to school, his volume has been limited to 800 hours. Still, that should not present any problems, given the massive base of fitness he's built during eleven years of racing, along with his age and muscular strength. His primary emphasis on force training will end the last week of March, but it will be maintained throughout much of the remainder of the season. Randy's Annual Training Plan is shown on page 168.

The first A race of the season for Randy will be the Bisbee Stage Race in late April, a five-day event that attracts a strong field. He will train through the Boulder Criterium Series and other races in March and early April, using them in combination with a buildup of intensity to peak for Bisbee. A top-ten placement in the general classification is well within his reach.

Following the Bisbee Stage Race, Randy will return to Build 1 as he is preparing for the Colorado State Road Race Championship in week 23. With this race coming so soon after Bisbee, he should be in excellent form.

The greatest challenge in Randy's race schedule will be maintaining race form for the three-day Colorado Cyclist Stage Race at the very end of the season (week 39). With fourteen weeks separating his last two A races, it will be best to reestablish his basic fitness by repeating Base 3 training in July, even though that may be seen as an unusual time to work on Base. The events during this period are all C races, so he can either train through them or skip a few.

Athlete: *Randy Stickler* Annual hours: *800*

Sample Annual Training Plan (Summer Base Training)

Seasonal goals:

1. *Top 10 in G.C. at Bisbee Stage Race.*
2. *Top 3 at Stage Road Race Championships.*
3. *Top 3 in G.C. at Colorado Cyclist Stage Race.*

Training objectives:

1. *Improve sprint: Average 800 w on Power Test by 4/20 and again by 9/14.*
2. *Improve anaerobic endurance: 5 min. anaerobic on LT test by 4/20 and 9/14.*
3. *Improve anaerobic endurance: Average 30 mph for 30 min. of AE intervals by 6/8.*

Wk#	Mon	Race	Pri	Period	Hours	Details	Weights	Endurance	Force	Speed Skills	Muscular Endur.	Anaerobic Endur.	Power	Testing
01	1/6			Base 2	17:00		MS	X		X	X			
02	1/13				20:00		SM	X	X	X	X			
03	1/20				23:00			X	X	X	X			
04	1/27			↓	11:30	*AT Test		X		X				*
05	2/3			Base 3	18:00			X	X	X	X			
06	2/10				21:30			X	X	X	X			
07	2/17				23:30			X	X	X	X			
08	2/24			↓	11:30	*LT, Power		X		X				*
09	3/3	Boulder Crit. Series	C	Build 1	20:30	*Race		X	X		X	*	X	
10	3/10	Boulder Crit. Series	C		↓	*Race		X	X		X	*	X	
11	3/17			↓	11:30	*TT		X		X				*
12	3/24	Boulder Crit. Series	C	Build 2	20:30	*Race		X	X		X	*	X	
13	3/31	Boulder RR	B		16:30	*Race		X	X		*	X	X	
14	4/7			↓	11:30	*TT		X		X				*
15	4/14			Peak	13:30	*TT, LT, Power	↓	X			X	X		*
16	4/21	Bisbee SR	A	Race	11:30	*Race		*	*		*	*	X	
17	4/28			Build 1	20:30		SM	X	X		X	X	X	
18	5/5	Sunburst Circuit/Crit.	C			*Race		X	X		*	*	X	
19	5/12	Pueblo Crit.	C		↓	*Race		X	X		X	*	X	
20	5/19			↓	11:30			X		X				
21	5/26	Ironhorse RR	B	Peak	17:00	*Race		X	X		*	X	X	
22	6/2	Meridian Crit.	C	↓	13:30	*Race			X		X	*	X	
23	6/9	State RR Champs	A	Race	11:30	*Race					*	X	X	
24	6/16			Peak	13:30			X	X		X	X	X	
25	6/23	Mt. Evans RR	A	Race	11:30	*Race			*		*	X	X	
26	6/30			Tran										
27	7/7	Peak to Peak RR	C	Base 3	18:00	*Race		X	*	X	*			
28	7/14	Grand Junct. RR/Crit.	C		21:30	*Race		X	*	X	*	*		
29	7/21				23:30			X	X	X	X			
30	7/28	Hummel Crit.	C	↓	11:30	*Race		X		X		*		
31	8/4	Coal Miner Crit.	C	Build 1	20:30	*Race		X	X		X	*	X	
32	8/11	Black Forest RR	B		16:30	*Race		X	X		*	X	X	
33	8/18			↓	11:30	*TT		X		X				*
34	8/25			Build 2	19:00			X	X		X	X	X	
35	9/1	Deer Creek HC	C			*Race		X	*		*	X	X	
36	9/8			↓	11:30	*TT, LT, Power		X		X				*
37	9/15			Peak	17:00			X	X		X	X	X	
38	9/22			↓	13:30				X		X	X	X	
39	9/29	Colorado Cyclist SR	A	Race	11:30	*Race		*	*		*	*	X	
40	10/6			Tran										
41	10/13													
42	10/20													
43	10/27			↓			↓							
44	11/3			Prep	13:30		AA	X		X				
45	11/10							X		X				
46	11/17							X		X				
47	11/24							X		X				
48	12/1							X		X				
49	12/8			↓	↓		↓	X		X				
50	12/15			Base 1	15:30		MS	X		X				
51	12/22				19:00			X		X				
52	12/29			↓	21:30		↓	X		X				

With no races in the three weeks preceding the Colorado Cyclist Stage Race, it's important that Randy make the best possible use of the dwindling group rides scheduled for that time of year and that he engage in race-intense workouts to peak his fitness.

Since Randy will not have done any strength training since March, he will begin six weeks of AA phase weight work in week 44 following a four-week Transition period. During the six-week Preparation period, Randy will mountain bike, run, and cross-country ski as the weather allows.

SAMPLE WEEKS

In week 21, as illustrated in the upper portion of Table 11.4, Randy will be starting to peak for an A-priority race—the Colorado State Road Championships. For him, the 17 weekly hours will be moderate as he begins tapering. The following week, volume will drop to just over 13 hours, with about 11 hours the week of State Roads. During these three weeks the emphasis will be on well-spaced, high-intensity training. Notice that in week 21 he will have only two hard training days—Wednesday and Sunday. The Sunday race is a B priority, so his training will be relatively light for the three preceding days. The group ride on Wednesday should last about 90 minutes and is expected to be quite intense, as most of the top riders in the area show up for this workout in the early summer months. To make that ride even more like State Roads, he will do hill intervals before the group ride. This workout should leave him quite fatigued, so two of the next three days are short recovery rides.

The Sunday road race is in the mountains, so there will be considerable climbing. After the race, a point-to-point event, he will ride back to the start area to log even more climbing. This will help prepare him for the Mount Evans Hill Climb, which is two weeks after State Roads.

Week 28 (lower portion of Table 11.4) is the second of a four-week Base period. It will include increased volume to reestablish Randy's endurance after eight weeks of reduced-duration training while he prepared for two A-priority races. This week will end with two races, but his volume will not be compromised because they are C priorities. With four rides of more than three hours each that week, he should make significant gains in aerobic endurance. Notice the instructions for Wednesday's group ride to "sit in." After eight weeks of high-intensity work, Randy doesn't need to further develop his power capabilities or anaerobic endurance. The plan shifts instead to increased endurance, and intensity must drop accordingly so that he can avoid injury or burnout later in the season.

Following three weeks of increased volume, Randy's aerobic endurance should be well established. That will allow him to emphasize intensity once again in preparation for his last A-priority race of the season. But if his aerobic endurance isn't sufficient, he will do more Base training starting in week 31 and continue until it is at the optimal level. See "Comparing Heart Rate with Power" in Chapter 4 for a discussion of how to determine this.

TABLE 11.4

Randy Stickler, Weeks 21 and 28

	DAY	TRAINING SESSION (see Appendix C for details)	DURATION (hrs:min)
Week 21 (Peak)	Mon.	Weights: Strength Maintenance (SM)	1:00
	Tue.	Endurance: Aerobic (E2)	2:30
	Wed.	Anaerobic Endurance: Hill Intervals (A4) before Group Ride (A1)	3:30
	Thur.	Endurance: Recovery (E1)	2:00
	Fri.	Endurance: Aerobic (E2). Within this ride do 4–6 Hill Sprints (P2).	2:00
	Sat.	Endurance: Recovery (E1)	2:00
	Sun.	Race: Ironhorse RR (B priority). Long cool-down after race.	4:00
Week 28 (Base 3)	Mon.	Weights: Strength Maintenance (SM), easy on legs	1:00
	Tue.	Endurance: Aerobic (E2)	3:30
	Wed.	Muscular Endurance: Group Ride (A1). Sit in. Long warm-up and cool-down.	4:00
	Thur.	Endurance: Recovery (E1)	2:30
	Fri.	Speed Skills: Form Sprints (S5)	2:00
	Sat.	Race: Crit. (C priority). Long warm-up and cool-down.	3:30
	Sun.	Race: Grand Junction RR (C priority). Long cool-down.	5:00

CASE STUDY 5: NEW TO TRAINING WITH POWER

PROFILE

Marlene Ziehl is a 39-year-old who has been competitive in her race category for the past five years. She started racing at age 32 and rapidly developed the fitness to become a contender at races throughout Arizona, where she lives. Since she moves up to a new age category this season, she would like to test herself at a higher level by racing masters nationals for the first time. Her focus will be on the time trial, which is her strongest event. This will require raising all of her fitness abilities, but especially force and muscular endurance, to higher levels.

She is a physical therapist with 10-hour workdays on Mondays, Wednesdays, and Fridays. Time for workouts is quite limited on these days. She can get in the bulk of her training on Tuesdays and Thursdays, when she works half-days, as well as on weekends, when she is off from work.

PLAN

Marlene purchased a power meter right at the start of this season and is learning how to use it. One of the first things she did was a CP30 test to establish her training zones. A 30-minute time trial done as a workout serves as an approximation of CP60. She could have raced a time trial of about 40 km to establish her CP60, but no such race was avail-

30-Minute Solo Workout Test

A 30-minute test done as a solo workout is a good substitute for a 60-minute test done during a race because it typically produces similar results in terms of power output. Think about it this way: If you were to ride a 20 km workout solo, or race in a 20 km event with several hundred competitors, which one would give you the faster time? The race, of course, because of the added motivation. In fact, your 20 km workout pace would be about equal to a 40 km race pace. That's because you ride about 5 percent faster in a race than in a workout of the same distance. So a 30-minute time trial as a workout will predict fairly accurately the power, pace, and speed you would achieve in a 60-minute race.

TABLE 11.5

Marlene Ziehl's Power Training Zones (watts)

ZONE 1	ZONE 2	ZONE 3	ZONE 4	ZONE 5	ZONE 6	ZONE 7
Recovery	Aerobic	Tempo	Threshold	Aerobic capacity	Anaerobic capacity	Power
<118	118–158	159–189	190–220	221–252	253–315	>315

Note: See Chapter 4 for details of how to establish power training zones.

able in November when she got the power meter. A 60-minute race is always preferable to a field test for establishing zones, since you go harder when racing than when training.

Marlene's CP30 test predicted her CP60 to be 210 watts, establishing her zones as shown in Table 11.5.

To accomplish her first season goal of winning the State Time Trial Championship (see her Annual Training Plan on page 172), Marlene would need to raise her CP60 from 210 to at least 220 watts. With a current body weight of 125 pounds (57 kg) and a CP60 of 210 watts, she produces about 3.7 watts per kilogram. She is already competitive in the time trial at the state level, and the extra 10 watts is a reasonable gain to expect by April 20 (as per her training objectives on the Annual Training Plan). Ultimately, she will need to be at 4 w/kg at CP60 to achieve her second season goal of becoming a top-ten contender at nationals. That means lifting her CP60 by at least 10 percent in eight months of training. This will not be easy, but it is realistic, given her profile.

Marlene will start in the weight room by focusing on building greater force. She will work to elevate her squat to 160 pounds (about 1.3 times her body weight), from a starting point of about 140 pounds—a 14 percent increase, which is reasonable to expect in this amount of time. That should be accomplished by the middle of January. At that point her training will shift toward developing greater bike-specific force with big gear intervals and, later, hill repeats done at zone 3 and, eventually, zone 4 power.

For her third goal of finishing with the field in the masters nationals, her greatest limiter is anaerobic endurance. Although this goal is not quite as challenging as the two time-trial goals, road racing requires a high level of anaerobic endurance. To ride strongly there, she will want to raise her CP6 from 4.5 w/kg (255 watts) to 4.8 w/kg (275 watts).

Sample Annual Training Plan (New to Training with Power)

Athlete: *Marlene Ziehl* Annual hours: *700*

Seasonal goals:
1. *Win AZ State TT (sub-65 min 40 km)*
2. *Top 10 at Nats TT (sub-63 min 40 km)*
3. *Finish with field at Masters Nats RR*

Training objectives:
1. *Refine RR strategy abilities by 7/20.*
2. *Squat 1.3 x body weight by 1/27 and 6/15.*
3. *Raise CP60 to 220 w by 4/20.*
4. *Raise CP60 to 230 w by 7/6.*
5. *Raise CP6 to 255 w by 7/6.*

Wk#	Mon	Race	PRI	Period	Hours	Details	Weights	Endurance	Force	Speed Skills	Muscular Endur.	Anaerobic Endur.	Power	Testing
01	11/5			Tran										
02	11/12			Prep	12:00		AA	X		X				
03	11/19				12:00		↓	X		X				
04	11/26			↓	12:00	*VO$_2$ Test	MT	X		X				*
05	12/3			Base 1	14:00		↓	X	X	X				
06	12/10				16:50		MS	X	X	X				
07	12/17				18:50			X	X	X				
08	12/24			↓	10:00			X		X				
09	12/31			Base 2	14:50			X	X	X	X			
10	1/7				17:50		↓	X	X	X	X			
11	1/14				19:50		SM	X	X	X	X			
12	1/21	Florence 20 km TT	C	↓	10:00	*Race		X		X	*			
13	1/28			Base 3	15:50			X	X	X	X		X	
14	2/4	Bartlett Lake HC	C		18:50	*Race		X	*	X	*		X	
15	2/11	McDowell RR	C		20:50	*Race		X	X	X	*	*	X	
16	2/18	Florence 20 km TT	C	↓	10:00	*Race, **VO$_2$ Test		X		X	*		X	**
17	2/25			Build 1	17:50			X	X		X	X	X	
18	3/3	Hungry Dog Crit.	C		17:50	*Race		X	X		X	*	*	
19	3/10	Tumacacori RR	B		14:50	*Race		X	X		X	*	*	
20	3/17			↓	10:00	*CP6-30 Field Tests		X		X				*
21	3/24			Build 2	16:50			X			X	X	X	
22	3/31	Superior RR	B		13:50	*Race		X			X	*	X	
23	4/7				16:50			X			X	X	X	
24	4/14			↓	10:00	*CP6-30 Field Tests		X		X			X	*
25	4/21			Peak	14:50			X			X	X	X	
26	4/28			↓	11:50		↓	X			X	X	X	
27	5/5	AZ State 40 km TT Champ	A	Race	10:00	*Race				X	*			
28	5/12			Build 1	17:50	*VO$_2$ Test (assess Base)	MT	X			X	X	X	*
29	5/19	Tucson Crit.	C		17:50		↓	X			X	X	X	
30	5/26	Tucson 20 km TT	B		14:50		MS	X			X	X	X	
31	6/2			↓	10:00	*CP6-30 Field Tests		X		X			X	*
32	6/9	Tucson Crit.	C	Build 2	16:50	*Race	↓	X			X	*	*	
33	6/16	Tucson 20 km TT	B		13:50	*Race	SM	X			*	X	X	
34	6/23				16:50			X			X	X	X	
35	6/30	Tucson RR	B	↓	10:00	*CP6-30 Field Tests			X			*	X	*
36	7/7	Tucson 20 km TT	B	Peak	13:50			X			X	X	X	
37	7/14			↓	11:50		↓	X			X	X	X	
38	7/21	Masters Nats	A	Race	10:00	*Race		*		X	*	*	*	
39	7/28			Tran										
40	8/4													
41	8/11	Eagle Vail Century	C			*Century		*	*					
42	8/18													
43	8/25	Copper Triangle Century	C	↓		*Century		*	*					

CP6 is a good predictor of aerobic capacity, which is improved by training at zone 5 power (see Table 11.5). In the Build periods she will devote one or two days each week to zone 5 training to lift her CP6.

We will field-test Marlene's CP6 and CP30 frequently throughout the season to gauge her progress. At the start of the Base and Build periods, she will also undergo lab testing to determine her aerobic capacity (VO_2max), pedaling economy, and metabolic efficiency. The lab technician will help her interpret the data and understand its implications for her training.

Table 11.6 shows the plan for Marlene's first Build period of the season. By this time she should have a well-established base of fitness, meaning that her aerobic endurance, force, and speed skills are progressing well. Her muscular endurance should also be coming along. In this sample week she will focus on beginning to raise her muscular endurance to the level necessary to set a personal best for a 40 km time trial. The Tuesday interval workout will be done in the time-trial position, but on hills to develop force while also boosting muscular endurance power. Essentially, the purpose is to improve her capacity to drive a bigger gear. Time trialing is all about who can turn the biggest gear the fastest—in other words, power. This is a workout she will do repeatedly in the Build period. The workout is conducted at CP30 power, which should rise over the course of several weeks. So the targeted power for this session will also change every few weeks.

On Sunday her long ride will be done on a hilly course on her road bike. She will stay seated on the climbs to boost her hip extension power while maintaining endurance. For further time-trial preparation she will perform Friday's recovery ride on her time-trial bike in the aero position. Riding the time-trial bike once each week is not sufficient when preparing for an important race against the clock. The extra day each week on this bike will allow her to continue to tweak her position and become comfortable with it.

In week 17, with the workouts on Thursday and Saturday, Marlene will also be working on building her anaerobic endurance and sprint power. The Saturday group ride should be done with preliminary masters nationals road-race strategy and tactics in mind. The purpose of this ride is not merely fitness, but also mental preparation. Over the next few weeks, the strategy she intends to use at nationals should take shape based on what she discovers works best for her in group rides.

Week 20 from Marlene's Annual Training Plan is shown in the lower portion of Table 11.6. This is a "rest and test" week. From experience she knows that it takes her about four consecutive days of rest to recover following a block of hard training. By Friday of that week she should be feeling rejuvenated and ready to go again. She will warm up well and then do a 6-minute time trial. On Saturday she will do a 30-minute time trial following her warm-up. Trying to do both on the same day is not a good idea for most athletes, as fatigue or low motivation is likely to affect the second test of the day. On Sunday she will do a long ride on a hilly course as usual, except this week it will be somewhat shorter.

TABLE 11.6

Marlene Ziehl, Weeks 17 and 20

	DAY	TRAINING SESSION (see Appendix C for details)	DURATION (hrs:min)
Week 17 (Build 1)	Mon.	Weights: Strength Maintenance (SM)	1:00
	Tue.	Muscular Endurance: 5 x 6 min. Hill Cruise Intervals (M3) + 20 min. Threshold (M6), all on TT bike in aero position	3:00
	Wed.	Endurance: Recovery (E1)	1:30
	Thur.	Anaerobic Endurance + Power: Jumps (P1) + 5 x 3 min. SE Intervals (A2) + Hill Sprints (P2)	3:00
	Fri.	Endurance: Recovery (E1) on TT bike in aero position	1:30
	Sat.	Anaerobic Endurance: Group Ride (A1) focusing on elements of proposed Nats RR strategy and tactics	3:30
	Sun.	Endurance + Force: Long ride on a course with Moderate Hills (F1). Stay seated on climbs to build/maintain force.	4:00
Week 20 (Build 1)	Mon.	Weights: Strength Maintenance (SM)	1:00
	Tue.	Endurance: Recovery (E1)	1:00
	Wed.	Endurance: Recovery (E1). Optional ride based on how you feel.	1:00
	Thur.	Endurance: Aerobic (E2)	1:00
	Fri.	Test: 6 min. TT on flat course to establish CP6 on road bike	1:30
	Sat.	Test: 30 min. TT on flat course to establish CP30 on TT bike	2:00
	Sun.	Endurance + Force: Long ride on a course with Moderate Hills (F1). Stay seated on climbs to build/maintain force.	2:30

CASE STUDY 6: THE AGING ATHLETE

PROFILE

Ralph Hearth is 56 and owns a successful business that takes a considerable amount of his time. He works around 50 hours weekly. His wife is supportive of his training and racing. He has two daughters who are away in college. Previously he raced both as a triathlete and as a road cyclist, with moderate success in both sports. With nagging running injuries, he has decided to focus on cycling this season to see what he can accomplish. There is a high likelihood that his bike fitness will bloom as a result of focused training.

PLAN

Let's take a close look at Ralph's Annual Training Plan as shown on page 176. His annual hours are based not only on what he has done in the past two seasons, but also on how much time he has available for training given the many demands on his time. I normally recommend that masters athletes don't train more than 500 hours a year. By using Table 8.5, he sees that his highest-volume week for a 500-hour year is 15 hours. That week, shown in Table 9.1, will be a challenge. He knows that he may not be able to achieve all of those hours. But missing a few hours in the peak-volume week is better than reducing his total annual hours. With a 500-hour seasonal volume, most of his weeks will be in the range of 10 to 13 hours, according to Table 8.5, which will fit well with his lifestyle.

Now let's examine his goals. It is not generally a good idea to set a goal of finishing in the top three in a race, as there are factors affecting that result that are outside an athlete's control. The exception, however, is when you know whom to expect on the starting line with you and how well prepared they are likely to be. Ralph has raced both of his A-priority events, the Wisconsin and Minnesota state road championships, many times and has seen the same riders contend for the podium spots. So he has a good idea of what to expect. He has no other goals for the season beyond winning these two races. That keeps the season and his training very simple. There is no doubt about what he needs to accomplish to have a successful year.

Ralph's training objectives fall into two categories, those related to power output and those having to do with race strategy. The goals relating to power illustrate how a power meter can simplify the planning and training process. The power meter takes much of the guesswork out of knowing what you need to accomplish and allows you to gauge your progress daily against an objective measure. Used correctly, it can be the single most important piece of training equipment you own, apart from your bike.

Ralph has determined that CP60 and CP6 power values (see Chapter 4 for more on power) are critical to his success this season. CP60 is closely related to muscular endurance, and having a high CP6 is a key to success in those brief episodes that often determine the outcome of races—making a breakaway attempt, bridging a short distance to a break that's up the road, climbing a short hill at a very high intensity, or hanging on when the group is guttered by a crosswind. CP6 is the intensity used for anaerobic endurance workouts (see Appendix C).

Ralph's CP60 and CP6 values at the end of last season were at 230 watts and 276 watts, respectively. Based on his body weight of 158 pounds (72 kg), his CP60 is 3.2 w/kg and his CP6 is 3.8 w/kg. To be competitive in his category for road races these need to be higher, probably at least 3.6 w/kg (260 w) and 4.2 w/kg (300 w), especially because he does not have a team to support him in races. He's done a lot of research on what his power should be relative to his weight, based on the averages for competitive male cyclists his age. Achieving these power levels by the dates specified in his training objectives will bring a clear focus to his training.

Ralph also needs to be better at having a race strategy and sticking to it. This has been his greatest limiter in the past. Simple race strategies are usually best. All Ralph needs to do is stay out of the wind and let others do most of the work, since he does not have a strong team to support him. He will rehearse this basic strategy in fast group rides in the Build period and in B- and C-priority races. His race tactics will evolve from the platform of this strategy.

Athlete: *Ralph Hearth* Annual hours: *500*

Sample Annual Training Plan (The Aging Athlete)

Seasonal goals:

1. *Podium at Wisconsin State Road Championships.*
2. *Podium at Minnesota State Road Championships.*

Training objectives:

1. *Raise CP60 to 3.6+ w/kg by 4/27.*
2. *Raise CP6 to 4.2+ w/kg by 5/18.*
3. *Rebuild CP60, CP6 as above by 8/10.*
4. *Establish and refine race strategy by 6/1.*
5. *Establish and refine race strategy by 8/17.*

Wk#	Mon	Race	PRI	Period	Hours	Details	Weights	Endurance	Force	Speed Skills	Muscular Endur.	Anaerobic Endur.	Power	Testing
01	12/3			Prep	8:50		AA	X		X				
02	12/10				8:50			X		X				
03	12/17			↓	8:50	*CP6 and CP30	↓	X		X				*
04	12/24			Base 1	10:00		MT	X	X	X				
05	12/31				12:00		↓	X	X	X				
06	1/7			↓	7:00		MS	X		X				X
07	1/14			Base 2	10:50			X	X	X	X			
08	1/21				12:50			X	X	X	X			
09	1/28			↓	7:00	*CP30	↓	X		X				*
10	2/4			Base 3	11:00		SM	X	X	X	X			
11	2/11				13:50			X	X	X	X			
12	2/18				7:00			X		X				X
13	2/25				13:50			X	X	X	X			
14	3/3				15:00			X	X	X	X			
15	3/10			↓	7:00	*CP6 and CP30		X		X				*
16	3/17			Build 1	12:50			X			X	X	X	
17	3/24				12:50			X			X	X	X	
18	3/31			↓	7:00			X		X			X	X
19	4/7			Build 2	12:00			X			X	X	X	
20	4/14	Durand RR	B		10:00	*Race		X			*	*	X	
21	4/21	Woods Memorial RR	C		7:00	*Race, **CP30		X		X	*	*	X	**
22	4/28				12:00			X			X	X	X	
23	5/5				12:00			X			X	X	X	
24	5/12	Denzer RR	C	↓	7:00	*Race, **CP6		X		X	*	*	X	**
25	5/19			Peak	10:50			X			X	X	X	
26	5/26	Sussex Crit	C	↓	8:50	*Race	↓	X			X	*	*	
27	6/2	WI State Road Champs	A	Race	7:00	*Race				X	*	*	X	
28	6/9	WI State Crit Champs	C	Tran	9:00	3-day Tran then Base 3	MT	X	X	*	X	*	*	
29	6/16			Base 3	15:00	14 days of Base 3		X	X	X	X			
30	6/23	Brice Prairie 40 km TT	B	↓	7:00	*Race, CP60	↓	X	X	X	*			*
31	6/30	Palmyra RR	B	Build 2	10:00	*Race	SM	X			*	*	X	
32	7/7				12:00			X			X	X	X	
33	7/14				7:00	*CP30		X		X			X	*
34	7/21				12:00			X			X		X	X
35	7/28	Firehouse 50-mile TT	B		10:00	*Race		X			*	X	X	
36	8/4			↓	7:00	*CP6 and CP30		X		X			X	*
37	8/11	Real Wheel RR	B	Peak	10:50	*Race	↓	X			*	*	X	
38	8/18	MN State Road Champs	A	Race	7:00	*Race				X	*	*	X	
39	8/25			Unstructured										
40	9/1	10 x 100 Ride	C	↓										
41	9/8	Cheq. Fat Tire 40-mile	B											
42	9/15			Tran										
43	9/22													
44	9/29													
45	10/6			↓										

As a 56-year-old athlete, Ralph needs to be much more concerned with his recovery than younger competitors. His periodization plan reflects this. Notice that he has scheduled three-week mesocycles instead of going with the more common four-week schedules, which will allow for a rest week after every two weeks of training. More frequent rest should boost the overall quality of his training. He will also carefully monitor how he is feeling and back off if he notices signs of overtraining.

Strength training is also critical for older athletes because they tend to lose muscle mass more quickly than younger athletes do. To counteract this, Ralph will continue to lift weights year-round, with one session per week when following his Strength Maintenance (SM) routine.

One of the suspected causes for muscle loss in older athletes has to do with diet. As it ages, the body has a tendency toward high levels of acidity. It responds by pulling nitrogen from the muscles to prevent the acidic shift, and this causes muscle loss. Ralph will emphasize fruits and vegetables in his diet to improve his acidity balance. This strategy is explained in greater detail in Chapter 14.

Ralph has very few races prior to the Wisconsin State Road Championships in week 27, so he will depend heavily on group rides in the Build period to become race ready. After that, Ralph may have too many B-priority races scheduled. Since he will need to rest for three to five days before each of these, there will be some loss of fitness. The most critical one is the Firehouse 50-mile team time trial in week 35, which comes just three weeks before his second A-priority race. The B-priority race the week before the Minnesota State Road Championship is not a problem since he will be peaking with reduced volume at that time anyway.

After the Minnesota State Road Championships in late August, he has no more A-priority races, but there are two other events he will participate in. This will be a time of unstructured training for Ralph. He should feel free to experiment with different training methods, such as block periodization, greater intensity with much less volume, or doing more group rides to see how they affect his performance. He may well find something that works even better for him.

The key to Ralph's season is lifting his CP60 and CP6 to all-time highs. Work on this begins as soon as training starts in December, and nearly all of his training points toward these two objectives. Week 8 in Table 11.7 is during Ralph's Base period, when he lays the groundwork for the Build period. It is critical that he focus on Base workouts so that he later has the fitness to train with greater emphasis on muscular endurance, anaerobic endurance, and sprint power.

Week 8 shows how Ralph will blend weight-room training with on-bike training. High power output at all durations results primarily from a cyclist having the muscular force to drive the pedal down when in a big gear. Maximum Strength (MS) training with weights, especially hip-extension exercises such as the squat, the leg press, and the step-up, builds such force. Notice that Ralph will be lifting weights twice this week, as he will have done for the previous seven weeks.

Due to the severity of Wisconsin's winters, which are characterized by limited daylight but no shortage of snow and ice, nearly all of Ralph's weekday bike training is expected to be done indoors on a trainer. To help prevent burnout from so much trainer time, the durations are held to no longer than 90 minutes. Some riders can easily manage more than that. Others find 90 minutes much too long.

The workouts Ralph has scheduled for this week are typical of Base 2. None of these bike workouts would be considered hard later in the season. But he will find these rides challenging, especially for the legs, because of the emphasis on heavy weight training in Base 2. Once strength work is cut back to Strength Maintenance (SM) in week 10, the on-bike sessions will become more challenging. The force and muscular endurance workouts will become much more intense as Base 3 starts. But he will be prepared for this as a result of the weight-room and on-bike training done in Base 2.

Week 28, shown in the lower portion of Table 11.7, is an interesting one. This is the week following his first A-priority race of the season. The first three days will be off the bike so that Ralph can get some much-needed rest before starting back to hard training. During these three days he will assess his fitness level to determine whether he needs to reestablish his endurance, force, or speed-skills abilities. He will also factor in how well he held up in the latter stages of the previous Sunday's race, how strong he was on climbs, how he did in time trial–like situations, and how well he has been pedaling. Ralph has a tendency to slip back into a low-cadence mashing if he doesn't stay focused on pedaling smoothly. When we created his Annual Training Plan, we assumed that he would need to

TABLE 11.7

Ralph Hearth, Weeks 8 and 28

	DAY	TRAINING SESSION (see Appendix C for details)	DURATION (hrs:min)
Week 8 (Base 2)	Mon.	Weights: Max Strength (MS)	1:00
	Tue.	Speed Skills: Spin-ups (S1)	1:30
	Wed.	Muscular Endurance: Tempo (M1)	1:30
	Thur.	Weights: Max Strength (MS)	1:00
	Fri.	Endurance: Recovery (E1)	1:30
	Sat.	Force: Moderate Hills (F1)	2:30
	Sun.	Endurance: Aerobic ride on rolling course (E2)	3:30
Week 28 (Transition)	Mon.	Weights: Max Transition (MT)	1:00
	Tue.	Day off	0:00
	Wed.	Day off	0:00
	Thur.	Muscular Endurance: Cruise Intervals on TT bike (M2)	2:00
	Fri.	Force: Long Hills (F2)	2:00
	Sat.	Endurance: Recovery (E1)	1:00
	Sun.	Race: State Crit. (C priority) + Endurance: Aerobic (E2)	3:00

return to Base training at this time. As a result, we included muscular endurance, force, and endurance training in the workouts for week 28. This three-day transition period may seem challenging for a masters-level athlete, but Ralph has a high fitness level, and he will monitor his fatigue closely and back off if necessary. After three days of inactivity at this point in the season, most athletes, including masters, are anxious to get back to training.

Even though it appears in the Annual Training Plan that Ralph will only be doing one week of Base training, he actually has 14 days devoted to endurance, force, speed skills, and muscular endurance. On Thursday of week 28 he starts back into the Base period. This Base period continues through week 29 and finally ends on Wednesday of week 30. Thursday through Saturday of week 30 will be rest days to prepare for the B-priority time trial on Sunday of that week.

Notice also that Ralph is returning to Maximum Transition (MT) training in the weight room on the Monday after the time trial (see Chapter 12 for details). He'll only do three such sessions—one each week for three weeks—and they won't be as intense as they were earlier in the year. At this point in the season, the focus of his training is on the bike. If he had twelve or more weeks until his next A-priority race, he could have gone back to Maximum Strength (MS) training with greater loads and fewer repetitions. But with such a short time to get ready for his next major event, there isn't time to recover adequately from the muscle soreness and reduced saddle time.

Each of these case studies includes elements that do not precisely follow the training plan guidelines discussed in Chapters 8, 9, and 10. Life rarely presents anyone with races, work, vacations, and other events neatly spaced to fit into annual plans. Don't be afraid to bend the rules a little so you can design a plan that fits your needs.

PART V

OTHER ASPECTS OF TRAINING
HISTORICAL PERSPECTIVES

CONDITIONING FOR CYCLING

by Willie Honeman

(as it appeared in *American Bicyclist Magazine,* June 1945)

Sleep eight to nine hours daily and try to make it a point of retiring and arising at about the same hour every day. Of course, when one races at night this may break up the routine, but otherwise try to follow this rule.

The question of food and what to eat is one that would take much space to cover. A good rule is to eat whatever foods appeal to you, but be sure they are of good quality and fresh. Avoid too many starchy foods, such as white bread, potatoes, pies, pastries, etc. Eat plenty of green and cooked vegetables.

Before a race meet, or road race, eat at least three hours before. If your appetite is good, and it should be, a good quality steak, cooked rare (when and if it can be had), spinach, or lettuce, toast, prunes, or some other fruit, black coffee, with a small quantity of sugar, makes up a good pre-race meal. If the time before a meet or race is limited, two soft-boiled eggs, toast, fruit, and black coffee is another menu. Lamb chops may be a good substitute for the steak. Avoid overeating. It is better to leave the table a little hungry than to overeat, which will interfere with the proper digestion of your food.

Physical culture and exercise should be indulged in each morning to develop the arms, chest, and to prevent getting too fat around the stomach. Small weights, or pulleys, can be used. Perform these exercises before an open window and practice deep breathing at the same time.

STRENGTH

12

Golf pros hit balls on the range, swimmers practice with paddles on their hands, and athletes in other sports do other things that improve performance by enhancing muscle memory. Too many cyclists just ride their bikes.

—MIKE KOLIN, CYCLING COACH

THERE ARE MANY FACTORS that go into determining who gets to the finish line first, not the least of which is the condition of the athlete's connective tissues—muscles and tendons.

The human body has more than 660 muscles making up some 35 to 40 percent of its mass. The strength and flexibility of these muscles contribute immensely to the athlete's race performance. Developing the ability to produce great force while maintaining a wide range of motion means greater racing speeds and a reduced risk of injury. If the muscles are even a bit weak, imbalanced, or inflexible, the rider never realizes his or her full potential, as power for climbing and handling the bike is too low and muscle pulls and strains are likely. Fortunately, the converse is also true: When you build your strength and flexibility in ways that complement cycling, you can reduce the likelihood of injury and significantly improve your racing at all levels.

Every successful athlete I have trained has lifted weights for at least part of the season. Those with a force limiter have improved their race performances the most via strength training. And, as we have seen, muscular force is a major component in time trialing, climbing, and sprinting. The rider who can apply the greatest force to the pedal has a leg up on the competition.

There was a time when endurance athletes avoided strength training like the plague. Today there are still reasons why some don't strength train. Many riders have a great fear of gaining weight, and they think that strength training will cause them to bulk up. This is unlikely. Although there are those who have a tendency to increase their muscle mass, very few cyclists have a genetic predisposition to become hulking monsters, especially on an endurance-based program. If three or four extra pounds result from weight training, the increased power typically more than offsets the mass to be carried. For most riders, strength training does not cause appreciable weight changes. This is not to say that some riders don't blame a little winter weight gain on their weight lifting. However, the problem typically lies elsewhere: They are probably eating as much as they did during the racing season even though they are riding infrequently. Fat naturally accumulates under these circumstances. In any case, a few extra pounds are not going to ruin their cycling career. By spring, when the mileage goes back up, this excess weight will usually disappear.

STRENGTH TRAINING BENEFITS

Research has demonstrated positive gains in cycling endurance performance resulting from strength increases, but no change in aerobic capacity (VO_2max). A possible reason for this apparent contradiction is that the greater strength of the slow-twitch, endurance muscles following weight training allows them to carry more of the burden of powering the bike, reducing the role of the fast-twitch muscles. Since the fast-twitch muscles fatigue rather quickly, decreasing their contribution to the total force results in greater endurance.

A study conducted at the University of Maryland found that greater strength from weight lifting was associated with a higher LT. Since LT is a major determiner of performance in bike racing, anything that elevates it is beneficial. The improvement may have resulted from the athletes using more slow-twitch and less fast-twitch muscle to power the bike. Since fast-twitch muscles produce abundant amounts of lactic acid, using them less means there will be less lactate in the blood at any given power output, which in turn means a higher LT.

Lifting weights also can increase the total amount of force applied to the pedals in every stroke. As you may recall from Chapter 4, as force rises at any given cadence, power increases. Greater power outputs are always associated with faster riding.

Other studies have shown that after participating in a leg-strengthening program for a few weeks, subjects enjoyed an increased "time to exhaustion"—that is, they could ride farther at a given intensity level than before. The endurance improvements have typically ranged from 10 to 33 percent, depending on the intensity of the effort. It should be pointed out, however, that the subjects in these tests have seldom been experienced cyclists. It is more likely they were moderately to poorly trained college students. We might conclude that weight training will provide this endurance enhancement to those who are newest to the sport, but not necessarily to the more experienced riders in a given group.

But the speed and endurance gains that may result from strength training are not the only reasons to include it in your training program. Strength training confers another advantage by protecting against injury. The weakest point in a muscle is where it attaches to the tendon. Most muscle tears occur at this point. Increasing the load capacity of these muscle-tendon unions with strength training reduces the risk of pulled muscles during a sudden change in power, as when accelerating quickly or sprinting.

Strength training also has the potential to improve muscle imbalances. These may be gross imbalances, such as a weak upper body and a strong lower body, or they may be relative imbalances between muscle groups that have opposing effects on a joint. Again, such enhancements reduce the chances of suffering an injury.

Whatever the mechanism of improvement may be, there is a high probability that strength work will make you a better racer. Even if you were to improve your pedal force by only a few percentage points, think how much better you could race. By adding strength training to your program, you will be able to ride faster or feel stronger at the end of a long road race, and you will reduce the likelihood of losing precious training days—or even sacrificing a season—because of an injury that takes time to heal.

GETTING STARTED

There are two main challenges for the rider determined to improve his or her racing with greater strength. The first is that there are as many strength programs as there are athletes, coaches, and weight training and cycling books. The average rider does not know whose advice to follow.

The second challenge is time. Many of the weight training programs suggested by these sources include an unrealistic number of exercises to complete, often a dozen or more. Given jobs, family, and life in general, most riders just can't afford to spend huge blocks of time in the gym. The program I have included below is pared down to fit into the "normal" athlete's busy lifestyle. Although you might be able to squeeze in more gym time, the racing benefits would not be much greater.

The sport of bodybuilding has had an unusually heavy influence on strength training in the United States. But for cyclists, using resistance exercise the same way bodybuilders do is likely to decrease endurance performance. Bodybuilders organize training to maximize and balance muscle mass while shaping their physiques for display. Function is not a concern. The goals of endurance athletes are very different, but all too often they learn the bodybuilder's methods at their gym and follow them for lack of a better way.

The purpose of strength training for cycling is about one thing: the application of force to the pedals for a prolonged period of time. To accomplish this task more effectively, the cyclist must improve the synchronization and recruitment patterns of muscle groups—not their size and shape. This means that resistance work must develop not only the muscles but also the central nervous system, which controls muscle use.

Based on comments from the athletes I train and their results over the years, I have continually refined the weight training program that I recommend. However, the basic rules of my program have stayed the same. Whatever program you follow, as far as sets, reps, and load go, be sure to lift by these rules:

1. Focus on Prime Movers. Prime movers are the big muscle groups that do the major work on the bike. Cycling's prime movers are the quadriceps, hamstrings, and gluteals. Well-developed deltoids may look nice, but they're only good for lifting your bike—not a common movement in road racing.

2. Prevent Muscle Imbalances. Some of the injuries common to riders result from an imbalance between muscles that must work in harmony to produce a movement. For example, if the lateral quadriceps muscle on the outside of the thigh is overly developed relative to the medial quadriceps above and inside the knee, a knee injury is possible.

3. Use Multijoint Exercises Whenever Possible. Biceps curls are a single-joint exercise involving only the elbow joint. This is the type of muscle-isolation exercise bodybuilders do. Squats, a basic cycling exercise, include three joints—the hip, knee, and ankle. This comes closer to simulating the dynamic movement patterns of the sport of cycling and, because it works several muscles at once, also reduces time in the gym.

4. Mimic the Positions and Movements of Cycling as Closely as Possible. When positioning your hands and feet for lifting weights, think about where they are placed on the bike and try to duplicate that placement. On a leg-press sled, for example, the feet should be the same width apart as the pedals. You don't ride with your feet spread 18 inches (45 cm) apart and your toes turned out at 45 degrees. Another example: When holding the bar for seated rows, position your hands as you would on handlebars.

5. Always Include the Core—Abdominals and Lower Back. The forces applied by your arms and legs must pass through the core of your body. If it is weak, much of the force is dissipated and lost. As you climb or sprint, it takes a strong core to efficiently transfer the force generated by pulling against the handlebars to the pedals. Weak abdominal and back muscles, in other words, make for wimpy climbing and sprinting. The seated row and abdominal with twist exercises detailed in this chapter will strengthen the lower back and core. You can find more exercises focusing on the core and lower back in *Weight Training for Cyclists,* second edition, by Ken Doyle and Eric Schmitz (VeloPress 2008).

6. As the Race Season Approaches, Make Strength Training More Specific and Less Time Intensive. Winter is a crucial time for developing force because this is when you will complete a Maximum Strength phase. Later, you will convert these gains into forms of strength usable in road racing—power and muscular endurance. The conversions are best accomplished on the bike while max strength is maintained in the weight room. If you have read earlier editions of this book, you will notice that this is an area where I have made significant changes to my recommendations for using weights to improve cycling performance.

7. Keep the Number of Exercises Low. To improve specific movements, focus on sets and reps rather than the number of exercises. Following the initial Anatomical Adaptation phase, gradually reduce the number of exercises you do. The idea is to spend as little time in the weight room as possible and yet still improve race performance.

8. Use Strength Training Fitness to Prepare for on-Bike Training Within Each Season Period. Specific exercise demands in the weight room must come before the same or similar demands on the bike. For example, the Maximum Strength training phase should occur in the weeks just prior to the start of hill training on the bike. In following this principle you will be preparing your muscles and tendons for the workloads you will experience on the bike, and you will therefore be able to start stressful workouts, such as hill repeats, at higher levels of performance with a lower risk of injury.

The following suggested strength program complies with the above guidelines. I designed it specifically for road cyclists. If you have been training like a bodybuilder, you may feel guilty at times using lighter weights, higher repetitions, and only a few exercises. Or you may question whether you will really see results this way. Stay with the program, however, and I think you'll find that your racing improves. You won't look much different in the mirror. But then again, that's not what you're after.

STRENGTH TRAINING PHASES

There are three strength training phases through which the cyclist should progress in approaching the most important races of the year.

PREPARATION PERIOD: ANATOMICAL ADAPTATION (AA) AND MAXIMUM TRANSITION (MT)

Anatomical Adaptation is the initial phase of strength training and is usually done in the late fall or early winter. Its purpose is to prepare the muscles and tendons for the greater loads of the next phases—Maximum Transition and Maximum Strength (MS). More exercises are done at this time of year than at any other, since improved general body strength is a goal. There is less time spent on the bike at this time of year as well, so more time is available for weight training.

Weight machines are convenient, but you should also use free-weight training during this period whenever possible as it recruits more muscles, especially the smaller muscles used for posture and balance. Circuit training, involving continuous movement from one station to the next, and doing several circuits in a workout can add an aerobic element to the AA phase for those who feel a need for more aerobic training at this time.

The Maximum Transition phase is just that—a phase that provides a transition from the light loads and high reps of the AA phase to the heavy loads and low reps of MS. With only a few of these workouts—and the loads increasing slightly each time—you will be ready to begin MS. Always be conservative when increasing loads, especially in the MS phase.

In the AA and MT phases the athlete should be able to increase loads by about 5 percent every four or five workouts. Sidebars 12.1 and 12.2 show details.

SIDEBAR 12.1

Anatomical Adaptation (AA) Phase

AA

Total sessions/phase	8–12
Sessions/week	2–3
Load (% 1RM)	40–60
Sets/session	2–5
Reps/set	20–30
Speed of lift	Slow
Recovery (min.)	1–1.5

EXERCISES

(in order of completion):

1. Hip extension (squat, leg press, or step-up)
2. Lat pull-down
3. Hip extension (use a different exercise than in #1)
4. Chest press or push-up
5. Seated row
6. Personal weakness (leg curl, knee extension, or heel raise)
7. Standing row
8. Abdominal with twist

BASE 1 PERIOD: MAXIMUM STRENGTH (MS)

As you gradually increase the resistance and decrease the number of repetitions in a set, your muscles will be generating more and more force. This phase is necessary to teach the central nervous system to easily recruit high numbers of muscle fibers. If you are new to weight training, omit this phase the first year and focus just on the MT phase throughout Base 1 and following. This is the most dangerous phase of strength training, and injury, possibly severe, is likely. Be particularly careful during this phase, especially with free-weight exercises such as the squat. If there is any question about whether you should even do the squat exercise—for example, because of a questionable back, knees, or any other joints—leave it out and do one of the alternatives (leg press or step-up). Don't take any risks during the MS phase. Select your loads conservatively at the start of this phase and in the first set of each workout. You can gradually increase the loads throughout the phase.

Loads are gradually increased throughout MS up to certain goal levels based on your body weight (BW). These are summarized in the instruction for MS training. Generally, women will aim for the lower ends of the ranges and men the upper ends. Those new to the MS phase of training should also set load goals based on the lower ends of the ranges. Sidebar 12.3 gives details for this phase.

SIDEBAR 12.2

Maximum Transition (MT) Phase

MT	
Total sessions/phase	3–5
Sessions/week	2–3
Load	Select loads that allow only 10–15 reps*
Sets/session	3–4
Reps/set	10–15*
Speed of lift	Slow to moderate, emphasizing form
Recovery (min.)	1.5–3*

**Note: Only boldfaced exercises below follow this guideline. All others continue AA guidelines.*

EXERCISES

(in order of completion):

1. **Hip extension (squat, leg press, or step-up)**
2. Seated row
3. **Abdominal with twist**
4. **Upper-body choice (chest press or lat pull-down)**
5. **Personal weakness (leg curl, knee extension, or heel raise)**
6. Standing row

It is tempting for some athletes to extend this phase beyond the recommended ranges in the table. Don't do it. Continuing this phase for several weeks is likely to result in muscle imbalances, especially in the upper leg, which may contribute to hip or knee injuries.

ALL OTHER PERIODS: STRENGTH MAINTENANCE (SM)

Carefully limited high-intensity lifting maintains the raw strength needed for racing. Stopping all resistance training once the Base 2 period starts may cause a gradual loss of strength and performance throughout the season unless serious strength training on hills is incorporated into your on-bike workouts. Even hill training may not be enough to maintain core strength. Maintenance is particularly important for women and those over the age of 40 because it takes longer for them to build muscle mass and less time for them to lose it compared to men below age 40.

Hip-extension training (squat, step-up, or leg press) is optional during the Strength Maintenance phase. If you find that hip-extension exercises help your racing, continue doing them. However, if working the legs only deepens your fatigue level, cut them out. Continuing to work on core muscles and personal weakness areas will maintain your strength needs. Sidebar 12.4 gives details for this phase.

SIDEBAR 12.3

Maximum Strength (MS) Phase

MS

Total sessions/phase	8–12
Sessions/week	2–3
Load (% 1RM)	BW goal*
Sets/session	2–6
Reps/set	3–6+*
Speed of lift	Slow to moderate
Recovery (min.)	2–4

**Note: Only boldfaced exercises below follow this guideline. All others continue AA guidelines.*

EXERCISES

(in order of completion):

1. **Hip extension (squat, leg press, or step-up)**
2. Seated row
3. **Abdominal with twist**
4. **Upper-body choice (chest press or lat pull-down)**
5. **Personal weakness (leg curl, knee extension, or heel raise)**
6. Standing row

LOAD GOALS BASED ON BODY WEIGHT (BW)

The goal is to complete three sets of six repetitions each at these loads by the end of the MS phase. If a goal is achieved early, maintain the load and increase the repetitions beyond six for the remainder of the MS phase.

Squat	1.3–1.7 x BW
Leg press (sled)	2.5–2.9 x BW
Step-up	0.7–0.9 x BW
Seated row	0.5–0.8 x BW
Standing row	0.4–0.7 x BW

To properly time your peak, eliminate all strength training for the seven days leading up to A-priority races.

SEASONAL PERIODIZATION OF STRENGTH TRAINING

Strength training with weights needs to dovetail with your cycling-specific training so that the two modes are complementary. If they don't mesh well, you may find that you are fre-

SIDEBAR 12.4

Strength Maintenance (SM) Phase

SM

Total sessions/phase	Indefinite
Sessions/week	1
Load (% 1RM)	60, 80 (last set)*
Sets/session	2–3*
Reps/set	6–12*
Speed of lift	Moderate*
Recovery (min.)	1–2*

**Note: Only boldfaced exercises below follow this guideline. All others continue AA guidelines.*

EXERCISES

(in order of completion):

1. **Hip extension (squat, leg press, or step-up)**
2. Seated row
3. **Abdominal with twist**
4. **Upper-body choice (chest press or lat pull-down)**
5. **Personal weakness (leg curl, knee extension, or heel raise)**
6. Standing row

quently tired and that your bike training isn't progressing. Table 12.1 shows you when you should do each phase of strength training during your season.

If you have two or more Race periods in a season, I recommend that you return to the MS phase whe ever you repeat the Base period. After four to six sessions, you can return to SM.

If your periodization plan has only one Race period, return to MS for four to six sessions about every 16 weeks. Reduce the intensity of your cycling-specific workouts during these short MS phases, especially the day after a strength session. In essence, you are inserting mini–Base periods into your plan every 16 weeks, with an increased emphasis on strength and a decreased emphasis on bike intensity. Emphasize duration in your rides; otherwise, your bike training may decline due to the intensity of the added heavy-lifting phase.

TABLE 12.1

Periodization of Strength Training

PERIOD	STRENGTH PHASE
Prep	AA–MT
Base 1	MS
Base 2	SM
Base 3	SM
Build 1	SM
Build 2	SM
Peak	SM
Race	(None)

DETERMINING LOAD

Perhaps the most critical aspect of lifting weights is the load you select during each phase. Although in this chapter I have suggested a load based on a percentage of the maximum you can lift for a single repetition (1RM), that is not always the best way to determine weight. Such heavy loads increase the possibility of injury, especially to the back, and of prolonged soreness that can negatively affect training for two or three days.

Another way to decide how much weight to use is to initially estimate the load and then adjust it as the phase progresses. Always start with less than you think is possible for the number of reps indicated. You can add more later, if you do it cautiously.

You can also estimate one-repetition maximums based on a higher number of reps done to failure. Start by doing a warm-up set or two. Select a resistance you can lift at least four times, but no more than ten. You may need to experiment for a couple of sets. If you do, rest for at least five minutes between attempts. To find your predicted 1RM, divide the weight lifted by the factor below that corresponds to the number of repetitions completed (see Table 12.2). Another way of estimating your 1RM from a multiple-lift effort is described in the Maximum Weight Chart found in Appendix A.

TABLE 12.2 Estimating One-Repetition Maximums

REPS COMPLETED	FACTOR
4	.90
5	.875
6	.85
7	.825
8	.80
9	.775
10	.75

During the MS phase, free weights are likely to bring greater results than machines, but if you use free weights, also include them in the MT phase. Again, be cautious whenever using barbells and dumbbells, especially with rapid movement.

MISCELLANEOUS GUIDELINES

In carrying out a strength development program, you will want to consider several other factors. They are discussed in detail in the following sections.

EXPERIENCE LEVEL

If you are in your first two years of strength training, your emphasis must be on building efficient movement patterns and bolstering connective tissue—not on heavy loads. Experienced athletes are ready to do more MS development.

DAYS PER WEEK

The weight phase tables suggest a range of days per week to lift weights based on the phase you are in. The period of the season you are in will help you to further refine this number. During Base 3, Build 1, and Build 2, reduce the number of days of strength training per week by one. In the Peak and Race periods, cut back to the minimum listed in the table. In a week preceding an A race, eliminate strength training altogether.

WARM-UP AND COOL-DOWN

Before an individual strength workout, warm up with about 10 minutes of easy aerobic activity. This could be running, rowing, stair-climbing, or cycling. Following a weight session, spin with a light resistance at a cadence of 90 rpm or higher for 10 to 20 minutes on a stationary bike. Allow your toes to relax. Do not run immediately following a strength workout, as this raises your risk of injury.

PHASING IN

Be cautious with load progression as you move into a new phase of strength training. This is as important at the start of the AA phase, as you return to weight training after some time off, as it is in the MS phase, as you progress to heavy loads. If you do it right, soreness will be minimal and there will be little or no need to modify any other workouts that week. If you do it wrong, you are likely to be quite sore for several days and could be forced to cut back on other forms of training.

EXERCISE ORDER

Exercises are listed in the phase tables in the order of completion to allow for a smooth progression and adequate recovery. In the AA phase you may want to use circuit training to give this phase an aerobic component. To do this, complete the first set of all exercises before starting the second set, and move rapidly from station to station taking little time for recovery. For example, in AA, do the first set of squats followed by the first set of seated rows. In the other phases, all sets of each exercise are done to completion before progressing to the next exercise, and you must allow for adequate recovery between sets by following the recommendations in the tables. This traditional form of completing sets is called "horizontal progression."

In some cases, you may do two exercises as a "superset" in the MS phase—alternate sets between two exercises to completion. Supersetting will make better use of your time in the gym since you'll spend less time waiting for recovery of a specific neuromuscular group. This does not eliminate the need to stretch following each set, however (see stretches specified with the exercises later in this chapter).

RECOVERY INTERVALS

In the tables, notice that the recovery time between sets is specified. During this time the muscle burn fades away, your heart rate drops, and breathing returns to a resting level as lactate is cleared and energy stores are rebuilt in preparation for the next set. These recovery periods are important, especially as the weight loads increase, if you expect to derive any benefit from strength work. Some phases require longer recovery intervals than others. During the recovery time, stretch the muscles just exercised. See Chapter 13 for instruction and illustrations of the stretches that accompany the strength exercises.

RECOVERY WEEKS

Every third or fourth week is a time of reduced training volume coinciding with your recovery weeks scheduled on the Annual Training Plan. Reduce the number of strength workouts that week, or reduce the number of sets within workouts. Keep the loads the same as in the previous week.

UNDULATING PERIODIZATION OF STRENGTH TRAINING

The strength training periodization model described above is called "linear" and was discussed in greater detail in Chapter 7. That chapter also mentioned that another model, "daily undulating" periodization, has been shown in scientific studies to be especially beneficial for the development of strength. You may find that it works better for you than linear periodization.

Using daily undulating periodization is simple. During the six weeks or so in which you would have been doing the MT and MS phases in succession, you instead combine them into one workout. You do both MT and MS for each weight lifting exercise in each workout. If, for example, you are doing three sets, the first set is done with a load you can only lift about 15 times. The second set is with a load you can lift 10 times. And the third set is with a load you lift only 5 times.

Except for the loads, reps, and sets, the guidelines for daily undulating strength periodization match those for the MS phase. Sidebar 12.5 shows details for this phase. During the six weeks you are using this daily undulating model, the loads should increase for each set, indicating that you are getting stronger. Of course, in the Base 1 and early Base 2 periods, on-bike workouts are low intensity with an emphasis on aerobic endurance, so this increased load from strength training should not be an issue. The AA and SM phases are unchanged.

SIDEBAR 12.5

Daily Undulating Strength Phase

Total sessions/phase	8–12
Sessions/week	2–3
Load (% 1RM)	BW goals*
Sets/session	2–6
Reps/set	3–6+
Speed of lift	Slow to moderate
Recovery (min.)*	2–4*

**Note: Only boldfaced exercises below follow this guideline. All others continue AA guidelines.*

EXERCISES

(in order of completion):

1. **Hip extension (squat, leg press, or step-up)**
2. Seated row
3. **Abdominal with twist**
4. **Upper-body choice (chest press or lat pull-down)**
5. **Personal weakness (leg curl, knee extension, or heel raise)**
6. Standing row

STRENGTH EXERCISES

HIP EXTENSION: SQUAT

QUADRICEPS, GLUTEUS, HAMSTRINGS

The squat improves force delivery to the pedals. For the novice, the squat is one of the most dangerous exercise options in this routine. Great care is necessary to protect the back and knees. *Please note that it is important to wear a weight belt during the Maximum Strength (MS) phase.*

1. Stand with the feet pedal-width apart, about 10 inches, center to center, with the toes pointed straight ahead.
2. Keep the head up and the back straight.
3. Squat until the upper thighs are just short of parallel to floor—about the same knee bend as at the top of a pedal stroke.
4. Point the knees straight ahead, maintaining their position over the feet at all times.
5. Return to the starting position.

Stretches: Stork Stand and Triangle.

FIGURE 12.1a

Squat

FIGURE 12.1b

Squat with Machine

HIP EXTENSION: STEP-UP

QUADRICEPS, GLUTEUS, HAMSTRINGS

Improves force delivery to the pedals. The step-up closely mimics the movement of pedaling, but the exercise takes more time than the squat or leg press, since each leg is worked individually. Caution is necessary to ensure a stable platform and overhead clearance. The platform should be a height equal to twice the length of the pedal cranks. That's approximately 14 inches (35 cm). A higher platform puts great stress on the knee and raises the possibility of injury.

1. Use either a barbell on the shoulders or dumbbells in the hands. Wrist straps may be used with dumbbells.
2. Place the left foot fully on a sturdy, raised platform with the toes pointing straight ahead.
3. With the back straight and the head erect, step up with the right foot, touching the top of the platform, and immediately return to the starting position.
4. Complete all left-leg reps before repeating with the right leg.
   Stretches: Stork Stand and Triangle.

FIGURE 12.2a

Step-up

FIGURE 12.2b

Step-up with Dumbbells

HIP EXTENSION: LEG PRESS

QUADRICEPS, GLUTEUS, HAMSTRINGS

Improves force delivery to the pedals. This is probably the safest of the hip-extension exercises and generally takes the least time. Be careful not to "throw" the platform, since it may damage the knee cartilage when it drops back down, especially because the knees could accidentally lock in trying to regain control.

1. Center the feet on the middle portion of a platform about 10 inches (25 cm) apart, center to center. The feet are parallel, not angled out. The higher the feet are placed on the platform, the more the gluteus and hamstrings are involved.
2. Press the platform until the legs are almost straight, but with the knees short of locking.
3. Release the platform until the knees are about 8 inches (20 cm) from the chest. Going deeper places unnecessary stress on the knees.
4. The knees remain in line with the feet throughout the movement.
5. Return to the starting position.

   Stretches: Stork Stand and Triangle.

FIGURE 12.3

Leg Press

SEATED ROW

UPPER AND LOWER BACK, LOWER LATS, BICEPS

This exercise simulates the movement of pulling on the handlebars while climbing a hill in a seated position. It also strengthens the core and lower back.

1. Grasp the bar with the arms fully extended and the hands about the same width apart as when gripping the handlebars.
2. Pull the bar toward the stomach, keeping the elbows close to the body.
3. Keep movement at the waist to a minimum, using the back muscles to stabilize the position.
4. Return to the starting position.
   Stretches: Pull-down and Squat.

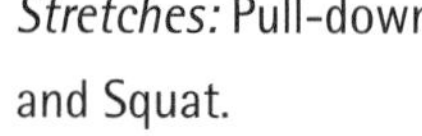
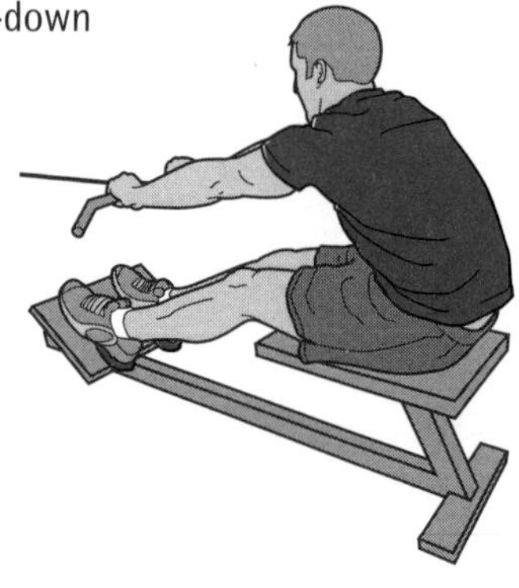
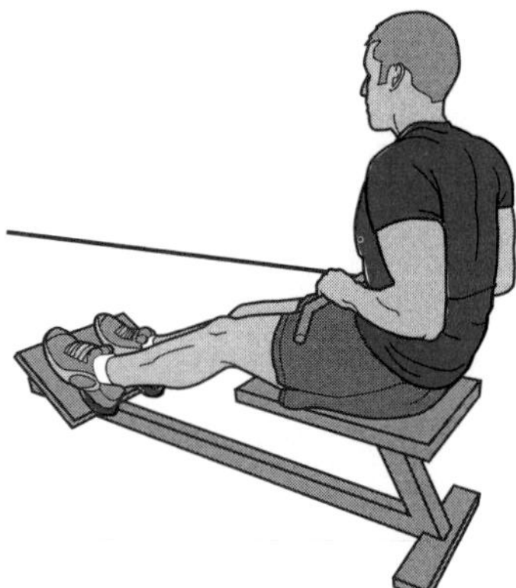

FIGURE 12.4

Seated Row

CHEST PRESS

PECTORALS, TRICEPS

The chest press, along with the lat pull-down and the standing row, strengthens muscles that will help support the shoulders in the event of a crash. With free weights, a spotter is necessary in the MS phase.

1. Grasp the bar with the hands above the shoulders and about as wide apart as when holding the handlebars.
2. Lower the bar to the chest, keeping the elbows close to the body.
3. Return to the starting position without raising the butt off the bench.
   Stretch: Pull-down.

FIGURE 12.5

Chest Press

PUSH-UP

PECTORALS, TRICEPS

The push-up provides the same benefits as the chest press. The advantage is that no equipment is necessary, so it can be done anywhere.

1. Place the hands slightly wider than the shoulders.
2. Keep the back straight and the head up.
3. Maintaining a straight-line, rigid body position, lower the body until the chest is within about 4 inches (10 cm) of the floor. This may be done with the knees on the floor as strength is developing.
4. Return to the starting position.
   Stretch: Twister.

FIGURE 12.6

Push-up

HEEL RAISE

GASTROCNEMIUS

This is a "personal weakness" exercise for athletes who experience calf and Achilles tendon problems. The heel raise may reduce susceptibility to such injuries, but be careful to use very light weights when starting, as it may also cause some calf or Achilles tendon problems initially. Progress slowly with this exercise. Never attempt a 1RM test with this exercise if the lower leg is an area of personal weakness.

1. Stand with the balls of the feet on a 1- to 2-inch (2.5 to 5 cm) riser, with the heels on the floor.
2. The feet are parallel and as wide apart as they would be on the pedals.
3. With straight knees, rise onto the toes.
4. Return to the starting position.
   Stretch: Wall Lean.

FIGURE 12.7

Heel Raise

KNEE EXTENSION

MEDIAL QUADRICEPS

If an athlete is plagued by a kneecap tracking injury, this exercise may help by improving balance between the lateral and medial quadriceps, keeping the injury under control.

1. Start with the knee fully extended and the toes pointing slightly to the outside. Work one leg at a time.
2. Lower the ankle pad only about 8 inches (20 cm)—do not go all the way down, as this may increase internal knee pressure, making the underside of the kneecap sore.
3. Return to the starting position.
   Stretch: Stork Stand.

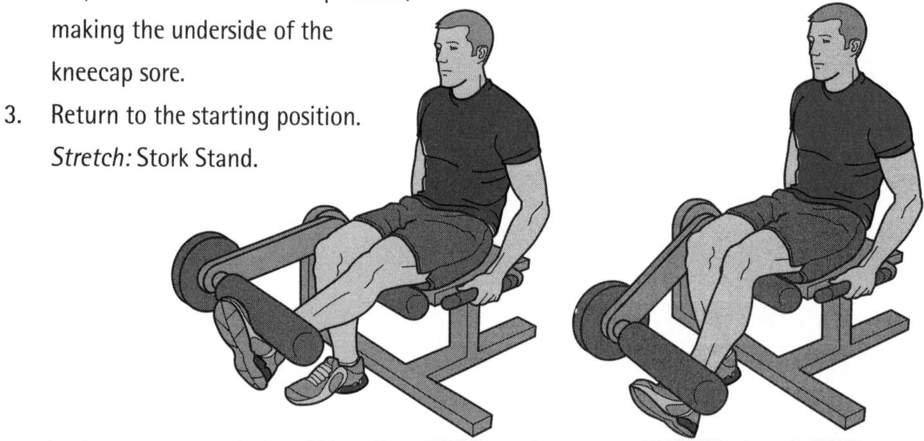

FIGURE 12.8
Knee Extension

LEG CURL

HAMSTRINGS

Hamstring injuries may result from an imbalance between the quadriceps and hamstrings. Strengthening the hamstrings can improve the strength ratio between these two major movers. Leg curls can be done on either prone or standing machines.

1. Bend the leg to about a 90-degree angle at the knee.
2. Return to the starting position.
   Stretch: Triangle.

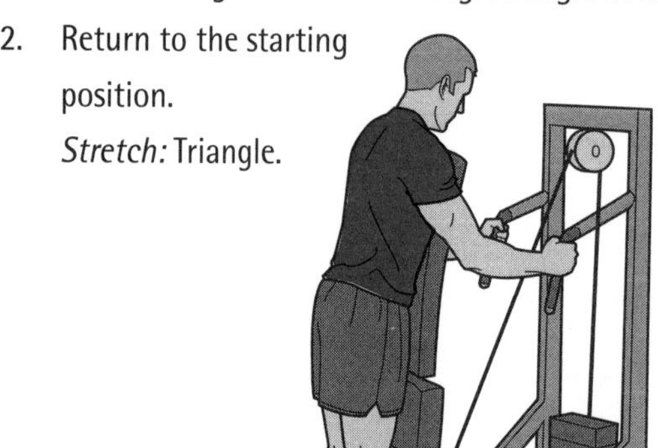

FIGURE 12.9
Leg Curl

ABDOMINAL WITH TWIST

RECTUS ABDOMINUS, EXTERNAL OBLIQUE

This is a core exercise to improve the transfer of energy from the upper to the lower body.

1. Sit on a decline board with the knees bent at about 90 degrees and the ankles held firmly in place.
2. The arms are crossed over the chest and may hold a weight plate.
3. Lower the upper body to about a 45-degree angle from parallel with the floor.
4. Return to the starting position with a twist. With each repetition, alternate looking over the right and left shoulders as the torso twists to the right and left.
   Stretch: Arch the back and extend the arms and legs.

FIGURE 12.10

Abdominal with Twist

LAT PULL-DOWN

LATISSIMUS DORSI, BICEPS

Just as with the chest press, the lat pull-down stabilizes the shoulder.

1. Grasp a straight bar with the arms fully extended and the hands placed about as wide apart as they would be on the handlebars.
2. Pull the bar toward the upper chest (not behind the head).
3. Minimize both movement at the waist and rocking back and forth to start the weight moving. Keep the body still, using the back muscles to stabilize this position.
4. Return to the starting position.
   Stretch: Pull-down.

FIGURE 12.11

Lat Pull-down

STANDING ROW

DELTOIDS, TRAPEZIUS, BICEPS

The standing row stabilizes the shoulder and improves the ability to lift the front wheel when clearing obstacles.

1. At the low-pulley station, or with a barbell or dumbbells, grasp the bar at thigh height with the hands as wide apart as they would be on the handlebars.
2. Pull the bar to the chest.
3. Return to the starting position.

   Stretch: Grasp a stationary object, such as a pole, behind the lower back with the hands as high as possible. Lean away from the pole, allowing the body to sag while relaxing.

FIGURE 12.12

Standing Row

COMPLEX TRAINING

One of the most effective ways to build muscular power is with plyometrics, a form of exercise involving explosive movements, such as jumping over or onto a high box. Including such exercises in your weekly training routine can be quite effective; the problem is that it takes more time than most of us have available. When you're already riding and lifting weights, adding one or two more workouts to the week is close to impossible. The answer is to combine plyometrics and weights into one session. This is known as "complex training."

Complex training not only saves time but also magnifies the benefit of the plyometrics. This is because lifting weights stimulates the nervous system to activate more muscle fibers for a few minutes following an exercise. And activating large numbers of muscle fibers during a plyometrics exercise means higher power generation. Combining the two disciplines into one workout radically improves power. This means less effort to ride at any given power output.

There's one complex exercise I've found to be very effective for improving power. It's a combination of hip extensions, plyometrics, and on-bike sprints. Here's how it's done.

COMBINATION EXERCISE

1. Do one SM set of a favorite hip-extension exercise (squat, leg press, or step-up). Proceed immediately with box jumps.
2. Do 20 box jumps. Stand on the floor facing a sturdy box. The box should be as high as possible, in order to jump onto it from a crouched position. Jump up, landing on the box with both feet, and then step down. *Do not do these in rapid succession.* Take a little time stepping down. Recovery is critical to building muscle power. If 20 are not possible, then there was not enough recovery.
3. Immediately after the last box jump go to a stationary bike and do five standing 30-second sprints at maximum effort with high resistance at a cadence 60 to 70 rpm. Sit down and spin easily to recover for 60 seconds. If possible, use your road bike on an indoor trainer instead of a stationary bike.
4. Do three sets of the above, alternating between hip extensions, box jumps, and bike sprints. This complex training session is best done in the Base 2 period eight to twelve times over four to six weeks.

FIGURE 12.14

Box Jump

13

STRETCHING

It doesn't get any easier; you just get faster.
—GREG LEMOND

PHYSIOLOGICALLY SPEAKING, cycling is not a perfect sport. (Then again, no sport is.) The repetitive movements of cycling cause a shortening and tightening of certain muscles. Leg muscles lose elasticity because they do not go through a full range of motion when pedaling—the leg stops both before reaching full extension and before complete flexion. Muscular tension affects the back, neck, arms, and shoulders on rides lasting several hours with little change of position. Such tightness can hold you back.

A good example of how tight muscles can limit your performance involves the hamstring muscle on the back of the upper leg. Of all the tightness that can result from cycling, this may be the most debilitating. Tight hamstrings restrain the leg during the downstroke. In this condition, they work to prevent the leg from straightening, and in so doing reduce the force produced by the leg. In an attempt to alleviate the tension felt in the back of the leg, the affected cyclist will often lower his or her saddle. A saddle that is set too low further reduces force generation, which in turn reduces power output.

Tight hamstrings can also contribute to a tight lower back, which haunts some riders on long rides as they wonder when it might lock up, forcing them to abandon a hard workout or race. Off the bike, this lower-back tightness may become lower-back pain. The solution to the problem of tight hamstrings is not to lower the saddle, or to live at the mercy of your back pain, but to incorporate regular stretching into your training plan so that you can avoid developing the tight muscles to begin with.

BENEFITS OF STRETCHING

A consistent and effective program of stretching can prevent or at least alleviate many such problems. Prevention is always more comfortable, less time consuming, and less expensive than treatment.

A study of 1,543 runners in the Honolulu Marathon found that those who stretched regularly following workouts had fewer injuries than those who did not stretch. Note that I said "following" workouts—in this same study, those who stretched only *before* workouts had the highest rate of injuries.

Stretching after workouts appears to aid the recovery process by improving the uptake of amino acids by the muscle cells. It therefore promotes protein synthesis within muscle cells, which is necessary for full and quick recovery, and maintains the integrity of muscle cells.

Stretching after a workout can take as few as 15 minutes, and you can do it while downing a recovery drink and chatting with your training partners. This is the optimum time to work on flexibility because your muscles are warm and supple after riding.

Another important time to stretch is during strength workouts. The act of forcefully contracting muscles against resistance in a weight lifting workout creates extreme tightness. As described in the previous chapter, following each strength set in the weight room you should stretch the muscles that were just used in any particular exercise. Correctly doing a strength workout means spending more time stretching in the gym than lifting weights.

Stretching a little bit throughout the day may also be beneficial to long-term flexibility and performance, though this is only an anecdotal observation; there's no research yet to back this up. But while sitting at a desk working or reading, you can gently stretch major muscle groups such as the hamstrings and calves. Work on flexibility while watching television, standing in line, talking with friends, and first thing in the morning when you are still in bed. After a while, you may make it such an integral part of your life that you no longer even think about stretching. It just happens. That's when your flexibility will be at its peak.

STRETCHING MODELS

Over the past forty years, four stretching methods have gained (and sometimes lost) popularity.

BALLISTIC

When I was in college in the 1960s, ballistic stretching was common. Bouncing movements were thought to be the best way to make muscles longer. Later we learned that this technique had just the opposite effect—muscles resisted lengthening and could even be damaged by overly motivated stretchers. Today almost no one stretches this way.

STATIC

Californian Bob Anderson refined a different stretching method in the 1970s, and in 1980 he released a book called *Stretching*. Anderson's approach involved static stretching with little or no movement. He instructed people to simply stretch the muscle to a level of slight discomfort and then hold it in that position for several seconds. Static stretching remains the most popular style today.

PNF

Another method also surfaced about the same time as static stretching, but it did not receive much exposure or support until the 1990s. Several university studies going back to the early 1970s found it to be 10 to 15 percent more effective than static stretching. This approach, called "proprioceptive neuromuscular facilitation," or PNF, has started to catch on over the past few years.

There are many variations on PNF stretching, some being quite complex. Here are the steps in one easy-to-follow version:

1. Static-stretch the muscle for about eight seconds.
2. Contract the same muscle for about eight seconds. (Leave out the contraction step when stretching between sets of strength training. Instead, hold static stretches for about fifteen seconds.)
3. Static-stretch the muscle again for about eight seconds.
4. Continue alternating contractions with stretches until you have done four to eight static stretches. Always finish with a static stretch.

You should find that the static stretches become deeper with each repeat as the muscles seem to loosen up. Using the PNF method, each stretch would take one to two minutes, slightly longer than static stretching.

ACTIVE-ISOLATED

A relatively new arrival on the fitness scene, active-isolated stretching involves brief, assisted stretches that are repeated several times. These stretches are usually performed lying down, when the targeted muscles are not bearing weight or otherwise actively engaged. Here is a typical routine:

1. Contract the opposing muscle group as you move into a stretching position.
2. Use your hands, a rope, or a towel to enhance the stretch.
3. Stretch to the point of light tension.
4. Hold for two seconds and then release.
5. Return to the starting position and relax for two seconds.
6. Do one or two sets of eight to twelve repetitions of each two-second stretch.

YOGA

Yoga has been around for thousands of years, but Western athletes have only used it since the 1970s. Starting with runners, it has grown to become a popular form of improving strength and flexibility in all sports. Countless cyclists have found that yoga not only improves their range of motion but also helps with core strength and balance, both of which are sorely lacking in many—if not most—riders. The best way to get started in yoga is to sign up for a class, such as one offered by a yoga center, health club, YMCA, or city recreation department. There are many different types of yoga, some more effective than others for athletes. For more information, refer to *The Athlete's Guide to Yoga* by Sage Rountree (VeloPress 2008).

POWER YOGA

Also sometimes called "Ashtanga," "Vinyasa," or "Flow" yoga, this is generally the preferred type of yoga for athletes. Based on a series of fast-moving poses, this type of yoga is also designed to raise your heart rate. The poses focus on strength, balance, and flexibility. It may take a few lessons to master the poses. Look for an instructor who offers corrections, guiding students into the proper positions as they learn the poses.

HATHA YOGA

This is a popular type of yoga for beginners and provides an excellent way to release stress. The poses are easy to master and involve slower, more fluid movements than in power yoga. Hatha yoga focuses less on strength and more on breathing, relaxation, and meditation. It would be a good class to take as an introduction to yoga, for a recovery day, or after a hard workout.

BIKRAM YOGA

Sometimes called "hot" yoga, Bikram yoga is performed in a humid room heated to a temperature of up to 105 degrees Fahrenheit. The hot, humid room is intended to make the muscles warm and limber so as to avoid injury. The heat also causes the body to sweat heavily, which is thought to help release toxins. Although this type of yoga has become popular in recent years, I don't recommend it for athletes because the sauna-type setting may have a dehydrating effect.

CYCLING STRETCHES

The following are a few of the many possible stretches for cyclists. You may find that some are more applicable to your specific needs than others. These are the ones to focus on every day and every time you ride. You should also blend some of these with your strength training in the gym. Those combinations are indicated here and also with the strength exercise illustrations in Chapter 12. I recommend following this stretching order at the end of every workout; you can even do most of these stretches while holding your bike for balance.

STORK STAND

QUADRICEPS

Use this stretch in the weight room during the hip-extension and seated-knee-extension exercises.

1. While balancing against your bike or a wall, grasp your left foot behind your back with your right hand.
2. Static-stretch by gently pulling your hand up and away from your butt.
3. Keep your head up and stand erect—do not bend over at the waist.
4. Contract by pushing against your hand with your foot, gently at first.
5. Repeat with the other leg.

FIGURE 13.1

Stork Stand

TRIANGLE

HAMSTRINGS

Use this stretch in the weight room during the hip-extension and leg-curl exercises.

1. Bend over at the waist while leaning on your bike or a wall.
2. Place the leg to be stretched forward with the foot about 18 inches from the bike.
3. The other leg is directly behind the first. The farther back you place this leg, the greater the stretch.
4. With your weight on the front foot, sag your upper body toward the floor. You should feel the stretch in the hamstring of your forward leg.
5. Contract the forward leg by trying to pull it backward against the floor. There will be no movement.
6. Repeat with the other leg.

FIGURE 13.2

Triangle

PULL-DOWN

LATISSIMUS DORSI, TRAPEZIUS, PECTORALIS, TRICEPS

In the weight room, do this stretch with seated lat pulls to chest, chest press, and seated rows.

1. Hold on to your bike or a railing for balance, with your weight resting on your arms.
2. Allow your head to sag deeply between outstretched arms to create a stretch in your lats.
3. To contract, pull down with your arms.

FIGURE 13.3
Pull-down

SQUAT

LOWER BACK, CALVES, QUADRICEPS, GLUTEUS

Do this stretch during back-extension strength exercises in the weight room.

1. Using your bike or a railing for balance, squat down while keeping your heels on the floor. (This is easier with your cycling shoes off.)
2. Allow your butt to sag close to your heels as you rock forward. Hold this position for about 30 seconds. (There is no contraction for this stretch.)

FIGURE 13.4
Squat

WALL LEAN

CALVES

Use this stretch in the weight room during the heel-raise exercise.

1. Lean against a wall with the leg to be stretched straight behind you and the other forward holding most of your weight.
2. Keep the heel of the rear foot on the floor with the toe pointed forward.
3. The farther forward your hips move, the greater the stretch in your calf.
4. To contract the calf, push against the wall as if trying to push it away using your leg.
5. Repeat with the other leg.

FIGURE 13.5

Wall Lean

TWISTER

PECTORALIS

Use this stretch in the weight room during the push-up exercise.

1. With your back facing a wall, grasp a stationary object at shoulder height.
2. Look away from the arm being stretched and twist your body away from it.

FIGURE 13.6

Twister

14

UNIQUE NEEDS

I'm a 42-year-old in a 20-year-old's body.
—KENT BOSTICK, OLYMPIAN AT AGE 42
AND AGAIN AT AGE 46

WOULDN'T IT BE EASY if there was a "training formula"? Sometimes I wish there was. Every day I get questions from athletes asking how they should do this or that in their training. They typically tell me their ages, how long they have been in the sport, and their categories. Then they present a training problem to me along with a question of how they should deal with it. I guess most athletes believe there is a body of information out there someplace that allows me to simply answer these questions much as a skilled auto mechanic might do when asked about an old Chevy that burns oil. It isn't that easy.

On the other hand, I think it's good that we don't have such a one-size-fits-all training formula. That would take all of the fun out of the individualized experience of training. As I've said throughout this book, training is as much an art as a science. A unique blending of personal experiences with research produces an "art form" called performance. While science can postulate and predict a lot about what to expect when certain elements of human physiology and exercise are combined, it is not even close to being able to state with certainty the outcomes of a given training program for a given individual. In the final analysis, every athlete is different and must experiment to find what works best in his or her own training. That's what makes it interesting.

Much of what is presented in this chapter is based on my experiences as a coach and not solely on scientific research. I have coached male and female athletes, both young and old—and with widely varying experience levels—since 1971. With each of those athletes I've had to make some adjustments in training—no two followed exactly the same program. Some of the adjustments were small, while others were significant. This chapter summarizes the most important factors specific to the training of women, masters, juniors, and novices.

WOMEN

Throughout most of the twentieth century there were few sports that women were officially allowed to compete in on a scale even approaching that of men. They were "protected." The most popular—and "ladylike"—sports throughout most of this period were tennis, golf, gymnastics, and figure skating. At about midcentury, women began challenging the restrictions placed on them, especially when it came to endurance sports. As a result, women made considerable progress toward full acceptance in endurance sports in the latter years of the century.

The change was quite evident in the sport of track and field. In the 1928 Olympic Games in Amsterdam, for example, the longest race in which women were allowed to compete was the 800-meter run. In that Olympiad, three female runners broke the world record for the distance, but they finished in "such a distressed condition" that officials were horrified and dropped the event from future competition. "Women just weren't meant to run that far" was the position of many male officials and even scientists. It wasn't until the 1964 Tokyo Games that the women's 800-meter run was resurrected in the Olympics.

Cycling has had its ups and downs when it comes to equality of the sexes but has generally reflected the same attitudes. In the 1890s, the "Golden Age" of cycling, at a time when society often closeted and sheltered the "weaker sex," women were nonetheless accepted into mass-start races alongside men. It wasn't until many years later that this attitude of near-equality changed and women were discouraged from racing bikes. Then, in the last few decades of the twentieth century, attitudes began to shift again.

A couple of years ago, a particularly thorough female professional cyclist was interviewing me as a potential coach. One of the questions she asked was a good one: Is there any difference between the way men and women should train? My answer was simple: No. Perhaps it was too simple. There are some things women can do differently than men to improve their performance.

There is no getting around the obvious male-female differences. Wider hips, shorter torsos relative to leg length, and a lower center of gravity all certainly affect the equipment a woman uses. There are other differences as well. Numerous studies have demonstrated that elite women athletes have aerobic capacities somewhat lower than those of elite men. The highest VO_2max ever recorded for a man was 94 ml/kg/min, whereas the highest recorded for a woman was 77 ml/kg/min—both were Nordic skiers. In comparison with male athletes, women riders carry a higher percentage of body weight as fat, and as a result of their smaller muscle mass, they generate less absolute force. These differences result in about a 10 percent variance in the results of world-class competitions involving males and females in events ranging from weight lifting to sprinting to endurance sports like bike racing.

In the real world of racing, there are actually more similarities between male and female athletes at comparable levels of sport than there are differences. Women are capable of training at the same volume levels as men, and they respond to training in essentially the same ways. Except for absolute magnitude of workload, there is not much difference in the way the two sexes should train. But women have some opportunities for improvement that men usually do not have. Here are five that may give them an edge over the competition.

QUANTITY VERSUS QUALITY

Women are fully capable of training at the same volume as men, but do they need to? Women's races typically evolve in a way unlike men's. First of all, women's road races aren't as long—sometimes no more than half the men's distance. I have no hard evidence to back this up, but it seems that women's races are therefore more likely to end in a pack sprint. But then a rider, or better, a couple of riders, who are strong enough to break from the women's field early in the race are more likely to stay off the front and finish ahead of the field than in a men's race.

What all of this means is that women road racers should concentrate more on the quality of their training than on their mileage. Not that building an aerobic base with long, steady rides is unimportant—it certainly is. Women, however, must place more emphasis than men on developing muscular endurance, power, and anaerobic endurance for the unique demands of their shorter and relatively faster races. A female racer who shifts her training emphasis from volume to working on these abilities is likely to see results in her race performance.

STRENGTH

The average woman's total body strength is about two-thirds of the average man's, but that difference isn't distributed equally. Women are relatively stronger in their legs and weaker in the abdominal region and arms. This comparison indicates where a woman's greatest opportunity for improvement lies. By increasing the strength of her arms and abdominal region, a woman racer can improve her climbing and sprinting ability relative to her competition. Powerful riding out of the saddle requires strength to stabilize the upper body against the torque applied by the legs. Spaghetti arms and an accordion abdominal muscle dissipate the force produced by the legs.

Upper-body strength work to improve this relative weakness involves pushing and pulling exercises that use all of the arm joints plus the back and the abdominals. Abdominal strength also needs emphasizing due to the larger size and wider shape of the female pelvis. Whenever possible, women should work the arms in conjunction with the abdominal and back muscles rather than in isolation. The seated-row exercise described in Chapter 12 is a good example of a multijoint exercise that benefits cycling. This station builds the arms and back much in the same way that climbing on a bike does. The chest press also provides muscular balance.

I generally recommend that women riders continue to lift weights year-round, scaling back to once a week during the summer racing months. Otherwise, a female athlete can quickly lose the benefits of her entire winter of focused weight-room work.

PSYCHOLOGY

Society expects less of women in sports and offers less—less media coverage, less prize money, less crowd support, and less time to train due to greater family responsibilities. That women make it in the sport anyway is a testament to their perseverance and dedication.

Despite the sociocultural obstacles, I have found that women tend to have a somewhat healthier view of winning and losing than men do. Since women typically strive to attain personal standards and are less preoccupied with defeating other riders, they are less devastated by losing and recover faster emotionally. Men take losing, when they feel they should have won, as a mark against their "manhood."

Women, however, carry even heavier and deeper psychological baggage than men in another area. Women are more likely to associate poor performance with lack of ability. After all, society taught most women that sports were for boys, and that girls were not particularly good at them. When men have a bad race, they tend to view the problem as a lack of effort—ability is not the issue.

Confidence is as important for success in sports as physical ability. No matter how talented you are, if you don't believe you can perform well, you won't. A female cyclist I once coached demonstrated this principle. She often felt she could not achieve high goals and generally thought of herself as inferior to the other women she raced with. She would comment on her limitations and failures. A lack of confidence was her greatest limiter.

I suggested that every night after turning the lights off and before falling asleep, she use those few minutes in bed to review and relive the biggest success of her day, no matter how small it seemed. It could simply be that she finished a tough workout feeling strong, that she climbed one hill particularly well, or that one interval felt especially good. She would recapture that experience in her mind and go to sleep feeling good about her ability.

I also told her to act as if she was the best rider in the peloton. Look at the best riders in your group. How do they sit on their bikes, talk with others, and generally behave? Mimic their behaviors by sitting proudly and confidently on the bike, by looking others in the eye when talking with them, and by acting as if you were the best woman in the field. It's amazing how the mind reacts when the body says, "I'm confident."

I knew that she had a voice in her head that was frequently telling her she was not any good. We all hear this voice from time to time. I told her that when she heard the voice starting to put her down, she should regain control of her mind immediately by mentally reliving her latest, greatest success. I reminded her again and again never to let the voice take control of her mind.

That year she had her best season ever, winning a national championship and finishing fifth at the world championship. It's hard to know exactly what the impetus was for her obviously improved confidence, but I believe part of it came from simply looking for success in her daily rides, acting as if she were the top rider, and taking control of her mind.

DIET

To counteract a greater propensity to store body fat, women athletes tend to restrict their caloric intake, especially from foods high in fat and protein. And yet it has been proven that endurance athletes need a higher protein intake than the population at large. A low-protein diet can not only cause a decline in aerobic capacity but also produce fatigue and anemia in women cyclists.

Many women cyclists consume fewer than 2,000 calories a day even though they require more than 3,000. With an average of 5 milligrams of iron per 1,000 calories in the typical American diet, a female athlete may only be getting 10 milligrams daily, but she needs 15 milligrams. The vegetarian diets favored by many women athletes are even lower in iron and provide a less absorbable type of iron. Exercise and menstruation further decrease iron levels. Over the course of several weeks, borderline iron deficiency or even anemia can creep up on a female athlete. Owen Anderson, Ph.D., the publisher of *Running Research News,* estimates that 30 percent of women athletes have an iron deficiency. One study linked low iron with an increase in running injuries in high school girls.

Eating more calories and including red meat are two easy solutions to these dilemmas, although they are not popular ones for many women. There are other ways to improve iron intake and absorption, including eating high-iron-content foods in combination with orange juice or vitamin C to boost iron absorption, eating certain foods such as spinach, and cooking acidic tomato sauces in an iron skillet. It may also be a good idea to talk with a health-care provider about supplementing with iron. Don't take an iron supplement without medical guidance, however. It is also wise to avoid food products that hinder iron absorption, such as tea, wheat bran, antacids, and calcium phosphate supplements. Women, indeed all riders, should have their blood tested in the winter during their annual physical to check their iron level. The symptoms of iron deficiency include loss of endurance, chronic fatigue, high exercise heart rate, low power, frequent injury, and recurring illness. Since many of these symptoms are also common to overtraining, the athlete may cut back on exercise, feel better, and return to training only to find an almost immediate relapse.

Dietary fat is also necessary for peak performance. A body deprived of essential fats is in danger of becoming run-down and susceptible to illness as a result of a weakened immune system. If you are sick, injured, or tired, you can't perform at your best. Include fat in your diet every day from good sources such as nuts, nut spreads, avocados, and canola and olive oil. Continue to avoid saturated fat and trans-fatty acids, which are found in foods with hydrogenated fat, such as snack foods and prepackaged meals. Chapter 16 provides more details on the athlete's diet.

CONTRACEPTIVES AND PERFORMANCE

A study at the University of Illinois showed that women who take birth control pills may have an advantage in endurance sports such as cycling. During long endurance runs at a low intensity, women taking oral contraceptives showed an increase in growth hormone. They used significantly fewer carbohydrates and more fat for fuel than women who were not taking the pill. This suggests that using oral contraceptives may improve a woman's capacity for burning fat, may allow her to get into shape faster, and may extend her endurance range in races. I am not aware of any other studies that have tested this finding, so the results should be taken with some reservation.

If you are not currently using an oral contraceptive, talk with your health-care provider before starting. Don't take the pill only for race-performance reasons.

MASTERS

Several years ago I spoke at an American College of Sports Medicine workshop in New York City. The topic for the workshop was masters athletes—those over the age of 40. For two hours before my presentation I listened as one doctor after another talked about "normal" performance declining with aging.

When I finally got my turn to speak, I was beginning to think we were all supposed to give up sports as we got older. I told the audience not to believe half of what they had been hearing. The reason people slow down so much after age 40 is not as much physiology as it is psychology. We think we should be slower.

I reminded the audience of 41-year-old Eamonn Coghlan, the first person over 40 to run a mile in under four minutes. He didn't do this by reading statistics on what is supposed to happen with age. I pointed to 40-year-old Dave Scott, who was planning a comeback at that year's Ironman—not just to finish, but to win (he finished second). Then there's 41-year-old Dara Torres and her amazing performance defeating swimmers less than half her age at the 2008 Beijing Olympics. At age 43, Dave Wiens outbiked Floyd Landis to win the Leadville 100, then beat Lance Armstrong the following year. Marathoner Dean Karnazes was 44 when he ran 50 marathons in 50 days. And Kent Bostick, 42, surprised everyone by qualifying for the 1996 Olympics, defeating 28-year-old Mike McCarthy by nearly one second in the 4,000-meter pursuit (Bostick qualified again for the 2000 Olympics at age 46).

These aging athletes are just the tip of the iceberg. There are hundreds of masters in the world of sport who are within seconds or inches of their best performances of all time. In the past 20 years, there has been tremendous growth in the number of USA Cycling (USAC) members who are over 40. From 1984 to 1993 there was a 75 percent increase in the number of members in their forties. In 1996, 20 percent of USAC racers were over 40. What just 20 years ago was a young man's sport has become a sport for both sexes and all ages.

ABILITY AND AGE

There's no denying that there's a loss of ability for racing with advancing age. The best indicators of this in road cycling are age-group records for the individual time trial (ITT). The 40 km records reveal an average slowing of 20 seconds per year, about 0.6 percent, after the age of 35. For the 20 km, ITT times slow about 12 seconds per year from ages 20 to 65—a 0.7 percent decline per decade of life.

These small drops in performance result from continuing losses of the three basic abilities—endurance, force, and speed skills. Although longitudinal studies of highly trained athletes are few and far between, it appears that the decline in each of these abilities is similar to what the ITT records show—about 6 percent per decade. That is far lower than the expected decline of 10 percent per decade that is found in the "normal" population after age 25.

Scientists have been studying the link between aging and physiological function since the 1930s. One inescapable conclusion has come from this research: Getting older inevitably means some degree of reduced function. Aerobic capacity (VO_2max) decline is a good example. You may recall from Chapter 4 that aerobic capacity is a measure of how much oxygen the body uses to produce energy at a maximal workload. The higher one's aerobic capacity, the greater his or her potential for performance in bike racing and other aerobic sports. Studies show that at about age 20, aerobic capacity begins to drop in the general population, in part because maximum heart rate decreases. A lowered maximum heart rate means less oxygen delivery to the muscles, and therefore a lowered aerobic capacity. The usual rate of decline measured in such research is in the range of six to ten beats per decade.

Similar results have come from aging studies on the pulmonary, nervous, muscular, thermal regulatory, immune, and anaerobic systems: Sometime in the third and fourth decades of life (ages 20 to 39), functional decreases begin to occur, with losses of up to 10 percent per decade. Compounding the problem is what appears to be a normal increase in body fat after the early twenties, obviously made worse by a sedentary lifestyle. Again, this is for the general population—not those who race bikes or are highly active.

Flexibility is also lost with age. This is in part due to a drop in the amount of body fluids the body can store in later life. An aging immune system doesn't work as well as it once did, either—a good reason to eat a diet rich in micronutrients such as antioxidants. Then there's heat. Getting older means not sweating as much as a younger athlete in hot, dry conditions, yet older athletes' urinary systems are more effective at flushing water. To make matters worse, the thirst mechanism isn't as sensitive as it once was. All of this means a decreased blood volume and a greater likelihood of overheating and becoming dehydrated.

THE AGING MYTH

A little skepticism is a healthy thing when it comes to evaluating research. Most studies of aging are based on "cross-sectional" analysis. This means, for example, that a group of 30-year-olds and a similar group of 40-year-olds are tested for some parameter of fitness, and the difference is assumed as the normal loss.

The alternative is "longitudinal" research, which involves following a group of subjects for several years, testing regularly to see how they change. This method has many benefits. Time is an obvious downside, however, adding to the difficulty and expense of a study, so few longitudinal studies of athletes are conducted.

Research on aging also raises the question of who the subjects are. Many studies that attempt to look specifically at athletes instead of a general cross section of the population characterize the subjects as "trained endurance athletes." This vague description is usually based on measures of training volume, such as years of activity or hours of training in a week. Definitions vary. One study's trained endurance athlete may be another study's novice. Seldom is the intensity of training used to categorize the groups studied, as it is hard to quantify. But since it appears that intensity is the key to maintaining race fitness, this is a crucial issue.

The few longitudinal studies that have been done show that when the intensity of training is maintained, aerobic capacity and other selected measures of fitness decline as little as 2 percent per decade. This is roughly a third to a fifth of what is usually discovered in sedentary subjects, or even in those who maintain their health and continue exercising at low intensities.

The "normal" decline in performance of 6 to 10 percent per decade is probably more a result of self-imposed training and lifestyle limitations than of human physiology. Aging may actually only account for a fourth of the losses, while disuse takes the bigger bite.

BEATING THE CURVE

Although slowing down with age to some extent may be inevitable beyond some number of years, many riders have found that the rate of decline can be dramatically reduced by a willingness to train with the same high intensity and volume as they did when they were younger. In fact, some of the top masters riders are even doing more now than in previous decades. Several scientific studies have shown that it's possible for an athlete to maintain aerobic capacity, a good indicator of fitness, well into his or her fifties.

The bottom line is that intense training keeps the heart, nerves, muscles, lungs, and other systems all working to their genetic potential. If you never exercise at high intensity, you will lose fitness, and possibly health, more rapidly than necessary. Even if average fitness does decline incrementally with aging among athletes as a group, that does not mean that your personal fitness must decline. Many older athletes improve their individual fitness through the years by training harder and training smarter. For those beyond the age of 40, the following training guidelines will help to keep fitness high.

TRAINING IMPLICATIONS

How willing and able are you to train as much as you did when younger—or even more? Here are some suggestions for improving your racing even as you get older.

- Keep strength training year-round. Although younger and more naturally muscular athletes can stop strength training in the late winter and maintain muscle mass during the race season, masters should continue throughout the year. The stronger you are, the more force you can apply to the pedal. Greater strength means lower perceived exertions at all levels of power output.
- Train a minimum of 7 to 10 hours a week on average throughout the year. That means a minimum annual volume of 350 to 500 hours.
- Take a full twelve weeks in the Base period. Don't cut this period short. You must maximize your endurance, force, and speed skills before upping the intensity. Be sure to stay proficient at spinning at high cadences.
- Once you have established your base fitness, put less emphasis than younger riders do on endurance, since older athletes have more years of training behind them and therefore greater depth of endurance fitness. Focus more on power, anaerobic endurance, and muscular endurance. That means greater attention to jumps, sprints, intervals, and time trialing than to long workouts. Your longest ride should be only as long as your longest race time.
- After you have established your base, allow for more recovery time between workouts than in the past. Few masters can handle more than two or three high-quality work-outs a week and get away with it for long. Many masters have found it possible to race quite well on two breakthrough workouts a week. For example, in the Build period, at midweek combine a muscular endurance workout with anaerobic endurance or power, doing the faster portion first. Then recover for two or three days and complete a high-intensity group ride or tune-up race on the weekend. Take at least one day off the bike every week. If you find recovery to be especially difficult, modify your weekly training hours so that you have only two weeks between recovery weeks instead of three (see Table 8.5). Omit the first week in each case. You may find that with only two weeks of hard training, you need only five days or so of recovery before starting the next cycle. So consider training with a pattern of sixteen days of hard training followed by five days of R&R. Or maybe you'll find

that a 15-6 pattern works best at certain times of the season. This will take some experimentation.

- Train in the heat once or twice a week during the summer, including higher-intensity workouts on hot days once you feel adapted. Be especially cautious with your levels of hydration. Drink a 16-ounce bottle of sports drink every hour during a ride whether you feel like it or not. Sip water throughout the day even if you don't feel thirsty.
- Stretch after every workout and again later in the day. Try to become more flexible now than you've been in years. You can do it if you are dedicated.
- In road races, stay in the front third from the start. The wide range in abilities and experience levels at masters races tends to cause the groups to break up sooner than they do in senior races.

DIET, AGING, AND MUSCLE

Popeye was right: Eating spinach can make you stronger and more muscular, especially if you're over age 50. Let me explain.

As we grow older, muscle mass is lost. Although this loss is slowed somewhat by weight lifting and vigorous aerobic exercise, it still happens. Even athletes in their sixties typically demonstrate considerably less muscle than they had in their forties.

Now there is research that shows why. Nitrogen, an essential component of muscle protein, is given up by the body at a faster rate than it can be taken in as we get older. This is due to a gradual change in kidney function that comes with aging, ultimately producing an acidic state in the blood. Essentially, we are peeing off our muscles as we pass the half-century mark in life.

Also, with a net loss of nitrogen, new muscle cannot be formed. This same acidic state of the blood explains why calcium is lost with aging, resulting in osteoporosis for many, especially women, with advanced age.

The key to reducing, or even avoiding, this situation is to lower the blood's acid level and increase its alkalinity. There are studies demonstrating that taking a supplement called potassium bicarbonate daily for as few as 18 days increases the blood's alkaline level by balancing nitrogen in the body. While it can be purchased relatively inexpensively in laboratory supply shops, potassium bicarbonate is not currently available as an over-the-counter supplement, and there are no long-term studies of its effects on health. There is some evidence that it contributes to irregular electrocardiogram (ECG) readings.

But there is also a natural way of achieving this same result through diet by eating foods that increase the blood's alkalinity—fruits and vegetables. Fats and oils have a neutral effect on blood acid. In other words, they don't make it either more acidic or more alkaline. All other foods, including grains, meats, nuts, beans, dairy, fish, and eggs, increase the blood's acidity. If your diet is high in these foods but low in fruits and vegetables, you can expect to lose muscle mass and bone calcium as you age.

A 1995 study by T. Remer and F. Manz ranked foods in terms of their effect on blood acidity and alkalinity. They found, for example, that among the foods they studied, parmesan cheese had the most acidic effect, and therefore contributed the most to a loss of nitrogen and ultimately muscle mass. The food they found to have the greatest alkaline effect, thus reducing nitrogen loss and muscle loss the most, was the humble raisin. Among vegetables, spinach was the most alkaline food. See what I mean? Popeye was right.

Table 14.1 ranks a sampling of the common foods (per 100-gram portions) that Remer and Manz studied and their effect on alkalinity and acidity. The higher a food's

TABLE 14.1

Acidic Ranking of Common Foods

ACID FOODS (+)	3.5-oz (100-g) SERVING
Grains	
Brown rice	+12.5
Rolled oats	+10.7
Whole wheat bread	+8.2
Spaghetti	+6.5
Corn flakes	+6.0
White rice	+4.6
Rye bread	+4.1
White bread	+3.7
Dairy	
Parmesan cheese	+34.2
Processed cheese	+28.7
Hard cheese	+19.2
Gouda cheese	+18.6
Cottage cheese	+8.7
Whole milk	+0.7
Legumes	
Peanuts	+8.3
Lentils	+3.5
Peas	+1.2
Meats, Fish, Eggs	
Trout	+10.8
Turkey	+9.9
Chicken	+8.7
Eggs	+8.1
Pork	+7.9
Beef	+7.8
Cod	+7.1
Herring	+7.0

ALKALINE FOODS (–)	3.5-oz (100-g) SERVING
Fruits	
Raisins	-21.0
Black currants	-6.5
Bananas	-5.5
Apricots	-4.8
Kiwifruit	-4.1
Cherries	-3.6
Pears	-2.9
Pineapple	-2.7
Peaches	-2.4
Apples	-2.2
Watermelon	-1.9
Vegetables	
Spinach	-14.0
Celery	-5.2
Carrots	-4.9
Zucchini	-4.6
Cauliflower	-4.0
Potatoes	-4.0
Radishes	-3.7
Eggplant	-3.4
Tomatoes	-3.1
Lettuce	-2.5
Chicory	-2.0
Leeks	-1.8
Onions	-1.5
Mushrooms	-1.4
Green peppers	-1.4
Broccoli	-1.2
Cucumber	-0.8

positive acidic ranking, the more likely it is to contribute to a loss of muscle mass and bone-mineral levels. The more negative the food's alkaline ranking, the more beneficial the effect is on these measures.

ATHLETES OVER 60

Everything described in the previous section on masters also applies to the over-60 age group—only more so. Whereas 40-something athletes can still make training mistakes and their bodies may well adapt and forgive them, riders over 60 have to be more careful to avoid pitfalls. This means getting the details exactly right for nutrition, rest and recovery, strength training, volume, intensity, equipment, and everything else that affects health and performance. Errors in judgment at this age can mean unusable joints, surgery, broken bones, and, at the very least, days lost to lingering fatigue.

The good news is that most members of this age category are patient and wise. They see cycling as a lifestyle, not as something to be defeated and vanquished. They're in it for the long haul. Younger athletes could learn a lot from them. If science could figure out how to put a grand master's wisdom into the mind of a 25-year-old physical specimen, it would create the ultimate athlete.

How should the grand master and the senior athlete train? To remain in top shape and to continue racing, they need to continue to challenge the muscular system, in particular. This means that strength training, hill work, and high-intensity efforts must be included regularly, yet spaced widely enough to allow for recovery. Strength training is especially important, and great gains can be made that will benefit not only the older rider's cycling but also his or her life in general. Research with 90-year-olds has found that their rate of improvement in strength is the same as that of 20-year-olds when they are put on a similar resistance-training program. By this age, cycling skills should be well honed. If not, the risk of injury is magnified.

Nutrition must emphasize alkaline-enhancing foods in the vegetable and fruit categories, as described above. The older we are, the more likely we are to have acidic body fluids, which ultimately mean the loss of muscle and bone. See Table 14.1 for more details. In this table the greater the number, indicated by plus (+) or minus (–) indicators, the greater the acidity or alkalinity of the food, respectively.

JUNIORS

In 1982, my son Dirk competed in his first bicycle race at age 12. On that cold September day, he raced three laps around the block in baggy windpants with a big smile on his face and finished dead last. But he was hooked. From this inauspicious start, Dirk went on to win the junior Colorado Road Race Championship and make the U.S. national team. He raced as an amateur in Europe for five years, turned pro at age 22, and continued racing as a pro into his thirties.

HOW TO IMPROVE

As a junior, Dirk was an exceptional athlete, one in whom I saw a great deal of promise. I wanted to coach him, but knew that would not work. A father is a young athlete's worst possible mentor. So I hired Pat Nash, a local coach who specialized in juniors, to work with my son. Dirk's early and continuing success was largely due to Pat's careful nurturing. I was not interested in how many races Dirk could win as a teenager. My major concern, which I expressed to Pat, was that Dirk still be enthusiastically riding, racing, and improving at age 25. A good coach helped to make that possible.

If you are a junior and new to racing, try to find a coach who has a local team and rides along on workouts. You and the coach will get to know each other better that way, and he or she will be better able to help you grow as a racer. Avoid coaches and teams more concerned about winning the next race than about developing the team tactics, skills, and fitness that come from a long-term approach.

Another way to speed up your progress is by attending a camp for juniors. These are usually staffed with one or more coaches and, sometimes, with elite riders. In a few days you can learn a lot about training and racing. Check in the advertising section at the back of cycling magazines and on the Web for camps that may be available in your area. If the only camps in your area are for senior riders, call the camp director and ask what accommodations they would make for training juniors.

Cycling clubs are also good for providing support, expertise, racing experience, and the camaraderie of other juniors. Join a club if there is one in your region, and try to ride with the members as often as you can. You'll learn a lot just from being around more experienced athletes. Also ask the club to provide events for juniors at their sponsored races, if they don't already do so.

On a slightly different note, you and your parents have probably come to realize that cycling is an expensive sport. Don't be concerned with having the latest and greatest frame, wheels, and pedals. Instead, concentrate on becoming the best motor and the most knowledgeable and skilled rider in your category. When it's time to replace a bike that is too small for you, talk with other juniors to see if you can purchase a bike one of them has outgrown. In the same way, see if younger athletes can use your old bike. Regardless of what you may read in the magazines and what others say, the key to improvement is not equipment but fitness, bike-racing savvy, and skills.

TRAINING

Many times junior riders are so enthusiastic about the sport that they try to do too much, training with an intensity that may not support healthy development. When your school sports end for the year and bike training starts, try to keep things in perspective. Remember that you're not an accomplished cyclist yet; there is a lot of room for improvement, and steady growth is necessary if you are to eventually achieve your potential. Professional cyclists didn't start off training with huge volumes and lots of intense workouts. They progressed steadily from year to year, a little at a time. Following are suggested guidelines for maintaining a healthy perspective and steady growth as a junior cyclist. (If you've been riding less than three years, you might find the "Novices" section in this chapter helpful as well.)

By the time you are 17, you and your coach should develop an Annual Training Plan like the one described in Part IV. Prior to this time, your training should be mostly centered on the basic abilities of force, endurance, and speed skills, with occasional races. In your early years as a cyclist, it is best for you to participate in at least one other sport. Even the top champions, such as Miguel Induráin and Lance Armstrong, did this. Lance was a world-class junior triathlete before he took up bike racing. Don't specialize in cycling before the age of 17—your long-term development will be greater for it.

In the first two years of riding, when you are participating in other sports, a total annual training volume in all sports of 200 to 350 hours is best. By age 17, you should be able to increase the volume, if you have been handling that level without difficulty. But do so gradually. More is not always better, and often worse.

Each year the number of races you enter should increase a little until, by age 18, you are racing as often as seniors. When you begin to race, emphasize team tactics more than winning. Learn what it takes to break away, to legally block, to work with other riders in a break, to lead out a teammate, and to sprint. Cycling is much like football or basketball in this respect—teamwork produces greater results than everyone riding only for themselves.

Regardless of your age when you begin to do weight-room strength workouts, the first year should include only the Anatomical Adaptation (AA) phase. Working with both machines and free weights, perfect your lifting form for each exercise in this first season. In the second year of strength training, it's okay to start the Maximum Strength (MS) phase in the weight room. The first time you do the MS phase, use a weight no greater than 80 percent of your estimated one-repetition maximum. Don't worry about finding a one-repetition max, however. Instead, use the guidelines for estimating it from multiple reps as described in Chapter 12. The most common injury that occurs in juniors starting to lift weights is to the lower back. Be careful, and wear a weight belt. By the third year you should be ready to move into more serious weight work, assuming you are at least 17 by then.

Before the start of each season, get a complete physical from your doctor. This is something even the pros do. It will allow you to start the year with a clean bill of health, and if you have a coach, he or she will want to know about any health concerns that may impact your training.

When you purchase a handlebar computer, look for one that displays cadence. It is a useful tool for helping you improve leg speed.

PATIENCE

Remember that you are in bicycle racing for the long haul. That's easy to say, but there will be times when you will want to accelerate the program and do more. Perhaps one of your friends is doing more training than you are, or you are just excited about your progress. But before you change the plan, talk with your coach. Any increase in your training should be done carefully to avoid overtraining and injury.

In his book *Greg LeMond's Complete Book of Bicycling,* LeMond describes how when he was 15 he wanted to ride more because one of his friends was putting in twice as much mileage. He was smart, however, and held back. The next year his friend was out of cycling, and LeMond went on to become one of America's greatest cyclists. Be patient.

HAVE FUN!

Always remember why you race. It certainly isn't for money or glory—these are far more abundant in sports like football and basketball. You're probably racing bikes for the personal challenge, for the enjoyment of having exceptional fitness, and, most of all, for fun. Keep that perspective. Win with humility, lose with dignity, congratulate those who beat you to the finish line—without offering excuses—and learn from mistakes.

NOVICES

Whatever your age, if you have been cycling seriously for less than three years, you are considered a novice. Whatever your reason for accepting the challenge of bicycle racing, it's important for you to know the ingredients for success, especially those that are central to the sport. As with all sports, success in cycling, no matter how it's measured, is only as great as your preparation. Training must steel you to the specific demands of the goal event. For example, a hilly course requires training in the hills, and long races demand great aerobic endurance. In fact, endurance is the single most important requirement of the sport regardless of the race. If you can't go the distance, nothing else matters.

TRAINING TO GO THE DISTANCE

If pressed, most riders will admit that they like training more than racing. Races are merely the carrot on the stick that gets them on the road as soon as they get home from work. Without races, there would be no feeling of necessity or sense of urgency about workouts. Races give focus and direction to training. Workouts, however, are the fun part. That's when you can drop all of the cares of the day and concerns for tomorrow, while living strictly in the present. Riding a bike reduces life to its most basic elements—breathing and movement.

Workouts are also when you may get together with your team or training partners who share common interests. Having partners to train with makes the effort seem easier and boosts motivation. And there will certainly be times when motivation wanes. Even the best in the sport find their desire to work out has highs and lows. This is not a sign of weakness, and may even have self-protection benefits, such as ensuring recovery. But too many workouts missed due to low enthusiasm means erosion of fitness and poor race performance. It is at such times that a training group is most beneficial. So find some other riders who want to do some of the same kinds of rides you are interested in doing—possibly through a local cycling club or by putting the word out for training partners through a local bike shop—and schedule your week to regularly work out with them.

A common mistake that novices make is to bring too much motivation to the sport. Compulsive training is likely to prevent you from achieving goals, as it frequently leads only to injury, illness, burnout, and overtraining. Chapter 2 presented an argument for training with moderation in a sport that appears, at least on the surface, to be extreme at times. At no time in your cycling career is a conservative approach to training more critical than in the early stages of your fitness development. Training with excessive volume and intensity at this time is counterproductive.

So how do you determine what is appropriate? Here are some tips that may provide guidance in your first year of training.

Volume

Are there externally imposed limits on the amount of time you have available to train? For example, if you realistically examine your workday and all other commitments, you may find that it is possible to fit in only one hour each day on the bike, perhaps even less. The weekends probably offer the most time for training. Winter brings fewer daylight hours and foul weather, further reducing training time.

Add up your available weekly hours using a conservative estimate, and multiply by 50 to find your projected annual training volume. This assumes that two weeks will be lost during the year to illness, travel, or other commitments. The number you come up with includes all training time in addition to cycling, such as weight lifting, cross-country skiing and any other crosstraining. Round off your annual hours to the closest 50 hours.

Next, go to Table 8.5 to find a suggested periodization plan for your volume. You may find that it is necessary to slightly increase the lighter training weeks or decrease the high-volume weeks in this table if your restrictions are imposed more by available time than by your physical capacity for training and recovery. Remember that this table is merely a suggested guideline, not a requirement.

Periodization

In your first year of bike racing, it's best to train primarily in the Base periods as described in Chapter 7. This means you will focus on the development of aerobic endurance, force, technique (speed skills), and muscular endurance. These are the most important and basic components of bike-racing fitness and will take a year, possibly more, to hone. There is no reason to build power and anaerobic endurance, the other fitness components, before the basics are well established.

Weekly Routines

There are endless possibilities for organizing your training week depending on time available, work schedule, experience with riding a bike, ability to recover, established group workouts, the times when a weight room is open, and numerous individual lifestyle issues. There is no standard way to arrange the week's workouts. Most new cyclists will find, however, that doing one workout a day, plus taking a weekly day off, produces good results.

Weights

If you have only a few hours to train each week and it is difficult to fit everything in, weight workouts are the first ones to omit so that you may concentrate available time on the bike. Your greatest need at this stage of training is aerobic fitness. If you have time for the gym, and weight training doesn't compromise your on-bike training, use only the Anatomical Adaptation (AA) and Maximum Transition (MT) phases, as discussed in Chapter 12. Concentrate first on perfecting your technique with light weights. You will probably be surprised at how strong you become by doing just this. In the second full year of weight training, you can introduce the other strength building phases.

SKILLS

As a newcomer to the sport of road racing, one of your greatest challenges in the first year will be developing and refining your bicycle skills. Riding with and observing experienced riders with good skills will help you hone yours. The starting point for building skills is getting your bike adjusted correctly by a professional fitter. Once your machine is properly fitted to your body and particular needs, the two basic skills of pedaling and cornering will be much easier to learn.

Pedaling Cadence

Economy in riding a bike is based on an interaction between a human and a machine. How well they fit together is a significant determining factor in selecting an economical cadence. For example, short crankarms favor pedaling at a high cadence, whereas a high saddle position slows the cadence.

The cadence you use determines how you will feel in a race and how effectively you ride. Low cadences, for example, put stress on the knees and muscles and require greater muscular force generation than high cadences. High cadences require great metabolic effort, which causes heavy breathing. This means that a high cadence minimizes muscle

Training Safety

Training for bike racing involves taking risks. Some of the risks you take may even be life-threatening, but you can minimize them by taking certain precautions. For example:

- Always wear a helmet when riding a bike.
- Avoid heavily trafficked areas whenever possible when riding.
- Ride only with safe groups while avoiding groups that run stop signs, ride in traffic, and generally do not obey traffic laws.
- Do not take undue risks on steep descents while riding.
- Make sure your bike is safe before starting a ride by testing your brakes, checking the quick releases to make sure they are tight, examining the tires to see if they have any cuts or show signs of too much wear, and tightening any loose bolts.

Also, if you experience any unusual physical conditions, such as chest pain, radiating arm or neck pain, an unusually high or erratic heart rate, joint soreness, back pain, unusual muscle or tendon discomfort, or blood in the urine, be sure to inform your doctor right away. Such conditions should also cause you to stop the workout immediately. Safety always comes first when riding a bike.

fatigue but may cause you to use more energy, at least until you are better adapted to the level of activity.

Observations of elite riders reveal a common cadence range of about 90 to 100 rpm. This range is also supported by much of the recent research. Studies dating back to 1913 have shown the most economical cadence to vary from 33 to 110 rpm. Recent, more sophisticated studies, however, have tended to favor higher cadences, at least when self-selected by accomplished riders.

The bottom line is that pedaling at a cadence in the range of 90 to 100 rpm on a flat course is probably best. If you typically turn the cranks at a slower rate than this, you should spend you first year focusing on cadence drills to improve your economy. Work on cadences as low as 60 rpm when climbing and as high as 120 rpm when sprinting.

Cornering

Cornering is both a safety and a performance issue. The most common cause of bicycle crashes is poor cornering skills. Improving your cornering skills will help you to maintain a position in the peloton on a course with lots of turns. As you can see in Figure 14.1, there are three ways to handle your bike when cornering—leaning, countersteering, and steering.

Leaning Method. The leaning method is the most common technique used by novice cyclists regardless of the cornering situation. But it is really best when making a wide, sweeping turn on dry, clean pavement. In the United States and other countries where

FIGURE 14.1

Bicycle Cornering Techniques

drivers and cyclists ride on the right side of the road, it is most effective when turning left. For those countries where drivers and cyclists ride on the left, this is the preferred right-turn method. To use the method, simply lean both the bike and your body into the turn with your weight on the outside pedal. If it is truly a wide, sweeping turn, you may be able to continue pedaling.

Countersteering Method. Few new to the sport use the countersteering technique, but it is quite effective for tight turns, such as right-hand turns in ride-on-the-right countries and left-hand turns in ride-on-the-left countries. Countersteering will get you around the corner with a much tighter radius than the leaning method will.

If you've learned countersteering on a motorcycle, the technique is the same. You must stop pedaling as you enter the turn because the bike tilt will be greater than with the leaning method. The inside pedal is up and your body weight is fully on the outside pedal. Here's where it feels counterintuitive: Straighten your arm on the inside of the turn and bend the elbow on the outside of the turn. It seems backward, as you're pushing on the opposite handlebar that you would use for a sweeping turn—in fact, you're actually steering the bike out from under you. This motion breaks the gyroscopic effect of the turning wheels and causes you to lean the bike sharply into the turn as your body stays upright. You will go around the corner on a tight radius. In order for this technique to be effective, your speed must be at least 15 miles per hour (24 kph) or so. It takes practice to make it habitual.

Steering Method. Use this method when cornering on wet pavement or when there is sand or gravel on the road surface. Regardless of whether this is a right or left turn, you will need to slow down. If it is a tight-radius turn, such as a right turn in the United States, you must also stop pedaling. The purpose is to safely get around the corner without falling. The proper method involves keeping the bike upright while leaning only your body into the turn. Keep both knees near the top tube of the bike—do not point your knee at the corner.

Other Cornering Considerations. When riding on wet pavement, reduce your tire pressure by about 25 percent. This will have minimal effect on your overall speed but will provide better traction in corners. The type of tire you use also plays a role when cornering. Tubular tires, also called "sew-ups," corner better than clinchers, as they have round sidewalls, whereas clinchers have flatter sidewalls. Be especially careful when cornering on wet pavement if there is a painted stripe on the road. When wet, this is like riding on ice. The same goes for utility-hole covers—they are extremely slippery when wet. Use extreme caution when cornering on wet pavement on steep descents. Apply your brakes well before you get to the corner to reduce speed. Do not use the brakes when cornering.

15

USING A TRAINING DIARY

The essence of a good training program is managing time.

—CONNIE CARPENTER,
1984 OLYMPIC GOLD MEDALIST, ROAD CYCLING

EVERY ATHLETE HAS a different response to training. If two cyclists test similarly at the outset of their training program, and then do exactly the same workouts day after day, one will eventually become fitter than the other. One may even become overtrained on a regimen that the other thrives on. So it is critical that you follow a program designed just for you. It is equally critical that once you have a plan, you adjust it over time as you learn more about what works—or does not work—for you personally. To do otherwise is to place limits on your potential.

How can you determine what constitutes the optimum training method for your unique needs? Race results and testing can help, because they are fairly objective measures of how you're doing. But these methods do not explain the causes of your performance improvements or declines. Fortunately, there is another way: Often, the causes can be discovered in your training records. Keeping a journal is your third most important task when not working out. It ranks right behind eating and resting.

In addition to offering the opportunity for keener analysis, a journal helps you grow by increasing your motivation. Motivation comes from recording successes. When you achieve a training goal, reach a higher level of training, or do well in a race, making a note of it in your journal can add to the sense of accomplishment you feel.

But be forewarned: Training diaries can be abused. I have known athletes who realized on Sunday afternoon that they were a few miles or minutes short of their weekly goal and felt compelled to go out for a short ride to reach the magic number. This is how you go about building "junk" miles. Becoming overly invested in the numbers that you record causes problems. Instead of using your journal as a scorecard, think of it as a diary—a place for important and personal information.

PLANNING WITH A TRAINING DIARY

The training diary is the best place to record your weekly training plan. Chapters 9 and 10 offered guidance on how to determine what workouts should be done each day. Figures 9.1 and 10.1 recommended a specific daily training structure. The blank training diary pages provided in Appendix D bring the final pieces of the training plan together by providing a space for you to outline your planned workouts each day. Figure 15.1, a sample diary, demonstrates how to log the critical information.

WORK WITH YOUR TRAINING PLAN AND GOALS

It's a good idea to plan the next week's training regimen at the end of each week. After reviewing how the preceding week went, sit down with your Annual Training Plan and jot down what you'll do and when you'll do it. Using the workout codes from Chapter 9 and the workout durations from Table 9.1 makes this quick and easy. Once you get used to it, planning an entire week in detail takes about ten minutes.

You don't have to use my training diary. Many athletes use a simple blank notebook in which they record as much data as they want in any way they want. The only problem with such a system is that it makes recall and analysis laborious, since you may have to search every page for the critical information. A standardized form makes these tasks much easier.

You can also choose to track and monitor your progress online. The Web-based training software available at www.TrainingBible.com offers a free daily workout log to record your workouts and graph your progress. The program also allows you to upload data from training devices such as heart rate monitors and power meters.

At the top of Figure 15.1, there are spaces to write in three weekly goals. These are specific actions you need to accomplish in order to stay on track with your training objectives, which are in turn tied to season goals. Consistent success in achieving short-term, weekly goals brings long-term success.

Weekly goals should focus on what the breakthrough (BT) workout and race objectives are for that week. If you properly selected weekly workouts based on your limiters and strengths, achieving their scheduled outcomes brings you one step closer to the season's goals. For example, if you've scheduled an aerobic endurance intervals (workout code A2) to include five 4-minute segments, building to zone 5b on each, a weekly goal may be "20 minutes of AE intervals." When you accomplish that goal, check it off. By periodically scanning your weekly goals, you can quickly see how you've been doing throughout the year.

WHAT TO RECORD

If you've never kept a journal, you may find record keeping a bit scattered at first. I ask the athletes I coach to record data in their journals in five categories.

- Morning warnings
- Workout basics
- Workout time by zone
- Physical comments
- Mental comments

Morning Warnings

Every morning on waking, your body "whispers" what it can handle that day. The problem is, most of us refuse to listen. A journal helps the body to be heard—if you pay attention to certain indicators of readiness. These are sleep quality, fatigue, stress level, muscle soreness, and heart rate. The first four should be rated on a scale of 1 to 7, with 1 being the best situation (for example, an excellent night's sleep) and 7 the worst (for example, extremely high stress).

Take your pulse while still lying quietly in bed and record it in beats per minute above (positive number) or below (negative number) your average morning pulse rate during an R&R week. If you record a 5, 6, or 7 for any of the first four indicators, or a positive or negative 5 or greater for heart rate, consider that to be a warning that something is wrong.

Another way of taking resting heart rate that has been shown as a more reliable indicator with some athletes is to take a lying-down pulse as described above, and then stand for 20 seconds and take your pulse again. A heart rate monitor is useful here. The variance in difference between the two is the indicator. An example may better explain this method:

Lying-down heart rate	46
Standing heart rate	72
Difference	26

Record your variance from a normal difference. For example, if your average difference over several days during a recovery week is found to be 26, but one day the difference is 32, record a variance of +6—a warning sign for that day. This may be a better warning method for you than simply tracking the lying-down heart rate. You may be able to determine which method works best for you by doing both for three to four weeks during a period of hard training.

Two morning warning scores of 5 or higher mean that you should reduce your training intensity that day. Three or more morning warnings mean your body is telling you to

WEEK BEGINNING: April 28 **PLANNED WEEKLY HOURS/MILES:** 13:30 ~240 miles

FIGURE 15.1

Sample of a Training Diary

NOTES

Mon.—3 sets of ME.
Felt strong.

Tue.—On trainer at 7 a.m.,
hard to get going.
Felt strong in zones 1–3,
4 was hard.
Good workout.

MONDAY 4/28

1 Sleep 2 Fatigue 2 Stress 1 Soreness

Resting heart rate 64 Weight 152

WORKOUT 1 Weights 3 x ME

Weather

Route

Distance

Time 1:00 Total 1:00

Time by zone 1 2

3 4 5

WORKOUT 2

Weather

Route

Distance

Time Total

Time by zone 1 2

3 4 5

TUESDAY 4/29

1 Sleep 1 Fatigue 1 Stress 2 Soreness

Resting heart rate 62 Weight 152

WORKOUT 1 M2, 4 x 6 min. (2 min. RI)

Weather 36°F

Route Trainer

Distance 29 mi

Time 1:30 Total 1:30

Time by zone 1 0:25 2 0:42

3 0:02 4 0:18 5 0:03

WORKOUT 2 E1

Weather 52°

Route Trainer

Distance 7 mi

Time 0:30 Total 0:30

Time by zone 1 0:30 2

3 4 5

NOTES

Wed.—Tired all day.
Stressful day at work. Rode
w/ Bill.
Nice and easy to unwind.

Thur.—Only did 3 intervals.
Haven't fully recovered from
Tuesday and work problems.
Power still pretty good.

WEDNESDAY 4/30

3 Sleep 2 Fatigue 3 Stress 1 Soreness

Resting heart rate 67 Weight 151

WORKOUT 1 E1

Weather 68°F

Route Frontage Rd.

Distance 46 mi

Time 3:00 Total 2:52

Time by zone 1 2:39 2 0:13

3 4 5

WORKOUT 2

Weather

Route

Distance

Time Total

Time by zone 1 2

3 4 5

THURSDAY 5/1

3 Sleep 5 Fatigue 4 Stress 1 Soreness

Resting heart rate 69 Weight 150

WORKOUT 1 A2, 5 x 3 min. (3 min. RI)

Weather 62°F, windy

Route Hwy 1

Distance 20 mi

Time 1:00 Total 1:09

Time by zone 1 0:18 2 0:30

3 0:10 4 0:04 5 0:08

WORKOUT 2 E1

Weather 56°F, raining

Route Trainer

Distance 6 miles

Time 0:30 Total 0:20

Time by zone 1 0:20 2

3 4 5

WEEK'S GOALS (CHECK OFF AS ACHIEVED)

- [x] 24 min. of cruise intervals
- [ ] 15 min. of SE intervals
- [x] Good effort for club ride

FRIDAY 5/2

2 Sleep 5 Fatigue 5 Stress 5 Soreness

Resting heart rate 68 Weight 151

WORKOUT 1 Off

Weather

Route

Distance

Time Total

Time by zone 1 2

3 4 5

WORKOUT 2

Weather

Route

Distance

Time Total

Time by zone 1 2

3 4 5

SATURDAY 5/3

1 Sleep 3 Fatigue 2 Stress 1 Soreness

Resting heart rate 64 Weight 152

WORKOUT 1 A1

Weather 75°F

Route Big Loop

Distance 58 mi

Time 2:30 Total 2:40

Time by zone 1 0:22 2 0:36

3 0:35 4 0:42 5 0:25

WORKOUT 2

Weather

Route

Distance

Time Total

Time by zone 1 2

3 4 5

NOTES

Needed to take Fri. off. Recovery came at the right time.

Sat.—Club ride, big crowd. Everyone rode hard today.

SUNDAY 5/4

2 Sleep 3 Fatigue 1 Stress 3 Soreness

Resting heart rate 67 Weight 151

WORKOUT 1 E2

Weather 77°F

Route to Lyons

Distance 63 mi.

Time 3:30 Total 3:32

Time by zone 1 1:44 2 1:48

3 4 5

WORKOUT 2

Weather

Route

Distance

Time Total

Time by zone 1 2

3 4 5

WEEKLY SUMMARY

	Weekly Total	Year to Date
Bike miles	229	2,800
Bike time	12:33	215:25
Strength time	1:00	29:30
Total	13:33	244:55

Soreness Quads were sore, probably from Saturday's ride.

NOTES Club ride was my first race effort of the year—a real eye opener! Long way to go. Stress didn't help. Feel great about Tuesday's intervals.

NOTES

Sun.—Nice day for a long ride. Feeling yesterday's workout in my quads. Will get massage tomorrow.

take the day off—you need more recovery. Failure to heed the morning warnings your body is whispering to you forces it to eventually shout by giving you a cold or by leaving you too exhausted to work out for several days. Ratings of 4 or less are generally good signs that your body is ready for serious training. The lower the scores, the harder the workout can be on any given day.

A study at the University of Queensland in Australia showed these indicators to be relatively reliable measures of overtraining and burnout. But they are not necessarily the best for everyone. You may find others that work better for you. If so, record them in the same manner.

Checking and recording body weight every morning after visiting the bathroom and before eating can also reveal some things about the state of your body. Short-term weight loss is a measure of fluid levels, so if your weight is down a pound from the previous day, the first thing you should do is drink water. A pint of water weighs about one pound. A study done in Oregon found that afternoon weight loss is also a good indicator of overtraining and may be the easiest-to-measure initial indicator. (Chapter 17 discusses overtraining in greater detail.)

Workout Basics

This is the detail stuff that will help you remember the workout months later. Specify any changes made to your training plan in the "Notes" section. Record the distance, weather, route, and other variables, such as equipment used (for example, mountain bike or fixed-gear bike).

Workout Time by Zone

Each day of the training journal has space to record data for two workouts. The first workout section provides spaces to record the time spent in each training zone for the first workout of the day. This could be heart rate or power data and serves as a good check of how the workout profile went in relation to the plan. A few weeks or even a year later you can compare this information following a repeat of the same workout.

Fill in the actual duration of your workout to the right of your planned time. This should be about the same as the planned duration.

The second workout section is completed in the same way for the second daily workout. If you worked out just once, leave it blank.

Physical Comments

Your observations about how you are performing in workouts and races are critical to measuring progress. After each workout, record such information as average heart rate, heart rate at the end of work intervals, highest heart rates observed, and average speed. If you have sophisticated equipment, you may record average power, maximum power, and lactate levels. Later, you may use any or all of these data for comparisons of workouts done under similar conditions. Also record aches or pains, no matter how trivial they may seem at the time. Season-wrecking injuries often start as insignificant discomforts. Later, it may be helpful to trace when, why, and how they occurred.

Women should record their menstrual periods to help them get a clearer picture of how they affect training and racing.

For races, you may want to record in your training diary your warm-up, key moves, limiters, strengths, gearing, results, and notes for future reference. Race information may also be recorded on the Season Results page in Appendix D. (See the sample provided in Figure 15.2.) This will come in handy when you need to seek sponsors or change teams. Putting together a race résumé is much easier when all of the information is in one location.

Mental Comments

Here is where most journal keepers fail to be thorough. Training and racing are usually thought of as strictly physical, whereas what's happening inside the head is deemed unimportant. But sometimes emotions are the most telling aspect of physical performance.

Always include your perception of how hard or easy the workout or race was. It's not necessary to be overly scientific about this. Just say something such as "Tough workout" or "Felt easy." These brief comments can tell you a lot about your experience. Commenting on how enjoyable the workout was can also be revealing. Repeated remarks about training being a "drag" are a good sign that burnout is imminent, just as frequent "Fun workout" comments speak volumes about your mental state.

From the Mental Skills Profile completed in Chapter 5, you should have a good idea of what needs work. If, for example, your confidence is lacking, look for and record the positive aspects of the workout or race. What did you achieve that was at the limits of your ability? What were your successes today? Remembering and reliving your accomplishments is the first step in becoming more confident.

Mental comments should also include unusual stresses in your life off the bike. Visiting relatives, working overtime, or experiencing illness, sleep deprivation, or relationship problems can all affect performance.

Week's Summary

At the end of the week, complete a short summary of how things went for you and total your training time. This will come in handy later in the year when it's time to decide on training volumes for the new season. Check how you felt physically this week. It's not a good idea to frequently feel "on the edge" of overtraining, though that feeling is inevitable whenever you're trying to become more fit. The third week of a four-week training block is when this typically happens. If you never feel on the edge, you are not working hard enough. However, it is seldom the case that serious riders are not working hard enough.

FIGURE 15.2

Season Results Form

SEASON RESULTS **YEAR** 2009

Date	Race	Distance	Time	Place (Starters)	Comments
4/25	Horsetooth	40-mi. road race	1:58	14th (38)	Cold day. Dropped on third lap on climb. Rode in with second group.
5/2	Durand	38-mi. road race	1:32	7th (35)	Field sprint. Felt good. Rode well.
5/10	Sussex	45-min. crit.	0:45	3rd (42)	Great race. Felt strong. Made break.
5/23	Boulder TT series	10.2-mi. time trial	22:36	8th (15)	Strong headwind. 352 watts. Need to improve aero position.
6/7	State Roads	56-mi. road race	2:22	3rd (45)	Good peak. Made break of 7 on 3rd lap. Hard race.

Keep track of any soreness you experienced during the week no matter how trivial it may have seemed at the time. There may be a pattern developing that will be easier to find if you note seemingly minor difficulties when you first notice them.

Summarize how the week went, noting your successes, the areas needing work, any racing or training revelations you had, and ideas for the future, such as how to deal with a problem you experienced during the week. For example, you may have had a head cold coming on and discovered something that helped you fight it off.

ANALYSIS

TRAINING

When training and racing aren't going so well, looking back in the journal at what was happening in more positive times can sometimes get you back on track. In addition, you'll find that comparing recent workouts with what you were doing a year or more ago can provide a solid gauge of your improvement. When trying to regain the top form from an earlier period, look for patterns, such as types of workouts you were doing then, morning warning levels, stress, recovery time between BT workouts, equipment used, training volume, training partners, and anything else that may provide a clue. Become a detective.

Here's an example of detective work. An athlete once asked me to review her training journal. She was training hard, putting in lots of quality miles, and was very focused on her goals. Yet she wasn't in top form at the A-priority races, and sometimes even had trouble finishing.

The first thing I noticed in her journal was that she was ignoring her warning signs. She faithfully took her resting heart rate every morning and recorded her hours of sleep and fatigue level. Yet she always did the planned workout regardless of what the morning warnings said. She was so driven to succeed that she let nothing get in her way—not even her own body. I told her about a 1968 study in which rats were forced to swim six hours a day, six days a week. After 161 hours of swimming, they showed great improvement in their aerobic capacities. But after 610 hours, their aerobic powers were no better than the untrained, control-group rats. She was an "overtrained rat," I told her.

We also talked about how to peak and taper for a big race. It was obvious that she had not been rested on race days. She trained through the A-priority races as if they were the same as her C-priority races. We discussed how backing off in the days and even weeks before an important event allows the body to absorb all of the stress that has been placed on it and grow stronger.

The next time I talked with this rider was several weeks later, and she was riding well and pleased with her results. Had it not been for the detailed journal she kept, I would never have been able to so quickly and definitively determine the causes of her lackluster performance.

RACING

If you want to improve your race performances, you must evaluate your race preparation and strategies after every race you are in. After cooling down, ask yourself why you performed as you did. Was there any particular aspect of your preparation or strategy that was especially strong or weak? What role did the pre-race meal, warm-up, start, pacing, power, technical skills, endurance, refueling, and mental skills play in the outcome? Did you have a sound strategy, and did you follow through on it?

The answers to such questions come from nothing more than your memory and conversations with other riders following the race. The longer you wait to answer them, the more your memory of the event fades. To enhance your recall, and especially to create a record for the future when you return to this same race, it is useful to write down what happened as soon as possible after finishing. The Race Evaluation form in Appendix D helps with this. You can also refer to the sample provided in Figure 15.3.

Race days on which you felt especially good or bad deserve special attention. Examine the days preceding the race to determine what may have led to this high or low. Perhaps it was a certain pattern of workouts, a period of good rest, excessive stress, or a particular diet that contributed to your results. If you can identify such trends, you are one step closer to knowing the secret of what works for you—and what doesn't work for you. Reproducing the positive factors while minimizing the negative ones can be invaluable for race peaking and performance.

SOFTWARE

There are now many computer software programs available to help you analyze the data downloaded from devices such as power meters, heart rate monitors, and GPS units. The manufacturers of these training tools nearly always include their own software with the purchase of the device. Some of the programs that come in the box are quite basic but others are fairly elegant.

FIGURE 15.3

Race Evaluation Form

RACE EVALUATION FORM

Race name: *State Road Championships*

Date and start time: *June 7, 10:30 am*

Location: *Minneapolis*

Type/distance: *56-mi. road race*

Competitors to watch: *Ralph H., Tom D., Rob W.*

Weather: *78°F, humid, slight wind out of south (headwind finish).*

Course conditions: *Roads newly paved. Wet pavement on last corner from sprinkler.*

Race goal: *Podium.*

Race strategy: *Stay out of wind early in race. Near front and on left coming to hill on each lap. Go with Ralph, Tom, or Rob on hill.*

Pre-race meal (foods and strategies): *Scrambled eggs, fruit, juice, coffee at 8 am. Banana and coffee at 9:30 am.*

Warm-up description: *20 min. on trainer followed by several 20-second repeats on road, finishing just before going to line.*

Start-line arousal level (circle one): Very low Low Moderate **(High)** Very high

Results (place, time, splits, etc.): *3rd*

What I did well: *Followed strategy, and it worked!*

What I need to improve: *Could not come around Ralph on sprint. Need to continue developing sprint power.*

Aches/pains/problems afterward: *A little tightness in low back the rest of the day, as usual. Legs good.*

Other comments: *Fast start. There were several moves early in race, but none were threats and brought back quickly. Went with Ralph, Rob, and 3 others on 3rd time up hill. We worked well together to hold off field. 3rd in sprint. 1,023 w!*

The problem with most of the software that comes with these devices is that it was designed by a company that makes excellent hardware but knows little about software. Unfortunately, the manufacturer rarely knows what's important in training either. Aftermarket training-analysis software designed by knowledgeable athletes in a software-focused company is usually better than the software that comes with the product.

One of the best software-analysis tools is called "WKO+" and is available online at http://TrainingPeaks.com. I admit I'm biased as I've played a small role in developing the software and use it to analyze all of my clients' training and racing. The reason I use it is that it is a powerful tool for the serious athlete and makes for easy analysis of almost any training device you own. It works with heart rate and power data regardless of your device's manufacturer, as long as the device comes with a cable or wireless capability for uploading information to a computer.

No matter what software you use, the key question it should help you answer is whether you are making progress toward your racing goals. By using the software, you should be able to figure out whether you are improving, and exactly how much you are improving. If the software doesn't easily help you do this, then it is useless. Make sure the software you are using offers these functions:

- Calculates the time you have spent in each heart rate and power zone by workout and for the entire season
- Indicates when you are ready to change your heart rate zones in training as a result of fitness changes
- Supplies a way for you to easily compare similar workouts
- Calculates changes in power relative to body weight
- Records improvements in workout power for similar workouts
- Predicts your capacity for handling greater training stress
- Estimates the level of fatigue you can manage without breaking down
- Provides a graphic or metric that shows how your fitness is progressing
- Includes a way of determining when you are ready to race

Even if you decide to use software to help you interpret your training data, it can still be incredibly useful to keep a diary. If the hard-copy approach provided here doesn't work for you, there are plenty of electronic formats that might suit you better. Regardless, a diary helps you see the big picture by keeping all the details in focus, both the hard data and the subjective feedback. When used effectively, it serves as an excellent tool for planning your steps, motivating you, and diagnosing your problems. It also provides a personal history of training and racing accomplishments. A well-kept diary ranks right up there with training, rest, and nutrition when it comes to developing a competitive edge.

FUEL

I get embarrassed when I see how slim I was.
—EDDY MERCKX

THE FOCUS OF THIS BOOK is training, not diet, but there is no denying the complex connections between nutritional practices and exhaustive exercise. Eating foods to which the human body is optimally adapted will reduce body fat, improve recovery, decrease downtime due to illness, and generally enhance athletic performance. The older you are, the more important diet is for performance. At age 20, you can make some dietary mistakes and get away with them. At age 50, everything is crucial, especially diet. Age is not the only individual variable that magnifies the role of good nutrition. The right diet is also essential for female athletes who are chronically low in iron stores or fighting a seemingly endless battle to keep off excess pounds. Any athlete who eats a junk-food diet low in micronutrients will eventually suffer from illness and constant fatigue, which lead to long recovery times and lagging performance. Even something as seemingly innocuous as eating the right foods but at the wrong times relative to training can postpone recovery and reduce performance levels. Other than training and rest, nothing is as important for your race results as what you eat and when you eat it.

So what should you eat? Suppose you were a zookeeper in charge of selecting food for the animals. It wouldn't be difficult to figure out that the lions thrive on a diet made up primarily of the protein in meat and the giraffes do best when allowed to graze on vegetation. You wouldn't feed leaves and grass to the lions. Nor would you feed the giraffes meat. Their health and well-being would decline if you did. So there are foods that are optimal for different types of animals. Why? Because they evolved eating such foods. For as long as lions and giraffes have been on the planet, they have eaten these foods. As the zookeeper, you will not change that. It's best to accept it.

What would you do if the zoo received an exotic animal that no other zoo had and for which the diet was unknown? Well, the obvious answer would be to study that animal in its natural environment to see what it ate there, and then feed the animal those same foods in your zoo. That would be the optimal food for that animal. Seems simple enough.

What foods are optimal for *Homo sapiens*—you and me? The way I answer that question is through the science of paleontology—the study of man before the advent of farming and civilization. Why would we not want to study human eating patterns after the introduction of farming? The reason has to do with time and evolution.

The evolutionary process is slow, taking hundreds of thousands of years to bring about very small changes. *Homo sapiens* have been on the planet for about 5 million years, but farming was introduced in the Middle East just 10,000 years ago or so. Consumption of dairy products by adults did not occur until even later in history, perhaps some 5,000 years ago. In the big picture, these developments are very recent. If our 5 million years on the planet were represented by a 24-hour clock, farming would have been with us for only the past 2 minutes and 52 seconds. Adult dairy consumption would have been around less than 90 seconds. These time spans are very short. There has simply not been enough time for humans to have fully adapted, through natural selection and the evolutionary process, to the foods that are unique to farming and dairy production.

What did humans eat prior to farming? What are the optimal foods for humans? Paleontology tells us that our hunting-gathering ancestors ate mostly vegetables, fruits, and lean meats (fish, poultry, and other wild or free-ranging game). Nuts, some seeds, berries, and honey are also foods that humans have eaten for millions of years, although in far smaller amounts than the foods listed above. The foods we have eaten only for the past 10,000 years or so, such as grains, milk, and cheese, are not optimal. Does this mean humans should never eat these nonoptimal foods? No, it merely means that we will thrive on a diet made up primarily of vegetables, fruits, and lean meats. The more of these nutrient-dense foods you eat, the better your health and athletic performance will be. The scientific evidence in support of the optimal foods as the best ingredients for a health-promoting diet is overwhelming. Replace them with nonoptimal foods and, like the exotic animal in the zoo that is fed the wrong things, your health and vitality will diminish. And that means your fitness will suffer.

Paleontology also tells us that our ancestors from the distant past would never have considered putting in multihour bouts of exercise, much of it at high intensity, day after day, week after week. This was unheard of until relatively recent times. Humankind evolved to do only what was necessary to provide food, shelter, and safety—and nothing more. We are meant to be lazy, making our couch potato friends the true descendants of the earliest humans, at least philosophically. Serious athletes are an anomaly.

Since as athletes we are a little different from our early ancestors, I believe we must "break the rules" to some extent when it comes to eating. We do need some of the energy-dense foods that were introduced with farming. We simply burn too many calories not to include certain nonoptimal foods, such as grains and other starches, in our diet from time to time. Although these foods are a disadvantage to our friend the couch potato, who is overweight and unhealthy, they can be quite advantageous to the athlete seeking quick restoration of glycogen stores following a hard workout. This does not contradict the basic rule: that the athlete's diet should be composed primarily of optimal foods. It merely suggests that there are small windows of time when nonoptimal foods may well be beneficial to recovery.

The details of how to blend all of these elements into the "athlete's diet" is the focus of this chapter. To learn more about the concept of optimal foods, read *The Paleo Diet* by Loren Cordain (2002).

FOOD AS FUEL

While the human genetic code has changed very little, dietary recommendations change often. In the mid–twentieth century, endurance athletes were advised to avoid starchy foods such as bread and potatoes and to eat more vegetables and meats instead. In the 1970s, a dietary shift away from protein began and nutrition experts recommended an increase in carbohydrates, especially starchy grains, for athletes. The 1980s brought concerns about fat in the diet, and low-fat and fat-free foods boomed, with an accompanying increase in sugar consumption. Now the pendulum is swinging back the other way, with the realization that certain fats are beneficial and that some carbohydrates, in large quantities, are deleterious.

The crux of the daily decisions you must make about your diet is the relative mix of the four macronutrients you consume—protein, fat, carbohydrates, and water. How much of each you include in your diet has a great deal to do with the current status of your training and racing.

PROTEIN

The word "protein" is derived from the Greek word *proteios,* meaning "first" or "of primary importance." That's fitting, because determining the right balance of macronutrients in your diet begins with a consideration of your protein intake.

Protein has a checkered history in the world of athletics. Greek and Roman competitors believed that the strength, speed, and endurance qualities of animals could be gained by merely eating their meat. Lion meat was in great demand. In the 1800s, too, protein was considered the best fuel for exercise, so athletes again ate prodigious quantities of meat. In the early part of the twentieth century, scientists came to understand that fat and carbohydrates provided most of the energy for movement. And by the 1960s, athletic diets began to change, reflecting this shift in knowledge. In fact, little interest was paid to the role of protein in sports throughout most of the 1970s and 1980s. Trends began to change again in the latter years of the twentieth century as more research was done on this almost forgotten macronutrient.

Protein plays a key role in health and athletic performance. It is necessary to repair muscle damage, maintain the immune system, manufacture hormones and enzymes, and replace red blood cells, which carry oxygen to the muscles. Moreover, protein produces up to 10 percent of the energy needed for long or intense workouts and races. It also stimulates the secretion of *glucagon,* a hormone that allows the body to use fat for fuel more efficiently.

Protein is so important to the athlete that it may even determine the outcome of races. A study of Olympians by the International Center for Sports Nutrition in Omaha, Nebraska, comparing the diets of medal winners and nonmedalists found just one significant difference between the two groups: The medal winners ate more protein than those who did not win a medal.

Performance is dependent on dietary protein because the body is unable to produce all it needs from scratch. And, unlike carbohydrates and fat, protein is not stored in the body at fuel depot sites for later use. The protein you eat is used to meet immediate needs, and excess intakes are converted to the storage forms of carbohydrates or fat.

Dietary protein is made up of 20 amino acids that the human body uses as building blocks for replacing damaged cells. Most of these amino acids are readily produced by the body when a need arises, but there are 9 that the body cannot manufacture. These "essential" amino acids must come from the diet in order for all the protein-related functions to continue normally. If your diet is lacking in protein, your body is likely to break down muscle tissues to provide what is necessary for areas of greater need, thus resulting in muscle wasting. This was evidenced in 1988 by a study involving the 7-Eleven cycling team during the Tour de France. It was discovered that the circumferences of the riders' thighs decreased during the three weeks of racing. After reviewing their diets, the team doctor determined that they were protein deficient.

Protein is more important for endurance athletes than for those in power sports, such as American football, baseball, and basketball. An intense, one-hour criterium can cause the depletion of up to 30 grams of protein, about the amount of protein contained in a 3-ounce can of tuna. Replacing these losses is critical to recovery and improved fitness. Without such replenishment, the endurance athlete's body is forced to cannibalize protein from muscle.

Unfortunately, there is no general agreement within the field of nutrition regarding the recommended protein intake for endurance athletes. The U.S. recommended daily allowance (RDA) for protein is 0.013 ounce per pound of body weight (0.8 gram per kilogram [g/kg]), but that is likely too low for an athlete. Peter Lemon, a noted protein researcher at Kent State University, suggests athletes eat about 0.020 to 0.022 ounce of protein per pound of body weight each day (1.2–1.4 g/kg). During a period of heavy weight lifting, such as in the MS phase described in Chapter 12, Lemon recommends a high of 0.028 ounce per pound (1.8 g/kg). The American Dietetic Association suggests a high-end protein intake of 0.032 ounce per pound (2.0 g/kg) each day. A nonscientific survey of sports scientists from around the world found a rather broad range of 0.020 to 0.040 ounce per pound (1.2–2.5 g/kg) suggested for endurance athletes daily. Applying these recommendations for a 150-pound (68 kg) athlete, the possible range, excluding the U.S. RDA, would be 3 to 6 ounces (84 to 168 g) of protein each day. Table 16.1 shows how much protein is found in common foods.

TABLE 16.1

Protein Content of Common Foods

FOOD 3.5 oz (100 g)	PROTEIN (oz)	(g)
Animal sources		
Sirloin steak, broiled	1.05	30
Chicken breast	1.05	30
Swiss cheese	1.01	29
Pork loin	0.92	26
Hamburger	0.92	26
Cheddar cheese	0.85	24.5
Tuna	0.82	23
Haddock	0.82	24
Venison	0.73	21
Cottage cheese, low-fat	0.43	12
Whole egg	0.42	12
Egg white	0.36	10
Milk, skim	0.12	3
Plant sources		
Almonds, dried	0.71	20
Tofu, extra-firm	0.39	11
Bagel	0.38	11
Kidney beans	0.30	9
Rye bread	0.29	8
Cereal, corn flakes	0.28	8
Refried beans	0.22	6
Baked beans	0.17	5
Hummus	0.17	5
Soy milk	0.10	3
Brown rice, cooked	0.09	2.5
Tomato, red	0.03	1

Protein is found in both vegetable and animal forms, and the quantity required, regardless of the source, can be difficult to consume unless you closely watch your diet. To get 127 grams of protein from vegetable sources would mean eating 17 cups of spaghetti, 14 cups of yogurt, or 21 bagels. The same 127 grams could also come from 15 ounces of chicken or lean steak or 17 ounces of tuna. This is a lot of food from either type, but there is an added benefit in getting protein from animal sources: All of the necessary amino acids are present in the right proportions (easily absorbable iron, zinc, calcium, and vitamin B-12), and the protein is more absorbable because of the lower fiber content of the meat.

So what happens if you fail to get enough protein when training hard? Occasionally missing out on your daily protein intake probably has no measurable impact on performance, but regular avoidance of high-quality protein, accompanied by a high volume of high-intensity exercise, can have a significant impact on training and racing. Besides being a minor fuel source during strenuous exercise, protein is responsible for building muscle, making hormones that regulate basal metabolic rate, and fighting off disease.

There's no doubt that during prolonged, high-intensity exercise, the body turns to stored protein, eventually resulting in the loss of muscle. A 1992 study looked at 16 hikers, who spent 21 days in the Andes Mountains traveling 5 hours a day on foot with an average elevation gain of 2,500 feet per day, and found significant loss of muscle mass over the course of their trip. This may explain why some endurance athletes have a gaunt look after several weeks of rigorous training with low intake of protein.

Without meat in the diet, the risk of low iron levels is also high. One study linked low iron levels with injuries in runners. Those lowest in iron had twice as many injuries as those highest in iron. Besides providing protein, lean red meat is also a good source of easily absorbed iron.

Are you getting enough protein? One way to determine the answer is to evaluate your physical and mental well-being. Signs that you need more protein in your diet include:

- Frequent colds or sore throats
- Slow recovery following workouts
- An irritable demeanor
- Poor response to training (slow to get in shape)
- Slow fingernail growth and easily broken nails
- Thin hair or unusual hair loss
- Chronic fatigue
- Poor mental focus
- Sugar cravings
- Pallid complexion
- Cessation of menstrual periods

Note that none of these indicators is certain proof of the need for more protein, as each may have other causes. A dietary analysis by a registered dietitian, or through the use of a computer software program such as DietBalancer, may help make the determination if you have concerns. Increasing your protein intake to see how it affects you is another simple option. It's unlikely that you will eat too much protein. Even at 30 percent of daily calories, as recommended in some diets, the excess should not be harmful. If you do consume excess protein, it will simply be converted to glycogen or fat and stored by your body in this form. There is no research suggesting that moderately high protein diets pose a health risk for otherwise healthy individuals, as long as plenty of water is consumed each day to help with the removal of nitrogen, a by-product of protein metabolism.

CARBOHYDRATES

Carbohydrates are critical for performance in endurance events because they provide much of the fuel, in the forms of glycogen and glucose, that is converted to usable energy. Low carbohydrate stores are likely to result in poor endurance and lackluster racing.

Many zealous athletes, upon learning about the role of carbohydrates in energy production for the first time, begin to overeat carbohydrates at the expense of protein and fat. A day in the life of such a person may include cereal, toast, and orange juice for breakfast; a bagel as a midmorning snack; a baked potato with vegetables for lunch; sports bars or pretzels in the afternoon; and pasta with bread for supper. Not only is such a diet excessively high in starch, with an overemphasis on wheat, but it is also likely to provide dangerously low protein and fat levels. Such a dietary plan could be improved by replacing the cereal with an egg-white omelet and including fresh fruit, topping the potato with tuna, snacking on mixed nuts and dried fruit, and eating fish with vegetables for supper.

When you eat a high-carbohydrate meal or snack, the pancreas releases insulin to regulate the level of blood sugar. That insulin stays in the blood for up to two hours, during which time it has other effects, such as preventing the body from utilizing stored fat, converting carbohydrates and protein to body fat, and moving fat in the blood to storage sites. This may explain why, despite serious training and eating a "healthy" diet, some athletes are unable to lose body fat.

Some carbohydrates enter the bloodstream more quickly than others, producing an elevated blood-sugar response and rapidly bringing about all the negative aspects of high insulin described above. These rapidly digested carbohydrates are high on the glycemic index—a food rating system developed for diabetics. Foods with a low glycemic index produce a less dramatic rise in blood sugar and help you avoid the cravings for more sugary food that come with eating high-glycemic carbohydrates. Table 16.2 lists some common foods with high, moderate, low, and very low glycemic indexes.

How a carbohydrate food is prepared and what other foods it is eaten with affect its glycemic index. Adding fat to a high-glycemic-index food lowers its glycemic index by slowing down digestion. An example of this is ice cream, which has a moderate glycemic index despite the presence of large amounts of sugar. In the same way, adding fiber to a meal that includes a high- or moderate-glycemic-index carbohydrate reduces the meal's effect on your blood-sugar and insulin levels and turns it into timed-release energy.

Notice in Table 16.2 that many of the foods that have a moderate to high glycemic index are the ones we have typically thought of as "healthy" and therefore eaten liberally. These include starchy foods such as cereal, bread, rice, pasta, potatoes, crackers, bagels, pancakes, and bananas. No wonder so many endurance athletes are always hungry and have a hard time losing excess body fat. Their blood-sugar levels are routinely kept at high levels, causing regular cascades of insulin. Not only do high insulin levels produce regular and frequent food cravings and excess body fat, they are also associated with such widespread health problems as high blood pressure, heart disease, and adult-onset diabetes.

But moderate- and high-glycemic-index foods have an important role in the athlete's diet. During long and intense training sessions and races it is important for you to replenish the carbohydrate stores in your muscles and liver. That's why sports drinks and gels are used during exercise. The 30 minutes immediately following a hard training session is another time when moderate- to high-glycemic-index carbohydrates and insulin are beneficial. This is the time to use a commercial recovery drink or starchy food. Combining protein with a high-glycemic-index food at this time has been shown to effectively boost recovery. For very hard workouts, this window of opportunity for enhancing recovery may extend as long as the duration of the preceding workout. So if you do a very intense two-hour ride, continue taking in high-glycemic foods with some protein for two hours post-workout.

Except for during and immediately after exercise, however, you should avoid sports drinks, gels, and soft drinks. Other high- and moderate-glycemic-index foods should also be consumed in strictly limited quantities throughout the day.

Despite the popular notion that athletes need to eat lots of carbs, eating a diet extremely high in carbohydrates is not unanimously supported by the sports science literature. A high-carbohydrate diet may cause your body to rely heavily on glycogen for fuel during exercise, with an associated increase in blood lactate levels, while reducing your use of fat as a fuel for exercise.

FAT

In the 1980s, Western society painted dietary fat as such a terrifying specter that many athletes still see all types of fat as the enemy and try to eliminate it entirely from their diet. In fact, not all fats are bad, although there are some types that should indeed be kept at low levels. The fats to minimize or avoid are saturated fats, which are found in prodigious quantities in feedlot cattle, and trans-fatty acids, the man-made fats found in many highly processed foods (called "hydrogenated" on the label). Both hydrogenated fats (or "trans fats") and saturated fats lead to artery clogging.

Don't confuse these "bad" fats with all types of fat. There are, in fact, "good" fats. These good fats prevent dry skin and dull hair, help maintain a regular menstrual cycle in women, and aid in the prevention of colds and other infections common to serious

TABLE 16.2

Glycemic Index of Common Foods

VERY LOW (<30%)	LOW (30–50%)		MODERATE (50–80%)	
Barley	Apple	Kiwifruit	All-Bran cereal	Bread, white
Beans, kidney	Apple juice	Oranges	Apricots	Corn chips
Cherries	Apple sauce	Pasta (whole wheat)	Bagels	Corn, sweet
Grapefruit	Beans, baked	Pears	Bananas	Cornmeal
Lentils	Beans, black	Peas, black-eyed	Barley	Couscous
Milk	Beans, lima	Peas, split	Beets	Crackers
Peaches	Beans, pinto	Rye	Black bean soup	Doughnuts
Peanuts	Chocolate	Tomato soup	Bread, pita	Ice cream
Plums	Grapefruit juice	Yogurt, fruit	Bread, rye	Mango
Soybeans	Grapes		Bread, wheat	Muesli

athletes. They also assist with the manufacture of hormones such as testosterone and estrogen, are necessary for healthy nerve and brain cells, and promote the absorption of vitamins A, D, E, and K. Fat is the body's most efficient source of energy. Every gram of fat provides nine calories, compared with four each for protein and carbohydrates. If you have been avoiding fats in general, you may find that eating some good fats improves your long-term recovery and capacity to train at a high level.

There is now compelling evidence that increasing intake of healthy fats, along with proper timing of carbohydrate consumption, may be good for endurance athletes, especially in events lasting 4 hours or longer. This is in contrast to the very-high-carbohydrate diets that coaches and nutrition experts advocated over the past three decades. Several studies have revealed that eating a diet high in fat causes the body to preferentially use fat for fuel, and that eating a high-carbohydrate diet causes the body to rely more heavily on limited stores of muscle glycogen for fuel. Theoretically, even the skinniest athlete has enough fat stored to last for 40 hours or more at a low intensity without refueling, but only enough carbohydrates for about 3 hours at most.

A study at State University of New York illustrated the performance benefits of fat. Researchers had a group of runners eat a diet with a higher-than-usual proportion of fat for one week, then a high-carbohydrate diet for one week. During the first week, 38 percent of the calories came from fats and 50 percent from carbohydrates. The second week, 73 percent of the calories came from carbs and 15 percent from fats. At the end of each week the researchers tested the subjects' maximum aerobic capacities and then asked them to run themselves to exhaustion on a treadmill. On average, the VO_2max of the participants was 11 percent greater when they were on the high-fat diet than when they were on the high-carbohydrate diet, and they lasted 9 percent longer on the run to exhaustion. One confounding element of the study, however, was that the subjects were depleted of their glycogen stores before starting the endurance run.

MODERATE (50–80%)		HIGH (≥80%)	
Muffins	Potatoes, sweet	Bread, French	Rice, instant
Oat bran	PowerBar	Corn flakes	Rice Krispies
Oatmeal	Pumpkin	Grapenuts	Rice, white
Orange juice	Raisins	Molasses	Tapioca
Pea soup	Rice, brown	Parsnips	Tofu frozen dessert
Pineapple	Rye crisps	Pasta	
Popcorn	Soft drinks	Potatoes, baked	
Potato chips	Taco shells	Potatoes, instant	
Potatoes, boiled	Watermelon	Rice cakes	
Potatoes, mashed	Yams	Rice Chex	

A 1994 study conducted by Tim Noakes, M.D., Ph.D., author of *The Lore of Running* (1991), and his colleagues at the University of Cape Town in South Africa found that after cyclists ate a diet of 70 percent fat for two weeks, their endurance at a low intensity improved significantly compared with cycling after consuming a diet high in carbohydrates for two weeks. At high intensities, there was no difference in the performances—fat did just as well as carbohydrates.

Other research has shown that our greatest risks associated with dietary fat—heart disease and weight gain—do not occur when eating a diet incorporating good fats. These

SIDEBAR 16.1

Are You Really Overtrained?

Low dietary intake of the mineral iron may be the most common nutritional deficiency for serious multisport athletes, especially women. Unfortunately, it goes undetected in most.

A 1988 university study of female high-school cross-country runners found that 45 percent had low iron stores. In the same study, 17 percent of the boys were low on iron. Other research conducted on female college athletes showed that 31 percent were iron deficient. And in a 1983 study, up to 80 percent of women runners were found to have iron stores below normal levels. Commonly accepted, although still debated, causes of iron depletion include high-volume running, especially on hard surfaces; too much anaerobic training; chronic intake of aspirin; travel to high altitude; excessive menstrual flow; and a diet low in animal-food products. Athletes most at risk for iron deficiency, in the order of their risk, are runners, women, endurance athletes, vegetarians, those who sweat heavily, dieters, and those who have recently donated blood.

The symptoms of iron deficiency include loss of endurance, chronic fatigue, high exercise heart rate, low power, frequent injury, recurring illness, and irritability. Since many of these symptoms are the same as for overtraining, the athlete may correctly cut back on exercise, begin feeling better, and return to training only to find an almost immediate relapse. In the early stages of iron depletion, performance may show only slight decrements, but additional training volume and intensity cause further declines. Many unknowingly flirt with this level of "tired blood" frequently.

If you suspect that you have an iron deficiency, check with your physician; he or she may want to have a blood test done. Even if you do not suspect a deficiency, it may be a good idea to be tested so that you will have a healthy baseline for later comparison. Then, repeat the test annually just to be on the safe side. The analysis should look at your levels of serum ferritin, hemoglobin, reticulocytes, and haptoglobin. The baseline test and annual checkups should be done during the Transition, Prep, or Base training period when training volume and intensity are low. If you have shown signs of a deficiency, however, don't wait for these periods for testing; check with your physician right away.

You should not eat anything or exercise for 15 hours prior to the test. Your health-care provider will help you understand the results. If they show a possible deficiency, your doctor will probably order a follow-up test to confirm this or rule out low iron as the culprit. Having a baseline test when you are not experiencing any symptoms of iron deficiency can be helpful because healthy iron levels can vary somewhat. Your blood indicators of iron status may be "normal" compared to the rest of the population, but low in relation to your baseline. Obviously, if your personal iron-level baseline is particularly high, then drops into what appears to be a "normal" range may adversely affect your health and performance.

Should the blood test indicate an abnormally low iron status, an increased dietary intake of iron is necessary. You may want to have a registered dietitian analyze your eating habits for adequate iron consumption. The RDA for women and teenagers is 15 milligrams per day. Men should consume 10 mg. Endurance athletes may need more. The normal North American diet contains about 6 mg of iron for every 1,000 calories eaten, so a female athlete restricting food intake to 2,000 calories a day while exercising strenuously can easily create a low-iron condition in a few weeks.

Dietary iron comes in two forms—heme and non-heme. Heme iron is found in animal meat. Plant foods are the source of non-heme iron. Very little of the iron you eat is absorbed by the body regardless of the source, but heme iron has the best absorption rate, at about 15 percent. Up to 5 percent of non-heme iron is taken up by the body. So the most effective way to increase iron status is by eating meat, especially red meat. Humans probably developed this capacity to absorb iron from red meat as a result of our omnivorous, hunter-gatherer origins. The reason that the iron in plant sources is not very available to the human body is that plants contain phytates, which bond with minerals like iron, preventing the body from absorbing the minerals. Plant sources of iron include raisins, leafy green vegetables, dates, dried fruits, lima beans, baked beans, broccoli, baked potatoes, soybeans, and Brussels sprouts. Other sources are listed in Table 16.1.

Iron absorption from any of these foods, whether plant or animal, is decreased if they are accompanied at meals by egg yolks, coffee, tea, wheat, or cereal grains. Calcium and zinc also reduce the ability of the body to take up iron. Including fruits, especially citrus fruit, in meals enhances iron absorption.

Don't use iron supplements unless it is under the supervision of your health-care provider. Some people are susceptible to iron overload, a condition called hemochromatosis that is marked by toxic deposits in the skin, joints, and liver. Other symptoms, including fatigue and malaise, may mimic iron deficiency and overtraining. Also note that ingesting iron supplements is a leading cause of poisoning in children, second only to aspirin.

include monounsaturated and omega-3 polyunsaturated fatty acids, which were plentiful in our Stone Age ancestors' diets, according to paleontology. Oils and spreads made from almonds, avocados, hazelnuts, macadamia nuts, pecans, cashews, and olives are high in these fats. Other good sources are the oils of cold-water fish such as tuna, salmon, and mackerel. The red meat of wild game or pastured animals (animals not raised in a feedlot or fed a diet of corn) also provides significant amounts of monounsaturated and omega-3 fats. Canola oil is another good source.

The bottom line on fat is to select the leanest cuts of meat (wild game or free-range livestock and fowl, if possible); trim away all visible fat from meat, including fish and fowl; eat low- or non-fat dairy in small quantities; avoid trans-fatty acids in packaged foods; and regularly include monounsaturated and omega-3 fats in your diet. Eating 20 to 30 percent of your calories from fat, with an emphasis on the good fats, is not harmful, and it may actually improve your training and racing performance if your fat intake has been low up to this point.

WATER

Many athletes don't drink enough fluids, which leaves them perpetually on the edge of dehydration. In this state, recovery is compromised and the risk of illness rises. Drinking throughout the day is one of the simplest and yet most effective means of boosting performance for these athletes. Since sports drinks and most fruit juices are high to moderate on the glycemic index, the best fluid replacement between workouts is water.

Dehydration results in a reduction of plasma, making the blood thick and forcing the heart and body to work harder when working out. Even with slight dehydration, exercise intensity and duration are negatively affected. A 2 percent reduction of body weight from fluid loss will slow a racer by about 4 percent—that's nearly 5 minutes in a 2-hour race. When race intensity is high, you must stay well hydrated to keep up.

A 150-pound (68 kg) adult loses just over half a gallon (2 liters) of body fluids a day just by living. Up to half of this loss is through urine, at the rate of about 2 ounces (30 milliliters) per hour. Heavy training or a hot and humid environment can increase the loss to 2 gallons (8 liters) daily through heavy sweating.

The thinking used to be that people required 8 to 12 cups of water a day. The advice to take in this amount was so widespread that it inspired many health-conscious people, and athletes, in particular, to carry around bottles of water or sports drink and sip on them constantly, especially prior to a race. Is this a good idea? Recent data indicate that it's not. Once our limited fluid storage areas are full, most of the excess is shunted to the bladder and removed as urine. In moderate cases, the excess water isn't a problem. However, hyperhydrating—which can be brought on by the habit of constantly sipping from a water bottle—can have serious consequences.

Excessive drinking has been shown to dangerously dilute the body's electrolyte stores, especially sodium. The high water intake may increase your risk of cramping, which can lead to hyponatremia, a sometimes fatal condition. In hyponatremia, sodium stores are so low that the body begins to shut down. In the early stages, someone with hyponatremia may experience nausea, headache, muscle cramps, weakness, and disorientation. Later on, seizures and coma are possible.

Although hyponatremia is unlikely to occur in athletes racing in events that take less than about four hours, it simply isn't a good idea to start any race, regardless of distance, with diluted electrolytes. Pay attention to your thirst mechanism. We've been taught over the past few years that it is not effective and that we shouldn't trust it. This "old wives' tale" refuses to go away. Drink when you are thirsty. When you are not thirsty, don't drink. It's that simple.

EATING FOR RECOVERY

It is well established that carbohydrates are necessary for high levels of performance in endurance sports such as bike racing. Just as critical to success is the timing of carbohydrate intake. In fact, if your carb intake is timed correctly, you can actually cut back a bit on the amount and take in a wider variety of nutrient-dense foods. Those foods can in turn help you recover faster and perform at a higher level.

First, accept that your workouts are the central events of each day, and that the types of foods you eat and when you eat them are determined by workout timing. This is likely a fairly easy notion to acquire since, as a serious athlete, you probably already have a "training is life, everything else is just the details" way of seeing the world.

Each workout has five feeding times linked with it. I call these "stages." Here's how they work.

STAGE 1—BEFORE THE WORKOUT

The goal of this stage is to store sufficient carbohydrates to get you through the workout. This is especially important for early-morning rides. For the perfect fuel, eat 200 to 400 calories, primarily from a moderate-glycemic-index, carbohydrate-rich food (see Table 16.2), two hours before the workout. Of course, few are willing to get up at 4 A.M. just to eat before a 6 A.M. ride. For these early-morning sessions, especially races and highly intense rides, try downing a bottle of your favorite sports drink or a couple of gel packets with 12 ounces of water about 10 minutes before the workout. This isn't quite as good as eating a real breakfast two hours beforehand, but it is far better than training on a low fuel tank.

STAGE 2—DURING THE WORKOUT

For an hour or less of training, water is all you need, assuming you refilled the tank in Stage 1. For longer workouts you also need carbohydrates, mostly in the form of liquids from a high-glycemic-index source. The best choice is your favorite sports drink. You could also use gels, chased immediately by lots of water. The longer the workout, the more important the carbohydrates are and the more of them you need. You'll need as few as 120 calories or as many as 500 calories per hour, depending not only on workout length but also on your body size, workout intensity, and level of experience. It's usually a good idea for this liquid fuel source to include sodium, especially if it's a hot day and you tend to sweat heavily. The research is less than overwhelming on other ingredients of sports drinks and gels, including potassium, magnesium, and protein. Include them if you want to. If you pay careful attention as you train and experiment with your nutrition, you can develop a sense of the type of carbohydrates that works best for you and the amount you need for different workouts.

STAGE 3—IMMEDIATELY AFTER THE WORKOUT

This and the next stage are the key times in the day for taking in carbohydrates. When athletes say that eating in stages, as described here, doesn't work for them, it's usually because they don't take in enough carbohydrates in Stages 3 and 4.

Your goal in Stage 3 is to replace the carbohydrates you used up during the workout. In the first thirty minutes or so after a workout, your body is several hundred times more sensitive to carbohydrates and will readily store more than at any other time of the day. The longer you wait to refuel, the less likely you are to completely refill the gas tank. Take in three to four calories per pound of body weight, mostly from carbohydrates, in this stage.

STAGE 4—AS LONG AS THE WORKOUT LASTED

Continue to focus your diet on carbohydrates, especially from moderate- to high-glycemic-index sources, along with some protein, for a time period equal to the amount

Recovery Drink

You can buy a commercial product for this type of refueling, but they are expensive. Make your own recovery drink with this simple list of ingredients.

16 oz fruit juice

1 banana

3–5 tbsp. glucose (such as Carbo-Pro, available at sportquestdirect.com), depending on body size

2–3 tbsp. protein powder (egg or whey sources are best)

2–3 pinches of salt

Consuming this drink during the 30-minute, post-workout window is critical for recovery. It should be your highest priority after a hard workout. If the workout lasted less than an hour and was low intensity, omit this stage.

of time you were working out. You may be ready to eat a meal during Stage 4 if the workout was long. Now is the time to eat low- to moderate-glycemic-index starches such as pasta, bread, bagels, cereal, rice, and corn to facilitate the recovery process. Perhaps the perfect foods to eat at this time are potatoes, sweet potatoes, yams, and bananas, since they also have a net alkaline-enhancing quality that reduces body acidity following workouts. Raisins are a great snack food for Stage 4. Eat until satisfied.

STAGE 5—UNTIL THE NEXT WORKOUT

Usually, by the time Stage 5 comes around, you will be at work, back in class, spending time with your family, mowing the grass, or doing whatever it is you do when not training or racing on a given day of the week. Although this part of your day may look ordinary to the rest of the world, it really isn't. You can still focus on nutrition for long-term recovery.

This is the time when many athletes get sloppy with their diets. The most common mistake is to continue to eat Stage 3 and 4 foods that are low in nutrient value and high in starch and sugar. Such foods are great for post-workout recovery but relatively poor in vitamins and minerals. The most nutrient-dense foods are vegetables, fruits, and lean

Diet and Reality

The Italians have a knack for living the good life, and with the help of a famous Italian economist, there's a way to apply la dolce vita to your training diet as well. The economist is Vilfredo Pareto, who in 1906 made the acute observation that 80 percent of the land in Italy was owned by 20 percent of the population. Experts in other fields soon discovered that Pareto's "80-20 Rule" applied to their areas of study as well.

For example, 80 percent of the productivity in a business typically comes from 20 percent of the employees. Schoolchildren spend 80 percent of their time with 20 percent of their friends. Investors find that 80 percent of their income comes from 20 percent of their stock.

We can apply Pareto's Principle to our diets, too. The lesson is simply this: You don't need to eat perfectly. Stage 5 of recovery, where we spend most of our eating life, is often viewed as being quite restrictive. We're supposed to eat "the perfect diet," focusing on fresh fruits, steamed vegetables, and lean protein. Happily, the 80-20 Rule tells us that it's okay to occasionally eat a cookie, a slice of pizza, a piece of garlic bread, or even a bit of creamy fettuccine Alfredo—so long as this makes up less than 20 percent of your food intake. In other words, it's perfectly acceptable to cheat a little. Just make sure that 80 percent of the food on your plate in Stage 5 is nutrient-dense, and you will be healthy, lean, fit, and fast. Pareto's Principle: another reason cyclists can thank the Italians.

protein from animal sources, especially seafood. Or you can snack on nuts, seeds, and berries. These are all good foods for Stage 5. They are all rich in vitamins, minerals, and other trace elements necessary for health and growth.

Avoid processed foods that come in packages, including those with labels that say "healthy." They aren't, and that even includes foods invented by sports nutrition scientists. They are still several million years behind nature in producing nutritious chow. Just eat *real* food in Stage 5.

If you are doing two workouts or race stages in a day, you may not get to Stage 5 until late in the day. Also, Stage 4 may replace Stage 1 with closely spaced workouts. That's not a problem.

That's all there is to it—a simple way to organize your day into five stages of eating to ensure adequate recovery and optimal health. You can find more details on this topic in my book *The Paleo Diet for Athletes*.

PERIODIZATION OF DIET

The optimal diet for peak performance must vary with the athlete just as the optimal training protocol must vary from person to person. We can't all eat the same things in the same relative amounts and reap the same benefits. Where your ancestors originated on the planet, and what was available for them to eat over the past 100,000 years or so, affect what you should eat now.

So the bottom line is that you must discover the mix of foods that works best for you. If you have never experimented with this, don't automatically assume you have found it already. You may be surprised by what happens when changes are made at the training table. A word of caution: Make changes gradually, and allow at least three weeks for your body to adapt to a new diet before passing judgment based on how you feel and your performance in training. It usually takes at least two weeks for someone to adapt to significant dietary changes before seeing any benefit. During the adaptation period you may feel lethargic and train poorly. For this reason, changes in diet are best done in the Transition and Preparation periods early in the season. Also, be aware that as you age, changes may occur in your body chemistry requiring further shifts in your diet.

That said, an optimal diet to enhance training, racing, and recovery involves not only eating moderate amounts of protein, carbohydrates, and fat, but also varying the mix of these macronutrients throughout the year. In other words, diet should cycle just as training cycles do within a periodization plan. Protein serves as the anchor for the diet and stays relatively constant throughout the year, whereas fat and carbohydrates rise and fall alternately with the training periods. Figure 16.1 illustrates this "seesaw" effect of the periodized diet. Note that the numbers used in this figure are merely an example, and the diet that is right for you may vary considerably.

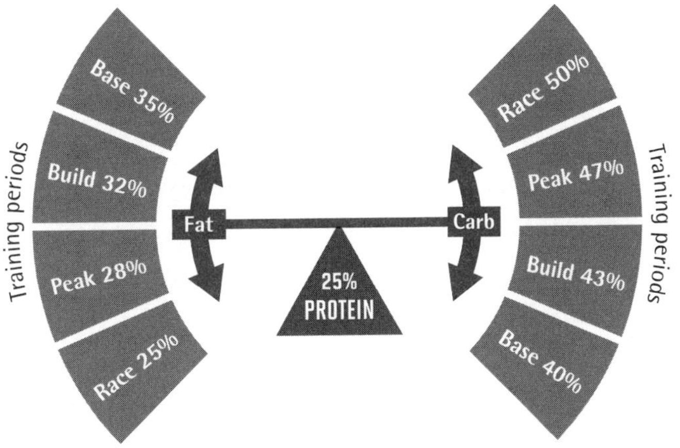

FIGURE 16.1

The Dietary Periodization "Seesaw"

Note: Exact percentages will vary depending on the athlete.

BODY WEIGHT MANAGEMENT

Cyclists are often concerned with losing weight to improve climbing. There's little doubt that being lighter means going up hills faster. A pound of excess body weight takes about two watts to get up a hill. That doesn't sound like much, but what if you could shed 10 pounds of fat? For most riders, that would mean ascending a hill 7 to 10 percent faster. That is a significant improvement in performance that would otherwise take lots of sweat and months of hard training to accomplish.

Although there is no question that excess body weight is a great handicap in climbing, this is not to say that all cyclists should lose weight. Trying to cut weight when you are already close to your optimal size is not a good idea. The key is to figure out what your optimal size is.

A good way to think about your body weight is in comparison to your height. For example, a 200-pound cyclist would be quite skinny if he were 7 feet tall. Your weight-to-height ratio is a simple and much more effective way to think about body mass than relying solely on the bathroom scale.

Determine your ratio by dividing your weight in pounds by your height in inches. Men who are good climbers are generally less than 2.1 pounds per inch. High-performance women climbers are generally under 1.9 pounds per inch. Men who exceed 2.5 pounds per inch and women above 2.3 are best advised to find flat racecourses where they have an advantage—particularly if the wind is blowing.

If you are above the climber weight-to-height-ratio range and you want to climb faster, what is the best way to drop those last few pounds? Unfortunately, studies on the best way for serious athletes to lose weight are rare. One group of researchers, however, has examined the issue in an interesting way. They compared eating less with exercising more to see which was more effective in dropping excess body fat.

The study followed six endurance-trained men who created a 1,000-calorie-per-day deficit for seven days. They did this in one of two ways, either by exercising more while maintaining their caloric intake, or by eating less while keeping exercise the same. The "exercise more" men added 1,000 calories of exercise daily—comparable to riding an additional 35 or so miles—and averaged 1.67 pounds of weight loss in a week. But the "eat less" men dropped 4.75 pounds on average for the week. Apparently, restricting food intake has a greater return *on the scales* than increasing the training workload does.

Notice that I said "on the scales." Unfortunately, the reduced-food-intake group in this study also lost a greater percentage of muscle mass than the increased-exercise group. That is an ineffective way to lose weight. If the scales show you're lighter, but you have less muscle to create power, the trade-off is not a good one.

How can you reduce calories and yet maintain muscle mass? Unfortunately, that question hasn't been answered for athletes. One study did address it for sedentary women, however. Perhaps the conclusions are still applicable to athletes.

In 1994, Italian researchers had 25 women eat only 800 calories a day for 21 days. Ten ate a relatively high-protein, low-carbohydrate diet. Fifteen ate a low-protein, high-carbohydrate diet. Both groups were restricted to 20 percent of calories from fat. The two groups lost similar amounts of weight, but there was a significantly greater loss of muscle for the women on the high-carbohydrate, low-protein diet.

So if cutting calories is more effective than increasing exercise for weight loss, it appears that the protein content of the diet must be kept at normal levels. This assumes that you're eating adequate protein before starting the diet, which many athletes aren't. If your protein intake is already low, typically less than about 20 percent of total calories, then dieting will negatively affect training quality and you are likely to lose muscle mass.

This leaves one question: When is the best time in the season to lose excess weight? When one of the athletes I coach needs to drop a few pounds, we try to accomplish this in the early Base period. The challenge for most athletes is that this generally includes the holiday season at year end. That can be a difficult time of year to reduce food intake. But by the time we reach Build 1—about 11 weeks before the first A-priority race—it's really too late. At that point we need to accept whatever his or her body weight is and move on to the more challenging race-like training.

ANTIOXIDANT SUPPLEMENTS

Generally it's a good idea to meet your nutritional needs with real foods and use food supplements sparingly. Scientists and supplement designers just aren't as smart as Mother Nature when it comes to deciding what to include and what to leave out of foods. Real food provides everything needed for health and fitness and is usually absorbed more efficiently than supplements. Antioxidant supplements are an exception. Here's why.

The process of metabolizing food and oxygen for exercise releases free radicals that cause damage to healthy cells. This is much like the rusting of metal—a breakdown caused by oxidation. Hard training produces large numbers of free radicals, which threaten both your health and your ability to recover following workouts.

One study measured by-products of free-radical damage in highly trained athletes, moderately trained athletes, and a sedentary group. The researchers found that the highly trained athletes had the highest levels of damage, while the moderately trained subjects had the least. The sedentary group was in the middle. A little exercise appears to be a healthy thing when it comes to free radicals, but extensive exercise or none at all causes problems.

In recent years, studies have shown that vitamins C and E reduce damage and prevent colds associated with extreme physical exertion by combining with the free radicals to stop the oxidative process. The research studies typically use large doses of each of these micronutrients—usually hundreds of times the RDA. Because the calculation involves variables such as age, sex, diet, body fat, size, and training load, it is difficult to determine the necessary amounts for each individual. Recommended daily intakes based on these studies generally fall into the following ranges:

Vitamin E	400–800 IU
Vitamin C	300–1,000 mg

The problem is that in order to get even the lowest of these dosages you would have to eat the equivalent of all of the following foods every day:

Asparagus	15 spears
Avocados	31
Broccoli	4 cups
Peaches	33
Prunes	30
Tomato juice	12 ounces
Spinach	17 cups
Wheat germ	1/4 cup

While some cyclists I know put away 3,000 to 4,000 calories a day, none eat such foods in these volumes.

Eating a wholesome diet from a wide-ranging menu is absolutely necessary for optimal health and fitness, but few people, including athletes, achieve the recommended standards. For example, it has been estimated that the minimum goal of eating five servings of fruits and vegetables per day is accomplished by less than 10 percent of the American population.

And although it is true that serious athletes tend to eat more than average citizens, they seldom eat enough of the right foods. A 1989 study of triathletes who competed in the national championship, the Hawaii Ironman, or the Huntsville, Alabama, Double Ironman found that as a group they had inadequate caloric intakes due to unusual eating habits. They also demonstrated poor food selection resulting from rigorous training schedules and limited time for eating.

Athletes often rely on daily multiple vitamins, but these seldom provide vitamins C and E in large enough quantities. Highly trained athletes may need to supplement their diets with individual vitamins, especially vitamin E. It appears that these supplements should be taken with meals twice a day for best results.

There are only low levels of risk associated with water-soluble vitamins such as vitamin A and the B-complex vitamins. High dosages of vitamin E can cause problems for those who are deficient in vitamin K. If you are on blood-thinning medications or high doses of pain relievers, you should also be cautious with vitamin E. Check with your health-care provider before starting supplementation with any vitamin. Even the water-soluble ones can cause problems for some individuals.

ERGOGENIC AIDS

Several years ago, university researchers asked a group of elite athletes to answer a question: "If you could take a pill that would ensure a gold medal in the next Olympics, but you would die within five years, would you take it?" The overwhelming answer, surprisingly, was yes.

Such attitudes have led elite athletes to experiment with anabolic steroids, erythropoietin (EPO), amphetamines, and other banned ergogenic aids. Some have consequently died in their quest for athletic excellence. Others have simply wasted their money on products that have no benefit beyond a placebo effect. Many of these substances have not withstood scientific investigation.

There is no magic pill that will guarantee an Olympic medal—or even a better-than-average race performance in your local crit. Training is still the single most important component of athletic excellence. There are, however, a few products that go beyond a normal diet and which science has generally found effective. I say "generally" because, as with the scientific study of almost anything, there have often been contradictory results. Also, not all ergogenic aids have the same benefits for everyone. Individualization applies here just as it does in training. Some of these products are discussed later in this chapter.

First let's look at ways to evaluate any ergogenic substance. There are five questions to ask concerning any product that claims to aid performance:

1. *Is it legal?* Products are often promoted to athletes despite the fact that they contain a banned substance. There have been many instances of blind trust resulting in a disqualification or worse for an elite athlete. To check on a specific product, call the U.S. Olympic Committee's Drug Hotline at 800-233-0393, or for a list of banned substances go to http://multimedia.olympic.org/pdf/en_ieport_542.pdf.
2. *Is it ethical?* Only you can answer this question. Some believe that a sport must be conducted in its purest form with absolutely no artificial assistance. But once we begin to ponder such ergogenic aids as carbohydrate loading and vitamin and mineral supplements, it becomes clear that it is difficult to draw a line in the sand.
3. *Is it safe?* Studies on the effects of various sports aids are often limited to a few weeks, as most subjects don't want to donate their entire lives to science. Such short periods of observation may not produce observable effects that might otherwise occur with long-term use. There is also the outside possibility that using multiple substances simultaneously or in combination with common medications will produce undesirable side effects. Another complication is that government safety regulations for supplements are more lenient than those for food products. Finally, it's always a good idea to check with your physician before supplementing, since your individual health or your family history may affect your decision about how to proceed.
4. *Is its use supported by the research?* There may be an isolated study on any product that shows evidence of a possible benefit, but does the bulk of the literature agree? To search the scientific journals for studies, point your browser at the government's PubMed Web site (www.ncbi.nlm.nih.gov/PubMed/), enter the substance of interest, and select "search." You'll be presented with a list of archived studies and their abstracts. Have fun reading the list—it could be a thousand or more items long. Better yet, ask a knowledgeable and trusted coach, trainer, registered dietitian, or medical professional for his or her insights on the product in question.
5. *Will it help in my race?* Even if generally supported by the research, not all ergogenic aids benefit all people in all events. There are many individual differences that may affect the use of a given product. It may not work well for you because of some combination of your age, sex, health status, medications used, and years of experience in the sport. Some aids have been shown to provide a benefit for short events such as the 100-meter dash, but not for events lasting for several hours.

The following is a discussion of several currently popular and legal ergogenic aids that are probably safe for most athletes and beneficial at some level in cycling. Before using any of these, consult with your health-care provider. Never use a product immediately before or during an important race without having first tried it in training or in a C-priority event.

BRANCHED-CHAIN AMINO ACIDS

During workouts lasting longer than about three hours, the body turns to protein to provide fuel. Protein can thus supply perhaps as much as 10 percent of the energy requirement in endurance sports. Three essential amino acids—out of the eight that must be present in the diet because they cannot be synthesized by the human body—make up about a third of the muscle tissue. These are leucine, isoleucine, and valine. Collectively they are called branched-chain amino acids (BCAAs).

Athletes who may not get enough protein, especially from animal sources, are likely to get the most benefit from using BCAA supplements. Since vegetarians are often deficient in protein intake levels, BCAA supplementation may prove especially helpful for them.

BCAA capsules may be purchased in many health-food stores and drugstores. They should come in a brown bottle to protect them from light, and the label should indicate each of the individual amino acids, preceded by an "L," as in "L-valine." This ensures adequate absorption.

Research on the use of BCAAs by athletes is inconclusive. Some studies have shown that supplementing the diet with BCAAs enhances endurance performance in long events, especially those lasting three hours or longer. A few have found that BCAAs even help in events of just one hour in duration. When benefits are seen in research, they typically fall into one of four categories:

- High workloads and exhaustive workouts and races are likely to weaken the immune system and lead to illness. BCAAs help to maintain the immune system following such events, reducing the likelihood of an athlete suffering training breakdowns. Thus they have the potential to speed recovery.
- Some studies have shown BCAAs to maintain muscle mass, power, and endurance during exhaustive, multiday endurance events such as stage races or crash training (see Chapter 10).
- BCAAs may help to reduce central nervous system fatigue, thus enabling an athlete to maintain performance late in a race. This is a recent theory that is still under investigation in the sports science community.
- BCAAs promote the use of fat for fuel while conserving glycogen.

There are four times in the training season when using BCAAs may be beneficial: during the Maximum Strength (MS) phase, in the Build and Peak training periods, for long and intense races, and while training intensely at high elevations. It is important to observe the following guidelines for supplementing with BCAAs:

- Take about 35 milligrams of BCAA for each pound of body weight daily, but only at the times indicated above. A 150-pound (68 kg) cyclist would take 5,250 milligrams, or about 5 grams daily. A 120-pound cyclist would consume 4,200 milligrams, or about 4 grams a day.

- One to two hours before an MS workout, a high-intensity workout in the Build or Peak period, or an A-priority race, take one-half of your daily dose. Then, one to two hours before bedtime the same day, take the other half.
- During a stage race, double your normal dosage, taking one-third before the race, one-third an hour or two before your post-race nap, and one-third before turning in for the day.

One potential negative side effect of taking BCAAs has to do with imbalances in the dietary intake of amino acids. When eating meat, all of the amino acids are present in the proper ratios; excessive supplementation with BCAAs may upset this balance. Some scientists and nutritionists are concerned that this may have long-term health implications.

MEDIUM-CHAIN TRIGLYCERIDES

Medium-chain triglycerides (MCTs) are processed fats that are metabolically different from other fats in that they are not readily stored as body fat and are quickly absorbed by the digestive system like carbohydrates, thus offering quick energy. They also provide about twice the calories per gram as carbohydrates. Some studies have shown that mixing MCTs and carbohydrates in sports drinks can improve endurance and help an athlete maintain the pace in the latter stages of races lasting two hours or more.

In a study at the University of Capetown in South Africa in the 1990s, six experienced cyclists rode for two hours at about 73 percent of maximum heart rate. Immediately after this steady but low-intensity ride, they time trialed for 40 kilometers at maximum effort. They did this three times over a ten-day period, using a different drink for each attempt. One drink was a normal carbohydrate sports drink. Another was an MCT-only beverage. The third ride used a sports drink spiked with MCT.

With the MCT-only drink, their average time for the maximum-effort ride was 1:12:08, and with the carbohydrate sports drink it was 1:06:45. With the mixed MCT-carbohydrate beverage, their average time was 1:05:00—a significant improvement. The study's authors believed that the MCT spared glycogen during the two-hour steady ride, allowing the riders to better utilize carbohydrates during the more intense time trial.

Consuming an MCT/sports drink mix may benefit your performance late in races that last three hours or longer. You can create a similar drink for yourself by mixing 16 ounces of your favorite sports drink with four tablespoons of MCT. You can purchase liquid MCT at most health-food stores. There are no known side effects for MCT used in this manner.

CREATINE

Creatine is one of the most recent additions to the ergogenics field, having its first known usage in athletics in 1993. Since then, the number of creatine studies has steadily increased, but a lot of questions remain unanswered.

Creatine is a substance found in dietary meat and fish, but it can also be created in your liver, kidneys, and pancreas. It is stored in muscle tissue in the form of creatine phosphate, a fuel used mostly during maximum efforts of up to about 12 seconds and, to a lesser extent, in intense efforts lasting a few minutes.

The amount of creatine made by the human body is not enough to boost performance for endurance events, but scientists have found that certain types of performance can be enhanced through supplementation with creatine for a few days preceding an event. In order to get an adequate amount of creatine from the diet to improve performance, an athlete would have to eat up to 5 pounds of rare meat or fish daily. Supplementation appears to be quite effective in increasing stored creatine.

A few years ago, scientists from Sweden, Great Britain, and Estonia studied the effect of creatine supplements on a group of runners. They tested the runners in a 4,000-meter interval workout (four intervals of 1,000 meters each) at maximum effort to obtain a baseline time, and then, following a creatine-loading period, tested them again in the same event. The creatine-supplemented subjects improved their total 4,000-meter times by an average of 17 seconds, while the athletes in the control group, who took only a placebo, slowed by 1 second. The relative advantage of the creatine users increased as the workout progressed. In other words, they experienced less fatigue and were faster at the end. Be aware, however, that a few other studies using swimmers and cyclists found no performance enhancement from creatine supplementation in repeated short, anaerobic efforts.

There is still not a lot known about creatine supplementation, but the benefits are probably greatest for maximizing the gains from interval and hill-repeat workouts, in races on the track, and in short races on the road such as criteriums. Some users believe that it decreases body fat, but it may only appear that way because creatine may cause total body weight to increase due to water retention, as fat stays the same. This would skew the results of certain forms of body-fat testing. Athletes have experienced total body weight gains in the range of 2 to 5 pounds (0.9 to 2.3 kg) during creatine supplementation. Also, creatine does not directly build muscle tissue. Instead it provides the fuel so that more power training is possible within a given workout, thus stimulating muscle-fiber growth.

The data on creatine use by endurance athletes are inconclusive. However, the best times to supplement with creatine for an endurance athlete, if at all, seem to be during the Maximum Strength weight-training phase and the higher-intensity Build period of training. Athletes who are low in force and power stand to benefit the most at these times. It is best to avoid its use in the Peak period, when weight gains due to water retention may be difficult to reduce prior to important races. About 20 to 30 percent of those who take creatine experience no measurable physiological changes. Vegetarian athletes may realize a greater gain from using creatine than meat-eating athletes since they typically have low levels.

Most studies have used very large dosages, such as 20 to 30 grams of creatine a day, taken in 4 to 5 doses over a period of 4 to 7 days. One found the same muscle levels, however, on as little as 3 grams daily for 30 days. After the loading phase, muscle creatine can be maintained at high levels for 4 to 5 weeks with 2 grams taken daily. Dissolving creatine in grape or orange juice seems to improve absorption. In these studies, not all the subjects experienced an increase in muscle creatine levels, despite high dosages.

According to scientists who have been working with creatine, there appears to be little health risk with supplementation because the creatine is passively filtered from the blood and puts no extra workload on the kidneys; however, the longest study lasted only 10 weeks, so the effects of long-term use are unknown. Scientists do know that once you stop short-term use, your natural production of creatine resumes. The only well-established side effect is the addition of body weight during the loading phase, which soon disappears. A greater concern is that creatine may give you a false positive in a urine test for kidney problems. There have also been anecdotal accounts of muscle spasm and cramping in power athletes using creatine on a long-term basis. This problem may be caused by a lowered concentration of electrolytes in the muscles.

Creatine can be purchased at health-food stores and will probably cost \$2–\$3 a day during the loading phase. Because of the potential kidney and cramping issues, it is wise to talk with your health-care provider before supplementing with creatine.

CAFFEINE

Caffeine is one of the oldest and most popular ergogenic aids. It has been shown to increase fatty acids in the blood, thus reducing the reliance on limited glycogen stores in the muscles. It also stimulates the central nervous system, decreasing the perception of fatigue, and may enhance muscle contractions. Most studies show benefits for intense events lasting an hour or longer when 300 to 600 milligrams of caffeine (two to four cups of coffee) are consumed 45 minutes to an hour prior to the start. Table 16.3 lists the caffeine content of common products.

TABLE 16.3 Caffeine Content of Common Products

BEVERAGE (6 oz/180 ml)	CAFFEINE (mg)
Drip coffee	180
Instant coffee	165
Percolated coffee	149
Brewed tea	60
Mountain Dew	28
Chocolate syrup	24
Coca-Cola	23
Pepsi Cola	19

Numerous scientific studies of caffeine's effects over the past 20 years have produced many contradictions. Most have shown benefits for endurance athletes. A recent English study, however, found no benefits for marathon runners, but significant aid for milers. The majority of studies have suggested that caffeine only helps in events lasting longer than 90 minutes, but others have shown improvement in 60- and even 45-minute competitions.

The author of one study concluded that caffeine causes a complex chemical change in the muscles that stimulates more forceful contractions during a longer period of time than would occur without it. However, most researchers have found that caffeine simply spares muscle glycogen during endurance exercise. The beneficial effects peak at about one hour after consumption and seem to last for three to five hours.

Glycogen is an energy source stored in the muscles. When glycogen runs low, the rider is forced to slow down or stop. Anything that causes the body to conserve this precious fuel, as caffeine appears to do, allows a cyclist to maintain a fast pace for a longer time. For example, one study of cyclists reported a 20 percent improvement in time to exhaustion following two cups of coffee one hour before testing.

The IOC's legal limit equates to about six to eight 5-ounce cups of coffee in an hour, depending on the athlete's size. While that's quite a bit to drink, it's certainly possible. It's interesting to note that other recent research has suggested that caffeine at the illegal level actually had a negative effect on performance.

Most studies find that 1.4 to 2.8 milligrams of caffeine per pound of body weight taken an hour before exercise benefits most subjects engaged in endurance exercise. That's about two or three cups of coffee for a 154-pound person. Athletes have also been known to use other products high in caffeine before and during competition.

While caffeine may sound like a safe and effective aid, be aware that there are possible complications. Most studies have shown it to have a diuretic effect on nonexercisers, although one using athletes found little increased fluid loss during exercise. In people not used to caffeine, it may bring on anxiety, muscle tremors, gastrointestinal cramps, diarrhea, upset stomach, and nausea. These are not good things to experience before a race. Caffeine also inhibits the absorption of thiamine, a vitamin needed for carbohydrate metabolism, and several minerals, including calcium and iron.

If you normally have a cup or two of coffee in the morning, you'll probably have no side effects when using it before a race. It appears that the benefits are greater, however, for non–coffee drinkers than for regular users. If you don't drink coffee but are considering using it before a competition, try it several times before workouts to see how it affects you.

The supplement industry in the United States is not closely regulated by the government, and consequently, product purity may be an issue for any supplement, especially if you purchase it from an unscrupulous manufacturer. A recent analysis of a widely advertised category of dietary supplements found unidentifiable impurities in most of the products. Some of these turned out to be banned substances that cost athletes their eligibility for several months. Buy only from reputable companies whose products are well established in the marketplace. Don't take anything unless you are sure that it does not contain banned substances.

Also, it is unknown how the ergogenic aids described here may interact if used in combination with each other, with other supplements, or even with many of the medications commonly used by athletes, such as ibuprofen or aspirin. It's always a good idea to talk with your health-care provider before taking any supplement, all the more so if you are also taking a prescribed or over-the-counter medication.

When using an ergogenic aid, it's important that you assess the benefits, if any, for your performance. Try one at a time, and keep careful notes in your training diary. Not only does using several aids concurrently increase your risk of side effects, it also clouds the issue of which one provided the most performance gain—or prevented it. In addition, you should always be skeptical of claims that you will experience better race performances as a result of supplementation. Advertisers have incentives to exaggerate the benefits. Was it really the pill, or was it the placebo effect? Look at these claims and studies with a critical eye. Taking the time to understand what helps you and what doesn't will ultimately lead to your best races.

In the final analysis, training and diet provide 99.9 percent of the impetus for performance improvements. Supplements offer only a small benefit. If your training and diet are less than desirable, ergogenic supplements won't solve your problem.

17

PROBLEMS

Ride lots.

—EDDY MERCKX, WHEN ASKED HOW TO TRAIN

CYCLING IS AN ADDICTION. The addictive nature of racing on two wheels is usually a positive, but from time to time problems do appear.

We so desperately want to excel in racing, and yet things get in the way. Sometimes it seems that life just isn't fair. Or is it? Where do our problems come from? In our greed to become more fit in less time, we may overtrain. We work out despite the scratchy throat and lose ten days to illness rather than five. Or our bodies seem invincible, so we push big gears in the hills repeatedly and wind up nursing a sore knee while watching the next race from the curb.

With rare exceptions, the problems we face in training and racing are of our own making. Our motivation to excel is exceeded only by our inability to listen to our bodies. The result is often overtraining, burnout, illness, or injury. This chapter describes how to avoid these problems, or, if they haven't been avoided, how to deal with them.

RISK AND REWARD

Choosing your workout for the day is a lot like investing in the stock market. When buying stock, the wise investor considers the risks and rewards each stock offers. There are blue chip stocks, which have a very low risk but increase in value slowly and steadily over time. Then there are penny stocks, generally offered by smaller or newer companies and considered quite volatile and speculative. They are risky—but the potential reward is also quite high. So you can play it safe with blue chip investments, or risk everything on striking it rich with the right penny stock.

Every workout you do has a similar risk/reward equation. Some workouts are low risk in terms of duration or intensity, but have a low return in terms of fitness. Others cost more in terms of your time and energy investment, but can allow your fitness to increase dramatically, particularly if you are wise enough not to overdo it.

Finding the right ratio of risk to reward for breakthrough workouts requires a delicate balance between pushing yourself to new levels and allowing yourself to get adequate rest so that your body can recover properly. The risks associated with these potentially high-paying workouts are the aforementioned overtraining, burnout, illness, and injury. Training time is lost when these setbacks occur, and so the overly aggressive athlete must return to basic, low-risk, low-reward training to reestablish a previously attained fitness level. Athletes who experience these conditions frequently may be addicted to high-risk training. Figure 17.1 illustrates the workout risk and reward curves.

FIGURE 17.1

The Risk/Reward Curves

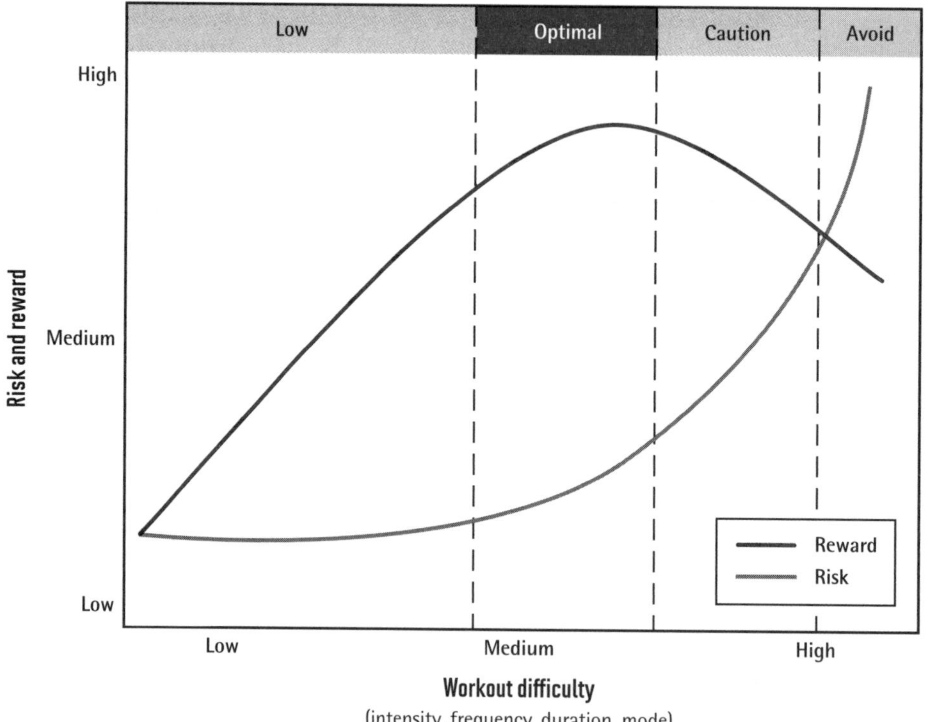

Note: A low degree of workout difficulty yields low to modest returns, but this range is the safest approach to training.

Risk is associated with the potential results from some combination of the frequency, intensity, duration, and mode of training and is unique for each athlete. What is high risk for one rider may be low risk for another. The difference has to do with experience, fitness levels, susceptibility to injury, previous training adaptations, age, and other factors.

Each athlete has a workout frequency and duration that is optimal. An elite cyclist may work out six hours a day for several days in a row and become more fit. But a novice trying to do this will soon break down and be forced to stop training for several days in order to recover. This is often referred to as "too much too soon." It's imperative that you find a workout frequency and duration that work for you and then stick to it.

The same holds true for the intensity of workouts. A lot of training done at high intensity, such as intervals, hard group rides, and races on consecutive days, makes for very risky but potentially rewarding training. If you survive it with your body and health intact, you will become a much fitter rider. Most can't safely sustain this level of training.

Whenever you work out for some period of time with high frequency, intensity, or duration, you must lower the risk by including substantial recovery time. Frequent recovery is the key to keeping this type of risk at a manageable level.

Risk associated with "mode" refers to the type of workout you do—including cycling, weight lifting, and crosstraining sports such as running and swimming. Of these modes, running is the riskiest because of the stress it places on bones and soft tissues. For some athletes, a lot of running is likely to cause injury; those who approach running cautiously, however—by strengthening their running-related tissues and bones gradually over a long period of time—may find that it produces good general aerobic conditioning, especially early in the training season.

Weight lifting also has the potential to be a high-risk mode of training. Going to high-load lifting before the body is ready can easily cause injury. I've seen it happen with many athletes who became too aggressive with the risks they took in the weight room.

Within a weight-training regimen, some exercises are riskier than others. Freebar squats are a good example of this. A heavily loaded bar placed on the shoulders may be especially risky for the athlete who is new to the weight room, who has experienced knee or hip injuries, or who is an older athlete with degenerating spinal disks. But if you can handle it, the reward reaped from squats is significant. Leg presses, step-ups, and lunges are less risky exercises: They work most of the same muscle groups as squats, but also carry a lesser reward.

Plyometric exercises—explosive movements done to build power, as described in Chapter 12—also have the potential to be both high risk and high reward. Eccentric-contraction plyometrics are riskier but potentially more rewarding than concentric-contraction plyometrics. An example of an eccentric-contraction plyometric exercise is jumping off a high box, landing on the floor, and then immediately springing back up to a second high box. A concentric-contraction version of this same exercise eliminates the jump down and landing, so you are simply jumping to the high box and stepping down. There is less potential for reward this way, but also less risk.

The purpose of this chapter is to help you realize that when selecting a workout, you need to consider the reward you hope to get from it and the risks involved in doing it. By investing wisely in your training, you will increase your likelihood of building excellent fitness through consistency while avoiding the common pitfalls of overly aggressive training. If you make a mistake in your training, make it on the side of low risk rather than high risk. I guarantee you will do better in the long run.

OVERTRAINING

Overtraining is best described as a decreased work capacity resulting from an imbalance between training and rest. In the real world of cycling, this means that decreasing performance is the best indicator of training gone awry. But when we have a bad race, what do most of us do? You guessed it—we train harder. We put in more miles, do more intervals, or both. It is a rare athlete who rests more when things aren't going well.

Of course, poor races don't always result from too much training. You could be exhausted from "overliving." A 40-hour-per-week job, two kids, a spouse, a mortgage, and other responsibilities all take their inevitable toll on energy. Training just happens to be the thing most easily controlled. You sure aren't going to call the boss to ask for the day off because your race performances are suffering (imagine how that conversation would go). Nor can you tell the kids to get themselves to the Scout meeting. Life goes on. Your smartest option is to train less and rest more.

Figure 17.2 shows what happens when we refuse to give in and insist on more, more, more. Notice that as the training load increases, fitness also increases, up to our personal limit. At that point, fitness declines despite an increasing load. Training beyond our limit causes a loss of fitness.

Increased training loads that eventually lead to overtraining stem from three common training excesses:

FIGURE 17.2

The Overtraining Curve

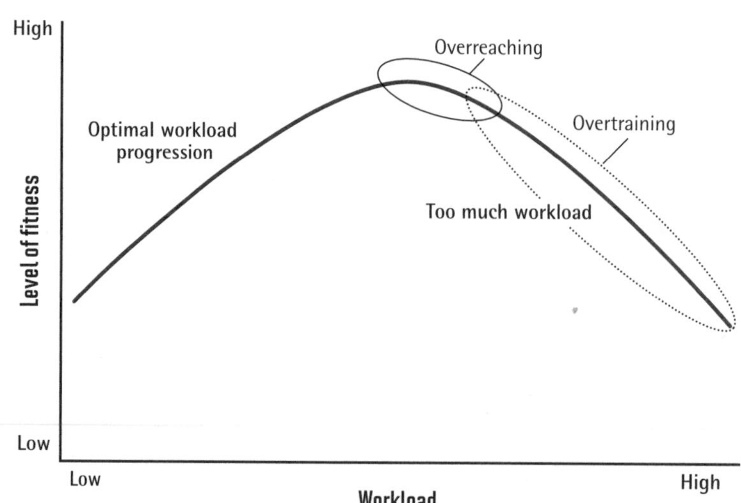

Note: Workload is frequency, intensity, and duration of training plus life's other responsibilities.

1. Workouts that are too long (excess duration)
2. A level of exertion that is too high too often (excess intensity)
3. Too many workouts done in too little time (excess frequency)

In my experience, the most common cause of overtraining in competitive cyclists is excess intensity. Road racing is roughly 90 percent aerobic and 10 percent anaerobic. Training should reflect that relationship. Placing too much emphasis on anaerobic training for a few weeks is a sure way to overtrain. That's why the Build period is limited to six weeks of high-intensity workouts plus two recovery weeks.

OVERTRAINING INDICATORS

The body responds to the overtrained state by issuing warnings in many forms. These reactions are the body's way of preventing death by making further increases in stress volume impossible.

If you've undergone blood testing during the Preparation or Base period of training, you have a healthy baseline for later comparison. When you suspect overtraining during other periods of the season, it's a good idea to have your blood tested again. The list below shows primary blood indicators of overtraining as reported in a 1992 study of experienced middle- and long-distance runners. Realize that you are comparing your recent

Overtraining Indicators

Although many of the problems listed below could have other causes, they could be signs of overtraining. In the blood-marker list, significant decreases from individual baseline markers may indicate overtraining.

BEHAVIORAL SYMPTOMS	PHYSICAL SYMPTOMS	BLOOD-MARKER SYMPTOMS
Apathy	Reduced performance	Albumin
Lethargy	Weight changes	Ammonium
Poor concentration	Morning heart rate changes	Ferritin Iron
Changes in sleep patterns	Muscle soreness	Free fatty acids
Irritability	Swollen lymph glands	Glycerin
Decreased libido	Diarrhea	Hemoglobin
Clumsiness	Injury	Iron
Increased thirst	Infection	LDL cholesterol
Sluggishness	Amenorrhea	Leukocytes
Sugar cravings	Decreased exercise heart rate	Magnesium
	Slow-healing cuts	Triglycerides
		VLDL cholesterol

test results with the baseline established when you were known to be healthy, not with standards for the general population.

None of the items listed are "sure" indicators of overtraining. Many of these situations may even exist in perfectly healthy athletes who are in top shape. In dealing with overtraining, there are no absolutes. You're looking for a preponderance of evidence to confirm what you already suspect.

STAGES OF OVERTRAINING

There are three stages on the road to becoming overtrained. The first stage is "overload." This is a part of the normal process of increasing the training load beyond what you are used to in order to cause the body to adapt. If great enough, but controlled, it results in supercompensation, as described in Chapter 10. During this stage it's typical to experience short-term fatigue, but generally you will feel great and may have outstanding race results. But it's also common during this stage to feel like your body is invincible. You can do anything, if you want to. That belief brings on the next stage.

In the second stage, "overreaching," you continue to train at the same abnormally high load levels, or even increase them for a period of two weeks or so. Extending the Build period of training, with its higher intensity, is a common cause of overreaching. Now, for the first time, your performance noticeably decreases. Usually this happens in workouts before it shows up in races, where high motivation often pulls you through. Fatigue becomes longer lasting than in the overload stage, but with a few days of rest it is still reversible. The problem is that you may decide that what is needed is harder training, which brings on the third stage.

The third and final stage is a full-blown overtraining syndrome. Fatigue is now chronic—it stays with you like a shadow. You are tired upon awaking as well as throughout the day, on the job, or in class, and yet you have trouble sleeping normally at night. Your adrenal glands are exhausted.

I tell the athletes I train that in order to get to the "peak of fitness" they must carefully manage the overloading process and the fatigue that comes as a result of it. At your optimal fitness level you are able to resist or delay fatigue, but there will still be limits to how long you can limit fatigue. Figure 17.2 shows how increasing your training load can cause a decline in fitness and bring you dangerously close to the edge of overtraining. The idea is to go to the edge infrequently, and then back off. By "infrequently," I mean once every four weeks or so. After three weeks of load increases, you need to allow for recovery and adaptation. Some athletes, especially masters and novices, may need to recover more frequently, perhaps after only two weeks. To do more is to fall over the edge.

As the body enters a chronically fatigued state, overtraining indicators begin to appear. You may experience poor sleep quality, excessive tiredness, or muscle soreness on a continuing basis. The indicators may be minor in number and severity, but with too great an increase or too prolonged a period of stress, you're in danger of overtraining. At this point, if you are wise, you reduce your training load (see Figure 17.2) and get the rest you need. Rest brings adaptation, with your fitness increasing to a level that exceeds the level you had started with four weeks before. After repeating this process several times, you are ready to peak.

If you fall over the edge into overtraining, the only option is rest. At the first signs of overtraining, take 48 hours of complete rest, and then try a brief recovery workout. If you are still not feeling peppy, take another 48 hours off and repeat the test ride. It could take five to eight weeks of this to fully beat back overtraining, at a great loss of fitness.

THE ART OF TRAINING

The art of training is based on knowing where the precipice is: When are you so fatigued that you are on the verge of overtraining? Highly motivated, young, or novice cyclists are less likely than seasoned riders to recognize when they are about to cross this line. That is why many cyclists are better off training under the guidance of an experienced coach.

Smart training requires constantly assessing your readiness to train. Chapter 15 provided a training diary format with suggested daily indicators to rate. Judiciously tracking these indicators will help you pay closer attention to your body's daily messages.

Unfortunately, there is no surefire formula for knowing when you have done too much and are starting to overreach. The best prevention is the judicious use of rest and recovery. Just as workouts must vary between hard and easy, so must weeks and months vary. It's far better to be undertrained, but eager, than to be overtrained. When in doubt, leave it out.

BURNOUT

By August every year, many riders begin to experience burnout. It is not overtraining—there are no physical symptoms—but more a state of mind. It is marked by decreased interest in training and racing, sometimes even frustration and a feeling of overwhelming drudgery when it comes time to get on the bike.

A mentally fried athlete may have been experiencing a slump for a couple of weeks. Negative reactions to the slump lower self-esteem and motivation, making focused concentration a thing of the past. This downward spiral leads to burnout.

A medical condition such as mononucleosis or anemia may be masquerading as burnout, but this is rare. For most of us, it is just a matter of timing. Still, this is a good time to get a blood test, just in case.

BURNOUT TIMING

That some cyclists become mental toast by August is not just bad luck or mere coincidence. About 220 to 250 days into heavy training without a break, athletes begin to experience burnout. If your serious workouts started in December or January, and there have been no breaks, August burnout fits right into that timeline.

Many riders race twice every weekend and do a hard club ride and BT workout at midweek. That is a lot of intensity and emotional investment week after week. For this reason, Build periods should last no longer than eight weeks, including the recovery weeks. Serious racing without time off the bike for more than six weeks—or fewer, for some—may also lead to August burnout.

Those who experience burnout are usually zealous athletes who set high racing goals. By August, they have either attained the goals or decided they are unattainable. Either situation may contribute to racing and training apathy.

Circumstances other than the two-wheeled variety may also contribute to an athlete becoming mental toast. Emotional stresses such as a job change, a divorce, or moving to a new home can definitely lead to burnout. Environmental factors, including heat, humidity, high altitude, and pollution, can also take a toll on enthusiasm. All of this may be compounded by a diet deficient in nutrients and water.

BURNOUT ANTIDOTE

If there is no doubt that you are burned-out, and yet you still have an important race at the end of the season, there are only three things you can do: rest, rest, and rest. Time off the bike is probably the hardest medicine to take for a usually enthusiastic rider. But a week to ten days of no training at all should have you ready to go again soon.

I can hear you now: "I'll lose all my fitness." No, you won't, but even if you did, which would be better: fit but apathetic, or unfit and ready to go? It takes months to develop endurance, force, and speed. They won't slip away in a few days. After a short break, you'll be ready to race again with two weeks of Build 1 training, three weeks tops.

More important, you need to learn something from the experience: Don't let it happen again next year. The way to avoid burnout in August is to plan on a two-peak season. This means bringing yourself into race form in the spring and then taking a short break of five to seven days off the bike. After that, rebuild your base fitness and be ready to go with another late-season peak.

The key to racing well when you want to is foresight. Good races in August don't just happen—they are planned well in advance.

ILLNESS

You would think that a lot of training would be healthy and help you avoid illness. That is not the case. Those who work out frequently are more likely to catch a bug than those who work out only occasionally.

A study of runners in the Los Angeles Marathon found that those who ran more than 60 miles per week were twice as susceptible to respiratory illness as those who ran less than 20 miles each week. Runners who completed the marathon were six times more likely to be ill in the week following the race as those who trained hard for the race but for some reason did not run it.

TIMING

The six hours following a hard workout or race has been shown to be the most critical phase for remaining healthy, as the immune system is depressed and less capable of fighting off disease. Unfortunately, this is also a time when many athletes are traveling and coming into contact with germs. If possible, avoid public places during this six-hour period. If you must be out and about, wash your hands frequently and try to minimize touching your face at this time.

NECK CHECK

What should you do when a cold or flu bug gets you down? Should you continue to train normally, cut back, or stop altogether? Doing a "neck check" will help you decide. If your symptoms are a runny nose, sneezing, or a scratchy throat (all symptoms above the neck), start your workout, but reduce the intensity to zone 1 or 2 and keep the duration short. If you feel worse after the first few minutes, stop and head home. If the symptoms are below the neck, such as a chest cold, chills, vomiting, achy muscles, or a fever, don't even start. You probably have an acute viral infection. Exercising intensely in this condition will increase the severity of the illness and can cause extreme complications, including death.

These below-the-neck symptoms are likely to be accompanied by the Coxsackie virus, which can invade the heart muscle and cause arrhythmia and other complications. I can speak from personal experience on this subject. In November 1994, I caught a bad cold with several below-the-neck symptoms, including fever, achy muscles, and coughing with mucus. Five months later, I had a full-blown Coxsackie virus in my heart. After a year of inactivity, I was finally able to start training again. No race or any amount of fitness is worth paying such a price. Don't take these symptoms lightly. Keep in mind that Coxsackie virus may be present whenever you have a respiratory infection with indicators below the neck.

RECUPERATING

After an illness has abated, you are likely to be run-down for some time. Many people experience a 15 percent reduction in muscle strength for up to a month following a bout of the flu. Your aerobic capacity may be reduced for up to three months, and your muscles may become acidic at lower levels of exercise intensity during this time. This means you will feel weak when working out even though the acute stage of your illness is past. Following a below-the-neck illness, return to the Base training period for two days for every day you had symptoms.

Trying to "push" past the flu will likely make your condition worse and cause it to last longer. It is best to get rid of the illness as soon as possible by allowing your limited energy reserves to go into fighting the disease rather than training.

INJURIES

For a serious athlete, there's nothing worse than an injury. As if it's not bad enough that it causes the athlete's fitness to slip away, depression may also set in, especially since so much of an athlete's life is tied to being physical.

Some people seem prone to injuries. They get them doing what others do routinely. One injury is more than a nuisance, but having to recuperate from injuries repeatedly can sideline an athlete often enough to ruin a racing career. Sidebar 17.1 provides some prevention tips that can help keep injury-prone people healthy.

SIDEBAR 17.1

Training Mistakes

It's amazing how often I see different athletes make the same mistakes. In fact, I've found that there are seven mistakes that are so common that nearly everyone makes them, from novice to experienced pro. I see it happen every season.

MISTAKE #1: NO DIRECTION

Almost every athlete has goals, but there are two problems with the goals they most often set. First, they are usually too vague. The typical athlete makes "I want to get better" goals for which it is impossible to measure whether progress is being made. Second, the goals are usually forgotten when hard training or racing begins. Many athletes become so absorbed in preparing for the next race that they become myopic about training, focusing on the short term instead of the long term.

MISTAKE #2: NO PRIORITIES

Without priorities, every race is treated as critical. It's easy to make this mistake, especially if you're doing a series of races that all count toward the final standings. Without priority races, you never have an opportunity to truly peak and can never fully realize what you're capable of doing in a race. That means permanent mediocrity.

MISTAKE #3: TRAINING THE WRONG STUFF

Most athletes have a pretty good idea of their weaknesses, but they don't work hard enough at correcting them. It's like the old saying, "A chain is only as strong as its weakest link." If your weak link is climbing, and the season's most important race is on a hilly course, you'd better be doing a lot to train yourself to climb better. Paying lip service to climbing while spending a lot of time and energy on flat courses, which you may enjoy more, won't do much to produce good race results. The weak link is still weak.

MISTAKE #4: INTERVALS TOO SOON

I've never figured out why an athlete who doesn't have a race until May is out doing gut-busting intervals in December. Why are athletes so eager to start intervals? I hope you're not doing this, but chances are good that you are. Wait until later in the season.

MISTAKE #5: NOT ENOUGH REST

This may be the most common mistake cyclists make. Nearly everyone who is even slightly serious about training ends up doing it sooner or later. I suspect it's so common because those who are successful in endurance sports tend to have certain personality traits. They learned at an early age that hard work produces results. So when things are going well, they work hard. And when things aren't going well, they work harder. In fact, they believe that hard work is the solution to all problems. This inevitably leads to overtraining (see mistake #6).

MISTAKE #6: IGNORING FATIGUE

Endurance athletes seem to believe they are Superman or Superwoman. Although they may understand that too much training and too little rest results in overtraining, they seem to think they are immune to the problem. When the signs of overtraining appear, they ignore them and continue as if they're just minor hindrances. "Overtraining can't happen to me" is the general belief.

MISTAKE #7: NOT TAPERING FOR BIG RACES

Either athletes don't know how to taper for important races or they're afraid of losing fitness by backing off. Every year I see athletes doing excessively long and hard workouts the week of an important race. They just don't understand that race-week rest is what will produce their best result on the weekend.

Preventing the above mistakes is essentially what a coach does for you. Coaches know that if they can just hold an athlete back a bit, the race results will take care of themselves. You'll be a better self-coach by eliminating such errors.

EQUIPMENT FIT AND SETUP

Get equipment that fits correctly. Riding a bike that is too big or too small sets you up for an injury. This is especially a problem for women cyclists, who all too often ride bikes designed for men, and for juniors, who sometimes ride bikes they'll "grow into."

Having poor biomechanics can easily injure a joint, especially the knee, as cycling involves repeating the same movement pattern hundreds or thousands of times under a load. Once you have the right equipment, ask an experienced bike shop employee, bike-fit specialist, or coach to take a look at your position and offer suggestions for improvement. Be especially concerned with saddle fore-aft position and height. If you don't have access to an experienced bike-fit expert, read *Andy Pruitt's Medical Guide for Cyclists,* which contains valuable guidance on proper bike fit.

TRAINING

The most likely times to get injured are in the two days after very long or very hard workouts or races. These days should be for short and easy rides, reserved for crosstraining, or days off altogether. In the same manner, two or three hard weeks of training should be followed by a week of reduced volume and intensity. This may be difficult to do when you know your cardiovascular and energy production systems are willing and able to handle it, but such restraint will help keep you injury free.

STRENGTH AND STRETCHING

The weakest link for most cyclists is the muscle-tendon junction. This is where tears and strains are likely to occur. Many muscle-tendon problems can be prevented early in the season by gradually improving the muscle's strength and range of motion. These are probably the most neglected areas for endurance athletes. Going for a ride is fun, but grunting through a combined strength and stretching session in the gym seems like drudgery. Hang in there, and you'll reap the benefits.

LISTEN

Pay attention to your body's signals to avoid injury. Learn to tell the difference between sore muscles that come from a high-quality effort and sore joints or tendons. Pinpoint any discomfort and try to put the sensation into words in your training journal. Don't just say "my knee hurts." Is it above or below the kneecap? Front or back of the knee? Is it a sharp pain or a dull ache? Does it hurt only while you are riding, or all the time? Is the pain worse when you are going up stairs or down? These are the sorts of questions you will be asked when you finally seek professional help. Be ready for them.

If the pain persists after five days of reduced activity, it is time to see a health-care provider. Don't put it off. Injuries are easier to turn around in the early stages than later on.

18

RECOVERY

My number one asset as a bike racer is my recovery.

—BOBBY JULICH

I HAVE EMPHASIZED RECOVERY throughout this book, occasionally providing guidelines for recovery days and periods. I have also discussed techniques for recovering from daily workouts through replenishing the nutrients and fluids your body needs. It should be clear by now that recovery is not just wasted time—during recovery your body is making adaptations to the training you have done and growing stronger in order to be able to meet greater challenges in the future.

In this chapter I will explain this important and often underrated aspect of training more fully. Due to the nature of the sport, with its stage races and double-race weekends, cycling often requires the athlete to be ready to go again within a few hours. In addition, the sooner a cyclist can do another breakthrough workout, the sooner his or her fitness will improve. Recovery holds the key to both of these situations.

THE NEED FOR RECOVERY

It is reasonably easy to get athletes to train hard. Give serious riders tough workouts and not only are they challenged, but most are even happy. Competitive cyclists are successful in part because they have a great capacity and affinity for hard work. Without such drive, they would never make it in the sport.

If daily, arduous training were the key to victory, everyone would be atop the winner's platform. The greater challenge for the self-coached cyclist is not formidable training sessions, but rather knowing how, when, and for how long to recover following tough workouts and races. Although that sounds like it should be easy, for most it is not. Recovery is the one area of training that athletes have the most difficulty getting right.

Recovery determines when you can go hard again, and ultimately it determines your fitness level. Cut recovery short frequently enough and the specter of overtraining lurks ever nearer. Go beyond the time needed to recover, and you may lose some components of your fitness as well as precious time. Most serious athletes err on the side of not allowing enough recovery. They believe that "training" only takes place on the bike. It is how many miles they ride, how hard the workouts are, and how often they ride that matter. They believe that what they do off the bike has no relevance to fitness—it is "non-training" time and therefore of no consequence.

If you think that way, you are wrong. Off-the-bike recovery time is critical to improving performance. Workouts provide the potential for increased fitness, but it's during recovery that the potential is realized. The time it takes for your body to realize this potential is also critical. The sooner you recover, the sooner you can do another quality workout. The sooner you can do another quality workout, the more fit you become. Another way of looking at it is as a formula:

$$\text{Fitness} = \text{workout} + \text{recovery}$$

In this formula, workout and recovery are of equal value. So the higher the intensity of the workout, the greater the depth of the recovery you need, not only in terms of time, but also in terms of method. The workout and the recovery must balance, and if the balance is right, your fitness is bound to improve. Get the balance wrong often enough, and you are initially suffering, then off the back, and finally overtrained.

If you truly understand this relationship between workouts and recovery, you will be as concerned about the quality of the recovery times you give yourself as you are about the difficulty of the workouts you undertake. The first question to answer in writing a weekly training schedule should be "How quickly can I recover?" With the answer to that question, the week can be scheduled.

RECOVERY PERIODIZATION

If you could wish for one athletic-enhancing gene, it should be the one that improves your capacity to recover quickly from workouts. Athletes with this gene seem to naturally become the best athletes in their respective racing categories. This is a conclusion I've drawn from my own observations, and while there aren't any scientific data to back it up, there seems to be a strong correlation between one's ability to recover and the rate of one's fitness progression. Recovering quickly also means getting in good shape quickly.

Why is this so? There is an easy explanation: It's during recovery following hard training that the body realizes the changes that we call "form," which is simply to say that one's potential for performance in a race or in subsequent training develops during rest. These changes may result in fat-burning enzyme increases, more resilient muscles and tendons, decreases in body fat, greater heart stroke volume, enhanced glycogen storage, and so on. Besides overloading your body with the stresses of hard exercise, focusing on recovery is the most powerful thing you can do in training to perform at a higher level. But this is the part of the training process that most self-coached athletes get wrong. They don't allow for enough recovery, and consequently, they overwhelm their bodies with stress.

Let's look at where recovery figures into the Annual Training Plan you created in Chapter 8.

Yearly Recovery. Recovery takes place during the Transition periods that come after the Race periods in your training plan. The purpose of these low-volume, low-intensity Transition periods is to allow your body and mind to rejuvenate themselves before you start back into another period of hard training. If you have two A-priority races in a season, you should generally have two Transition periods. The first may only be for three to five days, but the one that comes at the end of the season may well last for four weeks or more depending on the difficulty level of the previous season, especially the final part.

Monthly Recovery. Build recovery into your monthly training plan every third or fourth week (more frequently for masters riders). This regular period of reduced workload may be three to seven days, depending on what you did in the previous hard training weeks, how fit you are becoming, how quickly you tend to recover, and other individual factors.

Figure 18.1 illustrates what happens when you schedule a monthly recovery time. As your fatigue increases over the course of two to three weeks of increasing workloads, your form diminishes. Form is your potential for performance. In other words, how well you may train or race at any given point in time is based on how rested you are. Notice

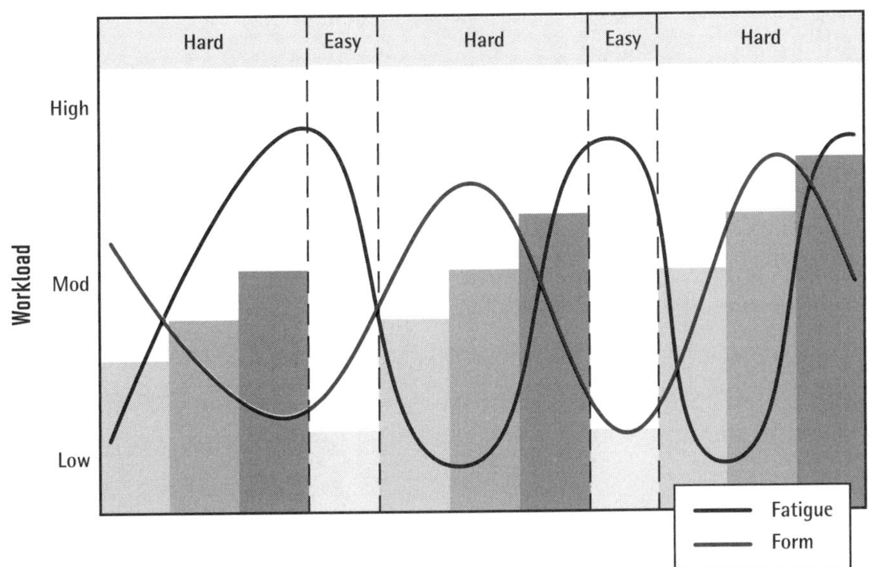

FIGURE 18.1

Impact of Recovery on Fatigue and Form

that fatigue and form follow nearly opposite paths. A key principle of training is to unload fatigue frequently, which has the effect of improving your readiness to train and race well again. If you do not unload accumulated fatigue, you become a zombie struggling through low-quality workouts with no enthusiasm.

Weekly Recovery. Within each week there should be hard and easy days. No one, not even elite athletes, can train hard every day with no recovery breaks. Just as with any part of training, "easy" is a relative term. Some athletes need a day completely off from exercise every week. Other athletes, especially those with the quick-recovery gene who also have a high capacity for work, can work out seven days a week. These elite athletes still need easy days each week, however. And even they need an occasional day off completely from exercise. A day off the bike aids not only physical recovery but mental recovery as well.

Daily Recovery. When you are doing two-a-day workouts, there will be times when both are challenging sessions, but there will also be days when both are light workouts or one is hard and one is easy. This is what makes training so complex and why having a coach is often necessary to achieving high levels of success.

How often you insert recovery into your training program, how long this period of recovery lasts, and exactly what recovery means to you in terms of workout duration, intensity, and frequency are an individual matter. The only sure way for you to know what will work best for you in terms of each of these factors is through trial and error. Some athletes will find they can recover quite nicely on short periods of infrequent recovery. Others will discover they need frequent long periods to recover adequately.

Be aware that the need for recovery is a moving target; it changes according to the total stress in your life and your fitness level. Be conservative when trying different recovery programs. "Conservative" in this case means erring on the side of too much recovery.

RECOVERY TIME

What happens inside the muscles during a hard workout is not a pretty sight. If you could look into your legs with a microscope after a hard race or BT workout, what you saw would look like a battleground. It would appear as if a miniature bomb had exploded in your muscles, with torn and jagged cell membranes evident. The damage can vary from slight to extreme, depending on how powerful the workout was. Under such conditions, it is unlikely the muscles and nervous system will be able to go hard again right away. Not until the cells are repaired, the energy stores rebuilt, and cellular chemistry back to normal will another all-out effort be possible. Your racing performance depends on how long that process takes.

Much of the time needed for recovery has to do with creating new muscle protein to repair the damage. Research conducted at McMaster University in Hamilton, Ontario, and at the Washington University School of Medicine in St. Louis found that this protein resynthesis process takes several hours. The study used young, experienced weight lifters and maximal efforts followed by observation of the muscle repair process. Reconstruction work started almost immediately following the workout. Four hours after the weight session, protein activity was increased about 50 percent. By 24 hours post-workout it reached a peak of 109 percent of normal. Protein resynthesis was back to normal, indicating that repair was complete, 36 hours after the hard workout.

While this study used exhaustive strength training to measure recovery time, the results are similar to what could be expected following a hard race or cycling workout.

RECOVERY PHASES

The recovery process can be divided into three phases in relation to the workout—before and during, immediately following, and long term. If you carefully plan each of these, your recovery will be quicker and your next quality session more productive.

RECOVERY BEFORE AND DURING THE WORKOUT

Recovery actually starts with the warm-up you do before a challenging workout or race. Starting with a good warm-up helps you to limit damage to your muscles by:

- Thinning body fluids to allow for easier muscle contractions
- Opening capillaries to bring more oxygen to the muscles
- Raising muscle temperature so that contractions take less effort
- Conserving carbohydrates and releasing fat for fuel

The recovery process should continue during the workout with the ongoing replacement of carbohydrate-based energy stores. By drinking 18 to 24 ounces of a sports drink every hour, you reduce the stress of the training session for your body and set the stage for the recovery of the energy production system. There is some research indicating that adding protein to your sports drink may also be beneficial. Other research has supported the addition of caffeine to the sports drink. These bodies of research are still growing.

There are individual differences among athletes in how well carbohydrate drinks are tolerated and emptied from the stomach. Find a sports drink that tastes good and doesn't upset your stomach when riding hard. Before a race, make sure you have plenty of whatever fluid works for you on your bike, and be prepared for hand-ups at feed zones. Making the drink more concentrated than is recommended on the label may cause you to dehydrate during a fast race, especially on a hot and humid day. You are most likely to benefit from a sports drink during races and workouts lasting longer than one hour. In races lasting longer than about four hours, solid food may also be necessary.

Gels may be used in place of or in addition to sports drinks. By using a gel with water, you are essentially mixing a sports drink in your gut. If you don't take in enough water with the gel, the risk of dehydration increases, as fluid will be pulled from the blood plasma into the gut to help break down the sugar of the gel. Due to this same mechanism, it's also best to wash down the gel with water rather than a sports drink.

Recovery continues with a cool-down. If you complete the interval portion of a workout and hammer all the way back to the front door and then collapse in a heap, your recovery will be prolonged. Instead, always use the last 10 to 20 minutes of a hard training ride to bring the body back to normal. The cool-down should be a mirror image of the warm-up, although it may be considerably shorter, ending with easy pedaling in zone 1 for several minutes.

SHORT-TERM RECOVERY FOLLOWING THE WORKOUT

As soon as you are off the bike, the most important thing you can do to speed recovery is to replace the carbohydrates and protein that you just used for fuel. A long, hard workout or race can deplete nearly all of your stored glycogen (a carbohydrate-based energy source) and consume several grams of muscle-bound protein. In the first 30 minutes after riding, your body is several times more capable of absorbing and replenishing those fuels than at any other time.

At this time, you don't want to use the same sports drink you used on the bike. It's not potent enough. You need something designed for recovery. There are several such products now on the market. As long as you like the taste and can get 15 to 20 grams of protein and about 80 grams of simple carbohydrates from one of them, it will meet your recovery needs. You can easily make a recovery "homebrew" by adding 5 tablespoons of table sugar to 16 ounces of skim milk. Whatever you use, drink all of it within that 30-minute window of opportunity. For nutrition tips, see "Eating for Recovery" in Chapter 16.

Short-term recovery continues for as long as the preceding workout or race lasted. So if the race was three hours long, this recovery phase lasts for three hours after you get off the bike. After the first 30 minutes, focus on moderate- to high-glycemic-index foods—breads, pasta, rice, potatoes, bananas, and apricots, for example—along with some protein. Following the short-term recovery phase, return to eating foods that are dense in vitamins and minerals and lower on the glycemic-index scale. The best foods for long-term recovery are vegetables, fruits, and lean meats, including fish and poultry. See Chapter 16 for more information on the glycemic index and nutrient-dense foods.

Hot Shower or Bath

Immediately following the cool-down and the recovery drink, take a hot shower or bath for 10 to 15 minutes. Do not linger, especially in the bathtub, as you will dehydrate even more.

Ice Bath

After the cool-down, fill a tub halfway with cold water. Add a large bag of ice, climb in, and remain in the tub for 7–10 minutes. The water should cover your legs completely (this will probably be the most painful part of your workout!). In the absence of ice, you can alternate hot and cold water in a shower for the same time period.

LONG-TERM RECOVERY

In the six to nine hours after a BT workout or race, you must actively seek recovery by using one or more specific techniques. This is critical during a stage race and can mean the difference between finishing well in subsequent stages and failing to finish at all.

The most basic method is to get plenty of sleep. Nothing beats a nap for rejuvenation. In addition to a 30- to 60-minute, post-workout nap, seven to nine hours of sleep are needed each night. Other recovery methods are unique to each individual, so you will need to experiment with several of these to find the ones that work best for you.

Most of these methods speed recovery by slightly increasing the heart rate, increasing blood flow to the muscles, accelerating the inflow of nutrients, reducing soreness, lowering blood pressure, or relaxing the nervous system.

ACTIVE RECOVERY

For the experienced rider, one of the best recovery methods is to pedal easily for 15 to 30 minutes several hours after the workout, perhaps in the evening before going to bed. Pressure on the pedals should be extremely light and cadence comfortably high, with very low power and the heart rate low in zone 1.

Another effective active recovery technique is better for the novice but also works well for seasoned riders. This technique is swimming, especially with a pull buoy between the legs, or simply moving around a bit in the water while floating.

Massage. Other than sleep, most riders find that a massage by a professional therapist is the most effective recovery technique. A post-race massage should employ long, flushing strokes to speed the removal of the waste products of exercise. Deep massage at this time may actually increase muscle trauma. If you get a massage 36 hours or more after the workout, the therapist can apply greater point pressure, working more deeply.

Due to the expense of massage, some athletes prefer self-massage. Following a hot bath or shower, stroke the leg muscles for 20 to 30 minutes, working away from the feet and toward the heart.

Sauna. Some athletes report that spending time in a dry sauna several hours after the workout or race speeds recovery. Do not use a steam room for recovery, however, as it will have the opposite effect. Stay in the sauna for no more than 10 minutes, and begin drinking fluids as soon as you are done.

Relax and Stretch. Be lazy for several hours. Your legs want quality rest. Give it to them by staying off your feet whenever possible. Never stand when you can lean against something. Sit down whenever possible. Better yet, lie on the floor with your feet elevated against a wall or furniture. Sit on the floor and stretch gently. Overused muscles tighten and can't seem to relax on their own. Stretching is best right after a hot bath or sauna and just before going to bed.

Walk in a Park or Forest. A few hours after finishing a workout or race, taking a short, slow walk in a heavily vegetated area such as a park or forest seems to speed recovery for some. Abundant oxygen and the aroma of the grass, trees, and other plants are soothing.

Other Methods. The sports program of the former Soviet Union made a science of recovery and employed several techniques with athletes that may or may not be available to you. They included electro-stimulation of the muscles, ultrasound, hyperbaric chambers, sports psychology, and pharmacological supplements such as vitamins, minerals, and adaptogens. These require expert guidance.

By employing some of the specific methods described here, you can accelerate the recovery process and return to action sooner than otherwise. Figure 18.2 illustrates how this happens.

FIGURE 18.2

Effect of Recovery Techniques on Performance

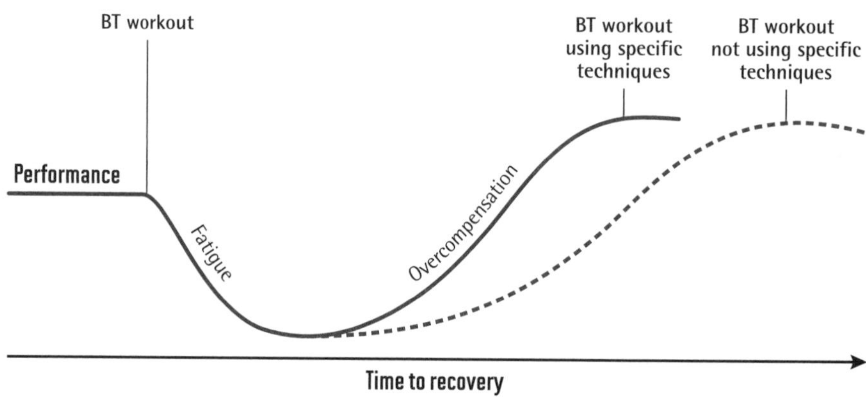

INDIVIDUALIZATION

Although I have listed several possible methods to speed recovery, you will find that some work better for you than others. You may also discover that a teammate doing the same workouts as you and following the same recovery protocol springs back at a different rate—either slower or faster. This goes back to the principle of individualization discussed in Chapter 3. While there are many physiological similarities among athletes, we are each unique and respond in our own way to any given set of circumstances. You must experiment if you want to discover how best to recover. As always, do your experimentation in training rather than in the first important stage race of the season.

Several individual factors affect recovery. Younger athletes, especially those who are 18 to 22 years old, recover faster than older athletes. The more race-experienced an athlete is, the more quickly he or she recovers from a race. If fitness is high, recovery is faster than if fitness is low. Females were shown in one study to recover faster than males. Other factors influencing the rate of recovery are climate, diet, and psychological stress.

How do you know if you are recovering adequately? The best indicator is your performance in races and hard workouts, but these are the worst times to find out that you're not ready. Typical signs that recovery is complete include a positive attitude, feelings of health, a desire to train hard again, high-quality sleep, normal resting and exercise heart rates, and balanced emotions. If any of these are lacking, continue the recovery process. By closely monitoring such signs, you should be able to determine not only the best procedure for your recoveries, but also the amount of recovery time you typically need in order to bounce back.

RECOVERY IN THE REAL WORLD

If you're following the periodization program suggested in this book, there will occasionally be periods of time when you experience an increasing load of fatigue. Despite your best recovery efforts, you will not unload all of the fatigue between planned workouts and will go into some BT workouts a bit heavy-legged and lacking snap. Don't expect to be fully recovered for every workout, all the time. In fact, a little workout fatigue sometimes can bring benefits in the form of supercompensation, which was discussed in earlier chapters. Supercompensation, in turn, can better prepare you for stage races and peak performances. You just don't want this to happen too often. Every three or four weeks, depending on your ability to avoid overtraining, include a recovery week to allow for the unloading of fatigue. Then start a new three- or four-week block of training.

EPILOGUE

A couple of hundred pages back I explained that my purpose in writing this book was to help you become a better cyclist. By now I hope you know what that means: work out with a purpose, listen to your body, train with a scientific method, and place a high value on rest and recovery. I have had so many cyclists tell me that this advice has helped them to produce better racing results that I feel confident you will also benefit.

Sometimes the hardest part of training is doing what you know is right rather than what others want you to do. Cycling is unique in many ways, beginning with the plethora of group rides available to most cyclists. Be careful of these rides, as they will divert you from the path of improved performance. The number of racing "opportunities" throughout the race season also makes cycling unique. Frequent racing means infrequent training. Be conservative with how often you race, regardless of whether it is an organized event or a weekday group ride. In the final analysis, you'll be better off because of it.

In the fourteen years since I first wrote this book there have been many changes in the world of cycling. Some have been technological. The most promising of these is the trend toward training with power. In 1995, power meters were almost unheard of. Practically no one had one. I had to import one from Germany just to see what they were all about. Now there are several companies making them, with more to come. If you aren't doing so now, within a couple of years you will consider training with power a necessity. There will still be some who don't fully grasp the value of such equipment, but they will be in the minority.

Expect other technological advances in training. Someday we may opt to have a small biometrics chip implanted that monitors heart rate, reports lactate levels, and helps us regulate blood glucose. Our friends and spouses may be able to track the progress of our daily rides or races from our homes and cars via Global Positioning Systems. All of these data and more will be easily uploaded from a single source to your pocket computer where a virtual coach will analyze it and alter your training schedule appropriately. And you will remember the days when your self-coaching was incredibly basic and naïve.

We haven't fully reached this technological training nirvana yet, but we are inching closer every year. In the meantime, if you want to succeed as a road racer, you need to understand the many subtle nuances of training. Or, you need to hire a coach. In 1995, only a handful of knowledgeable coaches were available. I knew most of them by name. Now USA Cycling has trained hundreds of coaches, and the career field is becoming more professional every year. If you have doubts about your capacity for self-coaching or the time you can devote to it, I'd highly recommend seeking out a professional coach to work with. It's truly amazing what a good coach can do for a rider.

I'd like to close this book with one guiding thought as you begin to plan for the best race performances of your career: Train hard—rest harder!

APPENDIX A
MAXIMUM WEIGHT CHART

To determine one repetition max (1RM) from a submaximal lift of 2 to 10 repetitions:

1. Select from the top row of the chart the number of reps completed (for example, 5).
2. In the reps completed column, find the weight used for the exercise (for example, 100).
3. From the weight used, look to the far left-hand "Max" column to determine predicted 1RM (for example, 115 pounds).

MAX	10	9	8	7	6	5	4	3	2
45	35	35	35	35	40	40	40	40	45
50	40	40	40	40	45	45	45	45	50
55	40	45	45	45	45	50	50	50	50
60	45	45	50	50	50	55	55	55	55
65	50	50	50	55	55	55	60	60	60
70	55	55	55	60	60	60	65	65	65
75	55	60	60	60	65	65	70	70	70
80	60	60	65	65	70	70	70	75	75
85	65	65	70	70	70	75	75	80	80
90	70	70	70	75	75	80	80	85	85
95	70	75	75	80	80	85	85	90	90
100	75	80	80	85	85	90	90	95	95
105	80	80	85	85	90	90	95	95	100
110	85	85	90	90	95	95	100	100	105
115	85	90	90	95	100	100	105	105	110
120	90	95	95	100	100	105	110	110	115
125	95	95	100	105	105	110	115	115	120
130	100	100	105	105	110	115	115	120	125
135	100	105	110	110	115	120	120	125	130
140	105	110	110	115	120	125	125	130	135
145	110	110	115	120	125	125	130	135	140
150	115	115	120	125	130	130	135	140	145
155	115	120	125	130	130	135	140	145	145
160	120	125	130	130	135	140	145	150	150
165	125	130	130	135	140	145	150	155	155
170	130	130	135	140	145	150	155	155	160
175	130	135	140	145	150	155	160	160	165
180	135	140	145	150	155	160	160	165	170
185	140	145	150	155	155	160	165	170	175
190	145	145	150	155	160	165	170	175	180
195	145	150	155	160	165	170	175	180	185
200	150	155	160	165	170	175	180	185	190
205	155	160	165	170	175	180	185	190	195
210	160	165	170	175	180	185	190	195	200
215	160	165	170	175	185	190	195	200	205
220	165	170	175	180	185	195	200	205	210
225	170	175	180	185	190	195	205	210	215
230	175	180	185	190	195	200	205	215	220
235	175	180	190	195	200	205	210	215	225
240	180	185	190	200	205	210	215	220	230
245	185	190	195	200	210	215	220	225	235
250	190	195	200	205	215	220	225	230	240
255	190	200	205	210	215	225	230	235	240
260	195	200	210	215	220	230	235	240	245
265	200	205	210	220	225	230	240	245	250
270	205	210	215	225	230	235	245	250	255
275	205	215	220	225	235	240	250	255	260

MAX	10	9	8	7	6	5	4	3	2
280	210	215	225	230	240	245	250	260	265
285	215	220	230	235	240	250	255	265	270
290	220	225	230	240	245	255	260	270	275
295	220	230	235	245	250	260	265	275	280
300	225	235	240	250	255	265	270	280	285
305	230	235	245	250	260	265	275	280	290
310	235	240	250	255	265	270	280	285	295
315	235	245	250	260	270	275	285	290	300
320	240	250	255	265	270	280	290	295	305
325	245	250	260	270	275	285	295	300	310
330	250	255	265	270	280	290	295	305	315
335	250	260	270	275	285	295	300	310	320
340	255	265	270	280	290	300	305	315	325
345	260	265	275	285	295	300	310	320	330
350	265	270	280	290	300	305	315	325	335
355	265	275	285	295	300	310	320	330	335
360	270	280	290	295	305	315	325	335	340
365	275	285	290	300	310	320	330	340	345
370	280	285	295	305	315	325	335	340	350
375	280	290	300	310	320	330	340	345	355
380	285	295	305	315	325	335	340	350	360
385	290	300	310	320	325	335	345	355	365
390	295	300	310	320	330	340	350	360	370
395	295	305	315	325	335	345	355	365	375
400	300	310	320	330	340	350	360	370	380
405	305	315	325	335	345	355	365	375	385
410	310	320	330	340	350	360	370	380	390
415	310	320	330	340	355	365	375	385	395
420	315	325	335	345	355	370	380	390	400
425	320	330	340	350	360	370	385	395	405
430	325	335	345	355	365	375	385	400	410
435	325	335	350	360	370	380	390	400	415
440	330	340	350	365	375	385	395	405	420
445	335	345	355	365	380	390	400	410	425
450	340	350	360	370	385	395	405	415	430
455	340	355	365	375	385	400	410	420	430
460	345	355	370	380	390	405	415	425	435
465	350	360	370	385	395	405	420	430	440
470	355	365	375	390	400	410	425	435	445
475	355	370	380	390	405	415	430	440	450
480	360	370	385	395	410	420	430	445	455
485	365	375	390	400	410	425	435	450	460
490	370	380	390	405	415	430	440	455	465
495	370	385	395	410	420	435	445	460	470
500	375	390	400	415	425	440	450	465	475
510	385	395	410	420	435	445	460	470	485
520	390	405	415	430	440	455	470	480	495
530	400	410	425	435	450	465	475	490	505
540	405	420	430	445	460	475	485	500	515
550	415	425	440	455	470	480	495	510	525
560	420	435	450	460	475	490	505	520	530
570	430	440	455	470	485	500	515	525	540
580	435	450	465	480	495	510	520	535	550
590	445	455	470	485	500	515	530	545	560
600	450	465	480	495	510	525	540	555	570
610	460	475	490	505	520	535	550	565	580
620	465	480	495	510	525	545	560	575	590
630	475	490	505	520	535	550	565	585	600
640	480	495	510	530	545	560	575	590	610
650	490	505	520	535	555	570	585	600	620
660	495	510	530	545	560	580	595	610	625
670	505	520	535	555	570	585	605	620	635
680	510	525	545	560	580	595	610	630	645
690	520	535	550	570	585	605	620	640	655
700	525	545	560	580	595	615	630	650	665

APPENDIX B
ANNUAL TRAINING PLAN TEMPLATE

Athlete: Annual hours:

Seasonal goals:

1.

2.

3.

Training objectives:

1.

2.

3.

4.

5.

Wk#	Mon	Race	Pri	Period	Hours	Details	Weights	Endurance	Force	Speed Skills	Muscular Endur.	Anaerobic Endur.	Power	Testing
01														
02														
03														
04														
05														
06														
07														
08														
09														
10														
11														
12														
13														
14														
15														
16														
17														
18														
19														
20														
21														
22														
23														
24														
25														
26														
27														
28														
29														
30														
31														
32														
33														
34														
35														
36														
37														
38														
39														
40														
41														
42														
43														
44														
45														
46														
47														
48														
49														
50														
51														
52														

APPENDIX C
WORKOUT MENU

These workouts are organized by ability area and are to be used in conjunction with the Annual Training Plan (Appendix B). Following the description of each workout is the suggested training period or periods in which to incorporate it. The workouts in each group are listed in a progressive manner, with the easiest, least stressful workouts first and the hardest ones last. It's best to follow this sequence as you continue to refine the ability that is the focus of training for a particular series of workouts.

This menu is hardly an exhaustive list of workouts. You can do many more simply by modifying some of the characteristics. You may also create others from scratch, based on conditions known to be in a given race. Combining workouts often provides a comprehensive race simulation, but be careful not to try to accomplish so much in a single session that the benefits are diluted. It's best to limit a multiple-benefit workout to two skills or abilities.

Each workout is preceded by an alphanumeric code that may be used as a scheduling shorthand. Chapter 15 discussed training diaries and provided a weekly scheduling format where such shorthand will come in handy.

Refer to Figure 9.1 for a visual representation of the duration and intensity of each workout. Individual indicators of intensity are discussed in greater detail in Chapter 4. I've also included race-industry workouts that may be ued to prepare for your A races.

ENDURANCE WORKOUTS

E1: RECOVERY

Done in zone 1 using the small chainring on a flat course. Do these the day after a BT workout. Best if done alone. May also be done on an indoor trainer or rollers, especially if flat courses are not available. Crosstraining is appropriate for recovery in Preparation, Base 1, and Base 2 periods. An excellent time to do a recovery spin is in the evening on a day when you've done intervals, sprints, a hard group ride, hills, or a race. Spinning for 15 to 30 minutes on rollers or a trainer hastens recovery for most experienced riders. Novices will typically benefit more from taking the time off. These workouts are not scheduled on the Annual Training Plan, but they are an integral part of training throughout the season. **(Periods: All)**

E2: AEROBIC

Used for aerobic maintenance and endurance training. Stay primarily in zones 1 and 2 on a rolling course of up to 4 percent grade. Remain seated on the uphill portions to build greater strength while maintaining a comfortably high cadence. Can be done with a disciplined group or on an indoor trainer by shifting through the gears to simulate rolling hills. Crosstraining is effective during Preparation and Base 1. **(Periods: All)**

E3: FIXED GEAR

Set up your bike with a gear that is appropriate for your strength level using a small chainring (39–42) and a large cog (15–19). If you are in your first two years of training, don't do this workout. Start by riding flat courses and gradually add rolling hills. Intensity should be mostly in zones 2 and 3. This is a multi-ability workout including endurance, strength, and speed—all elements required in Base training. **(Periods: Base 2, Base 3)**

STRENGTH (FORCE) WORKOUTS

F1: MODERATE HILLS

Select a course that includes several hills of up to 6 percent grade that take up to 3 minutes to ascend. Stay seated on all climbs, pedaling from the hips. Cadence should be at 70 rpm or higher. Stay in zones 1–4 on this ride. **(Period: Base 3)**

F2: LONG HILLS

Ride a course including long grades of up to 8 percent that take 6 or more minutes to climb. Remain mostly seated on the hills and keep your cadence at 60 rpm or higher. Go no higher than zone 5a. Concentrate on bike position and smooth pedaling. **(Periods: Base 3, Build 1)**

F3: STEEP HILLS

Ride a course that includes 8 percent or steeper hills requiring less than 2 minutes to climb. You can do repeats on the same hill with 3 to 5 minutes of recovery between climbs. Be sure to warm up thoroughly. Intensity may climb to zone 5b several times with recoveries into zone 1. Climb in and out of the saddle. Maintain a cadence of 50–60 rpm. Stop the workout if you cannot maintain at least 50 rpm. Do this workout no more than twice per week. Do not do this workout if you have knee problems. **(Periods: Build 1, Build 2, Peak, Race)**

SPEED WORKOUTS

S1: SPIN-UPS

On a downhill slope or on an indoor trainer set to light resistance, for 1 minute gradually increase cadence to maximum—this is the cadence that you can maintain without bouncing. As the cadence increases, allow your lower legs and feet to relax, especially the toes. Hold your maximum for as long as possible. Recover for at least 3 minutes and repeat several times. These are best done with a handlebar computer that displays cadence. Heart rate and power ratings have no significance for this workout. **(Periods: Preparation, Base 1, Base 2, Base 3)**

S2: ISOLATED LEG

With light resistance on an indoor trainer or on a downhill slope, do 90 percent of the work with one leg while the other is "along for the ride." Spin with a higher-than-normal cadence. Change legs when fatigue begins to set in. This exercise can also be done on a trainer with one foot out of the pedal and resting on a stool while the other works. Focus on eliminating "dead" spots at the top and bottom of the stroke. Heart rate and power ratings have no bearing on this workout. **(Periods: Base 1, Base 2)**

S3: CORNERING

On a curbed street with a clean surface and 90-degree turns, practice cornering techniques: Lean both the bike and your body into the turn, lean your body while keeping the bike upright, and keep your body upright while leaning the bike. Avoid streets with heavy traffic. Practice several speeds with different angles of approach. Include two or three sprint efforts into the turn. Heart rate and power ratings are not important for this workout. **(Periods: Base 3, Build 1, Build 2)**

S4: BUMPING

On a firm, grassy field, practice making body contact with a partner while riding slowly. Increase speed as skill improves. Also include touching overlapped wheels. **(Periods: Base 3, Build 1, Build 2)**

S5: FORM SPRINTS

Early in a ride, do six to ten sprints on a slight downhill or with a tailwind. Each sprint should last about 15 seconds, followed by a 5-minute recovery. This exercise is done for form, so hold back a bit on intensity. Heart rate is not an accurate gauge. Power/RPE should be in zone 5b. Stand for the first 10 seconds while running smoothly on the pedals, building leg speed. Then sit for 5 seconds and maintain a high cadence. This workout is best done alone to avoid "competing." **(Periods: Base 3, Build 1, Build 2, Peak, Race)**

S6: SPRINTS

Within an aerobic ride, include several 10- to 15-second race-effort sprints. These can be done with another rider or with a group. Designate sprint primes such as signs. Employ all of the techniques of form sprints, only now at a higher intensity. Power/RPE should be in zone 5c. Heart rate is not a good indicator. There should be at least 5-minute recoveries between sprints. **(Periods: Build 1, Build 2, Peak, Race)**

MUSCULAR ENDURANCE WORKOUTS

M1: TEMPO

On a mostly flat course or on an indoor trainer, ride continually in zone 3 without recovery at time-trial cadence. Avoid roads with heavy traffic and stop signs. Stay in an aerodynamic position throughout. Start with 20 to 30 minutes and build to 75 to 90 minutes by adding 10 to 15 minutes each week. This workout may be done two or three times weekly. **(Periods: Base 2, Base 3)**

M2: CRUISE INTERVALS

On a relatively flat course or on an indoor trainer, complete three to five work intervals that are 6 to 12 minutes long. Build to zones 4 and 5a on each work interval. If training with a heart rate monitor, start the work interval as soon as you begin pedaling hard—not when you reach zone 4. Recover for 2 or 3 minutes after each interval. Rest intervals should be 2 to 3 minutes long and your heart rate should drop into zone 2. The first workout should total 20 to 30 minutes of combined work-interval time. Stay relaxed and aerodynamic, and listen closely to your breathing while pedaling at time-trial cadence. **(Periods: Base 3, Build 1, Build 2, Peak, Race)**

M3: HILL CRUISE INTERVALS

These are the same as the M2 cruise intervals except that you do them on a long 2–4 percent grade. These are good if strength is a limiter. **(Periods: Build 1, Build 2, Peak, Race)**

M4: MOTOR-PACED CRUISE INTERVALS

These are the same as the M2 cruise intervals except that you do them in a motor-paced workout. Whenever doing motor-pace sessions, use only a motorcycle for pacing. Do not use a car or truck. Not only do they make the workout too fast, they also make it more dangerous. Be sure the driver of the motorcycle has experience with motor-paced workouts and will always be thinking about your safety. Discuss the workout details with the driver before starting. **(Periods: Build 1, Build 2, Peak)**

M5: CRISSCROSS THRESHOLD

On a mostly flat course with little traffic and no stops, ride 20 to 40 minutes in zones 4 and 5a. Once you have reached zone 4, gradually build the effort to the top of zone 5a, taking about 2 minutes to do so. Then begin backing off slightly, and slowly drop back to the bottom of zone 4, taking about 2 minutes again. Continue this pattern throughout the ride. Cadence will vary. Complete three or four cruise interval workouts before attempting this workout. **(Periods: Build 2, Peak)**

M6: THRESHOLD

On a mostly flat course with little traffic and no stops, ride 20 to 40 minutes nonstop in zones 4 and 5a. Stay relaxed and aerodynamic, and listen closely to your breathing throughout the workout. Don't attempt a threshold ride until you've completed at least four cruise interval workouts. This workout definitely should be included in your training, preferably on your time trial bike. **(Periods: Build 2, Peak)**

M7: MOTOR-PACED THRESHOLD

This workout is the same as the M6 threshold workout, except that it is done as a motor-paced workout. Follow the safety guidelines explained in the section for the M4 workout. **(Periods: Build 2, Peak, Race)**

ANAEROBIC ENDURANCE WORKOUTS

A1: GROUP RIDE

Ride however you feel like riding. If you are tired, sit in or break off and ride by yourself. If you are fresh, ride hard if you want to, going into zones 5a–5c several times. **(Periods: Build 1, Build 2, Peak, Race)**

A2: AE INTERVALS

After a good warm-up, on a mostly flat course with no stop signs and only light traffic, do five work intervals of 3 to 6 minutes each. Build to zone 5b on each with a cadence of 90 rpm or higher. If you are unable to achieve zone 5b by the end of the third work interval, stop the workout. This means you aren't ready for this type of interval. Recover to zone 1, with the duration of the rest interval matching the preceding work interval. **(Periods: Build 1, Build 2, Peak, Race)**

A3: PYRAMID INTERVALS

These are the same as AE intervals, except that the work intervals are for the following numbers of minutes in succession: 1, 2, 3, 4, 4, 3, 2, and 1, building to zone 5b. The recovery after each should be equal to the preceding work interval. **(Periods: Build 1, Build 2, Peak, Race)**

A4: HILL INTERVALS

Following a thorough warm-up, go to a hill with a 6–8 percent grade that takes 3 to 4 minutes to complete and do five climbs. Stay seated with cadence at 60 rpm or higher. Build to zone 5b on each. Recover to zone 1 by spinning down the hill and riding at the bottom for a total of 3 to 4 minutes depending on the duration of the climb. **(Periods: Build 2, Peak)**

A5: LACTATE TOLERANCE REPS

This workout is to be done on a flat or slightly uphill course or into the wind. After a long warm-up and several jumps, do four to eight repetitions of 90 seconds to 2 minutes each. Intensity is zone 5c. Cadence is high. The total of all work intervals must not exceed 12 minutes. Recovery intervals are 2.5 times as long as the preceding work interval. For example, after a 2-minute rep, recover for 5 minutes. Build to this workout conservatively, starting with 6 minutes total and adding no more than 2 minutes weekly. Do this workout no more than once a week and recover for at least 48 hours afterward. If you are unable to achieve zone 5c after three attempts, stop the workout. Do not do this workout if you are in the first two years of training for cycling. **(Periods: Build 2, Peak)**

A6: HILL REPS

After a good warm-up, go to a hill with a 6–8 percent grade and do four to eight reps of 90 seconds each. Stay seated for the first 60 seconds as you build to zone 5b at 60–70 rpm. In the last 30 seconds, shift to a higher gear, stand, and sprint to the top, attaining zone 5c. Recover completely for 4 minutes after each rep. If you are unable to achieve zone 5c after three attempts, stop the workout. Do not do this workout if you are in the first two years of training for cycling. **(Periods: Build 2, Peak)**

POWER WORKOUTS

P1: JUMPS

Warm up well. Then, early in the workout, on an indoor trainer or the road, do 15–25 jumps to improve explosive power. Complete three to five sets of five jumps each. Each jump is 10 to 12 revolutions of the cranks (each leg) at high cadence. Recover for 1 minute between efforts and 5 minutes between sets. Power/RPE should be zone 5c. Heart rate is not a good indicator of exertion for this workout. **(Periods: Build 1, Build 2, Peak, Race)**

P2: HILL SPRINTS

Early in the workout, after a good warm-up, go to a hill with a 4–6 percent grade. Do six to nine sprints of 20 seconds each. Use a flying start for each sprint, taking 10 seconds to build speed on the flat approach while standing. Climb the hill for 10 seconds, applying maximal force while standing on the pedals and using a high cadence. Recover for 5 minutes after each sprint. Power/RPE should be zone 5c. Heart rate is not a good indicator of exertion for this workout. **(Periods: Build 1, Build 2, Peak)**

P3: CRITERIUM SPRINTS

Warm up and then go to a course with curbed corners, clean turns, and little traffic. Do six to nine sprints of 25–35 seconds each, including corners just as in a criterium. Recover to zone 1 for 5 minutes after each. This workout can be done with another rider. When you have a partner, take turns leading the sprints. **(Periods: Build 2, Peak, Race)**

TEST WORKOUTS

T1: AEROBIC TIME TRIAL

This test works best on an indoor trainer with a rear-wheel computer pickup, or on a CompuTrainer. It may also be done on a flat section of road, but weather conditions will have an effect. After a warm-up, ride for 5 miles with your heart rate 9–11 beats below LTHR. Use a standard gear without shifting. Record your time. The conditions of this workout must be as similar as possible from one test to the next. This includes the amount of rest you've had since your last BT workout; the length and intensity of your warm-up; the weather, if you are conducting the test on the road; and the gear used during the test. As your aerobic fitness improves, your time should decrease. **(Periods: Base 1, Base 2)**

T2: TIME TRIAL

After a 15- to 30-minute warm-up, complete an 8-mile time trial on a flat course. Go 4 miles out, turn around, and return to the starting line. Mark your start and turn for later reference. Look for faster times as your anaerobic endurance and muscular endurance improve. In addition to time, record average power and heart rate and peak power and heart rate. Keep the conditions the same from one time trial to the next, as in the aerobic time trial. Use any gear, and feel free to shift during the test. **(Periods: Build 1, Build 2)**

RACE-INTENSITY WORKOUTS

CRITERIUM

On a criterium-style course do 15–30 sets, each a 10-second sprint out of corners. Do one set for every 3 minutes of race duration, so for a 45-minute crit do 15 sprints and for a 90-minute race do 30. Follow each with a 20-second recovery, including an extra minute of rest after every fifth sprint. This is best done by training partners who take turns leading. Reduce the number of sprints by three to five each time this workout is done during the Peak period. **(Period: Peak)**

HILLY ROAD RACE

Find a challenging hill similar to one in the race. Do repeats on it totaling 20 to 40 minutes at your target power level or heart rate, or at what feels like race intensity. Your total climbing time should equal the time you will spend climbing in the race. On each climb, once every 30 to 60 seconds, stand while shifting to a higher gear and accelerate for 12 pedal strokes. Recover after each climb for as long as it took to do the climb. Reduce the session's total climbing time by about 20 percent each time this workout is done during the Peak period. **(Period: Peak)**

FLAT ROAD RACE

Start by riding in heart rate zones 3 to 5 (or CP90 to CP60 if using a power meter) for 20 to 40 minutes in a very aero position, alternating pulls with a training partner every 3 to 5 minutes. The rider pulling should briefly attempt to drop the other rider once in each pull. This should be when the trailing rider least expects it. Finish the workout by doing six to eight maximum-effort 20-second sprints. Reduce the duration of the steady-state portion by about 20 percent each time you do this workout during the Peak period. **(Period: Peak)**

TIME TRIAL

On a time-trial bike, do 20 to 40 minutes of total time, depending on the race length. Make the hard-effort portion of the workout about 60–70 percent of your anticipated race finish time. Do a series of intervals, each 4 to 8 minutes long at race perceived exertion, power, or heart rate. For longer races, such as 40 km time trials, use longer intervals; for shorter races, use shorter intervals. Follow each with a recovery that is one-fourth as long as the preceding work interval. Reduce the total interval time by about 20 percent for this session each time you do this workout during the Peak period. **(Period: Peak)**

APPENDIX D
RACE EVALUATION FORM, SEASON RESULTS FORM, DIARY PAGES

RACE EVALUATION FORM

Race name: ______________________________

Date and start time: ______________________________

Location: ______________________________

Type/distance: ______________________________

Competitors to watch: ______________________________

Weather: ______________________________

Course conditions: ______________________________

Race goal: ______________________________

____

Race strategy: ______________________________

____

Pre-race meal (foods and strategies): ______________________________

____

Warm-up description: ______________________________

____

Start-line arousal level (circle one): Very low Low Moderate High Very high

Results (place, time, splits, etc.): ______________________________

____

What I did well: ______________________________

____

What I need to improve: ______________________________

____

Aches/pains/problems afterward: ______________________________

____

Other comments: ______________________________

____

____

____

SEASON RESULTS				YEAR ____	
Date	Race	Distance	Time	(Starters)	Place Comments

WEEK BEGINNING: **PLANNED WEEKLY HOURS/MILES:**

NOTES

MONDAY / /

☐ Sleep ☐ Fatigue ☐ Stress ☐ Soreness

Resting heart rate Weight

WORKOUT 1

Weather

Route

Distance

Time Total

Time by zone 1 2

3 4 5

WORKOUT 2

Weather

Route

Distance

Time Total

Time by zone 1 2

3 4 5

TUESDAY / /

☐ Sleep ☐ Fatigue ☐ Stress ☐ Soreness

Resting heart rate Weight

WORKOUT 1

Weather

Route

Distance

Time Total

Time by zone 1 2

3 4 5

WORKOUT 2

Weather

Route

Distance

Time Total

Time by zone 1 2

3 4 5

NOTES

WEDNESDAY / /

☐ Sleep ☐ Fatigue ☐ Stress ☐ Soreness

Resting heart rate Weight

WORKOUT 1

Weather

Route

Distance

Time Total

Time by zone 1 2

3 4 5

WORKOUT 2

Weather

Route

Distance

Time Total

Time by zone 1 2

3 4 5

THURSDAY / /

☐ Sleep ☐ Fatigue ☐ Stress ☐ Soreness

Resting heart rate Weight

WORKOUT 1

Weather

Route

Distance

Time Total

Time by zone 1 2

3 4 5

WORKOUT 2

Weather

Route

Distance

Time Total

Time by zone 1 2

3 4 5

WEEK'S GOALS (CHECK OFF AS ACHIEVED)

☐ __________
☐ __________
☐ __________

FRIDAY / /

☐ Sleep ☐ Fatigue ☐ Stress ☐ Soreness

Resting heart rate Weight

WORKOUT 1

Weather

Route

Distance

Time Total

Time by zone 1 2

3 4 5

WORKOUT 2

Weather

Route

Distance

Time Total

Time by zone 1 2

3 4 5

SATURDAY / /

☐ Sleep ☐ Fatigue ☐ Stress ☐ Soreness

Resting heart rate Weight

WORKOUT 1

Weather

Route

Distance

Time Total

Time by zone 1 2

3 4 5

WORKOUT 2

Weather

Route

Distance

Time Total

Time by zone 1 2

3 4 5

NOTES

SUNDAY / /

☐ Sleep ☐ Fatigue ☐ Stress ☐ Soreness

Resting heart rate Weight

WORKOUT 1

Weather

Route

Distance

Time Total

Time by zone 1 2

3 4 5

WORKOUT 2

Weather

Route

Distance

Time Total

Time by zone 1 2

3 4 5

WEEKLY SUMMARY

	Weekly Total	Year to Date
Bike miles		
Bike time		
Strength time		
Other		
Total		

Soreness

NOTES

NOTES

GLOSSARY

aerobic In the presence of oxygen; aerobic metabolism utilizes oxygen.

aerobic capacity The body's maximal capacity for using oxygen to produce energy during maximal exertion. Also known as VO_2max.

agonistic muscles Muscles directly engaged in a muscular contraction.

anaerobic In the absence of oxygen; nonoxidation metabolism.

anaerobic endurance (AE) The ability resulting from the combination of speed skills and endurance allowing the athlete to maintain a high cadence for an extended period of time.

anaerobic threshold (AT) When aerobic metabolism no longer supplies all the need for energy, energy is produced anaerobically; indicated by an increase in lactic acid. Also known as lactate threshold.

anatomical adaptation (AA) The initial phase of strength training.

antagonistic muscles Muscles that have an opposite effect on movers (see "agonistic muscles"), or against muscles, by opposing their contraction. For example, the triceps is an antagonistic muscle for the biceps.

Base period The period during which the basic abilities of endurance, speed skills, and force are emphasized.

bonk A state of extreme exhaustion during a workout caused mainly by the depletion of glycogen in the muscles.

breakaway A rider or group of riders that rides away from the main pack.

BT Breakthrough workouts that provide the stress to start the adaptive process.

Build period The specific preparation mesocycle during which high-intensity training in the form of muscular endurance, anaerobic endurance, and power is emphasized and endurance, force, and speed skills are maintained.

capillaries A fine network of small vessels located between arteries and veins where exchanges between tissue and blood occur.

carbohydrate loading (glycogen loading) A dietary procedure that elevates muscle glycogen stores.

cardiorespiratory system Cardiovascular system and lungs.

cardiovascular system Heart, blood, and blood vessels.

chase The attempt to catch a breakaway.

circuit training Selected exercises or activities performed rapidly in sequence; used in weight training.

criterium A road race that is generally held on city streets or inparks. The course is usually 1 mile or less and is marked by short straights and tight turns.

crosstraining Participating in one sport to train for another.

duration The length of time of a given workout.

endurance The ability to persist despite the onset of fatigue.

ergogenic aid A substance or phenomenon that can improve athletic performance.

fast-twitch fiber (FT) A muscle fiber characterized by fast contraction time, high anaerobic capacity, and low aerobic capacity, all making the fiber suited for high-power-output activities.

force The ability of a muscle or muscle group to overcome a resistance.

free weights Weights not part of an exercise machine (i.e., barbells and dumbbells).

frequency The number of times per week that one trains.

glucose Simple sugar.

glycogen The form in which glucose (sugar) is stored in the muscles and the liver.

growth hormone A hormone secreted by the anterior lobe of the pituitary gland that stimulates growth and development.

hamstring Muscle on the back of the thigh that flexes the knee and extends the hip.

individuality, principle of The theory that any training program must consider the specific needs and abilities of the individual for whom it is designed.

intensity The qualitative element of training, such as speed skills, maximum force, and power.

interval training A system of high-intensity work marked by short but regularly repeated periods of work stress interspersed with periods of recovery.

jump A sudden burst of speed that provides the initial acceleration for a sprint.

lactate Formed when lactic acid from the muscles gives off a hydrogen atom upon entering the bloodstream.

lactate threshold (LT) The point during exercise of increasing intensity at which blood lactate begins to accumulate above resting levels. Also known as anaerobic threshold.

lactic acid A by-product of the lactic acid system resulting from the incomplete breakdown of glucose (sugar) in the production of energy.

limiter A race-specific weakness.

long, slow distance (LSD) training A form of continuous training in which the athlete performs at a relatively low intensity.

macrocycle A period of training including several mesocycles; usually an entire season.

maximum strength (MS) The phase of strength training during which loads gradually increase up to certain goal levels.

maximum transition (MT) The phase of strength training that provides a transition between the AA and MS phases.

mesocycle A period of training generally two to six weeks long.

microcycle A period of training approximately one week long.

motor-pacing Riding behind a motorcycle or other vehicle that breaks the wind.

muscular endurance (ME) The ability of a muscle or muscle group to perform repeated contractions for a long period of time while bearing a load. The combination of force and endurance abilities.

overload, principle of A training load that challenges the body's current level of fitness.

overtraining Extreme fatigue, both physical and mental, caused by training at a volume or intensity higher than that to which the body can adapt.

Peak period The mesocycle during which volume of training is reduced and intensity is proportionally increased, allowing the athlete to reach high levels of fitness.

periodization A process of structuring training into periods.

power The ability to apply maximum force in the shortest time possible.

Preparation period The mesocycle during which the athlete begins to train for the coming season; usually marked by the use of crosstraining.

progression, principle of The theory that workload must be gradually increased, accompanied by intermittent periods of recovery.

quadriceps The large muscle in front of the thigh.

Race period The mesocycle during which workload is decreased, allowing the athlete to compete in high-priority races.

Rating of Perceived Exertion (RPE) A subjective assessment of how hard one is working.

recovery interval The relief period between work intervals within an interval workout.

repetition The number of work intervals within one set.

repetition maximum (RM) The maximum load that a muscle group can lift in one attempt. Also called "one-repetition maximum" (1RM).

road race A mass-start race that goes from point to point, covers one large loop, or is held on a circuit longer than those used for criteriums.

set The total number of repetitions performed before an extensive recovery interval is taken.

slow-twitch fiber (ST) A muscle fiber characterized by slow contraction time, low anaerobic capacity, and high aerobic capacity, all making the fiber suited for low-power endurance activities.

specificity, principle of The theory that training must stress the systems critical for optimal performance in order to achieve the desired training adaptations.

speed skill In cycling, the ability to turn the cranks quickly and efficiently.

stage race A multiday event consisting of road races, time trials, and often criteriums.

strength maintenance (SM) The phase of strength training during which strength is maintained.

tapering A reduction in training intensity and volume prior to a major competition.

time trial (TT) A race against the clock in which individual riders start at set intervals.

Transition period The mesocycle during which the workload and structure of training are greatly reduced, allowing for physical and psychological recovery from training and racing.

ventilatory threshold (VT) The point during increasing exertion at which breathing first becomes labored. Roughly corresponds with lactate threshold.

VO_2max The maximal capacity for oxygen consumption by the body during maximal exertion, also known as aerobic power and maximal oxygen consumption.

volume A quantitative element of training, such as miles or hours of training within a given time.

work interval High-intensity efforts separated by recovery intervals.

workload Measured stress applied in training through the combination of frequency, intensity, and duration.

REFERENCES AND RECOMMENDED READING

Abraham, W. M. "Factors in Delayed Muscle Soreness." *Medicine and Science in Sports and Exercise* 9 (1977): 11–20.

Allen, H., and A. Coggan. *Training and Racing with a Power Meter*. Boulder: VeloPress, 2006.

Alter, M. J. *Sport Stretch*. Champaign, IL: Human Kinetics, 1998.

"Altering Cardiorespiratory Fitness." *Sports Medicine* 3, no. 5 (1986): 346–356.

Anderson, B. *Stretching*. Bolinas, CA: Shelter Publications, 1980.

Anderson, O. "Carbs, Creatine and Phosphate: If the King Had Used These Uppers, He'd Still Be Around Today." *Running Research News* 12, no. 3 (1996): 1–4.

———. "The Search for the Perfect Intensity Distribution." *Cycling Research News* 1, no. 10 (2004): 1, 4–10.

Angus, D. J., et al. "Effect of Carbohydrate or Carbohydrate Plus Medium-Chain Triglyceride Ingestion on Cycling Time Trial Performance." *Journal of Applied Physiology* 88, no. 1 (2000): 113–119.

"Antioxidants and the Elite Athlete." Proceedings of Panel Discussion, Dallas, Texas, May 27, 1992.

"Antioxidants: Clearing the Confusion." *IDEA Today* (Sept. 1994): 67–73.

Avela, J., et al. "Altered Reflex Sensitivity after Repeated and Prolonged Passive Muscle Stretching." *Journal of Applied Physiology* 84, no. 4 (1999): 1283–1291.

Baker, A. "Training Intensity." *Performance Conditioning for Cycling* 2, no. 1 (1995): 3.

Balsam, P. D. "Creatine Supplementation Per Se Does Not Enhance Endurance Exercise Performance." *Acta Phys Scand* 149, no. 4 (1993): 521–523.

Bemben, D. A., et al. "Effects of Oral Contraceptives on Hormonal and Metabolic Responses during Exercise." *Medicine and Science in Sports and Exercise* 24, no. 4 (1992).

Berdanier, C. D. "The Many Faces of Stress." *Nutrition Today* 2, no. 2 (1987): 12–17.

Billat V. L., A. Demarle, J. Slawinski, M. Paiva, and J. P. Koralsztein. "Physical and Training Characteristics of Top-Class Marathon Runners." *Medicine and Science in Sports and Exercise* 33, no. 12 (2001): 2089–2097.

Billat, V. L., and J. P. Koralsztein. "Significance of the Velocity at VO_2Max and Time to Exhaustion at This Velocity." *Sports Medicine* 22, no. 2 (1996): 90–108.

Billat, V. L., et al. "A Comparison of Time to Exhaustion at VO_2Max in Elite Cyclists, Kayak Paddlers, Swimmers, and Runners." *Ergonomics* 39, no. 2 (1996): 267–277.

Billat, V. L., et al. "Interval Training at VO_2Max: Effects on Aerobic Performance and Overtraining Markers." *Medicine and Science in Sports and Exercise* 31, no. 1 (1999): 156–163.

Birkholz, D., ed. *Training Skills*. Colorado Springs, CO: United States Cycling Federation, 1991.

Blomstrand, E., et al. "Administration of Branched Chain Amino Acids during Sustained Exercise—Effects on Performance and on Plasma Concentrations of Some Amino Acids." *European Journal of Applied Physiology* 62 (1991): 83–88.

Bompa, T. *From Childhood to Champion Athlete*. Sedona, AZ: Veritas Publishing, 1995.

———. *Periodization of Strength*. Sedona, AZ: Veritas Publishing, 1993.

———. *Periodization, Theory and Methodology of Training*. Champaign, IL: Human Kinetics, 1999.

———. "Physiological Intensity Values Employed to Plan Endurance Training." *New Studies in Athletics* 3, no. 4 (1988): 37–52.

———. *Power Training for Sports*. New York: Mosaic Press, 1993.

———. *Theory and Methodology of Training*. Dubuque, IA: Kendall Hunt, 1994.

Borg, G. *An Introduction to Borg's RPE Scale*. Ithaca, NY: Movement Publications, 1985.

Borysewicz, E. *Bicycle Road Racing*. Boulder: VeloNews, 1995.

Bouchard, C., and G. Lortie. "Heredity and Endurance Performance." *Sports Medicine* 1 (1984): 38–64.

Bouchard, C., et al. "Aerobic Performance in Brothers, Dizygotic and Monozygotic Twins." *Medicine and Science in Sports and Exercise* 18 (1986): 639–646.

Boulay, M. R., et al. "Monitoring High-Intensity Endurance Exercise with Heart Rate and Thresholds." *Medicine and Science in Sports and Exercise* 29, no. 1 (1997): 125–132.

Brenner, I. K. M. "Infection in Athletes." *Sports Medicine* 17, no. 2 (1994): 86–107.

Brown, C., and J. Wilmore. "The Effects of Maximal Resistance Training on the Strength and Body Composition of Women Athletes." *Medicine and Science in Sports and Exercise* 6 (1974): 174–177.

Brown, R. L. "Overtraining in Athletes: A Round Table Discussion." *The Physician and Sports Medicine* 11, no. 6 (1983): 99.

Brunner, R., and B. Tabachnik. *Soviet Training and Recovery Methods*. Pleasant Hill: Sport Focus Publishing, 1990.

Brynteson, P., and W. E. Sinning. "The Effects of Training Frequencies on the Retention of Cardiovascular Fitness." *Medicine and Science in Sports and Exercise* 5 (1973): 29–33.

Brzycki, M. "Strength Testing—Predicting a One-Rep Max from Reps to Fatigue." *Journal of Physical Education, Recreation and Dance* 64 (1993): 88–90.

Bull, Stephen J. *Sport Psychology*. Wiltshire, UK: Crowood Press, 2000.

Burke, E. *Serious Cycling*. Champaign, IL: Human Kinetics, 1995.

Cade, J. R., et al. "Dietary Intervention and Training in Swimmers." *European Journal of Applied Physiology* 63 (1991): 210–215.

Cade, R., et al. "Effects of Phosphate Loading on 2,3-Diphosphoglycerate and Maximal Oxygen Uptake." *Medicine and Science in Sports and Exercise* 16, no. 3 (1984): 263–268.

Cera, F. B., et al. "Branched-Chain Amino Acid Supplementation during Trekking at High Altitude." *European Journal of Applied Physiology* 65 (1992): 394–398.

Chamari, K., et al. "Anaerobic and Aerobic Peak Power and the Force-Velocity Relationship in Endurance-Trained Athletes: Effects of Aging." *European Journal of Applied Physiology* 71, nos. 2–3 (1995): 230–234.

Child, J. S., et al. "Cardiac Hypertrophy and Function in Masters Endurance Runners and Sprinters." *Journal of Applied Physiology* 57 (1984): 170–181.

Clement, D. B., et al. "Branched Chain Metabolic Support: A Prospective, Randomized Double-Blind Trial in Surgical Stress." *Annals of Surgery* 199 (1984): 286–291.

Cohen, J., and C. V. Gisolfi. "Effects of Interval Training in Work-Heat Tolerance in Young Women." *Medicine and Science in Sports and Exercise* 14 (1982): 46–52.

Cordain, L. *The Paleo Diet.* New York: Wiley and Sons, 2002.

Cordain, L., and J. Friel. *The Paleo Diet for Athletes.* Emmaus, PA: Rodale Press, 2005.

Costill, D. "Predicting Athletic Potential: The Value of Laboratory Testing." *Sports Medicine Digest* 11, no. 11 (1989): 7.

Costill, D., et al. "Adaptations to Swimming Training: Influence of Training Volume." *Medicine and Science in Sports and Exercise* 23 (1991): 371–377.

Costill, D., et al. "Effects of Repeated Days of Intensified Training on Muscle Glycogen and Swimming Performance." *Medicine and Science in Sports and Exercise* 20, no. 3 (1988): 249–254.

Costill, D. L., et al. "Effects of Reduced Training on Muscular Power in Swimmers." *The Physician and Sports Medicine* 17, no. 2 (1985): 94–101.

Coyle, E. F., et al. "Cycling Efficiency Is Related to the Percentage of Type I Muscle Fibers." *Medicine and Science in Sports and Exercise* 24 (1992): 782.

Coyle, E. F., et al. "Physiological and Biomechanical Factors Associated with Elite Endurance Cycling Performance." *Medicine and Science in Sports and Exercise* 23, no. 1 (1991): 93–107.

Coyle, E. F., et al. "Time Course of Loss of Adaptations after Stopping Prolonged Intense Endurance Training." *Journal of Applied Physiology* 57 (1984): 1857.

Cunningham, D. A., et al. "Cardiovascular Response to Intervals and Continuous Training in Women." *European Journal of Applied Physiology* 41 (1979): 187–197.

Czajkowski, W. "A Simple Method to Control Fatigue in Endurance Training." *Exercise and Sport Biology, International Series on Sport Sciences* 10 (1982): 207–212.

Daniels, J. "Physiological Characteristics of Champion Male Athletes." *Research Quarterly* 45 (1974): 342–348.

———. "Training Distance Runners—A Primer." *Sports Science Exchange* 1, no. 11 (1989): 1–4.

Daniels, J., et al. "Interval Training and Performance." *Sports Medicine* 1 (1984): 327–324.

David, A. S., et al. "Post-Viral Fatigue Syndrome: Time for a New Approach." *British Medical Journal* 296 (1988): 696–699.

Dill, D., et al. "A Longitudinal Study of 16 Champion Runners." *Journal of Sports Medicine* 7 (1967): 4–32.

Doherty, M. "The Effects of Caffeine on the Maximal Accumulated Oxygen Deficit and Short-Term Running Performance." *International Journal of Sports Nutrition* 8, no. 2 (1998): 95–104.

Dragan, I., and I. Stonescu. *Organism Recovery Following Training.* Bucharest: Sport-Turism, 1978.

Dressendorfer, R., et al. "Increased Morning Heart Rate in Runners: A Valid Sign of Overtraining?" *The Physician and Sports Medicine* 13, no. 8 (1985): 77–86.

Drinkwater, B. L. "Women and Exercise: Physiological Aspects." *Exercise and Sports Science Review* 12 (1984): 21–51.

Drinkwater, B. L., ed. *Female Endurance Athletes.* Champaign, IL: Human Kinetics, 1986.

Droghetti, P., et al. "Non-Invasive Determination of the Anaerobic Threshold in Canoeing, Cycling, Cross-Country Skiing, Roller and Ice Skating, Rowing and Walking." *European Journal of Applied Physiology* 53 (1985): 299–303.

Dunbar, C. C., et al. "The Validity of Regulating Exercise Intensity by Ratings of Perceived Exertion." *Medicine and Science in Sports and Exercise* 24 (1992): 94–99.

Eaton, S. B. "Humans, Lipids and Evolution." *Lipids* 27, no. 1 (1992): 814–820.

Eaton, S. B., and M. Konner. "Paleolithic Nutrition: A Consideration of Its Nature and Current Implications." *New England Journal of Medicine* 312, no. 5 (1985): 283–289.

Eaton, S. B., and D. A. Nelson. "Calcium in Evolutionary Perspective." *American Journal of Clinical Nutrition* 54 (1991): 281S–287S.

Ekblom, B. "Effect of Physical Training in Adolescent Boys." *Journal of Applied Physiology* 27 (1969): 350–353.

"Elevation of Creatine in Resting and Exercised Muscle of Normal Subjects by Creatine Supplementation." *Clinical Science* 83 (1992): 367–374.

Elliott, Richard. *The Competitive Edge.* Mountain View, CA: TAFNEWS Press, 1991.

Ericsson, K. A., R. T. Krampe, and S. Heizmann. "Can We Create Gifted People?" *CIBA Foundation Symposium* 178 (1993): 221–231.

Ernst, E. "Does Post-Exercise Massage Treatment Reduce Delayed Onset Muscle Soreness? A Systematic Review." *British Journal of Sports Medicine* 32, no. 3 (1998): 212–214.

"An Evaluation of Dietary Intakes of Triathletes: Are RDAs Being Met?" *Brief Communications* (November 1989): 1653–1654.

Evans, W., et al. "Protein Metabolism and Endurance Exercise." *The Physician and Sports Medicine* 11, no. 7 (1983): 63–72.

Faria, I. E. "Applied Physiology of Cycling." *Sports Medicine* 1 (1984): 187–204.

Fitts, R. H., et al. "Effect of Swim-Exercise Training on Human Muscle Fiber Function." *Journal of Applied Physiology* 66 (1989): 465–475.

Fitzgerald, L. "Exercise and the Immune System." *Immunology Today* 9, no. 11 (1988): 337–339.

Fowles, J. R., and D. G. Sale. "Time Course of Strength Deficit after Maximal Passive Stretch in Humans." *Medicine and Science in Sports and Exercise* 29, no. 5 (1997): S155.

Francis, K. T., et al. "The Relationship between Anaerobic Threshold and Heart Rate Linearity during Cycle Ergometry." *European Journal of Applied Physiology* 59 (1989): 273–277.

Frassetto, L. A., et al. "Effect of Age on Blood Acid-Base Composition in Adult Humans: Role of Age-Related Renal Function Decline." *American Journal of Physiology* 271, no. 6-2 (1996): F1114–F1122.

Frassetto, L. A., et al. "Potassium Bicarbonate Reduces Urinary Nitrogen Excretion in Postmenopausal Women." *Journal of Endocrinology and Metabolism* 82, no. 1 (1997): 254–259.

Freeman, W. *Peak When It Counts*. Mountain View, CA: TAFNEWS Press, 1991.

Freund, B. J., et al. "Glycerol Hyperhydration: Hormonal, Renal, and Vascular Fluid Responses." *Journal of Applied Physiology* 79 (1995): 2069–2077.

Friel, J. *CompuTrainer Workout Manual*. RacerMate, 1994.

———. *The Mountain Biker's Training Bible*. Boulder: VeloPress, 2000.

———. *Training with Power*. Cambridge, MA: Tune, 1999.

Frontera, W. R., et al. "Aging of Skeletal Muscle: A 12-Year Longitudinal Study." *Journal of Applied Physiology* 4 (2000): 1321–1326.

Fry, R. W., and D. Keast. "Overtraining in Athletes." *Sports Medicine* 12, no. 1 (1991): 32–65.

Fry, R. W., et al. "Biological Responses to Overload Training in Endurance Sports." *European Journal of Applied Physiology* 64 (1992): 335–344.

Galbo, H. *Hormonal and Metabolic Adaptations to Exercise*. Stuttgart: Georg Thieme Verlag, 1983.

Gibbons, E. S. "The Significance of Anaerobic Threshold in Exercise Prescription." *Journal of Sports Medicine* 27 (1987): 357–361.

Gleim, G. W., and M. P. McHugh. "Flexibility and Its Effects on Sports Injury and Performance." *Sports Medicine* 24, no. 5 (1997): 289–299.

Goedecke, J. H., et al. "Effects of Medium-Chain Triaclyglycerol Ingested with Carbohydrate on Metabolism and Exercise Performance." *International Journal of Sports Nutrition* 9, no. 1 (1999): 35–47.

Goforth, H. W., et al. "Simultaneous Enhancement of Aerobic and Anaerobic Capacity." *Medicine and Science in Sports and Exercise* 26, no. 5 (1994): 171.

Goldspink, D. F. "The Influence of Immobilization and Stretch on Protein Turnover of Rat Skeletal Muscle." *Journal of Physiology* 264 (1977): 267–282.

Gonzalez, H., and M. L. Hull. "Bivariate Optimization of Pedaling Rate and Crank-Arm Length in Cycling." *Journal of Biomechanics* 21, no. 10 (1988): 839–849.

Graham, T. E., and L. L. Spriet. "Caffeine and Exercise Performance." *Sports Science Exchange* 9, no. 1 (1996): 1–6.

Graham, T. E., et al. "Metabolic and Exercise Endurance Effects of Coffee and Caffeine Ingestion." *Journal of Applied Physiology* 85, no. 3 (1998): 883–889.

Greiwe, J. S., et al. "Effects of Endurance Exercise Training on Muscle Glycogen Accumulation in Humans." *Journal of Applied Physiology* 87, no. 1 (1999): 222–226.

Guilland, J. C., et al. "Vitamin Status of Young Athletes Including the Effects of Supplementation." *Medicine and Science in Sports and Exercise* 21 (1989): 441–449.

Hagberg, J. M. "Physiological Implications of the Lactate Threshold." *International Journal of Sports Medicine* 5 (1984): 106–109.

Heath, G. "A Physiological Comparison of Young and Older Endurance Athletes." *Journal of Applied Physiology* 51, no. 3 (1981): 634–640.

Heath, G. W., et al. "Exercise and Upper Respiratory Tract Infections: Is There a Relationship?" *Sports Medicine* 14, no. 6 (1992): 353–365.

Heil, D. P., et al. "Cardiorespiratory Responses to Seat-Tube Angle Variation during Steady-State Cycling." *Medicine and Science in Sports and Exercise* 27, no. 5 (1995): 730–735.

Herman, E. A., et al. "Exercise Endurance Time as a Function of Percent Maximal Power Production." *Medicine and Science in Sports and Exercise* 19, no. 5 (1987): 480–485.

Hickson, R. C., et al. "Potential for Strength and Endurance Training to Amplify Endurance Performance." *Journal of Applied Physiology* 65 (1988): 2285–2290.

Hickson, R. C., et al. "Reduced Training Intensities and Loss of Aerobic Power, Endurance and Cardiac Growth." *Journal of Applied Physiology* 58 (1985): 492–499.

Hickson, R. C., et al. "Strength Training Effects on Aerobic Power and Short-Term Endurance." *Medicine and Science in Sports and Exercise* 12 (1980): 336–339.

Hoffman-Goetz, L., and B. K. Peterson. "Exercise and the Immune System: A Model of the Stress Response?" *Immunology Today* 15, no. 8 (1994): 382–387.

Holly, R. G., et al. "Stretch-Induced Growth in Chicken Wing Muscles: A New Model of Stretch Hypertrophy." *American Journal of Physiology* 7 (1980): C62–C71.

Hooper, S. L., and L. T. MacKinnon. "Monitoring Overtraining in Athletes: Recommendations." *Sports Medicine* 20, no. 5 (1995): 321–327.

Hooper, S. L., et al. "Markers for Monitoring Overtraining and Recovery." *Medicine and Science in Sports and Exercise* 27 (1995): 106–112.

Hopkins, S. R., et al. "The Laboratory Assessment of Endurance Performance in Cyclists." *Canadian Journal of Applied Physiology* 19, no. 3 (1994): 266–274.

Hopkins, W. G. "Advances in Training for Endurance Athletes." *New Zealand Journal of Sports Medicine* 24, no. 3 (1996): 29–31.

Horowitz, J. F., et al. "Pre-exercise Medium-Chain Triglyceride Ingestion Does Not Alter Muscle Glycogen Use during Exercise." *Journal of Applied Physiology* 88, no. 1 (2000): 219–225.

Hortobagyi, T., et al. "Effects of Simultaneous Training for Strength and Endurance on Upper- and Lower-Body Strength and Running Performance." *Journal of Sports Medicine and Physical Fitness* 31 (1991): 20–30.

Houmard, J. A., et al. "The Effects of Taper on Performance in Distance Runners." *Medicine and Science in Sports and Exercise* 26, no. 5 (1994): 624–631.

Houmard, J. A., et al. "Reduced Training Maintains Performance in Distance Runners." *International Journal of Sports Medicine* 11 (1990): 46–51.

Howe, M. J., J. W. Davidson, and J. A. Sluboda. "Innate Talents: Reality or Myth?" *Behavior and Brain Science* 21, no. 3 (1993): 399–407.

Ivy, J. L., et al. "Muscle Respiratory Capacity and Fiber Type as Determinants of the Lactate Threshold." *Journal of Applied Physiology* 48 (1980): 523–527.

Jackson, Susan A., and Mihaly Csikszentmihalyi. *Flow in Sports*. Champaign, IL: Human Kinetics, 1999.

Jacobs, I., et al. "Blood Lactate: Implications for Training and Sports Performance." *Sports Medicine* 3 (1986): 10–25.

Janssen, P.G.J.M. *Training, Lactate, Pulse Rate*. Kempele, Finland: Polar Electro Oy, 1989.

Jeukendrup, A. E., et al. "Physiological Changes in Male Competitive Cyclists after Two Weeks of Intensified Training." *International Journal of Sports Medicine* 13, no. 7 (1992): 534–541.

Johnston, R. E., et al. "Strength Training for Female Distance Runners: Impact on Economy." *Medicine and Science in Sports and Exercise* 27, no. 5 (1995): S47.

Jung, A. P. "The Impact of Resistance Training on Distance Running Performance." *Sports Medicine* 33, no. 7 (2003): 539–552.

Kearney, J. T. "Training the Olympic Athlete." *Scientific American*, June 1996, 52–63.

Keast, D., et al. "Exercise and the Immune Response." *Sports Medicine* 5 (1988): 248–267.

Kent-Braun, J. A., et al. "Skeletal Muscle Oxidative Capacity in Young and Older Women and Men." *Journal of Applied Physiology* 89, no. 3 (2000): 1072–1078.

Kindermann, W., et al. "The Significance of the Aerobic-Anaerobic Transition for the Determination of Workload Intensities during Endurance Training." *European Journal of Applied Physiology* 42 (1979): 25–34.

Klissouras, V. "Adaptability of Genetic Variation." *Journal of Applied Physiology* 31 (1971): 338–344.

Knuttgen, H. G., et al. "Physical Conditioning through Interval Training with Young Male Adults." *Medicine and Science in Sports and Exercise* 5 (1973): 220–226.

Kokkonen, J., et al. "Acute Muscle Stretching Inhibits Maximal Strength Performance." *Research Quarterly for Exercise and Sport* 69 (1998): 411–415.

Kovacs, E. M. R., et al. "Effect of Caffeinated Drinks on Substrate Metabolism, Caffeine Excretion and Performance." *Journal of Applied Physiology* 85, no. 2 (1998): 709–715.

Kraemer, W. J., et al. "Compatibility of High-Intensity Strength and Endurance Training on Hormonal and Skeletal Muscle Adaptations." *Journal of Applied Physiology* 78, no. 3 (1995): 976–989.

Kreider, R. B., et al. "Effects of Phosphate Loading on Metabolic and Myocardial Responses to Maximal and Endurance Exercise." *International Journal of Sports Nutrition* 2, no. 1 (1992): 20–47.

Kreider, R. B., et al. "Effects of Phosphate Loading on Oxygen Uptake, Ventilatory Anaerobic Threshold, and Run Performance." *Medicine and Science in Sports and Exercise* 22, no. 2 (1990): 250–256.

Kubukeli, Z. N., T. D. Noakes, and S. C. Dennis. "Training Techniques to Improve Endurance Exercise Performances." *Sports Medicine* 32, no. 8 (2002): 489–509.

Kuipers, H., and H. A. Keizer. "Overtraining in Elite Athletes: Review and Directions for the Future." *Sports Medicine* 6 (1988): 79–92.

Kuipers, H., et al. "Comparison of Heart Rate as a Non-Invasive Determination of Anaerobic Threshold with Lactate Threshold When Cycling." *European Journal of Applied Physiology* 58 (1988): 303–306.

Legwold, G. "Masters Competitors Age Little in Ten Years." *The Physician and Sports Medicine* 10, no. 10 (1982): 27.

Lehmann, M., et al. "Overtraining in Endurance Athletes: A Brief Review." *Medicine and Science in Sports and Exercise* 25, no. 7 (1993): 854–862.

Lehmann, M., et al. "Training-Overtraining: Influence of a Defined Increase in Training Volume versus Training Intensity on Performance, Catecholamines and Some Metabolic Parameters in Experienced Middle- and Long-Distance Runners." *European Journal of Applied Physiology* 64, no. 2 (1992): 169–177.

LeMond, G., and K. Gordis. *Greg LeMond's Complete Book of Bicycling*. New York: Perigee Books, 1988.

Lindsay, F. H., et al. "Improved Athletic Performance in Highly Trained Cyclists after Interval Training." *Medicine and Science in Sports and Exercise* 28, no. 11 (1996): 1427–1434.

Loehr, James. *Mental Toughness Training for Sports*. Brattelboro, VT: Stephen Greene Press, 1982.

———. *The New Mental Toughness Training for Sports*. New York: Penguin Books, 1995.

Loftin, M., and B. Warren. "Comparison of a Simulated 16.1-km Time Trial, VO_2Max and Related Factors in Cyclists with Different Ventilatory Thresholds." *International Journal of Sports Medicine* 15, no. 8 (1994): 498–503.

Luis, A., H. Joyes, and J. L. Chicharro. "Physiological Response to Professional Road Cycling: Climbers vs. Time Trialists." *International Journal of Sports Medicine* 21 (2001): 505–512.

Lynch, Jerry. *Creative Coaching*. Champaign, IL: Human Kinetics, 2001.

———. *Running Within*. Champaign, IL: Human Kinetics, 1999.

———. *Thinking Body, Dancing Mind*. New York: Bantam Books, 1992.

———. *The Total Runner*. Englewood Cliffs, NJ: Prentice Hall, 1987.

Lynch, Jerry, and Chungliang Al Huang. *Working Without, Working Within*. New York: Tarcher and Putnam, 1998.

MacLaren, C. P., et al. "A Review of Metabolic and Physiologic Factors in Fatigue." *Exercise and Sports Science Review* 17 (1989): 29.

Maglischo, E. *Swimming Faster*. Palo Alto, CA: Mayfield, 1982.

Marcinik, E. J., et al. "Effects of Strength Training on Lactate Threshold and Endurance Performance." *Medicine and Science in Sports and Exercise* 23, no. 6 (1991): 739–743.

Martin, D. E., and P. N. Coe. *Training Distance Runners*. Champaign, IL: Leisure Press, 1991.

Massey, L. K., et al. "Interactions between Dietary Caffeine and Calcium on Calcium and Bone Metabolism in Older Women." *Journal of the American College of Nutrition* 13 (1994): 592–596.

Matveyev, L. *Fundamentals of Sports Training*. Moscow: Progress Publishing, 1981.

Mayhew, J., and P. Gross. "Body Composition Changes in Young Women and High Resistance Weight Training." *Research Quarterly* 45 (1974): 433–440.

McArdle, W. D., F. I. Katch, and V. L. Katch. *Exercise Physiology*. Baltimore: Williams and Wilkins, 1996.

McCarthy, J. P., et al. "Compatibility of Adaptive Responses with Combining Strength and Endurance Training." *Medicine and Science in Sports and Exercise* 27, no. 3 (1995): 429–436.

McMurray, R. G., V. Ben-Ezra, W. A. Forsythe, and A. T. Smith. "Responses of Endurance-Trained Subjects to Caloric Deficits Induced by Diet or Exercise." *Medicine and Science in Sports and Exercise* 17, no. 5 (1985): 574–579.

McMurtrey, J. J., and R. Sherwin. "History, Pharmacology and Toxicology of Caffeine and Caffeine-Containing Beverages." *Clinical Nutrition* 6 (1987): 249–254.

Milne, C. "The Tired Athlete." *New Zealand Journal of Sports Medicine* 19, no. 3 (1991): 42–44.

Mujika, I., and S. Padilla. "Creatine Supplementation as an Ergogenic Aid for Sports Performance in Highly Trained Athletes: A Critical Review." *International Journal of Sports Medicine* 18, no. 7 (1997): 491–496.

Myburgh, K. H., et al. "High-Intensity Training for 1 Month Improves Performance but Not Muscle Enzyme Activities in Highly Trained Cyclists." *Medicine and Science in Sports and Exercise* 27, no. 5 (1995): S370.

Nelson, A. G., et al. "Consequences of Combining Strength and Endurance Training Regimens." *Physical Therapy* 70 (1990): 287–294.

Nelson, A. G., et al. "Muscle Glycogen Supercompensation Is Enhanced by Prior Creatine Supplementation." *Medicine and Science in Sports and Exercise* 33, no. 7 (2001): 1096–1100.

Neufer, P. D., et al. "Effects of Reduced Training on Muscular Strength and Endurance in Competitive Swimmers." *Medicine and Science in Sports and Exercise* 19 (1987): 486–490.

Newham, D. J., et al. "Muscle Pain and Tenderness after Exercise." *Australian Journal of Sports Medicine and Exercise Science* 14 (1982): 129–131.

Nicholls, J. F., et al. "Relationship between Blood Lactate Response to Exercise and Endurance Performance in Competitive Female Masters Cyclists." *International Journal of Sports Medicine* 18 (1997): 458–463.

Nieman, D. C., et al. "Infectious Episodes in Runners before and after the Los Angeles Marathon." *Journal of Sports Medicine and Physical Fitness* 30 (1990): 316–338.

Niles, R. "Power as a Determinant of Endurance Performance." Unpublished study at Sonoma State University, 1991.

Noakes, T. D. "Implications of Exercise Testing for Prediction of Athletic Performance: A Contemporary Perspective." *Medicine and Science in Sports and Exercise* 20, no. 4 (1988): 319–330.

O'Brien, C., et al. "Glycerol Hyperhydration: Physiological Responses during Cold-Air Exposure." *Journal of Applied Physiology* 99 (2005): 515–521.

Okkels, T. "The Effect of Interval and Tempo Training on Performance and Skeletal Muscle in Well-Trained Runners." Acoteias, Portugal: Twelfth European Track Coaches Congress (1983): 1–9.

Orlick, Terry. *Psyched to Win*. Champaign, IL: Leisure Press, 1992.

———. *Psyching for Sport*. Champaign, IL: Leisure Press, 1986.

Parizkova, J. "Body Composition and Exercise during Growth and Development." *Physical Activity: Human Growth and Development* (1974).

Pate, R. R., et al. "Cardiorespiratory and Metabolic Responses to Submaximal and Maximal Exercise in Elite Women Distance Runners." *International Journal of Sports Medicine* 8, no. 2 (1987): 91–95.

Paton, C. D., and W. G. Hopkins. "Combining Explosive and High-Resistance Training Improves Performance in Competitive Cyclists." *Journal of Strength and Conditioning Research* 19, no. 4 (2005): 826–830.

Peyrebrune, M. C., et al. "The Effects of Oral Creatine Supplementation on Performance in Single and Repeated Sprint Training." *Journal of Sports Science* 16, no. 3 (1998): 271–279.

Phillips, S. M., et al. "Mixed Muscle Protein Synthesis and Breakdown after Resistance Exercise in Humans." *American Journal of Physiology* 273, no. 1 (1997): E99–E107.

Phinney, D., and C. Carpenter. *Training for Cycling*. New York: Putnam, 1992.

Piatti, P. M., F. Monti, and I. Fermo, et al. "Hypocaloric, High-Protein Diet Improves Glucose Oxidation and Spares Lean Body Mass: Comparison to Hypocaloric, High Carbohydrate Diet." *Metabolism* 43, no. 12 (1994): 1481–1487.

Pollock, M., et al. "Effect of Age and Training on Aerobic Capacity and Body Composition of Master Athletes." *Journal of Applied Physiology* 62, no. 2 (1987): 725–731.

Pollock, M., et al. "Frequency of Training as a Determinant for Improvement in Cardiovascular Function and Body Composition of Middle-Aged Men."

Archives of Physical Medicine and Rehabilitation 56 (1975): 141–145.

Pompcu, F. A., et al. "Prediction of Performance in the 5000m Run by Means of Laboratory and Field Tests in Male Distance Runners." *Medicine and Science in Sports and Exercise* 28, no. 5 (1996): S89.

Poole, D. C., et al. "Determinants of Oxygen Uptake." *Sports Medicine* 24 (1996): 308–320.

Rankin, J. W. "Weight Loss and Gain in Athletes." *Current Sports Medicine Reports* 1, no. 4 (2002): 208–213.

Rasmussen, B. B., et al. "An Oral Essential Amino Acid–Carbohydrate Supplement Enhances Muscle Protein Anabolism after Resistance Exercise." *Journal of Applied Physiology* 88, no. 2 (2000): 386–392.

Ready, S. L., et al. "Effect of Two Sports Drinks on Muscle Tissue Stress and Performance." *Medicine and Science in Sports and Exercise* 31, no. 5 (1999): S119.

Remer, T., and F. Manz. "Potential Renal Acid Load of Foods and Its Influence on Urine pH." *Journal of the American Dietetic Association* 95, no. 7 (1995): 791–797.

Rhea, M. R., S. D. Ball, W. T. Phillips, and L. N. Burkett. "A Comparison of Linear and Daily Undulating Periodized Programs with Equated Volume and Intensity for Strength." *Journal of Strength Conditioning Research* 16, no. 2 (2002): 250–255.

Rhea, M. R., W. T. Phillips, L. N. Burkett, W. J. Stone, S. D. Ball, B. A. Alvar, and A. B. Thomas. "A Comparison of Linear and Daily Undulating Periodized Programs with Equated Volume and Intensity for Local Muscular Endurance." *Journal of Strength Conditioning Research* 17, no. 1 (2003): 82–87.

Rogers, J. "Periodization of Training." *Endurance Training Journal* 2 (1992): 4–7.

Rogers, M. A., et al. "Decline in VO_2max with Aging in Masters Athletes and Sedentary Men." *Journal of Applied Physiology* 68, no. 5 (1990): 2195–2199.

Romijn, J. A., et al. "Regulation of Endogenous Fat and Carbohydrate Metabolism in Relation to Exercise Intensity and Duration." *American Journal of Physiology* 265 (1993): E380.

Roth, S. M., et al. "High-Volume, Heavy-Resistance Strength Training and Muscle Damage in Young and Older Men." *Journal of Applied Physiology* 88, no. 3 (2000): 1112–1119.

Rountree, S. *The Athlete's Guide to Yoga*. Boulder: VeloPress, 2008.

Roy, B. D., et al. "Effect of Glucose Supplement Timing on Protein Metabolism after Resistance Training." *Journal of Applied Physiology* 82 (1997): 1882–1888.

Roy, B. D., et al. "The Influence of Post-Exercise Macronutrient Intake on Energy Balance and Protein Metabolism in Active Females Participating in Endurance Training." *International Journal of Sport Nutrition, Exercise and Metabolism* 12, no. 2 (2002): 172–188.

Sale, D. G., and D. MacDougall. "Specificity in Strength Training: A Review for the Coach and Athlete." *Canadian Journal of Applied Sciences* 6 (1981): 87–92.

Sale, D. G., et al. "Comparison of Two Regimens of Concurrent Strength and Endurance Training." *Medicine and Science in Sports and Exercise* 22, no. 3 (1990): 348–356.

Schatz, M. P. "Easy Hamstring Stretches." *Physician and Sports Medicine* 22, no. 2 (1994): 115–116.

Schneider, D. A., et al. "Ventilatory Thresholds and Maximal Oxygen Uptake during Cycling and Running in Biathletes." *Medicine and Science in Sports and Exercise* 22, no. 2 (1990): 257–264.

Schumacher, Y. O., and P. Mueller. "The 4000-m Team Pursuit Cycling World Record: Theoretical and Practical Aspects." *Medicine and Science in Sports and Exercise* 34, no. 6 (2002): 1029–1036.

Seals, D. R., et al. "Endurance Training in Older Men and Women." *Journal of Applied Physiology* 57 (1984): 1024–1029.

Sebastian, A., et al. "Improved Mineral Balance and Skeletal Metabolism in Postmenopausal Women Treated with Potassium Bicarbonate." *New England Journal of Medicine* 330, no. 25 (1994): 1776–1781.

Seiler, K. S., and G. O. Kjerland. "Quantifying Training Intensity Distribution in Elite Endurance Athletes: Is There Evidence for 'Optimal Distribution?" *Scandinavian Journal of Medicine & Science in Sports* 16, no. 1 (2006): 49–56.

Shangold, M. M., and G. Mirkin, eds. *Women and Exercise: Physiology and Sports Medicine*. Philadelphia: F. A. Davis, 1988.

Sharkey, B. *Coaches' Guide to Sport Physiology*. Champaign, IL: Human Kinetics, 1986.

Sharp, N. C. C., and Y. Koutedakis. "Sport and the Overtraining Syndrome." *British Medical Journal* 48, no. 3 (1992): 518–533.

Shasby, G. B., and F. C. Hagerman. "The Effects of Conditioning on Cardiorespiratory Function in Adolescent Boys." *Journal of Sports Medicine* 3 (1975): 97–107.

Simon, J., et al. "Plasma Lactate and Ventilation Thresholds in Trained and Untrained Cyclists." *Journal of Applied Physiology* 60 (1986): 777–781.

Skinner, J. S., et al. "The Transition from Aerobic to Anaerobic Metabolism." *Research Quarterly for Exercise and Sport* 51 (1980): 234–248.

Sleamaker, R. *Serious Training for Serious Athletes*. Champaign, IL: Leisure Press, 1989.

Sleivert, G. G., and H. A. Wenger. "Physiological Predictors of Short-Course Biathlon Performance." *Medicine and Science in Sports and Exercise* 25, no. 7 (1993): 871–876.

Smith, L. L., et al. "The Effects of Athletic Massage on Delayed Onset Muscle Soreness, Creatine Kinase, and Neutrophil Count: A Preliminary Report." *Journal of Orthopedic Sports Physical Therapy* 19, no. 2 (1994): 93–99.

Snell, P., et al. "Changes in Selected Parameters during Overtraining." *Medicine and Science in Sports and Exercise* 18 (1986): abstract #268.

Somer, E., and Health Medical of America. *The Essential Guide to Vitamins and Minerals*. New York: Harper Perennial, 1992.

Stahl, A. B. "Hominid Dietary Selection before Fire." *Current Anthropology* 25, no. 2 (1984): 151–168.

Steed, J. C., et al. "Ratings of Perceived Exertion (RPE) as Markers of Blood Lactate Concentration during Rowing." *Medicine and Science in Sports and Exercise* 26 (1994): 797–803.

Steinacker, J. M., W. Lormes, M. Lehmann, and D. Altenburg. "Training of Rowers before World Championships." *Medicine and Science in Sports and Exercise* 30, no. 7 (1998): 1158–1163.

Stewart, I., et al. "Phosphate Loading and the Effects on VO_2max in Trained Cyclists." *Research Quarterly for Exercise and Sport* 61, no. 1 (1990): 80–84.

Stone, M., et al. "Overtraining: A Review of the Signs, Symptoms and Possible Causes." *Journal of Applied Sport Sciences* 5, no. 1 (1991): 35–50.

Stone, M. H., et al. "Health- and Performance-Related Potential of Resistance Training." *Sports Medicine* 11, no. 4 (1991): 210–231.

Stucker, M. "Training for Cycling." Unpublished manuscript, 1990.

Tanaka, H., and T. Swensen. "Impact of Resistance Training on Endurance Performance: A New Form of Cross-Training?" *Sports Medicine* 25, no. 3 (1998): 191–200.

Tanaka, K., et al. "A Longitudinal Assessment of Anaerobic Threshold and Distance-Running Performance." *Medicine and Science in Sports and Exercise* 16, no. 3 (1984): 278–282.

Tiidus, P. M. "Massage and Ultrasound as Therapeutic Modalities in Exercise-Induced Muscle Damage." *Canadian Journal of Physiology* 24, no. 3 (1999): 267–278.

Tiidus, P. M., and J. K. Shoemaker. "Effleurage Massage, Muscle Blood Flow and Long-Term Post-Exercise Strength Recovery." *International Journal of Sports Medicine* 16, no. 7 (1995): 478–483.

Ungerleider, Steven. *Mental Training for Peak Performance.* Emmaus, PA: Rodale Sports, 1996.

USA Cycling. *Expert Level Coaching Manual.* Colorado Springs, CO: USA Cycling, 1995.

Vanderburgh, H., and S. Kaufman. "Stretch and Skeletal Myotube Growth: What Is the Physical to Biochemical Linkage?" In *Frontiers of Exercise Biology,* edited by K. Borer, D. Edington, and T. White. Champaign, IL: Human Kinetics, 1983.

Van Hall, G., et al. "Muscle Glycogen Resynthesis during Recovery from Cycle Exercise: No Effect of Additional Protein Ingestion." *Journal of Applied Physiology* 88, no. 5 (2000): 1631–1636.

Van Handel, P. J. "Periodization of Training." *Bike Tech* 6, no. 2 (1987): 6–10.

———. "Planning a Comprehensive Training Program." *Conditioning for Cycling* 1, no. 3 (1991): 4–12.

———. "The Science of Sport: Training for Cycling I." *Conditioning for Cycling* 1, no. 1 (1991): 8–11.

———. "The Science of Sport: Training for Cycling II." *Conditioning for Cycling* 1, no. 2 (1991): 18–23.

———. "Specificity of Training: Establishing Pace, Frequency, and Duration of Training Sessions." *Bike Tech* 6, no. 3 (1987): 6–12.

VanNieuwenhoven, M. A., et al. "Gastrointestinal Function during Exercise: Comparison of Water, Sports Drink, and Sports Drink with Caffeine." *Journal of Applied Physiology* 89, no. 3 (2000): 1079–1085.

Vanzyl, C. G., et al. "Effects of Medium-Chain Triglycerides Ingestion on Fuel Metabolism and Cycling Performance." *Journal of Applied Physiology* 80, no. 6 (1996): 2217–2225.

Viitsalo, J. T., et al. "Warm Underwater Water-Jet Massage Improves Recovery from Intense Physical Exercise." *European Journal of Applied Physiology* 71, no. 5 (1995): 431–438.

Wallin, D., et al. "Improvement of Muscle Flexibility: A Comparison between Two Techniques." *American Journal of Sports Medicine* 13, no. 4 (1985): 263–268.

Wells, C. L. *Women, Sport, and Performance: A Physiological Perspective.* Champaign, IL: Human Kinetics, 1991.

Weltman, A. *The Blood Lactate Response to Exercise.* Champaign, IL: Human Kinetics, 1995.

Weltman, A., et al. "Endurance Training Amplifies the Pulsatile Release of Growth Hormone: Effects of Training Intensity." *Journal of Applied Physiology* 72, no. 6 (1992): 2188–2196.

Wemple, R. D., et al. "Caffeine vs. Caffeine-Free Sports Drinks: Effects on Urine Production at Rest and during Prolonged Exercise." *International Journal of Sports Medicine* 18 (1997): 40–46.

Wenger, H. A., and G. J. Bell. "The Interactions of Intensity, Frequency and Duration of Exercise Training in Altering Cardiorespiratory Fitness." *Sports Medicine* 3, no. 5 (1986): 346–356.

Weston, A. R., et al. "Skeletal Muscle Buffering Capacity and Endurance Performance after High-Intensity Training by Well-Trained Cyclists." *European Journal of Applied Physiology* 75 (1997): 7–13.

Wilber, R. L., and R. J. Moffatt. "Physiological and Biochemical Consequences of Detraining in Aerobically Trained Individuals." *Journal of Strength Conditioning Research* 8 (1994): 110.

Wilcox, A. R. "Caffeine and Endurance Performance." *Sports Science Exchange* 3, no. 26 (1990).

Wilmore, J., and D. Costill. *Physiology of Sport and Exercise.* Champaign, IL: Human Kinetics, 1994.

———. *Training for Sport and Activity: The Physiological Basis of the Conditioning Process.* Champaign, IL: Human Kinetics, 1988.

Wilmore, J., et al. "Is There Energy Conservation in Amenorrheic Compared with Eumenorrheic Distance Runners?" *Journal of Applied Physiology* 72 (1992): 15–22.

Wyatt, F. B., et al. "Metabolic Threshold Defined by Disproportionate Increases in Physiological Parameters: A Meta-Analytic Review." *Medicine and Science in Sports and Exercise* 29, no. 5 (1997): S1342.

Zappe, D. H., and T. Bauer. "Planning Competitive Season Training for Road Cycling." *Conditioning for Cycling* 1, no. 2 (1991): 4–8.

Zatiorsky, V. M. *Science and Practice of Strength Training.* Champaign, IL: Human Kinetics, 1995.

INDEX

ABOUT THE AUTHOR

Joe Friel has trained endurance athletes since 1980. His clients have included amateur and professional road cyclists, mountain bikers, triathletes, duathletes, swimmers, and runners. They have been from all corners of the globe and have included American and foreign national champions, world championship competitors, and an Olympian.

In addition to *The Cyclist's Training Bible*, he is the author of *Cycling Past 50*, *Precision Heart Rate Training* (coauthor), *The Triathlete's Training Bible*, *The Mountain Biker's Training Bible*, *Going Long: Training for Ironman-Distance Triathlons* (coauthor), *The Paleo Diet for Athletes* (coauthor), *Total Heart Rate Training*, and *Your First Triathlon*. He holds a master's degree in exercise science and is a USA Triathlon and USA Cycling coach certified at their highest levels.

He is also a columnist for *VeloNews* and *Inside Triathlon* magazines and writes feature stories for other international publications and Web sites. He is frequently interviewed as an authority on sports training by media such as the *New York Times*, *Outside* magazine, the *Los Angeles Times*, and other leading publications. In addition, he consults with national Olympic federations.

Joe speaks at seminars and camps around the world on training and racing for endurance athletes and provides consulting services for corporations in the fitness industry. Every year he selects a group of the brightest coaches with the greatest potential and closely oversees their progress as they advance into the ranks of elite-level coaching.

For more information on personal coaching, seminars, camps, developmental coach mentoring, certification of coaches in the Training Bible methodology, coaching symposia, and consulting, go to www.TrainingBible.com. There you will also find training plans, a blog, a newsletter, and other free resources that provide updates to the Training Bible methodology described in this book. For all of the tools necessary for effective self-coaching using the concepts of this book, including a "virtual coach," go to http://TrainingPeaks.com.

Joe Friel may be contacted with questions or comments via e-mail at jfriel@trainingbible.com.